FIRST AMONG UNEQUALS

First among Unequals

The Premier, Politics, and Policy in Newfoundland and Labrador

EDITED BY

Alex Marland and Matthew Kerby

McGill-Queen's University Press

Montreal & Kingston · London · Ithaca

© McGill-Queen's University Press 2014

ISBN 978-0-7735-4344-7 (cloth)
ISBN 978-0-7735-4345-4 (paper)
ISBN 978-0-7735-9056-4 (ePDF)
ISBN 978-0-7735-9057-1 (ePUB)

Legal deposit second quarter 2014
Bibliothèque nationale du Québec

Printed in Canada on acid-free paper that is 100% ancient forest free (100% post-consumer recycled), processed chlorine free

This book has been published with the help of a grant from the Canadian Federation for the Humanities and Social Sciences, through the Awards to Scholarly Publications Program, using funds provided by the Social Sciences and Humanities Research Council of Canada. Funding has also been received from Memorial University of Newfoundland's Publications Subvention Program and the University of Ottawa's Faculty of Social Sciences Publication Assistance Program.

McGill-Queen's University Press acknowledges the support of the Canada Council for the Arts for our publishing program. We also acknowledge the financial support of the Government of Canada through the Canada Book Fund for our publishing activities.

Library and Archives Canada Cataloguing in Publication

First among unequals : the premier, politics, and policy in Newfoundland and Labrador / edited by Alex Marland and Matthew Kerby.

Includes bibliographical references and index.
Issued in print and electronic formats.
ISBN 978-0-7735-4344-7 (bound). – ISBN 978-0-7735-4345-4 (pbk.). – ISBN 978-0-7735-9056-4 (ePDF). – ISBN 978-0-7735-9057-1 (ePUB)

1. Newfoundland and Labrador – Politics and government – 2003– 2. Politics, Practical – Newfoundland and Labrador – Case studies. 3. Power (Social sciences) – Newfoundland and Labrador – Case studies. 4. Premiers (Canada) – Newfoundland and Labrador – Case studies. 5. Newfoundland and Labrador – Social policy – Case studies. 6. Newfoundland and Labrador – Economic policy – Case studies. 7. Williams, Danny, 1949–. 8. Dunderdale, Kathy. I. Marland, Alex, 1973–, author, editor of compilation II. Kerby, Matthew, 1973–, author, editor of compilation

FC2177.2.F57 2014   971.8'05   C2013-908673-0
                                             C2013-908674-9

Typeset by Jay Tee Graphics Ltd. in 10.5/13 Sabon

Contents

Tables and Figures

TABLES

FIGURES

Foreword

Alex Marland and Matthew Kerby have invited me to write a foreword for this long-awaited, badly needed, and welcome book. Fine biographies exist of some of Newfoundland & Labrador's leading politicians before and after Confederation in 1949, but until now there has not been as detailed and thorough a treatise as this. It is my view that this learned and interesting survey of politics and public policy is a first-class piece of work that will become the standard on this area of life in our province.

First among Unequals: The Premier, Politics, and Policy in Newfoundland and Labrador contains excellent research concerning the concentration of power in the office of the premier. Throughout Canada there has been a shift in the power of making policy from party caucuses and cabinet ministers, as a collective, towards the heads of government as individuals. Many now feel there is too much power in the Prime Minister's Office at Ottawa or in premiers' offices and within supporting central agencies such as the Privy Council Office and Treasury Board, known collectively as "the centre" federally and also now provincially. As this volume notes, party discipline is strong, a leader's supremacy over the party is vast, and the supremacy of a popular head of government even more so. Clearly, except when a general election is lost, in Canada the forcible removal of a prime minister or premier is rare.

The prime minister in Ottawa and most premiers throughout the country are no longer the first among equals in cabinet. Rather, as Alex Marland notes in chapter 1, they have vast authority. Furthermore, it is more common at the provincial level for elections to result in a landslide of seats. Opposition parties may be few in members and in disarray, suffering from poor organization, weak financing, and tenuous relationships with their national counterparts. It has also been pointed out that the intensity of investigative journalism is lower in the provinces and that local media outlets tend to be more prone to government messaging and to defer to a premier's celebrity status, as well as to the perceived need to communicate regional grievances. As the authors in this book observe, a premier's control over provincial politics can be ominous. While it enables swift government action to be mobilized, it comes at a cost to consultation, scrutiny, and accountability.

This book submits that democracy has been a fragile proposition in Newfoundland & Labrador and that it remains a work in progress. The authors note that the province has experienced prolonged periods of one-party dominance and that premiers have at times behaved in a quasi-autocratic manner while often cultivating an image of defenders of Newfoundland. Though readers will need to look elsewhere for a detailed account of the administrations of Joey Smallwood, Brian Peckford, Clyde Wells, and Brian Tobin, this book indicates that the Danny Williams administration was the latest to have commanded an astonishing concentration of power in the Office of the Premier.

As the authors point out, there are many reasons for this, one of which was Newfoundlanders' expectation that their premier must punch above his or her weight when lobbying Ottawa. Newfoundlanders pride themselves on being distinct, with a distinctive culture. They are frustrated with the federal government, which is perceived to treat them with disrespect, to ignore their concerns, to favour other provinces in revenue sharing, and to have too much control over our province's natural resources. Even so, Newfoundlanders are enthusiastic supporters of Canada's social programs, such as universal health care and employment insurance, and believe that being part of Canada has been a benefit. It is my view that Newfoundland & Labrador has had a much greater influence on federal policy and treatment of the province than one would expect of a place with only seven MPs in Parliament in Ottawa.

The plan of this book is to focus on executive power and public policy during the Williams era, seeking to increase our knowledge of the state of democracy, the public policy processes, government priorities, and election campaigning in the most recent addition to Confederation. It examines a significant period of public policy in the province. The public believes that it was a major economic and psychological achievement in 2008 when Newfoundland shed its "have not" status and joined Alberta as a "have" province, no longer qualifying for federal equalization payments. An interesting fact that emerges in this book is that while provincial royalties accounted for $88 million or 2 percent of the government's total revenues just before Williams became premier, by the fiscal year of his departure royalties had ballooned to $2.4 billion, accounting for 35 percent of the government's total revenues, which had more than doubled during a period of low inflation. The authors point out that from 1981 to 2010, Newfoundland experienced the strongest growth in an index of provincial economic well-being in Canada, so that in 2010 Newfoundlanders' consumption, wealth, economic equality, and economic security were deemed second only to those of Albertans.

First among Unequals: The Premier, Politics, and Policy in Newfoundland and Labrador succeeds in offering a modern perspective on the realities of provincial politics and will certainly be welcomed by readers interested in Canadian politics, governance, and public policy. The authors tackle a range of important subjects intelligently and clearly. They conclude, and I agree, that Newfoundland's political system does not tend to provide enough checks and balances on the executive authority of its premiers and that, unfortunately, there is often no credible opposition. We have been very lucky, especially in recent years, to have had excellent histories of this province written by scholars such as Patrick O'Flaherty, Sean Cadigan, Peter Neary, and others, but this fine work should certainly be added to the list of books that must be read by anyone interested in the political history of Newfoundland & Labrador, our politics, and our public policy. I have no hesitation in recommending it to all men and women in Newfoundland & Labrador who are interested in how our political system operates and in the development of public policy in this province.

I recommend, without qualification, this book's wide circulation, not only within Newfoundland & Labrador but throughout Canada, wherever there are people interested in the politics and political systems and public policy of the various provinces of Canada. It will be very helpful to those who engage in further research into ways to improve our system of democratic government.

The Honourable John C. Crosbie, PC, OC, ONL, QC

Preface

The Latin expression *primus inter pares*, which means first among equals, is routinely used to describe the unpretentious role of the head of cabinet in a parliamentary system of government. The idea is that the leader of the political party that controls the legislature is surrounded by peers, many of whom could themselves be suitable leaders if called on to serve. But *primus inter pares* does not appropriately describe the norm in a media-centred democracy like Canada. Some have gone so far as to declare that government is now all about the primus, and that there are no pares (Savoie 1999, 71). Others counter that the evidence to suggest that cabinet government is "dead" simply does not exist (Weller 2003, 719). This nevertheless raises the spectre of the growing influence of a prime minister or premier over central agencies that in turn exercise authority over ministers, the civil service, and public policy.

Academics worldwide have observed that governments are becoming "centralized" and that the parliamentary system of government is becoming "presidentialized." Canadian scholars such as Donald Savoie have presented convincing evidence that ministers and departments in the government of Canada prioritize accountability to the prime minister's office. Popular books such as *The Friendly Dictatorship* and *Harperland*, written by political journalists, similarly express a frame of executive dominance that is common in the media. Furthermore, a narrative that political party leaders are powerful is eagerly promoted by partisans themselves, as well as by their critics. It is therefore not a question of *whether* political power is concentrated in the office of the head of government but, rather, a question of *to what extent* such perceptions are valid.

Does a premier have as much power over government policy decisions as is popularly perceived? Little is known about the case of Newfoundland & Labrador, a place where representative and responsible government was slow to develop, where democracy was suspended during the Commission of Government era (1934–49), and where premiers are expected to be passionate defenders of local interests. Although political decision making in Newfoundland & Labrador is considerably more democratic than it has ever been, the perception persists that its premiers are policy saviours and/or policy dictators.

Centring on a case study of the administration of Newfoundland & Labrador premier Danny Williams, with some treatment of the early years of the Kathy Dunderdale administration, this book seeks to fill a gap in academic research about politics and public policy at the provincial level generally and in Newfoundland & Labrador specifically. It begins from the normative *de rigueur* position in Canadian political science that the power to make policy decisions resides foremost in the office of the head of government. When we contacted McGill-Queen's University Press (MQUP) in mid-2010 about the idea of an edited volume, the Williams administration had been in power for nearly seven years, and Premier Williams had become Newfoundland & Labrador's foremost celebrity and its national ambassador. Journalists from across Canada, as with the local media and most citizens in Newfoundland, were captivated by his use of unconventional methods to achieve policy objectives, by personality politics, and by the astoundingly high approval numbers that he achieved as the leader of the province's Progressive Conservative (PC) Party.

At the time, Newfoundland & Labrador was going through an economic transformation on its way to becoming a "have" province. Unemployment rates, while still the highest in Canada, were gradually declining. Within the government of Newfoundland & Labrador there was also a renewed interest in expanding policy capacity after cuts in the 1990s and an awareness of the need for policy change in response to the province's significant demographic changes (Brett 2003). On 25 November 2010, not long after MQUP signalled that it was on board, Danny Williams suddenly announced that he was resigning as premier, effective 3 December. How the Canadian Press chose to lead its news report that day speaks to how he was perceived across Canada at the time: "Premier Danny Williams, the political pugilist from Newfoundland and Labrador whose popularity was the envy of politicians across Canada, is leaving politics" (Bailey 2010a). The emotional attachment

to Mr Williams, both genuine and manufactured, that Newfoundlanders and Labradorians felt should not be underestimated. Party staff and
public servants jammed the lobby of the Confederation Building to listen to his announcement, some weeping openly. Local media reported on
mass public disbelief and sadness. At Memorial University, students were
abuzz, worried about what would happen to the province; one relayed
that while they were driving to campus, both she and her mother had
burst into tears when the news was reported on the radio. A custodian
acted as though there had been a death in the family, shaking his head
and staring at the floor as he walked along the Department of Political
Science hallway muttering, "It's a sad day for Newfoundland, b'y."

The media emphasized this collective mourning and initially pushed
aside discussion about Williams' proclamation that Kathy Dunderdale
would become the province's first female premier. For those paying
attention, the timing made sense. The PC Party's agenda, which had
been so ambitious in 2003, had waned by 2010. Their leader had had
heart surgery in February 2010; his "fighting Newfoundlander" style
was becoming predictable, and he had reached a stalemate with Prime
Minister Stephen Harper; on 18 November 2010 Williams had signed a
multi-billion dollar deal with Nova Scotia to develop the Lower Churchill hydroelectric megaproject, which seemed to be a legacy project; and
the fall session of the legislature had yet to begin. Furthermore, in its first
term his administration had passed legislation requiring that an election
be held within a year of a party selecting a new leader. With an election
scheduled for October 2011, in which Ms. Dunderdale would go on to
lead the PCs to the party's third consecutive majority government, the
timing was right.

Circumstance further affected this project when the swearing in of
Premier Dunderdale's post-election cabinet was announced for 28 October 2011. The editors had obtained a Social Sciences and Humanities
Research Council of Canada (SSHRC) grant to fund a workshop about
politics and public policy on 28–29 October at Memorial University.
The idea was for authors to present their draft chapters and for civil servants in the provincial government to act as discussants. The event was
a success, and fortunately the cabinet reshuffle proved to be a minor
inconvenience, in part owing to the recognition of its importance within
the senior public service.

On 22 January 2014, just as this book was going to print, Kathy
Dunderdale announced her resignation. Her decision followed years of
declining popularity, the retirement of key minister Jerome Kennedy,

several by-election losses, including Kennedy's seat, and two floor cross-
ings. The tipping point was public and caucus anger at her perceived
mishandling of electricity power outages earlier that month. Public reaction to her announcement was muted compared with the collective sadness and anxiety when Williams resigned three years earlier; as well, her
departure was barely noticed by major Canadian news media and not
mentioned at all on the homepage of the *Globe and Mail*. The outgoing
premier's perceived right to choose party stalwart Tom Marshall as her
(interim) successor was the height of elitism, as was Williams' choice of
Dunderdale before that, and raises important questions about to what
extent the parliamentary system of government is democratic. However,
unlike Ms Dunderdale, Mr Marshall seems likely to stick to his word
that he will hold the position only on an interim basis. This would set
the stage for the badly needed leadership campaign and policy renewal
that the party should not have bypassed with Dunderdale's coronation
in 2010.

While it is too early to judge Williams' legacy, let alone Dunderdale's,
she does appear to have fallen victim to what media scholars refer to as
"the game frame." This theory maintains that the treatment of politics
and government as a horserace reduces complex political and public
policy matters into a simple narrative of winners and losers. In Newfoundland & Labrador, this is epitomized by the fascination among political and media elites (as well as academics) with the latest results of the
Corporate Research Associates (CRA) opinion survey. Towards the end
of his reign, over 80 percent of Newfoundlanders preferred Williams as
premier, whereas Dunderdale's support consistently declined until her
polling numbers settled into a range of 75 percent of electors preferring
someone *else*. Thus, for most of the Williams era, every three months
the CRA poll results were treated as staggering proof of the supremacy
of the premier's authority; for most of the Dunderdale era, each poll
contributed to a damning narrative that the leader of the "new energy"
party was running out of power. Readers are encouraged to bear in mind
the implications of a game frame for the premier, politics, and policy in
Newfoundland & Labrador.

ACKNOWLEDGMENTS

The editors are grateful for input, support, and guidance from a number
of people. First and foremost we wish to thank the many fine researchers

who contributed chapters and whose commitment made this project possible. Senior provincial public servants who participated in this project include, but are not limited to, Ross Reid, Robert Thompson, Diana Dalton, Sean Dutton, and Alaistair O'Reilly. David McGrane (St Thomas More College, University of Saskatchewan) kindly provided feedback on a draft chapter, and we are particularly grateful to the two anonymous referees who were contracted by McGill-Queen's University Press for their thoughtful comments on earlier drafts of the manuscript. Political science students Sean Fleming, Michael Penny, and Stephen Power provided outstanding copyediting support. The impressive editorial stewardship of McGill-Queen's University Press was led by MQUP senior editor Kyla Madden and managing editor Ryan Van Huijstee, and expert copyediting was provided by Ron Curtis. Appreciation is extended to the office of Premier Dunderdale and to the Government of Newfoundland and Labrador for permission to reproduce figures in chapter 5. While we regret that Mr Williams turned down an invitation to be interviewed for this book, when he did so we pledged to provide him with one of the first copies. The editors wish to extend special thanks to John Crosbie for writing the foreword.

The editors also wish to acknowledge three publishing subsidy awards. This book has been published with the help of a grant from the Canadian Federation for the Humanities and Social Sciences, through the Award to Scholarly Publications Program, using funds provided by the Social Sciences and Humanities Research Council of Canada. Its publication is also possible thanks to financial awards provided by Memorial University of Newfoundland's Publications Subvention Program, Office of Research Services, and the University of Ottawa's Faculty of Social Sciences Publication Assistance Program.

GENERAL CONCLUSION OF THE BOOK

The general conclusion of *First among Unequals: The Premier, Politics, and Policy in Newfoundland and Labrador* is that a modern premier cannot possibly have as much power over public policy as is publicly perceived. True, at times a premier may micromanage a file, but government is too big and public policy too complex for any one individual to dictate policy. Rather, the public policy process invites a variety of inputs as it passes through various stages, and this often includes interaction with the centre. The executive authority of a populist warrants additional scrutiny, and yet by definition excessive trust is placed in him. However, in a small polity like Newfoundland there are too few people in the premier's office to steer every issue, even if the government is headed by a premier who appears to be larger than life.

Alex Marland, lead editor

FIRST AMONG UNEQUALS

1

Introduction: Executive Authority and Public Policy in Newfoundland & Labrador

ALEX MARLAND

In 1949, Newfoundland premier Joey Smallwood,[1] who was stumping for a federal Liberal candidate, infamously warned electors in Ferryland that "I don't need you. I've been elected. But you need me. I'm sitting on top of the public chest, and not one red cent will come out of it for Ferryland unless Greg Power is elected [to Ottawa]. Unless you vote for my man, you'll be out in the cold for the next five years ... Those settlements which vote against Greg Power will get nothing – absolutely nothing" (Gwyn 1999, 151).

This is one of many instances of Newfoundlanders being advised that their premier wields considerable sway over politics and public policy. In the post-Confederation era successful leaders in Newfoundland have won convincing election victories, have faced limited organized opposition, and have verbally jousted with prime ministers and any other opponents who have stood in their way. He – or, since Premier Kathy Dunderdale, she – is expected to be Newfoundland's chief spokesperson, a patriotic defender of provincial interests, and the decision maker who brokers competing policy priorities (Cadigan 2009; House 1985; Marland 2010).

Perceptions of a premier's influence over public policy vary and may be based on that individual's public persona. Premiers such as Frank Moores and Beaton Tulk freely delegated the authority of their office to ministers and acted as "chairmen of the board" (Crosbie 1997, 134). Smallwood occupied the other extreme: he has been described as "a demagogue [ruling] over an unsophisticated and uninformed electorate" (Gwyn 1999, 152) and "a complete one-man show" who micromanaged government policy (Crosbie 1997, 56). In between is a range of characterizations of Newfoundland premiers: Clyde Wells was praised for his honesty, intelligence, and integrity, but critiqued for an "autocratic style" (Hoy 1992, 296) and likewise for running "a one-man show" (e.g., Newfoundland and Labrador 1991). A similar narrative has emerged for Danny Williams, Newfoundland & Labrador's ninth premier, who held that office from November 2003 to December 2010. As *Telegram* editor Russell Wangersky put it, "[Premier] Williams was so involved in the daily workings of his government that a feeling grew over the years: if you really wanted an issue dealt with by the government as a whole, you had to garner Williams' personal interest first. Williams was criticized as being a one-man show, a controlling leader with his hands on everything" (2011, 136).

Given Newfoundland's political history and a dearth of scholarly analysis, it is difficult to assess whether this public "feeling" of executive control was justified. What little research there is on the matter suggests that the actions and statements of premiers, their parties, and their critics tend to convince followers, pundits, and electors that the Premier's Office has the unilateral ability to shape public policy. This may be symptomatic of a global trend of central government offices steering policy (Dahlström, Peters, and Pierre 2011) and, within parliamentary systems, of one-party cabinets (Lijphart 2012) and "presidentialization" (Poguntke and Webb 2005). At the federal level of government in Canada, the prevailing wisdom is that the power to influence public policy is concentrated within central agencies, which are comprised of the Privy Council Office (PCO), the Treasury Board, the Department of Finance, and the Prime Minister's Office (PMO) (Bakvis and Wolinetz 2005; Bernier, Brownsey, and Hollett 2005; Doern and Aucoin 1979; Malloy 2004; Martin 2010; Savoie 1999, 2005, 2010, 2011; Thomas 2003; White 2005). The prime minister is not a "first among equals" in cabinet; rather, journalists decry what they perceive as autocratic leadership, framing Prime Minister Jean Chrétien as a "friendly dictator," or Stephen Harper as a control freak at the head of "Harperland" (Martin 2010; Simpson 2001). At the provincial level, power is likewise thought to reside with premiers, who face fewer constraints, especially in the case of populists (Bernier, Brownsey, and Hollett 2005; Chandler and Chandler 1979; Dunn 1996, 2006a; Martin 2002; Malloy 2004; Miljan 2008; Savoie 1999; White 2005).

While it is true that government departments no longer operate in silos, such academic and media frames can downplay the considerable constraints faced by the head of a democratic government. Even in small polities like Newfoundland, modern government is so big, so complex, and so process-oriented that it operates as a machine with many interlocking parts and is subject to external forces. Thus despite public impressions, a premier may act first as a broker of competing policy demands and defer to the course of action recommended by a minister (Bernier, Brownsey, and Hollett 2005; White 1994). In this view the diffusion of power depends on the degree of pluralism and an engaged public sphere (Bachrach and Baratz 1962).

The question of "who decides" matters because how much we pay in taxes, the quality of medical services, and the condition of roads are some of the many outcomes of government policies that are shaped by an appointed cabinet, elected legislators, and a non-partisan bureaucracy. Provincial governments are responsible for policies in areas such as health care, education, local transportation, municipalities, lands, and non-renewable natural resources. Every so often, voters express their dissatisfaction with provincial policies and elites by voting for another party or coalition of parties to control the government. This book is about one such instance; it is an exploration of some of the policy decisions taken by the Progressive Conservative (PC) government led by Premier Williams. It focuses on the administration of an influential leader as it seeks to answer the following question: Does the premier really have as much power over government policy decisions as is popularly perceived?

WHAT IS PUBLIC POLICY?

Public policy is the framework that guides government decisions, resulting in action or inaction, particularly with respect to the distribution of finite government resources. Policies are introduced, updated, and repealed in response to the myriad of changing dynamics of society. The process of renewing public policy ranges from responding to crisis situations to acting on proactive ideas and normative ideals: it is both political and apolitical. In a democracy, we expect the governing party to listen to the expertise of public servants, we hope that affected people and organizations will be engaged and consulted, and we believe that governments can be pressured to reverse unpopular decisions.

The policy process is rarely simple, since it "involves an extremely complex set of elements that interact over time" (Sabatier 2007, 3). Academics typically teach detailed and complex policy models that are based on generalizations of case studies of controversial issues. In theory, elected representatives deliberate on government policy and consider diverse perspectives that take various forms, including the following: laissez-faire pluralism, whereby political elites respond to powerful competing interests; corporate pluralism, which sees interest groups capturing government authority by projecting grassroots representation while commanding a semi-monopoly of power; and public pluralism, which features the state's regulation of conflicting interests to ensure competition (Kelso 1978, 12–29).

Deborah Stone explains that the "fields of political science, public administration, law, and policy analysis have shared a common mission of rescuing public policy from the irrationalities and indignities of politics, hoping to make policy instead [using] rational, analytical, and scientific methods" (1997, 6). She confronts the idealism of rational policy analysis with the realism of political decisions. Public policies that are advocated by the political executive, even in the face of contrary scientific evidence, are the positions that are most likely to be implemented. In other words, academics and the bureaucracy preach careful policy analysis and caution, whereas politicians are more likely to follow their instincts and demand expedience, for they are the ones who are accountable to the public.

Political reasoning is very different from rational decision making. It can be the art of persuasion through the use of metaphors and analogies, of personal and mass communication, and of the propagation of emotion over reason. It often pits the short-term sensitivities of politicians and political advisors against the permanent executive's long-term experience and bureaucratic culture. Political executives are forever mindful that what is rational to party members and/or public policy experts may conflict with public preferences. For instance, remarking on suggestions for program expenditure cuts that the political executive had requested from provincial public servants in 2004, Premier Williams observed the following: "If in fact we had taken the advice of our civil service during the budget process, there would be people on social assistance today who don't have dentures, who can't get glasses. The Kids Eat Smart program would be cut back [and] the school lunch program would be cut back dramatically" (Sweet 2004, 1).

More often than not, the non-partisan advice of experienced and impassionate civil servants is followed. Their preference for evidence-based decision making and a concern for longer-term implications are valued when circumstances allow. This may explain why some political pledges, such as the PC government's steadfast insistence in 2007 that Sir

Wilfred Grenfell College in Corner Brook become an independent university (CBC News 2007a), are not fulfilled and are moved off the government's agenda.[2]

Politicians, not civil servants, are embroiled in the game of setting the public agenda, which enables a democratic government to take action. Agenda setting occurs early in the policy process, when political actors identify a problem and establish a need for government action (Howlett, Ramesh, and Perl 2009, 92; Soroka 2002). In their efforts to build and establish a public agenda, political actors seek to influence public opinion through strategic media relations, advertising, and the repetition of key messages. The debate is further mediated by journalists, who may have their own agenda and exhibit a range of slants (Entman 2007; Kiousis, Mitrook, and Wu 2006; Scheufele and Tewksbury 2007), as do the citizens who interpret this information. This mediation of different perspectives leads to a perceived reality that in turn influences public policy.

The balance of internal and external pressures, sources of policy data, and forms of policy analysis are illustrated in table 1.1. Generally speaking, the public service prioritizes the status quo, prefers standardized policies, and draws on quantitative data. Bureaucrats engage in more complex and objective analysis than the politicians who push for change, prefer that policies reflect local dynamics, draw on qualitative data (though this is changing), and who employ a simpler and more subjective method of analysis.

THE NATURE OF DEMOCRATIC GOVERNMENT

Students of political science will be acquainted with the differences in systems of government and debates about effective governance. For our purposes of assessing the relationship between executive power and public policy we need only establish what democracy is. Newfoundland meets the minimum conditions of a democratic system of government: there are regular and non-violent legitimate elections where the winner takes office; the head of government is selected by means of those elections; members of the legislature are elected; more than one party contests elections; and power alternates (Cheibub, Gandhi and Vreeland 2010; also Barro 1999). The rule of law and civil rights are also upheld. Optimally, this should lead to the ruling elite being responsive to a society that is engaged in policy decisions and therefore empowered. As a result, the "public good is achieved, citizen preferences are represented,

Table 1.1
Public policy priorities of the bureaucracy and the political executive

	Bureaucrats	*Cabinet*
Internal pressures	Status quo • Preservation of long-standing policies and processes within established framework	Change • Shaping of policies to reflect party priorities as channelled through the party leader
External pressures	Standardization • Updating of policies to reflect broad societal changes, other jurisdictions' policies, and legal rulings	Localization • Shaping of policies in response to local public, party, and interest group demands
Policy data	Quantitative • Demographics, economics, external studies, internal reports, user statistics, census	Qualitative • Caucus, constituent interaction, media monitoring, opinion research, party members, political staff, stakeholder consultation
Policy analysis	Complex • Analytical, computers, institutional memory, trained policy evaluators, multiple "lenses," long-term view, concerned about precedents	Simple • Emotional, instinctive, ideological, political memory, advocates of policy victims, short-term view, concerned about resolving problems

governments become accountable, citizen participation in political life is maximized, economic equality is enhanced, rationality is implemented, economic conditions improve" (Cheibub, Gandhi, and Vreeland 2010, 72). Democracy is an attractive concept.

Yet democracy is messy. In reality there is competition for government resources; electoral systems overrepresent some voices to the detriment of others; government transparency is paralyzed by the prospects of outside criticism; voter turnout is low; and politicians are rewarded when they promote short-term policy over a more rational long-term outlook. There are further variations depending on the concentration of power in the executive versus legislative branches, the vibrancy of political parties, the degree of pluralism, the flexibility of a constitution, and so on (Lijphart 2012). A democracy must also uphold political freedoms, including free speech and protections for political minorities. In contrast, dictatorships and authoritarian rule occur in crisis situations where constitutional rules are suspended by a centralized leadership, which tends to assume and maintain power through the use of force (Linz 2000).

In a parliamentary system of democracy there are considerable constraints on executive authority compared with non-democratic systems. Broadly speaking, the executive branch (e.g., the cabinet) is bound by statutes and regulations and by parliamentary principles such as responsible government and collective and individual ministerial responsibility. The public service may release policy details in response to freedom of information requests and through annual reports. Senior public servants, notably deputy ministers, may have performance contracts. In the legislature, ministers defend their decisions to opposition parties during question period and in legislative committees; budget estimates are debated and scrutinized; and statutory offices such as the auditor general, the ombudsman, and the chief electoral officer deliver non-partisan reports to all members of the legislature. The judicial branch upholds the rule of law by rendering judgments on whether statutes and regulations have been followed, as well as on their constitutionality. All these constraints are observed and pressure is exerted by the press gallery, citizen journalists and pundits, party donors, pollsters, interest groups, business owners, organized labour, lobbyists, and ultimately the general public.

In a democracy, support for policy change is related to societal factors, including a balance of rational citizens seeking to maximize their personal self-interest and the broader interests of their political community. In response to public demands, government policy is biased towards spending finite resources on short-term policy benefits, as opposed to exercising spending restraint for the benefit of longer-term policy (Jacobs and Matthews 2012). There is a place for production models of policy-making that describe the stages of idea germination, movement through political and bureaucratic channels, implementation of policy, and revisions based on external challenges. But an arena of agenda setting where political actors and government elites use available levers – including influence, cooperation, loyalty, group dynamics, information, passion, and power – is what often prevails in smaller communities like Newfoundland & Labrador.

THE POWER OF PREMIERS AND THE POLITICAL EXECUTIVE

A democratic principle in the parliamentary system holds that the cabinet is accountable to the citizens' elected representatives: the political executive must maintain the confidence of a majority of members of the

Table 1.2
Governing parties' control of legislatures in Canada (election results, 1949–2013)

Jurisdiction	Number of majority governments	Number of minority governments	Percentage of majority outcomes	Examples of prolonged party government
Canada	12	9	57	Liberal, 1935–57, 1993–2004
British Columbia	18	1	95	Social Credit, 1952–72, 1975–91
Alberta	17	0	100	Social Credit, 1935–1971; PC, 1971–
Saskatchewan	15	1	94	NDP, 1944–64, 1991–2007
Manitoba	15	3	83	PC, 1958–69, 1988–99; NDP, 1999–
Ontario	13	4	76	Conservative, 1943–1985
Quebec	15	2	88	Union Nationale, 1944–60
New Brunswick	16	0	100	PC, 1970–87; Liberal, 1987–99
Nova Scotia	15	4	79	Liberal, 1933–56; PC, 1956–70, 1978–93
PEI	18	0	100	Liberal, 1935–59, 1966–79, 1986–96
Newfoundland & Labrador	18	1	95	Liberal, 1949–71, 1989–2003; PC 1971–89; 2003–

legislature. However, the quality of responsible government is related to the design of the electoral system. In the provinces, it is normal for the governing party to win only a plurality of election votes yet be rewarded with a majority of seats, bringing into question the ability of the single-member plurality electoral system to reflect the electorate's preferences. Supermajorities, whereby the governing party dominates the unicameral legislature, and extended periods of the same party controlling the government are also common (table 1.2; see also table 4.1 in chapter 4). Sometimes the governing party so thoroughly dominates the legislature that there is no credible opposition, as when Frank McKenna's Liberals won all fifty-eight seats in the 1987 New Brunswick election; Pat Binns' PC party won twenty-six of twenty-seven seats in the 2000 Prince Edward Island general election; Gordon Campbell's Liberals took seventy-seven of seventy-nine seats in British Columbia in 2001;

and Williams' PCs won forty-four of forty-eight seats in Newfoundland in 2007. This fusion of the executive and legislative branches inhibits responsible government and in such circumstances a premier's control over provincial politics can be ominous. While it means that swift government action can be mobilized, it comes at a price of reduced consultation, scrutiny, and accountability.

There are other institutional reasons why premiers hold more sway over public policy than prime ministers do. In most circumstances the head of a provincial government is subject to less scrutiny than her national counterpart is. A provincial executive does not face a bicameral legislature, it represents the interests of a more homogenous polity, and it is less constrained by international agreements. Internal power struggles are limited by the lack of aspiring successors who can successfully mobilize against an incumbent. Premiers cultivate a loyal personal following by meeting with constituents, with municipal leaders, and with interest group representatives. Political finance rules do not tend to be as rigorous as those at the federal level, where, since 2007, donations from corporations and trade unions to political parties, candidates, and leadership contestants have been banned. Local media outlets have less capacity to fund investigative journalism. Compared with national public affairs, provincial electors are therefore more susceptible to government messaging, the communication of regional grievances, and the treatment of their leader as a celebrity.[3]

Some premiers, especially those who belong to the same political party as their federal counterparts, tend to work cooperatively within the federal system of government. But others espouse an asymmetrical style of federalism as they compete for more beneficial policies and a greater share of the federal spending power. They build their province by acting as powerful champions of local causes and by presenting themselves as protectors of a shared regional identity. A prime minister who cedes to a province's demands does so with no guarantee of satisfying its premier and also risks inflaming political tensions elsewhere in Canada. Former federal minister John Crosbie has remarked that, in his experience, Newfoundland premiers were "totally selfish and ungrateful, no matter what Ottawa did for them. If a billion dollars in cash or benefits was delivered to them one day, they'd be howling twenty-four hours later that they hadn't received a second billion dollars ... The more we did for the province, the more they asked for, the more they attacked, the more unreasonable they were, and the more arrogant they grew" (Crosbie 1997, 354–5).

Regardless of what, if any, policy changes result from intergovernmental lobbying, there is a good chance that the premier will personally benefit from the masses unifying behind a "selfless superhero" (Overton 1985, 87). By taking on outsiders, the premier indirectly gains increased executive power over her party, over the unicameral legislature, over the local media, and over the public service. An us-versus-them dynamic is election fodder that can exploit the weaknesses of opposition parties and the public's emotions. The most powerful premiers tend to be populists who readily employ this tactic.

Populists present themselves as outsiders who champion the public's preferences. These charismatic figures embody a political identity and bypass institutional norms to achieve their policy objectives. When faced with obstacles, they may ignore established government processes and be ruthless with opponents, all in the name of the greater good (Canovan 1999; Lukacs 2005; Taggart 2000). Even though elites are shocked at such nonconformity and grow concerned about the concentration of power in a single individual, the public tolerates this situation when they like and trust the leader to represent their interests. Such leaders are framed as strong commanders-in-chief whose personalities and alleged micromanaging supersedes all other decision frameworks. As long as the rule of law is upheld, it is a matter of debate whether populists embody democracy or are an affront to democratic principles.

For all their political power, real or perceived, premiers do face challenges in achieving their policy goals. The Charter of Rights and Freedoms places legal constraints on government and has increased the counterbalance of the courts against executive dominance. Changes in communications technology, notably the Internet, have favoured the media, opposition parties, and interest groups, who can mobilize and share information more quickly than ever before. The constitution provides the federal government, not the provinces, with authority over the regulation of trade and commerce, currency, banking, interest rates, and indirect taxation. Provincial actors do not control monetary policy; they are subject to financial pressures and international agreements and the forces of capitalism and globalization.

The ability of the provinces to fund social programming is contingent on federal funding, and in the 1990s the Canadian government unilaterally introduced significant cuts to social program transfers. The nature of integrated programs and the issues that arise from them lead to federal, provincial, and territorial (FPT) dialogue, as well as meetings of all premiers at the Council of the Federation and regional meetings such as the Council of Atlantic Premiers. There remain significant issues associated with interprovincial trade, labour force training, health care, and environmental policy, despite the signing of the Agreement on Internal Trade (1995) and the Social Union Framework Agreement (1999). As a consequence, Canada has moved away from executive federalism to cooperative federalism, although it is a fragile model that continues to place premiers at the centre (Cameron and Simeon 2002, 64).

The most significant challenges to premiers' authority are unpopular decisions and elector unrest. News of government mismanagement, a poor showing in a public opinion poll, or an abuse of office knocks the premier off her agenda and can weaken her authority to lead. Intense pressure can result from internal reforms that trigger political activism and media frenzy. Examples include the following: spending cuts, the proposed sale of provincial assets, the negotiation of collective bargaining agreements with organized labour, and tax increases. Taking a hard line in the name of good financial management occurs at the risk of media criticism and reduced popularity (e.g., Hoy 1992). When such problems emerge, exerting control over cabinet and the legislature is paramount if she is to implement a political agenda.

PUBLIC POLICY AND PREMIERS IN NEWFOUNDLAND & LABRADOR

The analysis of policy-making involves a variety of long-standing theories (Simon 2007, 26–45). Group theory posits that political parties and interest groups may prioritize policy solutions, while incrementalism maintains that policies are made through a series of small decisions. Public choice theory explores the nature of collective action in the government sphere, whereby the pursuit of self-interest is constrained by the need to ensure the delivery of public goods and common pool resources. Conversely, systems theory suggests that public responses to policies serve to re-shape those policies. Numerous recently developed approaches also explain the flow of public policy. They include the punctuated-equilibrium framework, which indicates that incrementalism is periodically interrupted by major policy change, and the advocacy coalition framework, which promotes a view that elites from various institutions unite to achieve a shared policy goal (Sabatier 2007).

Two theories of public policy appear to be highly relevant for Newfoundland & Labrador. Elite theory views control of the government as resting with a powerful minority (Stewart, Hedge, and Lester 2008). The masses generally accept elites' power and are unengaged except when a

policy affects them directly or when they express discontent in an election. In this scenario, citizens are "pawns" who follow the requests of
political leaders and/or interest groups who persuasively mobilize political action to satisfy a policy goal or ideology that is shared by a cohesive
group (Adams 2007, 8). This pattern is prevalent in cases of demagogic
leadership, patriarchy, paternalism, and populist government.

While the elite model contravenes notions of a pluralistic democracy,
institutionalism, by comparison, theorizes that policies emerge because
of the nature of government institutions – specifically, the power of the
executive, legislative, and judicial branches. They act major constrain-
ing elements on the power of political actors – the rules, processes, and
frameworks of institutions, and the negotiation and competition that
takes place between institutions. Though policy outcomes are often
visible, the behaviour of elites and the powers of institutions can be
informal and invisible, making them difficult to examine empirically
without conjecture (Simon 2007, 37, 41).

Elite theory and institutionalism are applicable to Newfoundland for a
number of reasons. First, immediately before Newfoundland joined Canada in 1949, the Commission of Government operated as a "benevolent
dictatorship" (Mayo 1949; for more on Newfoundland's political history see Cadigan 2009, as well as chapter 2, by Christopher Dunn, in this
book). Second, since adopting the parliamentary system of government,
Newfoundland has experienced prolonged periods of one-party dominance and premiers who have cultivated an image as public defenders but
have been criticized for behaving in a quasi-autocratic manner. Third,
the executive branch's power has stemmed from strong majority governments and feeble oppositions (see table 4.1), from political homogen-
eity and interest group accommodation, from a tendency towards media
reporting rather than investigative journalism, and from a premier's cult
of personality. That Newfoundlanders often refer to their premiers on a
first name basis – e.g., "Joey," "Danny," or "our Brian" – speaks to the
personal connection they feel with their political leaders.

Perceptions that power is concentrated in the Office of the Premier
have been prevalent since Newfoundland joined Canada. It is said that
Smallwood unilaterally made his government's policy decisions and that
he regarded most of his cabinet "with a disdain he often made no effort
to conceal" (Gwyn 1999, 159; also Chandler and Chandler 1979, 102).
In 1950 a British high commissioner reported to London that Smallwood
enjoyed being "the head of a 'one-man government' and commented
... on the benefits of 'democratic dictatorship' which he said was only

possible in a small place like Newfoundland" (Crosbie 1997, 44). By comparison subsequent premiers have operated an institutionalized cabinet that features a more complex institutional structure and reduced departmental autonomy (Dunn 2005a).[4] There has been an increase in the size and professionalism of central agencies such as the Treasury Board Secretariat and the Finance Department. Political staffers in the Premier's Office work closely with informed specialists in those agencies and especially in the Executive Council. This development has added layers of internal review to the policy process, has expanded the scope of interdepartmental and public consultation, and has increased ministers' and public servants' awareness of the importance of evidence-based policy-making. Nevertheless, the image of the premier as an autocrat persists.

Innumerable policy accomplishments and controversies are associated with Newfoundland's premiers (for an overview see table 1.6, in the appendix to this chapter). Over time, the capacity of the provincial government for policy analysis has improved, but it is still limited. To illustrate, in 2009–10 the Executive Council had a number of policy arms, which included the Intergovernmental Affairs Secretariat, the Rural Secretariat, the Office of Climate Change, and the Women's Policy Office. Government agencies dealing with policy included the Human Rights Commission and the Research and Development Corporation. At that time, about 180 government departmental employees had "policy" in their formal job title; of these, nearly a quarter (24 percent) were employed by the department dealing with income support, even though it was responsible for just 5.3 percent of government expenditures (table 1.3). Central agencies reporting to the Premier's Office also employed a sizeable share of policy personnel. While this outline is not intended to be a precise measure of the capacity for policy analysis – after all, the public service as a whole, especially at the executive level, is inherently involved in policy creation, implementation, or evaluation – it does indicate the importance of policy attached to unemployment programs and central agencies. Moreover, it does not necessarily indicate that the province's policy analysis capacity is a problem. In Crosbie's experience, policies shaped by "a rat's nest" of democratic inputs ranging from feasibility studies to interdepartmental task forces are often no more rational than unilateral decisions made by "a despot" like Smallwood (Crosbie 1997, 473).

As table 1.3 shows, the main business of a provincial government tends to be the administration of welfare state programming. Cabinet's

Table 1.3
Number of policy personnel, Government of Newfoundland & Labrador (2010)

Department	Divisions with policy personnel (number of policy personnel)*	Expenditures (% of all)**
GENERAL GOVERNMENT		
Executive Council	Climate Change, Energy Efficiency & Emissions Trading; Communication & Consultation Branch; Intergovernmental Affairs Secretariat; Office of the Chief Information Officer; Public Service Secretariat; Rural Secretariat; Transparency & Accountability Office; Voluntary & Non-Profit Secretariat; Women's Policy Office (n=20)	$103 million (1.9)
Finance	Fiscal Policy; Newfoundland & Labrador Statistics Agency; Policy, Planning, Accountability, and Information Management; Professional Services and Internal Audit Division; Project Analysis; Tax Policy (n=13)	$81 million (1.5)
Government Services	Board Services; Executive Support; Financial Services Regulation; Government Purchasing Agency; Policy & Planning (n=9)	$28 million (0.5)
Labrador and Aboriginal Affairs	Aboriginal Affairs (n=1)	$4 million (0.07)
Transportation and Works	Policy and Planning (n=6)	$470 million (8.6)
RESOURCE SECTOR		
Business	Red Tape Reduction Initiative; Regulatory Reform; Strategic Policy Development (n=6)	$13 million (0.2%)
Environment and Conservation	Environment; Land Management; Sustainable Development & Strategic Science; Tourism; Wildlife (n=9)	$29 million (0.5)
Fisheries and Aquaculture	Aquaculture; Licensing and Quality Assurance; Planning Services; Seafood Marketing and Support Services; Sustainable Fisheries and Oceans Policy (n=8)	$22 million (0.4)
Innovation, Trade and Rural Development	Business; Research and Development Corporation; The Strategic Partnership; Trade and Export Development (n=8)	$83 million (1.5)
Natural Resources	Energy Economics; Petroleum Projects Monitoring; Policy & Strategic Planning; Natural Resources (n=13)	$154 million (2.8%)
Tourism, Culture and Recreation	Planning, Research & Promotion (n=2)	$64 million (1.2)
SOCIAL SECTOR		
Child, Youth and Family Services	Policy and Planning (n=2)	$125 million (2.3)

Table 1.3 continued

Education	Adult Learning and Literacy; Evaluation and Research; Planning and Accountability; Policy and Planning; Post-Secondary Research and Analysis; School Services; Student Financial Services (n=18)	$1.21 billion (22.1)
Health and Community Services	Child, Youth and Family Services Act; Planning and Evaluation; Policy Development (n=8)	$2.35 billion (43.1)
Human Resources, Labour and Employment	Finance and General Operations; Income Support; Labour Market Development Agreement; Labour Relations Agency; Office of Immigration and Multiculturalism; Policy, Planning and Evaluation; Poverty Reduction Strategy; Workplace Health, Safety and Compensation Review (n=43)	$291 million (5.3)
Justice	Civil Division; Corrections Administration; Inland Fish Enforcement Program; Legal Information Management; Policy and Strategic Planning; Public Prosecutions (n=9)	$217 million (4)
Municipal Affairs	Policy and Strategic Planning; Waste Management (n=5)	$217 million (4)

Note: Policy personnel total n=180; total departmental expenditures = $5,458,310 million.
*Presents position titles that include "policy" on an illustrative basis. Does not show related positions such as deputy ministers. Includes management (n=25) such as assistant deputy ministers, assistant secretaries to Cabinet, directors and managers, and policy analysis positions (n=155) such as senior policy advisors, policy development specialists, and policy analysts. Table does not include House of Assembly staff (n=5) or administrative support staff (n=2). Calculated from Newfoundland and Labrador (2010h).
**Rounded figures. Shows budgetary expenditures for government departments only (e.g., excludes the legislative brand and government agencies such as the Newfoundland and Labrador Housing Corporation). Expenditures expressed as a percentage of current and capital account expenditures using 2009–10 revised (net) data. Calculated from Newfoundland and Labrador (2010c). Actual total of all government expenditures was $6,043,340 million.

most significant policy decisions tend to involve health care, which accounts for over two dollars of every five dollars spent on government departments and which together with education is responsible for nearly two-thirds of provincial government expenditures. Social sector departments account for the majority of provincial government spending and, anecdotally, nearly half of Newfoundland's policy labour force (85 of 180 positions). The proportion of government policy personnel involved with social assistance matters is consistent with a comparative but dated study that has remarked on the high per capita spending by the Newfoundland government, the comparatively low employment and income levels of Newfoundlanders, and the province's homogeneous British

ethnicity (Chandler and Chandler 1979). Indeed, although Newfoundland's financial situation has improved, its annual average unemployment rate was the worst of all the provinces *every single year* from 1976
to 2011 (Newfoundland and Labrador Statistics Agency 2012). Related
to this, the province's 38,500 Employment Insurance (EI) beneficiaries
in April 2012 represented 6.8 percent of the national total, pointing to a
disproportional dependency for a province comprising less than 1.5 percent of the Canadian population (Statistics Canada 2012b).

The harsh effects of a modern global political economy on small, rural
economies, especially those that can no longer rely on the fishery, contribute to lingering public sentiments that federalism has not worked
out for Newfoundland. There is some truth to this feeling, given that
Newfoundland elects just seven of the more than three hundred members of parliament (MPs) in the House of Commons, that it is represented in the Senate by just six of the more than one hundred senators,
that it is among the smallest of the federation's ten provinces, and that
it is located in the Canadian hinterland far from major centres. Newfoundlanders tend to be frustrated with the federal government, which
is perceived to treat them with disrespect, to ignore their concerns, to
favour other provinces in revenue sharing, and to have too much control over Newfoundland's natural resources (Ryan Research and Communications 2003). Yet Newfoundlanders are enthusiastic supporters of
Canada's social programs, such as universal health care and Employment Insurance, and they believe that being part of Canada has been a
net benefit for the province.

These feelings of low national efficacy translate into expectations
that Newfoundland's premier will punch above her weight when lobbying Ottawa. There is a rotation between the joint federal-provincial
policy approach to cooperative federalism and the adversarial relationships of competitive federalism, which often depend on the presence of
a powerful regional minister (Bakvis 1989; Marland 2010; Skogstad
2000, 58). Premier Smallwood leveraged federal funds by ensuring he
had a Liberal "man at Ottawa" (Gwyn 1999, 208), but intergovernmental cooperation was interrupted by Smallwood's animosity towards
Progressive Conservative prime minister John Diefenbaker. Such conflict
receded under Premier Moores, who prioritized government reform and
ministerial autonomy (Wells 2008, 214). Progressive Conservative premier Brian Peckford became a controversial figure for his political rhetoric against Liberal prime minister Pierre Trudeau over natural resource
ownership, but the "bad boy of Confederation" image solidified the

premier's popularity at home (Summers 2001, 37). The image of Premier Wells, a Liberal, was of both a "selfless saint" and a "dogmatic sinner" (Hoy 1992, xii) for holding firm against Progressive Conservative prime minister Brian Mulroney's intent to recognize Quebec as a distinct society, but cooperative federalism prevailed when Chrétien's Liberals took over. The rhythm of cyclical federalist cooperation and nationalist conflict continued when Brian Tobin, a minister in Chrétien's administration, capitalized on a "Captain Canada" reputation to succeed Wells and leverage his Ottawa connections. As voter unrest with over a decade of federal-provincial Liberal governance grew, Premier Roger Grimes called the Royal Commission on Renewing and Strengthening Our Place in Canada, setting the scene for Newfoundland's premier to demand a more favourable economic relationship with Ottawa with respect to offshore oil resources (Boswell 2002).

PUBLIC POLICY IN THE PREMIER WILLIAMS ERA

While it is not possible to provide a full profile of Premier Williams' government here, some further context is needed to set the scene for each chapter's case study analysis. Three interconnected thematic areas – economic conditions, executive authority, and political communication – warrant particular consideration.

Economic Conditions

First, if public policy involves government decisions about the allocation of finite resources, then in the early twenty-first century Newfoundland enjoyed an unprecedented range of policy options. The period was marked by significant economic growth owing to major increases in the value of offshore oil royalties. When Danny Williams became premier in 2003, the price of a barrel of crude oil was US$29.12; when he resigned in 2010, it was US$90.01 (World Bank 2012). It was a major economic and psychological achievement in 2008 when, for the first time, Newfoundland shed its "have not" status to become a "have" province that no longer qualified for federal equalization payments, whereas Ontario was suddenly "have not" (e.g., Peckford 2012). A sign of Newfoundland's growing confidence was Premier Williams' insistence that the federal government offer compensation to offset declining transfer payments as oil revenues increased, which Valérie Vézina and Karlo Basta discuss in chapter 3. Moreover, in keeping with his party's "no more

Table 1.4
Revenue sources, Government of Newfoundland & Labrador (2002–03 and 2010–11)

	Revenues (% of total)	
Revenue source	2002–03	2010–11
Provincial taxes (e.g., personal and corporate income, sales, gasoline, payroll, tobacco, insurance companies, corporate capital, forest management)	$1.7 billion (46)	$2.9 billion (41)
Provincial royalties (e.g., offshore oil, mining, forestry)	$88 million (2)	$2.4 billion (35)
Provincial licenses, permits, fines, and fees (e.g., vehicle and driver licenses, registry of deeds, fines and forfeitures, inland fish and game, water power rentals, registry of personal property, crown lands, mining)	$80 million (2)	$262 million (4)
Other provincial sources (e.g., Newfoundland Liquor Corporation, lottery revenues, interest income, other)	$270 million (7)	$150 million (2)
Federal transfer payments (e.g., equalization, Atlantic Accord, health transfers, social transfers, statutory subsidies, other)	$1.5 billion (42)	$1.2 billion (18)
Total provincial government revenues	$3.7 billion (100)	$6.9 billion (100)

Source: 2002–03 and 2010–11 revised data. Calculated from Newfoundland and Labrador (2003, viii; 2011b, v).

Note: Figures are rounded.

giveaways" rallying cry, Williams negotiated provincial government ownership in oilfield production so that the public would benefit when the price of crude increased.

A look at government revenues shows why natural resource issues have attracted so much attention in Newfoundland and what a significant impact they have had on the provincial government's ability to finance its policy objectives (table 1.4). In the last full fiscal year of Liberal government before the PC era began, provincial royalties accounted for $88 million, which amounted to 2 percent of the government's total revenues. By the fiscal year of Williams' departure, royalties had ballooned to $2.4 billion, accounting for 35 percent of the government's total revenues, which themselves had more than doubled during a period of low inflation. The broad societal benefits of such wealth are undeniable: from 1981 to 2010, Newfoundland experienced the strongest growth in an index of provincial economic well-being, such that in 2010 Newfoundlanders' consumption, wealth, economic equality, and economic security were deemed second only to those of Albertans (Osberg and Sharpe 2011). As well, for the first time in the province's history, an administration made headway in paying down debt and liabilities, though perhaps not aggressively enough given the non-renewable nature of oil reserves.

People tend to approve of a government's policies when the economy is strong. Thus, we would anticipate that Newfoundlanders were satisfied with the PC administration during this period. Judging by the opinion poll data reported elsewhere in this volume, the public was *extremely* satisfied with the government, with the PC Party, and with Premier Williams. As we will see, one of the factors in this success was skilled media management, for even when economic times are good, a governing party and its leader can achieve positive approval ratings only if they have a public image as responsible economic managers (Powell and Whitten 1993; Gavin and Sanders 1997).

Executive Authority

Second, the substance and tone of a leader's policy decisions contribute to impressions of the scope of her executive authority. Newfoundlanders became acquainted with Premier Williams' populist style in 2004. He began by setting the public agenda by means of a televised address to inform citizens of an "evolving financial crisis" and of government restraint that would require "sacrifice by everyone," including public servants (Newfoundland and Labrador 2004e). During an ensuing public sector strike, with reporters in tow, the premier bypassed union leaders and approached strikers on the picket line to explain the government's offer. That September, the minister of health resigned when Williams bypassed the minister to authorize the settlement of a nurses' strike in his electoral district (CBC News 2004). "I could not continue in a portfolio when I would make decisions and then the premier would publicly overturn them and not tell me," Beth Marshall would explain (Moore 2005). Days later, when the deputy minister of health was fired, Williams remarked that it was "one of my best days at the office" (Sweet 2004, 1). Christopher Dunn concluded that in the early days of the Williams administration Newfoundland's cabinet structure had thus evolved into a premier-centred one, as it already had in other provinces (Dunn 2005a). This kind of executive governance features ministers and committees who discuss but who do not decide. Central agencies urgently prioritize and analyze the premier's issues over those of other ministers. Performance management indicators are introduced, and bureaucratic briefings freeze out some members of cabinet. But there is also a willingness to pander to local policy preferences when there are electoral gains to be had.

Two by-election episodes illustrate this nicely. During a 2005 by-election in Exploits, the premier reversed a school board decision to close Leo Burke Academy in Bishop's Falls. He defended his pronouncement by saying that as the leader of a democratic government, he was obliged to overrule what he deemed to be unreasonable policies made by unelected public servants. "You'll see it again," he remarked. "That's not the practice, that's not the intention. But if boards or groups or reports or consultants make decisions that are wrong decisions, then we have a responsibility as a government to make the right ones" (Antle 2005). The PCs won the seat and the school stayed open. But, as Maria Mathews describes in chapter 8, a different policy outcome occurred during a 2009 by-election in The Straits-White Bay North. During that campaign, the cabinet overturned an unpopular government decision to cut laboratory and x-ray services in Flower's Cove. This time the PC candidate was defeated, and while the health care services were preserved as promised, a subsequent cabinet decision to relocate the Northern Peninsula's air ambulance service to Labrador was interpreted as Tory payback for the by-election defeat (Roberts 2010).[5]

In public, Williams disagreed with the characterization that government policy always required his approval. "Despite the opinion by some people that this might be a one-man show – which [my government] has been termed – in fact, these ministers are managers of their department and they are delegated with the authority to run their own departments," he said in 2008 (Antle 2008). Testimony at the Cameron Inquiry (see chapters 7 and 8 in this book) presented mixed evidence for ministerial independence. Senior civil servants in the Department of Health and Community Services had sent important briefing notes directly to the Premier's Office without their minister's knowledge and at times had decided not to provide information to anyone in cabinet (Sweet 2008a, 2008b). Some public servants suggested that the Premier's Office practised "unusual interference" in public administration; however, others indicated that the premier's staff behaved no differently from other ministerial staffers (Sweet 2008c, 2008d). Ministers may have formally been in charge of their own departments but, as Matthew Kerby observes in chapter 6, over time many of the cabinet's more independently minded ministers exited, and the number of people willing to challenge the premier's policy ideas diminished. Allegations that Premier Williams had excessive power persisted after he had left office; interim Liberal leader

Yvonne Jones told her party in 2011 that he had "ruled this province with somewhat of an iron fist," which was possible because of a "cult of personality" (McLeod 2011a).

Political Communication

Third, perceptions of executive authority are linked to political communication. Jones's remarks were a common theme, as with the NDP leader's use of the word "dictator" in the legislature, which led to a point of order debate (Newfoundland and Labrador 2005b). The media paid considerable attention to the premier's disputes, which served to inform his critics that they risked a public confrontation. The media's interest in such power struggles dated back to Williams' oft-repeated remark in the 1990s that the deputy mayor of St John's needed "someone to give him a good shit-knocking" (*Telegram* 2010). The premier's willingness to joust with outsiders on a national or an international stage – including with big oil, Quebec, former Beatle Paul McCartney, and successive prime ministers – increased his image as a patriotic defender of his homeland and as a businessman who opposed economic liberalism. Locally, Williams sparred with the leaders of opposition parties, business organizations, and unions, and with departing members of caucus (e.g., CBC News 2005, 2008d). The media reported on his criticisms of the Newfoundland Oceans Industries Association (NOIA), the federal government's nominee to the Canada-Newfoundland Offshore Petroleum Board (C-NLOPB), and the mayor of Marystown. It also dissected instances where the premier responded angrily when his private life entered the public sphere (e.g., CBC News 2010k). Occasionally local journalists were themselves part of the story. In 2006 the *Independent* searched for details about where the premier's salary was donated, and as a consequence Williams ceased communicating with that newspaper's reporters, and his office cancelled its subscriptions (Cleary 2006). In 2008 when CBC journalist David Cochrane asked whether it was appropriate for the premier to attend a fundraising dinner, Williams pointed to Cochrane and said, "He's cut off" (*Telegram* 2008, A6). In 2009 the premier chastised the host of VOCM Open Line on live radio for musing that too much attention was being given to oil development deals (CBC News 2009j; see also chapter 4, by Royce Koop). Such confrontations fuel an anti-democratic narrative and public fear of a leader (e.g., Furedi 2005; Martin 2010).

This populist style fulfilled the media's need for infotainment, contributing to a "hyperreality" where the wider community was left to

Table 1.5
Premiers' approval ratings in their provinces (November 2010)

Province	Premier (party)	Premier since	Approval rating(%)
Newfoundland & Labrador	Danny Williams (Progressive Conservative)	November 2003	67
Saskatchewan	Brad Wall (Saskatchewan Party)	November 2007	60
New Brunswick	David Alward (Progressive Conservative)	October 2010	32
Manitoba	Greg Selinger (New Democratic Party)	October 2009	28
Alberta	Ed Stelmach (Progressive Conservative)	December 2006	21
Nova Scotia	Darrell Dexter (New Democratic Party)	June 2009	20
Ontario	Dalton McGuinty (Liberal)	October 2003	16
British Columbia	Gordon Campbell (Liberal)	June 2001	16
Quebec	Jean Charest (Liberal)	June 2003	14

Source: Angus Reid (2010).
Note: Respondents were asked "Do you approve or disapprove of the performance of...?"
Disapproval and unsure responses not shown.
PEI residents were not surveyed about Liberal premier Robert Ghiz.

arrive at its "own interpretation of political reality" (Delli Carpini and Williams 2001, 177). It is part of a broader tendency of the media and electors to pay attention to personalities over policy and the amplification of leaders' celebrity status (Bittner 2011; Marsh, Hart, and Tindall 2010). The oxygen that fed the premier's political power was the media coverage of his staggering popularity. From 2006 onwards – coinciding with Stephen Harper becoming prime minister – Newfoundlanders' preference for Williams as premier never dipped below 71 percent and reached as high as 85 percent in February 2008 (Marland 2007b; Corporate Research Associates 2012). Just before he announced his resignation in 2010, Williams' approval rating among Newfoundlanders stood at 67 percent, which was higher than all other premiers at the time (table 1.5). This figure is even more impressive in view of the fact that his popularity registered 80 percent earlier in the year and that he had been in power for seven years (Angus Reid 2010). Moreover, it is a startling contrast with the unpopularity of his successor, Kathy Dunderdale, who at just 20 percent voter approval placed last among Canadian premiers in mid-2013 (Angus Reid 2013). Such polling data matters because it speaks to a Newfoundland premier's ability to set the agenda through skilled media management, including a focus on achieving favourable polls.

RESEARCH QUESTIONS

Does Newfoundland's political system provide enough checks on executive authority? Is there a need for significant constraints on executive power if residents are enamoured with their premier and she respects the rule of law? Such questions are worth examining in a case study of one provincial administration. Academic knowledge of executives' role in public policy development in provincial government generally, and in Newfoundland & Labrador specifically, is limited.

While there is an industry of history and folklore publications, some of which delve into politics (such as Malone 2012; Webb 2008), most scholarly literature about Newfoundland politics has not encompassed entire volumes (but see Jackson 1984; Noel 1971). To date, political insights before the Williams era have been communicated in journal articles (Cadigan 2006; Conrad 2003; Hiller 1987; House 1982, 1985; King and Clarke 2002; Mayo 1949; Overton 2000; Penney 1981; Rothney 1962), book chapters (Graesser 1992; McCorquodale 1972, 1989; Overton 1979; Perlin 1974), monographs (House 1999; Overton 1985), and commissioned studies such as the aforementioned Royal Commission.[6] The exception to this rule is provided by accounts in the popular press of political biographies, autobiographies, and memoirs (e.g., Crosbie 1997; Gwyn 1999; Peckford 2012; Rowe 2010). The existing policy literature concerning Newfoundland & Labrador is likewise largely atheoretical and heavily concentrated on the natural resource and economic development arenas (Byron 2003; Feehan and Baker 2010; Summers 2001) as well as on social policy (Neville et al. 2005; Tomblin and Braun-Jackson 2006, 2009) and intergovernmental relations (Feehan 2006). Notable exceptions include analyses of reforms for democratic accountability (Dunn 2004), of municipal governance (Dunn 2006b), and of sociological observations (House 2005).

As mentioned, the central research question of this book is whether the premier has as much power over government policy decisions as is popularly believed. In the context of Newfoundland & Labrador, and specifically during the Williams era, we seek to understand (1) the authority of the political executive, (2) public policies of the government of Newfoundland & Labrador, and (3) how the former shapes the latter. Questions specific to Newfoundland & Labrador include the following: What public policies are prioritized? Which policies achieve group consensus and which spark political debate? To what extent are democratic ideals upheld, particularly with respect to the principle and spirit of responsible government? What are the positive and negative implications for public policy? Is reform needed and, if so, what opportunities for improvement exist? By enriching our understanding of how these questions were interrelated in the early 2000s, we hope to provide a theoretical and case-specific context for subsequent multidisciplinary analysis of past and future administrations, both in Canada's most easterly province and elsewhere.

PLAN OF THE BOOK

This book looks at the questions just mentioned through a multidisciplinary lens and is anchored by political science. By focusing foremost on executive power and public policy during the Premier Williams era, the authors seek to increase our knowledge of the state of democracy, public policy processes, provincial government policies, and election campaigning in Canada's most recent addition to Confederation. It adds to an emerging literature about the Williams era that features material dealing with the institutionalized cabinet (Dunn 2005a), elections (Marland 2007b, 2009), fiscal issues (Dunn 2005b; Lecours and Béland 2009; Mackenzie 2004), the legislature (Franks 2008; Green 2007; Marland 2007a, 2011; Moss 2009), image management (Marland and Kerby 2010), intergovernmental relations (Rowe 2010), nationalism (Marland 2010), and rural economic development (Close, Rowe, and Wheaton 2007; Vodden 2010).

The chapters cover an array of topics from a various perspectives. The early chapters of the book deal with politics and public administration in the Williams era. In chapter 2, Christopher Dunn provides some broad historical context of public administration in Newfoundland & Labrador. In chapter 3, Valérie Vézina and Karlo Basta explore nationalism and its pervasiveness in Newfoundland politics. Chapter 4, by Royce Koop, looks at party politics and how policy ideas are brokered. It is followed by a discussion about political parties and their leaders as brands in chapter 5, by Alex Marland. In chapter 6 Matthew Kerby presents a comparative analysis of ministerial turnover in the Williams cabinet.

Subsequent chapters of the book profile recent cases of public policies. In chapter 7, Kate Puddister and James Kelly look at the role of the judicial and executive branches in sorting out serious scandals in health care and the House of Assembly. Maria Mathews, in chapter 8, provides further detail about health care policy; that chapter is followed by Gerald Galway's analysis of education policy in chapter 9. In chapter 10, Mario Levesque examines provincial fisheries policy, and in chapter 11 Kelly Vodden, Ryan Gibson, and Michelle Porter discuss rural and regional development in Newfoundland & Labrador. In Chapter 12, James Feehan provides an overview of the contentious development of the Lower Churchill hydroelectric megaproject. The implications of economic growth for organized labour in Newfoundland are then discussed in chapter 13 by John Peters, Angela Carter, and Sean Cadigan. Finally, the book's concluding chapter considers the context and research questions presented in this first chapter in light of the various case studies and seeks to address the overarching issue of the first minister's power over government policy.

Most chapters follow a common structure. Applicable scholarly theory related to the topic is briefly summarized, the case study of the issue during the Progressive Conservative government from its election in 2003 to its re-election in 2011 is profiled, and this theory is then applied to the case study to arrive at insights about political decision making in the province. Readers should bear in mind that the diversity of theoretical approaches reflects the authors' backgrounds, since this volume brings together scholars whose area of research is not only Canadian and/or Newfoundland political science but also education, economics, geography, history, and medicine. The result is a strong multidisciplinary comprehension of how politics and public policy operate in Newfoundland & Labrador. Moreover, the use of theoretical concepts should allow the application of authors' findings to a variety of situations, regardless of the province studied or who happens to be premier.

Table 1.6
Major policy decisions by premiers of Newfoundland & Labrador

Premier	Policy accomplishments and controversies	Reason for departure
Joey Smallwood (Liberal, April 1949 – January 1972)	• Accessed federal funds to develop the welfare state and improve citizens' standard of living. • Expanded education, public health care, electricity, roads, communications. • Prioritized offshore trawlers and processing in fish plants; decline of small-boat inshore salt fishery. • Supported programs to resettle remote rural communities. • Decertified International Woodworkers of America (IWA) union after bitter Grand Falls loggers' strike. • Lobbied Ottawa for more transfer payments under term 29 of Terms of Union. • Moved legislature from Colonial Building to new Confederation Building. • Initiated royal commission on education (Warren Report) that would recommend secularization of education delivery. • Bungled economic deals and resource giveaways, including Come By Chance oil refinery, Stephenville linerboard mill, and Churchill Falls. • Budget deficits added to provincial debt.	Party did not win a majority of seats in the 1972 election.
Frank Moores (Progressive Conservative, January 1972 – March 1979)	• Sought to improve bad economic deals from Smallwood era. However, the Moores government's own questionable deals included millions for the Come By Chance oil refinery and the Stephenville linerboard mill. • Promoted rural development by funding small business start-ups. • Modernized the legislature, including the introduction of oral question period and the Ombudsman's Office; introduced the Public Tendering Act and an independent Public Service Commission; reformed the province's legal system. • Promoted offshore oil exploration. • Defended Newfoundland against international protesters against the seal. • Lobbied Ottawa for more rights to natural resources. • Budget deficits added to provincial debt.	Retired from politics.

Table 1.6 (continued)

Brian Peckford (PC, March 1979 – March 1989)	• Lobbied Ottawa for rights to offshore oil and fisheries; modernized inshore fishery. • Sinking of Ocean Ranger oil rig in 1982 spawned a royal commission. • Negotiated 1985 Atlantic Accord funding to offset reduced federal equalization payments owing to increased oil royalties. • Attempted to renegotiate terms of Churchill Falls contract. • Agreed to close the railway in exchange for roads funding. • Supported repatriation of the Canadian constitution, passage of the Charter of Rights and Freedoms, and the Canada-US Free Trade Agreement. • Supported constitutional amendment to give Pentecostal Church rights to administer education. • Adopted new provincial flag to replace Union Jack. • Appointed the first women to cabinet (Hazel Newhook and Lynn Verge) and the first woman to the provincial Supreme Court (Margaret Cameron). • Funded wasteful hydroponic cucumber development project. • Budget deficits added to provincial debt. • Public sector strike in 1983 reduced public servants' eligibility for labour union rights.	Retired from politics.
Tom Rideout (PC, March 1989 – May 1989)	• Initiated royal commission into Mount Cashel orphanage abuse scandal.	Party did not win a majority of seats in the 1989 election.
Clyde Wells (Liberal, May 1989 – January 1996)	• Emphasized education and entrepreneurship after cod moratorium. • Opposed Meech Lake constitutional accord and its proposed "distinct society" status for Quebec. • Promoted Senate reform and supported Charlottetown constitutional accord. • Initiated referendum on changing denominational education. • Abandoned plans to privatize NL Hydro amidst public opposition. • Signed agreement to develop Hibernia oilfield. • Made significant attempts to reduce public expenditures; nevertheless, budget deficits added to provincial debt.	Retired from politics.

Table 1.6 (continued)

Brian Tobin (Liberal, January 1996 – October 2000)	• Encouraged development of tourism industry. • Signed agreement to develop Terra Nova oilfield; Hibernia oilfield begins production. • Funded post-secondary tuition freeze policy. • Initiated referendum on further change of denominational education; supported constitutional amendments to end church-based administration of education under term 17 of Terms of Union. • Budget deficits added to provincial debt.	Resigned to become federal minister of industry.
Beaton Tulk (Liberal, October 2000 – February 2001)	• Supported constitutional amendment to formally change name of province to "Newfoundland and Labrador" under term 1 of Terms of Union (moved in House of Commons by Minister Tobin).	Permanent Liberal Party leader selected.
Roger Grimes (Liberal, February 2001 – November 2003)	• Lobbied Ottawa for better equalization payments formula; initiated royal commission on NL's place in Canada. • Terra Nova oilfield begins production; White Rose oilfield development begins. • Funded reductions in post-secondary tuition fees. • Signed deal to develop Voisey's Bay nickel mine. • Introduced televised proceedings of the legislature. • Budget deficits added to provincial debt.	Party did not win a majority of seats in the 2003 election.
Danny Williams (PC, November 2003 – December 2010)	• Amalgamated hospital and school boards. • Failed attempt at fisheries rationalization. • Introduced poverty-reduction strategy, including significant increases to minimum wage. • Negotiated renewed Atlantic Accord. • Negotiated equity shares in Hebron and Hibernia South oilfield developments. • Signed the Labrador Inuit Lands Claims Agreement leading to the creation of the Nunatsiavut Government. • Appointed judges to recommend reforms after House of Assembly spending scandal and flawed results of breast cancer tests. • Lobbied for increased equalization funding; launched "ABC" campaign against Harper Conservatives in 2008 federal election. • Bungled expropriation of AbitibiBowater assets. • Signed memorandum of understanding with Nova Scotia on development of Lower Churchill project (Muskrat Falls).	Retired from politics.

Table 1.6 (continued)

	• Paid down provincial debt and pension liabilities.	
Kathy Dunderdale (PC, December 2010 – January 2014)	• Defended Muskrat Falls deal; secured loan guarantee from the federal government. • Continued policy of funding post-secondary tuition freeze. • Overhauled access to information legislation ("Bill 29"). • Amalgamated school boards into one English-language board and one French-language board.	Retired from politics.

Sources: Include Bailey (2011), Baker (2003), Cadigan (2009), CBC News (2011j), Rowe (2010), Tobin (2002), Wells (2008) and miscellaneous government of Newfoundland and Labrador news releases.

NOTES

1 In 2001 a constitutional amendment officially changed the province's name from "Newfoundland" to "Newfoundland and Labrador." For the sake of readability in this book we alternate between the two and employ the provincial government's brand signature's use of an ampersand in "Newfoundland & Labrador."

2 The college was instead rebranded in 2010 as "Grenfell Campus, Memorial University of Newfoundland."

3 In Newfoundland the CBC is better resourced and less beholden to provincial government advertising revenues. Major and community newspapers in Newfoundland & Labrador, including the *Telegram*, are operated by Transcontinental, and the only private sector radio station that discusses politics is VOCM-AM, which draws extensively on open line calls and news releases. Television media is more competitive, with NTV News and Rogers community TV producing political programming. In recent years the blogosphere has emerged to offer a variety of competing policy perspectives, and political conversation has gravitated to microblogging on Twitter.

4 For further discussion about the unaided, institutionalized, and prime minister-centred cabinets see Dunn (2002).

5 Premiers' anger is a recurring theme in literature about the Newfoundland political executive. For instance, Hoy mentions that Clyde Wells's outbursts came to be known as "Clyde's Irk" (1992, 284).

6 For an example of the range of literature concerning Newfoundland studies, see Ritcey (2002).

2

The Public Sector of Newfoundland and Labrador

CHRISTOPHER DUNN

INTRODUCTION

This chapter provides some historical and contemporary context about public policy and public administration in Newfoundland & Labrador, in order to set the scene for the ensuing chapters. First and foremost it must be noted that there is no single provincial public administration: there are multiple public administrations, those for the departmental public service, for the legislature and judiciary, and for the health and education sectors, the Crowns, and various ABCs (agencies, boards, and commissions). Together they constitute what can be termed "the public sector of Newfoundland & Labrador." They have developed according to different historical rhythms and as a result of multiple factors.

This chapter primarily offers an overview of the provincial public sector at large and some of the factors that shape it, its recent evolution, and some new challenges. The chapter also yields passing observations about a premier's power, noting that those holding the dominant-power thesis should also consider the continuing collegiality the provincial cabinet manifests. That there are differing imperatives facing the public sector complicates governance. The public sector is difficult to govern; this chapter will explain why.

Each component of the public sector tends to be linked in particular with one set of imperatives (see figures 2.1 and 2.2). First, there are the constitutional imperatives. The departmental executive is particularly affected by responsible government and the prerogative power. The legislative bureaucracy is attentive to the separation of powers, parliamentary supremacy, and parliamentary privilege. Judicial administration

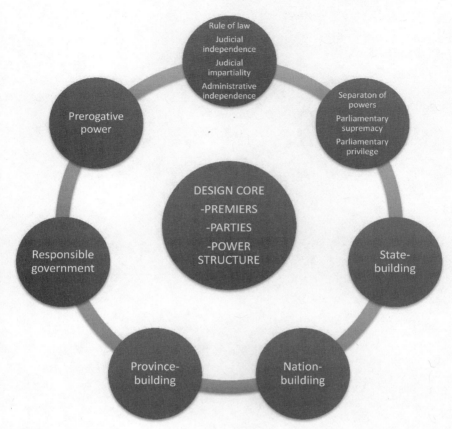

Figure 2.1
Constitutional and political imperatives affecting the design of the Newfoundland &
Labrador public sector

is marked by the rule of law, judicial independence, judicial impartiality, and the need for administrative independence.

Second, there are political imperatives, of which province-building is the dominant consideration in the case of resource Crowns and regulators. Nation-building drives the health and post-secondary education sectors; it is manifested in the drive for national standards and in the power of professional groups. State-building provides the reason for the existence of the ABC sector. The degree to which the imperatives dominate is variable, of course, and is determined by the "design core" of the society, the "three Ps": premier, parties, and power structure.

Figure 2.2
Dominant imperatives in the design of public sector elements

ERAS IN THE DEPARTMENTAL PUBLIC SERVICE

The imperatives that affect the design of the departmental public service are those of responsible government and the prerogative power (figure 2.1). The governance of departments is confided not to cabinets, but to ministers of the Crown, who exercise responsibility of an individual nature to the House of Assembly, as well as collective, and who exercise multiple accountabilities. The prerogative power to organize government departments and determine their number belongs to the premier, and this power also extends to the choice of deputy minister. The exercise of responsible government and the prerogative power are affected by political and fiscal trends, and some of these have been dramatic in the case of Newfoundland.

There have been three public services in Newfoundland: those serving the first period of responsible government, then the Commission of Government, and then the Province of Newfoundland. There are three "traditions" of the public service in play.

Responsible Government (1855–1934)

The first public service – which served responsible government – was by no stretch of the imagination a career public service. The responsible government period covered the years 1855 to 1934 and was characterized by such a lack of public sector probity that it ultimately necessitated the loss of self-government.

A number of distinct themes marked government in this period: sectarianism, patronage, and departmentalism (Channing 1982, 4–9). The "denominational principle" reigned. It had been a way of settling the violent sectarian arguments that had split the colony of Newfoundland before the 1860s, but over time, it achieved the status of a constitutional convention (Noel 1971, 24). As well, since a spoils system flourished, governments changed with the civil service in train. Post-election changes were often sweeping, with effects that were felt throughout the colony.

Departmentalism – the autonomy of individual ministers – accompanied sectarianism and spoils. In effect, political parties controlled public finances, acting through the departmental minister, and centralized control was almost entirely absent. The Audit Act, 1899, established a comptroller and auditor general, but no treasury board. The auditor general had only a minimal staff, and his complaints about lax guardianship of public funds, when made, were almost uniformly to no avail. Ministers continued to broach no interference from him, the Department of Finance, or even from other cabinet or legislative members.

By the 1930s, a treasury board or other reforms probably would not have helped. The public debt had doubled between 1920 and 1933 (from $49 million to close to $101 million), service charges amounted to more than 60 percent of annual revenue, and in 1931 attempts to tender for a new loan of $8 million were met with no response from the money markets (Channing 1982, 2–3). A series of short-term financial requests to Britain culminated in a request by Newfoundland for a royal commission to investigate the future of the country.

The Amulree Commission recommended the cessation of self-government until Newfoundland could once again support itself. In its place would be governance by a special commission composed of a chairman and six members, three from Britain and three from Newfoundland. The commission supported its drastic recommendation with references to political corruption and the wastefulness of the public administration of the colony. Many historians have disputed the causes of the imposition of commission government (Rowe 1980, chap. 20; Noel 1971, chap. 14). Whatever the cause, the die was cast, and Newfoundland entered into one of the more unusual forms of government in recent Commonwealth history.

Commission of Government (1934–49)

The public service of the Commission of Government period (1934–49) was in several respects the antithesis of that in the responsible government era. The commission aimed to bring Newfoundland public policy and public administration into line with that of the United Kingdom (Noel 1971, 228). The commissioners reorganized the numerous government departments into more functional groupings, each one under a commissioner, and standardized departmental administrative practices. The commission replaced patronage and religion as the bases for appointment and promotion with the more legal-rationalistic bases familiar to students of modern public administration (Channing 1982, 20). The Treasury Control Act of 1932 was finally strengthened by making the comptroller and auditor general directly responsible to the commissioner of finance, and there was to be an expanded auditor general's staff. While the salary and expenditure responsibilities of the departments remained as before, the commission would discipline employees who engaged in unauthorized or wasteful expenditures.

The first public service had not in fact been a career public service. There were now some signs of a single, professional, merit-based public service: a rulebook outlining ethical and disciplinary matters; ad hoc recruitment boards for new staff selected by the governor-in-commission and composed of representatives of the department affected, the Department of Finance, and the Auditor General; and designation of positions along British lines along with a regime of fixed salary scales and annual increments determined by the commissioner of the Treasury, who had general authority in staff matters under the Treasury Control Act (Channing 1982, 20–6). The degree of professionalism was incomplete, however. Salary and expenditure matters, as noted, were decentralized to the departmental level, and recruitment board recommendations did not bind the department. Still, the commission was able to bequeath to the new province a cadre of trained professional deputies from its own deputies (called "secretaries") and senior officials (Dunn forthcoming). The size of the bureaucracy grew from 2,600 public servants in 1934 to 4,737 in 1948–49 (Channing 1982, 20–6).

Confederation (1949–)

If the public service of the commission period epitomized the antithesis of the first era of responsible government, then public administration in Newfoundland when responsible government returned under Confederation was a synthesis of practices from both (table 2.1). What resulted was a hybrid public administration. A career public service took shape, but its implementation and scope were restricted to an extent because of the conflicting themes at the heart of the political/administrative machine. The restriction was most notable in the first political era, that of Joseph "Joey" Smallwood (Liberal, 1949–72) and thereafter declined gradually in the subsequent administrations of Frank Moores (Progressive Conservative, 1972–79), Brian Peckford (Progressive Conservative, 1979–89), and Clyde Wells (Liberal, 1989–96).

On the one hand, Newfoundland administrations would continue certain themes from the commission period. Among these were an emphasis on centralized policy-making and financial administration and a respect for the advantages of the merit system. Centralization in policy and financial matters manifested itself in different ways in different eras. Yet Newfoundland would also continue some practices from its responsible government era, which, after all, had a hold on the memories of adults in the new province. The early reliance on patronage under Smallwood was such a practice, together with some vestiges of sectarianism. However, there were innovations deriving from provincial status as well. The government adopted or copied "Canadian" institutions such as a Treasury Board (1953), Public Service Commission (1953), and later reforms like collective bargaining (1970), a cabinet committee system (1973) and affirmative action (intent, 1984), pay equity (intent, 1988), deregulation and privatization (1994–95), and New Public Management reforms (2003–10).

Another commonality with provincial counterparts was the heightened policy direction over the deputy minister cadre exercised by the

Table 2.1
Evolution of the Public Sector in Newfoundland & Labrador

Premier	Nature of regime	Public sector footprint
J.R. Smallwood 1949–72	Partial emulation of Canadian public administration. Paternalism. Patronage for first part of regime. Premier dispensed senior appointments and contracts with partisanship. Denominationalism in school system constitutionalized historical compromise of Education Act of 1876. Centralization: premier chose all Liberal candidates, dominated cabinet (Johnson 1976).	Civil Service Commission established in 1953 with modest remit. Posts excluded from its reach, non-binding. The *Revenue and Audit Act* creates Treasury Board as a committee of cabinet, but Smallwood declines to endow it with a secretariat until 1967. One-man Treasury Board in practice. No other cabinet committees. In June 1970 the legislature passes the *Public Sector (Collective Bargaining) Act* granting collective bargaining rights, including the right to strike. However, the act allows the government to exclude categories of employers or employees from the effect of the act, to regulate the bargaining process, and to use emergency wording to end a strike. Postponed.
Frank Moores 1972–79	Rationalist. Centralist: much emphasis on building up strength of the central executive. Impacted by federal planning models and influence.	Committee on Government Administration and Productivity modernizes cabinet system. Centralist bent evident in hierarchical institutionalized cabinet structure and a control-oriented financial system and Public Service Commission (PSC). Five cabinet committees, one of which was the Planning and Priorities Committee. Public Service Commission Act (PSCA), 1973: powerful PSC remit to enforce the merit approach in the public service. PSC now has central personnel directory, effective promotion procedure, personnel planning, staff training and evaluation (with Treasury Board), and staff procedure manuals (Newfoundland & Labrador). Appointments to or promotions within the public service are not to be made without the recommendation of the commission. Government accedes to union pressures to introduce meaningful collective bargaining. Regular service covered by Public Service Collective Bargaining Act (PSCBA). Police covered by Labour Relations Act/Royal Newfoundland Constabulary Act. Firefighters by Labour Relations Act/ City of St John's Fire Department Act.

Table 2.1 (continued)

		Treasury Board is responsible for financial management, administrative policy, personnel management, and other matters referred to it. In personnel policy, controls classification, pay, hours of work, leave, pensions, and other terms and conditions of employment and determines the conduct of collective bargaining negotiations for the public service and public bodies.
Brian Peckford (1979–89)	Peckford interested more in policy than administration, yet takes tentative steps toward streamlining. "Randell Committee" of DMs recommends a balanced budget over a four-year period, consolidation of government departments, selected privatizations, and new ways to generate revenues. No action.	Royal Commission on Employment and Unemployment (the House Commission) established. Its 1986 report says more regionally sensitive program and planning approach needed; Wells would later implement. The pay equity policy, initiated in the collective agreements of 1988, intended to redress "systemic gender discrimination in compensation." Implemented in health first; rolled over to subsequent agreements. Some action on gender equality. Advisory Council on the Status of Women created 1980. Announcement, 1984, of intention to establish affirmative action plan for women and a Task Force on Affirmative Action to draft the policy, but no explicit action by Peckford or Wells.
Clyde Wells (1989–95)	Emphasis on planning. Emphasis on fighting deficit and achieving economies. Province joins movement to "New Public Management": planning, deregulation, service quality, downsizing, and productivity. Regional development pushed, new information technologies emphasized. Centralization of power in the hands of Premier Wells and a handful of officials: the cabinet secretary, the secretary to cabinet for intergovernmental affairs, and treasury board secretary. Wells established direct links to the deputy ministers	Economic Recovery Commission (ERC) established 1989. ERC is an economic restructuring agency reporting to the Cabinet to perform follow-up measures to the House Commission. However, it is another cabinet body that produces the "Strategic Economic Plan" (Newfoundland and Labrador 1992). The strategic plan contains 134 recommendations applying to education and training, income security, labour relations, government operations, taxes, manufacturing, tourism, energy, natural resources, government operations, and regionalization. The same group later produces a Strategic Social Plan. Government retains central executive design. As well, budgetary and personnel management policies remain.

Table 2.1 (continued)

and tended to bypass ministers in the decision-making process.	In the wake of the 1993 Cod Moratorium, seeks rural rebuilding by introducing twenty Regional Economic Development Boards in 1995.
	The *Public Employees Act* of 1990 outlines the conditions that may lead to dismissal for public employees.
	Deficits attacked by wage freezes, wage-reduction talks, and executive government reorganization. The 1993 budget announces the merging of the administrative divisions of the Executive Council, the Public Service Commission, and the Department of Finance. The Works, Services and Transportation Department undertakes a reorganization in 1994–95 and announces significant savings. In 1995 the government signals the impending consolidation of the administrative divisions of the Departments of Environment; Employment and Labour Relations; and Tourism, Culture and Recreation.
	Full-service Government Service Centres introduced.
	Total Quality Management movement reflected in the Service Quality Initiative.
	1994 Regulatory Reform Initiative headed by an independent commissioner, the Honourable Nathaniel S. Noel.
	Several (modest) privatizations: the sale of Newfoundland and Labrador Computer Services in 1993, Newfoundland Farm Products Corporation in 1994, and both Newfoundland Hardwoods Limited and Hotel Buildings Limited in 1995. Some activities of the Newfoundland and Labrador Housing Corporation are privatized as well.
	1995 sees the introduction of fourteen Regional Health Authorities (RHAs) that come under three models: integrated, institutional, and community-based.
	In 1995 government announces plan to merge two St John's hospitals, the Grace and the Janeway (Paediatric) Hospital, with the existing Health Sciences Centre in three years, but later acts only on Grace.
	1995 Denominational Education System referendum won by government, which plans constitutional amendment to replace the denominational with "inter-denominational" school boards.

Table 2.1 (continued)

Brian Tobin/ Roger Grimes et al. (1996–2003)	Emulation of the federal cabinet style and ministerial discretion is pronounced. Emphasis on role of cabinet. Tobin aim: cut the ties that led to the premier's office and to make fiscal control a corporate issue. Differences in tone between Tobin and Grimes in central government. Central agencies less often called on as a policy resource in the Grimes years, whereas they were called on more often with Tobin. With Grimes, mostly facilitating role for agencies. Some emphasis on planning. Grimes sees need to establish new models of "strategic co-operation" between government, business, and labour to guide economic renewal.	Cabinet Secretariat, Intergovernmental Affairs, and Treasury Board Secretariat continues as parts of the Executive Council Office (ECO). New Aboriginal and Labrador Secretariat in the ECO with its own deputy minister. He moves to revivify the committee system, so that policy would go through them first and only then on to cabinet; cabinet was not going to decide everything. The role of P&P was de-emphasized. The wide-ranging renewal of the deputy minister (DM)/assistant DM cadre begins in 1996: doubling of women in the senior public service, from 15 percent at the end of the Wells era to around 30 percent under Tobin. Broad-sweeping replacement of deputies and assistant deputies. Role of the Treasury Board in enforcing spending freezes ended. Departments now to enjoy staffing delegation, with only nominal involvement by the Public Service Commission. Tobin ends the denominational school system entirely. Several attempts to control health care expenses, especially those by RHAS. Withholds provincial approval of the Voisey's Bay development pending a promise from INCO for a provincial smelter. Grimes approves deal for equivalent policy. Formation in 2002 of a provincial royal commission on the province's place in the federation, to report 2003. *Final Report on a Renewal Strategy for Jobs and Growth*, is released in March 2001. To give effect to the report's vision, Grimes creates the new Department of Industry, Trade and Rural Development in 2001, and, as well, in January 2002 founds the Strategic Partnership Forum, a semi-annual meeting among business, labour, and government leaders. Premier chairs.
Danny Williams (2003–10)	Business orientation: Williams favours private sector management techniques like business plans, productivity and performance measurement, client-centred service, and managerial accountability.	The emphasis on management skills and private sector experience is unmistakable. Of the fifteen deputies in 2010 (a few of the categories overlap), two were trained as chartered accountants; three were MBAs (notably, even the deputy in justice had one); six were bachelors of commerce; and two

Table 2.1 (continued)

Embraces new management style. Dissatisfied with the standard Whitehall approach, in which the permanent public service views itself as the protector of the public interest, and more comfortable with direction by political executive.	were in the process of partial postgraduate-level management training. This made about 87 percent of deputies with management training. In addition, a third (five) had sat on private sector boards, and four had significant private sector experience.
Emphasis on big revenue sources to dig out of deficits/debt.	Transparency and Accountability Act, 2002, contains new principles of legislative reporting.
	Annual reports mandatory for departments and Crown agencies.
	Establishment of a new financial regime for administration of the House of Assembly.
	Performance planning and reporting for all government departments and agencies.
	Performance contracts for all DMs and chairpersons of public bodies, the non-performance of which could be reported to cabinet by the responsible minister.
	Incentive-pay arrangement plan set in motion, includes independent committee to oversee it.
	Atlantic Accord renegotiated.
	Offshore deals negotiated with enhanced NL financial shares and decision making power.
	The federal treatment of resource revenues in relation to the equalization formula sparks bitter Williams political response.

premier and cabinet, as the present collection demonstrates. In the Williams administration this was manifest in the increased role of party political manifestos in setting government policy, private sector-type performance contracts, an incentive program for deputies, and cultural change in the public sector elite.

Whether this direction was indicative of a deeper-set premier-dominated public service is open to debate. Chapter 1 has cited Mr Williams' comment denying the oft-repeated characterization of his government as a one-man show. Comments by senior cabinet officials in successive administrations leave the same impression, and academic commentary leaves a more nuanced provincial picture than that of the Savoie (1999, 2008) centralization of power thesis. White (2005) does not believe the autocratic premier myth; Rasmussen and Marchildon

(2005) note that institutionalization (collegiality) is the common coin of Saskatchewan cabinet tradition; Glenn (2005) says that dominance has given way to collegiality according to need in Ontario's history; and Bernier (2005) says the instability of premierial tenure in Quebec militates against court government.

A more nuanced view in Newfoundland & Labrador is warranted. Having an influential premier does not rule out collegial cabinets. In this province, the same sort of cabinet committees have remained in place for forty years, and there has been a priorities and planning committee and a deputy premier for most administrations, including Williams's. However, the vision of the administration is plainly provided by the premiers: witness the central importance of the leader in the PC Party election manifestos of 2003 and 2007, and in the government's energy plan of 2007 (see also chapter 5 of this volume).

In spite of the varying exercises in public sector renewal and experimentation, the provincial public service has remained relatively stable in number, ranging from roughly seven to eight thousand for most of the last quarter century, expanding and contracting as a function of budget stringencies and the mission of government (see table 2.2 in the appendix to this chapter).

THE LEGISLATIVE BUREAUCRACY

The dynamic in the legislative administration has been the need to uphold responsible government. The organizational framework of the House of the Assembly is based on the fundamental principles of parliamentary supremacy and the independence of the legislative branch of government from the executive branch, and it has seen three changes in regime since 1989: in 1989–96, 1996–2007, and 2007 to the present.

In 1988, the House of Assembly amended the Internal Economy Commission (IEC) Act, requiring an independent commission, following each general election, to make binding recommendations regarding compensation and expense reimbursement for members of the House of Assembly (MHAs). In 1989, the first (and as it turned out, the only) such independent commission, chaired by Dr M.O. Morgan, recommended a revised and comprehensive governance framework. The Morgan era introduced significant and complex changes to MHA compensation and expenses, with limits prescribed for each MHA and with expenses to be supported by receipts. In 1993, amendments to the IEC Act lifted the obligation to appoint an independent commission after each election, leaving the appointment – then still required in legislation – to the discretion of the IEC. It never did appoint another commission.

The Morgan recommendations added complexity to the House administration, but the executive did not respond to the issue by increasing the legislature's budget significantly. The very small administrative staff was not increased. While the clerk was responsible for the overall administration of the House, in practice he delegated most financial management and administrative functions to the director of administration (later called the director of financial operations). In theory, the executive branch had no authority to direct the affairs of the House; however, the financial control framework, administered by the comptroller general of the government, appeared to apply to the House of Assembly.

Beginning in 1996, there were changes in the policy framework governing MHA allowances and key aspects of House administration. The IEC spearheaded a series of permissive funding decisions that benefitted its fellow legislators, all without the appointment of an independent commission. As well, as the Green Commission would later remark, there were "notable discrepancies between the minutes of the IEC tabled in the House and the official minutes maintained by the Clerk" (Green 2007, 6). The IEC Act was progressively weakened after 1996: the House, at the instigation of the IEC, removed the requirement for review by an independent commission; changed the act to bar the auditor general from auditing the accounts of the legislature and, in particular, MHA allowances; denied the comptroller general access to expenditure documentation of the House; and effectively exempted itself from 2000–01 and possibly 1999–2000 audits of House administration. Weaker oversight led to abuses.

In 2006, the auditor general alleged that several MHAs had apparently submitted misleading expense claims, and in 2007, his annual report commented on the inaccurate financial reporting by the Commission of Internal Economy to the House of Assembly, together with spending in excess of legislative appropriations, in violation of the Financial Administration Act (see chapter 7 in this book for more on this). The "constituency allowances scandal" led to the establishment of the Review Commission on Constituency Expenses and Related Matters in 2006. It reported the next year and recommended a new administrative and regulatory regime for the House, to which the government and House agreed.

The key administrative changes agreed to were the following: access to information legislation was to apply to the House and its administration;

there was a publication scheme; there was a new House of Assembly Management Commission (HOAMC) to replace the IEC; an energized Public Accounts Committee was to review the House expenditures; and there was an expansion of the Order of Mandamus avenue for ordinary citizens to enforce statutory duties. The direct administration was to be affected by changes to the clerk's appointment process (to promote independence), the designation of the clerk as an "accounting officer" (to provide the focus for administrative responsibility), an Audit Committee for HOAMC, and the establishment of the same financial regime for the public service and the House (FAA, comptroller general, audits).

This is not the only way that the legislature's operations are monitored and assisted. "Statutory officers" aid the House in providing independent oversight of the executive. At present, there are six such offices: auditor general (brought under the aegis of the IEC in 1990), chief electoral officer (added 1993), commissioner for members' interests (2001), information and privacy commissioner (2004), child and youth advocate (2001), and citizens' representative (2001).

Justice Green, in his Review Commission report, made incidental comments about a lack of clarity in the financial relationship between the clerk and the statutory offices. Accordingly, the report recommended a system, but one that fell short of independence for these offices. The clerk is designated in legislation as the chief financial and administrative officer for both the House operations and the general administration of the statutory offices. The clerk monitors and reports to the House of Assembly Management Commission and to the Public Accounts Committee on the budget submissions and budgetary performance of the offices. As before, the commission approves staff appointments to the offices, and they are subject to the Public Service Commission Act, as are the general staff of the House.

ADMINISTRATION OF THE COURTS

The dynamics organizing the administration of the courts are the basic constitutional principles of the rule of law, judicial independence, judicial impartiality, and, to some extent, the division of powers.

The requirement for an impartial judiciary requires that it also be independent; the two terms are intimately related, as Justice LeDain says in the *Valente* decision (2 S.C.R. 673 [1985], para. 15). To ensure the fairness and impartiality of outcomes, there must be some judicial autonomy or independence.

The modern Anglo-Canadian concept of judicial independence begins over three hundred years ago. The Act of Settlement of 1701 mandated that judges serve during good behaviour and are dismissible only for cause and only by address of both houses of Parliament.[1] Judicial independence is further protected in the Canadian context by various constitutional arrangements (ss. 97–100 of the 1867 Act, Section 11 (d.) of the Charter), statutes (the federal Judges Act, 1985; the Federal Courts Act of 1985; the Supreme Court Act, 1985; and provincial statutes), judicial decisions, and conventions.

Much post-Charter jurisprudence is relevant to judicial independence, and it has revealed several elements that apply to all levels of courts. These, McCormick says, cover matters such as personal independence, adjudicatory or decisional independence, collective or institutional independence, the activities of a chief judge, the role of a judicial council, internal independence, budgets regarding judicial independence, and those affecting court operations (2004, 28–9).

The basic structures of the court system in the province follow the dictates of the constitution. The court system of the provinces is sometimes referred to as "quasi-unitary," in the sense that the federal government appoints provincial judges and Parliament pays them. The federal governor general in council appoints the judges of the superior, district, and county courts in each province by authority of section 96 of the Constitution Act, 1867. However, section 92(14) provides the provinces with the power to make laws for "the administration of justice in the province," which includes the "constitution, maintenance and organization of provincial courts, both of civil and criminal jurisdiction." Federal judges therefore staff courts designed by the provinces. The dismissal of the Superior Court judges is, under section 99, also federal, removable by the governor general on address of the Senate and the House of Commons. The salaries, allowances, and pensions of section 96 judges are fixed by Parliament. In Newfoundland & Labrador, the section 96 courts are combined under the rubric of its Supreme Court. However, section 92(4) of the Constitution Act, 1867 enables provinces to make laws in relation to "the establishment and tenure of provincial offices and the appointment and payment of provincial officers." This provides the basis for the appointment and payment of judges of the "provincial courts."

The Supreme Court is the highest section 96 court in Newfoundland & Labrador and is federally appointed and paid. It deals with appeals, as well as civil and criminal matters, and includes the Court of

Appeal, Trial Division (General), and Trial Division (Family). The various components of the Provincial Court (provincially appointed and paid) are the Youth Court, Traffic Court, Small Claims Court (for most civil claims below twenty-five thousand dollars), and the Family Court (for most family law matters, other than divorce or division of property under the Family Law Act and other than cases arising on the Avalon Peninsula, Corner Brook, and the West Coast, which fall under the jurisdiction of the Family Division of the Supreme Court). It is the court of first instance for criminal and regulatory offenses, and most such offenses conclude in Provincial Court. The Provincial Court is organized into eleven court centres, with the numbers of judges and staff assigned on the basis of population distribution and caseloads. St John's is the largest court centre and the headquarters.

It was of more than passing interest when the chief justice of the Supreme Court – Trial Division, Derek Green, felt compelled in 2004 to express concerns about the degree of what he called institutional, or administrative, independence in the province. He was concerned about the level of funding to courts and the method of funding (Green 2004). Regarding the level of funding, Justice Green flagged a number of ongoing concerns.

As for the method of funding, Justice Green questioned the dominant management model. Impatient with the pervasive "executive model," which featured the government deciding all matters relating to the courts short of court dockets and case assignments, he suggested alternatives, such as a judicial model with greater financial control by chief justices. Another approach, suggests McCormick (2004, 57) is to have a neutral third party make reviewable decisions based on applications by both government and courts on objective grounds, established procedures, and a judicially reviewable basis.[2]

There has been no review of the state of judicial independence since the early 2000s, but more resources have been dedicated to the courts (Newfoundland and Labrador 2004a, 228; 2011b, 247). The only structural change in court administration involves consultation, information exchange, and planning, but not financial decision making, notes a Canadian Judicial Council report. A Court Advisory Board performing such functions was established in September of 2004, composed of the minister of justice and the attorney general, the three chief justices of Newfoundland's courts, the deputy minister of justice and the assistant deputy minister (Canadian Judicial Council 2006, 100). It has fallen into disuse, not having met for several years.

ADMINISTRATION OF THE HEALTH SECTOR

Administration in the health sector is driven by a general nation building imperative (Fierlbeck 2011, 56). Nation building expresses itself through dedication to national standards, of which there are several for and by professionals, several sets of professional groups and unions involved in promoting them, and two levels of government whose directing forces have their own views on standards of care and organization. Organization in the health care sector matters, as Maria Mathews also indicates in chapter 8.

The workforce of the Regional Health Authorities, at about 20,000 full-time and casual employees (see table 2.3 in the appendix to this chapter), overshadows that of the core public service, which had about 8,250 positions in 2010. One of the health authorities, Eastern Health, has more employees (13,500) than the entire departmental service. At a glance, appendices 2.2 and 2.3 show that the growth rate of the health sector has been greater than that of the departmental service. Facts like these have important implications for collective bargaining and the ability to manage.

Katherine Fierlbeck (2011, 85) has observed that "the way in which health care is administered is very much influenced by larger trends in governance." The New Public Management (NPM) approach to the health sector, she argues, pits professionals on the side of politicians, with managers and citizens on the other. This view echoes that of the late Peter Aucoin (1995).

In the case of health, NPM was a good technique for identifying who should be displaced as the primary decision makers in the system and how the system should be structured in Canadian jurisdictions. Historically, governments provided health care providers, principally physicians, with decision-making authority on their behalf and supplemented this with extensive measures of self-regulation. This proved to be too expensive, uncoordinated, and asymmetrical in power.

So physician-centered administration – or the *provider-centred model* – was replaced by what we will call here, *faute de mieux*, the management model. This model had a number of characteristics, two of which will seem immediately recognizable to students of the Newfoundland & Labrador health care system and its pan-Canadian variants: results-based management and regionalization.

Results-based management has at various points included performance indicators, benchmarks, business plans, user feedback, and comparative information across jurisdictions.[3] Regionalization figured as well. NPM took various forms elsewhere, but in Canada, for reasons of culture and federalism, it took the form of territorial decentralization – that is, regionalization. It was integration that was regionalization's great success story, promoting less of a silo mentality and seamless care (Fierlbeck 2011, 84–5).

Such was largely the story in Newfoundland. First, its health care went from physician-centred to board governance. Second, data collection became more pronounced. Third, facilities were eliminated to reduce overlap. Fourth, the integration of health records became quite sophisticated. Lastly, there were attempts, of varying success, to integrate the various levels of health care, namely acute care, secondary or long-term care, and community-based care.

Organized health care is characterized by different delivery models in Newfoundland & Labrador. Acute care is typically of short duration, provided in a hospital for brief, severe illness, and can involve intensive or emergency care. Long-term care, sometimes referred to as secondary care, deals with longer-term, high-maintenance care. Community-based care is typically provided for by specialized personnel and organizations: examples are home care workers, workers in public health care and care for dementia, social workers, nurses, and other allied health professionals.

After Confederation, several long-term facilities were established, some being the St Patrick's Mercy Hospital, the Agnes Pratt Home, St Luke's, Glenbrook, and later Hoyles-Escasoni and others throughout the province. At first, they were established by churches, but in the 1960s, most incorporated separately from church groups.

Community-based care has grown in sophistication and elaboration in the province. Like long-term care, it is not funded by Medicare, so individuals can be charged. However, the province provides subsidies for community support and residential options based on assessments provided by regional health authority staff.

Acute care in the late nineteenth and early twentieth century was comprised of three separate eras. The first saw a number of hospitals founded in the capital and larger centres. Military hospitals were the first long-term establishments; then came religious and charitable institutions such as St Clare's Mercy Hospital, founded by the Sisters of Mercy in 1922, and the Grace Maternity Hospital (later called the Grace General Hospital), founded in 1923 by the Salvation Army. By the late 1920s, the government was providing financial aid to six of the twelve hospitals in Newfoundland (Perlin 1958, 210).

Second came the cottage hospital, a model borrowed from Scotland, which had been foreseen in recommendations of the Royal Commission on Public Health and Charities. Cottage hospitals, begun in 1935, were operated by the government administration and by senior nurses (matrons). Foreshadowing later socialized medicine in Canada, a premium of ten dollars allowed Newfoundland families to receive medical and hospital care in publicly owned hospitals staffed by salaried doctors.

Third were the boards. By the 1950s, "voluntary boards" provided more sophisticated hospital administration. Over the period of the 1950s to the 1980s, there were about fifty such boards. As more facilities came into existence, more came to be run directly by government.

Fiscal and financial crises brought changes in board governance. In pursuit of fiscal health, the Wells government amalgamated the fifty-odd boards into fourteen in 1994, which would stay in operation until 2005 (and, in the same spirit, set in motion the events that would lead to the closing of the Grace Hospital in 2000). The move was influenced by broader national developments in the health field, like the establishment of New Brunswick-style regional health authorities (RHAS) in most provinces except for Ontario (Parfrey, Barrett, and Gregory 2005). The specific contours of the Newfoundland & Labrador reform, however, were influenced by the 1993 Dobbin Report on the reduction of hospital boards (Dobbin 1993).

The reform introduced by the subsequent provincial policy (*Health Reform Initiatives: Changing Realities*, 1994) introduced three different types of boards, depending on the circumstances of the region: integrated boards, institutional boards, and community health boards. Integrated boards combined all three delivery models; institutional boards combined two, acute and long-term; and then there were the community health boards (Parfrey, Barrett, and Gregory 2005).

The reduction of the fourteen to four RHAS in 2005 occurred as a result of a combination of financial and planning reasoning (Parfrey, Barrett, and Gregory 2005). St John's had been the most expensive facility and had caused significant concern for government policy-makers, who struggled to make the corporation live within its budget (Hay-Group 2002, i). The government established four regional health authorities: Eastern, Western, Central, and Labrador/Grenfell. At first, the RHAS managed only acute care facilities. Community-based care later became a part of the remit of the authorities in 2006–07. Faith-based nursing homes remained outside the system.

The design of the health boards is predicated on a divide between policy and administration, but it is getting harder to maintain. Political micromanagement is prevalent, and it is often inconsistent: in 2007 alone, there were three deputy ministers of health, and in 2009 alone there were three successive ministers (see Matthew Kerby's chapter 6 for more on ministerial turnover).

ADMINISTRATION OF THE POST-SECONDARY AND K-12 EDUCATION SECTORS

The post-secondary (PSE) and elementary (K–12) sectors are also driven by national standards. Even though education is a provincial responsibility, the national standards aspect comes out in the harmonization exercises of the Council of Ministers of Education (CMEC) and various federal initiatives. There are also supplemental imperatives in the PSE sector. The notion of university institutional autonomy and the strength of a professional teaching corps complicate the relationship with government, and the government's general concern with enhancing its stock of human capital animates its relations with the education sector.

Post-Secondary Education

The publicly funded post-secondary education delivery system in Newfoundland & Labrador consists of Memorial University of Newfoundland, which includes the Fisheries and Marine Institute and Memorial University, Grenfell Campus, and the College of the North Atlantic. The latter has seventeen campuses in the province and one under contract with the State of Qatar. Student enrollment at Memorial in September of 2010 was more than 18,600, and at the College of the North Atlantic approximately 7,200 were in attendance. Approximately 3,200 students were enrolled in twenty-five Private Training Institutions (Newfoundland and Labrador 2011a).

University institutional autonomy involves a balance between the prerogatives of government and those of the university. According to the Association of Universities and Colleges of Canada (AUCC), university "institutional autonomy includes, *inter alia*, the following powers and duties: to select and appoint faculty and staff; to select and admit and discipline students; to set and control curriculum; to establish organizational arrangements for the carrying out of academic work; to create programs and direct resources to them; to certify completion of a program of study and grant degrees" (Association of Universities and Colleges of Canada 1988). Government's role for its part is generally thought to be suitable within a narrow band: funding, setting fee structures, and introducing new programs (Council of Ministers of Education 2005).

Memorial possesses such hallmarks of operational autonomy, but lacks certain bulwarks of governance autonomy. One has only to witness the refusal of government to appoint the University's nominee for president in summer of ·2008. A subsequent ad hoc committee of the Board of Regents of Memorial University studied the matter of the status of the university in 2008. It noted that certain factors that contributed to autonomy were compromised in the Memorial case. The Memorial University Act (article 51) provides that the president is chosen by the Board of Regents with input from the Senate but is approved by the cabinet, a provision that almost no university in Canada endures. Government chooses the majority of members on the Board of Governors. Cabinet also appoints the chair of the board, rather than allowing election or appointment by board members, which was the case in all other universities surveyed. Cabinet removes board members, whereas the national norm is to have the board itself do this, or at least to recommend it (Memorial University 2008). These legislative provisions are still in effect, despite representations to change them from Memorial.

Governments enjoy wider latitude over colleges. They are, after all, one of the important economic instruments in the provincial public sector. The College of the North Atlantic is the only public college in the province and is governed by the College Act (1996). The cabinet appoints nine to eighteen members of the college's board (s. 10(1), and the provincial personnel administrative policy applies to the college unless the minister orders otherwise (s. 15(h)). The minister "may require the modification, establishment, suspension or termination of the administration, courses, programs or facilities of the college that he or she considers necessary" and "may approve or disapprove a budget submitted by the board" (s. 21(3)).

Human capital theory – making decisions based on an evaluation of future economic returns possible from different kinds and lengths of schooling (Blaug 1976) – has become the dominant outlook on education in the province and country. An Organization for Economic Co-operation and Development (OECD) study group noted that the Atlantic provinces were considering "the creation of a human capital strategy for the region that takes the 'cradle to the grave' concept of linked education (schools, vocational education, community colleges, and universities) and connect it more directly to regional strategies and priorities" (OECD 2006, 41).

The provincial government's 2005 *White Paper on Public Post-Secondary Education* aimed to put the human capital approach into effect. The white paper, led by Commissioner Wayne Ludlow, recommended that the province's Council on Higher Education (CHE) be reconfigured and recognized in legislation. Joint appointments (three) would be made to the two (university and college) boards, and appointees who would presumably report provincial intentions to them. As well, the province would enter into three-year outcomes-based performance contracts with the university and the college. The report provides a lengthy and detailed list of areas to be included in these performance contracts (Newfoundland and Labrador 2005a, 77). This was a pretty direct statement of *dirigisme*.

In 2006, there was a partial recognition of the spirit of the white paper's recommendations. The respective acts were changed to feature the conjoint appointees in each of the boards. While the act did not mention a reconfigured CHE, the strategic planning exercises of Memorial took on the same tone as the recommendations, and Ludlow's direct approach was replaced by financial incentives from the provincial government. There is no need to coax the college, since it is under the control of the government at any rate.

Elementary and Secondary Education

The elementary and secondary education sector is also concerned with national standards, but in this case the levers of influence of the provincial government are greater, as Gerald Galway points out in chapter 9 of this volume. This is especially the case where public, provincially controlled educational institutions are involved. There are a number of federally or First Nations-controlled educational institutions, as well as private or independent schools, but the total number of all these is not significant when compared to that in the provincial public system. Figures from Statistics Canada in table 2.4 in the appendix to this chapter show an especially daunting challenge for education policy-makers in Newfoundland & Labrador compared to other provinces. The hollowing out of the source population for K–12 schools (and the PSE sector for that matter) is especially daunting in this province. K–12 enrolments declined by nearly 20 percent in the past decade – the highest of any province – as opposed to a 6 percent decline nationally.

A diminishing number of teaching staff has followed. In 2001–02, there were 6,264 full-time equivalent teachers in the system, with a pupil-teacher ratio (PTR) of 13.4 and 74.4 teachers per 1,000 pupils. In 2011–12, the number had shifted downward to 5,529 teachers, a PTR of 11.9, and 84.4 teachers per 1,000 students (Newfoundland and Labrador 2012a).

Provincial control over education has grown since Confederation. Moving to non-denominationalism helped. Term 17 of the Terms of Union with Canada (1949) allowed six denominations to operate publicly funded schools. In 1987, Term 17 was amended give the Pentecostal assemblies the same right. Now there were four school systems operating: the Integrated School System (Anglican, Presbyterian, Salvation Army, and United Church); the Pentecostal System; the Roman Catholic System; and the Seventh Day Adventist System. In 1997, the second of two referenda on schools resulted in elimination of the denominational system, and the first elections for nondenominational school boards took place in 1998. The role of the denominations in the operation of the department was at an end.

Consolidation of school boards also increased provincial control. In the 1950s and 1960s, the number of school boards in the province had gone from 270 to a tenth of that, which was in part a reflection of the national movement that equated educational excellence with more streamlined delivery. The 1992 royal commission report, *Our Children, Our Future*, and a supplemental report, *Adjusting the Course: Restructuring the School System for Educational Excellence* (1993), advocated reducing the number of school boards from twenty-seven to ten, together with a greater operational delegation to the local level. In 1998, the number of boards in fact became eleven with the addition of a francophone school board. In 2004, the number of boards in the Island portion of the province shrank to three (Eastern [number 4], Nova Central [number 3] and Western [number 2]); there were in addition the Conseil Scholaire Francophone, covering the whole province, and the Labrador board [number 1], which remained unchanged (Fleming 1997).

Elementary and secondary education may be a provincial government responsibility, but education delivery is essentially a partnership. An outline of some of these partners, and their roles, follows. The legislature passes legislation and the budget. The premier and cabinet provide leadership, make regulations pursuant to education acts, and establish legislative timetables. The minister and the Department of Education provide leadership in the education sector, draft laws and regulations, regulate early childhood learning, oversee provincial libraries, certify new teachers, fund school divisions, operate distance education and Web-based instruction, oversee curriculum development and assessment, and plan construction and infrastructure renewal. The Department of Education is responsible for administering the following legislation: the Public Libraries Act; the School Boards' Association Act; the Schools Act, 1997; the Teacher Training Act; the Teachers' Association Act; and School Bus Transportation Policies. In late 2011, the government created a new Department of Advanced Education and Skills, incorporating the Advanced Studies (post-secondary) component of the former Department of Education and most of the former Department of Human Resources, Labour and Employment and establishing the new Workforce Development Secretariat.

There are also actors at the local level. School boards are mandated through the Schools Act, 1997, as amended to oversee the delivery of K–12 educational services in each of five districts. Each district holds an election every four years to elect fifteen trustees on each of the boards. They provide day-to-day administration of schools, set school budgets, hire teachers, open or close schools, plan and administer transport systems, and administer and modify curricula. In the case of the province-wide francophone board, individual school councils elect the trustees separately. School councils were established in the Schools Act, 1997, to allow parental and community-mandated input into the quality of education. They are elected or appointed and serve in an advisory capacity, and they bring together educational professionals, parents, students, and various community members.

There are national actors as well. Federal responsibilities imply some ancillary educational responsibilities for national defence, corrections, registered or status Indians, the territories, and foreign affairs. They also play a role in minority language education and tax supports. The Council of Ministers of Education (CMEC) operates on a unanimity principle. It is concerned with national standards, established voluntarily, and devises cross-Canada achievement tests. Others, such as the Canadian Education Association (CEA), the Canadian Teachers' Federation (CTF), the Canadian Association of School Administrators (CASA), the Canadian Association of Principals (CAP), and the Canadian School Boards Association (CSBA), speak on behalf of their members on matters of education.

THE CROWN CORPORATION SECTOR

The imperative animating the Crown corporation sector is clearly "province-building." Maxwell and Pestieau write that "each province seeks to maximize incomes, employment and population growth in its own territory" (1980). They observe that such objectives imply a number of policy orientations, including a push for industrial diversification with an emphasis on the processing of natural resources and a drive to acquire provincial decision-making powers and influence on relevant federal powers. One might add to these orientations the establishment of backward and forward economic linkages that would aid in growth in income, employment, and population.

There are presently three large Crown corporations, namely the Newfoundland & Labrador Housing Corporation (NLHC), the Newfoundland & Labrador Liquor Commission, and Nalcor Energy. Of these, Nalcor provides the greatest evidence of involvement in the vital business of province-building.

The NLHC has province-building overtones in its series of initiatives to devolve decision-making powers away from the federal authority. It should also be remembered, however, that the uptake in the provincial role came at the same time as the federal authorities abandoned a direct role in social housing. In the early part of the last decade, several federal initiatives involved the province. One was the Canada-Newfoundland & Labrador Social Housing Agreement; another was the Provincial Home Repair Program (PHRP, now renamed the Housing Renovation Program Agreement, HRPA); and a third was the Affordable Housing Agreement.

The Social Housing Agreement was signed in 1998 between the province and the federal government. Also known as the Devolution Agreement, it was part of a nationwide effort by the federal authorities to disengage from social housing. By this agreement, the provincial government took over the social housing component of the Canada Mortgage and Housing Corporation (CMHC) programs and assumed responsibility for properties that had previously been run directly by it. There is to be a gradual withdrawal of financial contributions by the federal authorities over forty years (1997–2037), after which the federal contributions will stop.

The province announced its intention to enter into a cost-shared Affordable Housing Agreement with the federal government through CMHC in the 2003–04 fiscal year, and the Canada-Newfoundland & Labrador

Affordable Housing Agreement was signed with Newfoundland early in 2004. There is no management committee, as there is in other programs. The program is administered by the NLHC according to the provisions of the federal-provincial agreement; the current agreement lasts from 2011 to 2014. The whole corporation does not cost much in the larger order. Newfoundland & Labrador Housing had a gross budget of $122 million in 2011–12, of which $53 million came from federal funding and $51 million from the province. The rest, $18 million, came from rental/other sources (Newfoundland and Labrador Housing Corporation 2011, 2). The total personnel resources devoted to the NLHC have been relatively low as well, just under or over four hundred between 2001 and 2011.

The Newfoundland & Labrador Liquor Commission (commonly abbreviated as NLC) plays a mix of province-building and societal-protection roles. The province-building role comes by virtue of its monopoly on the sale of liquor products and its significant contribution to provincial revenues (Newfoundland and Labrador 2004d). Each year, the commission transfers a distribution of its net income, which is in the tens of millions of dollars, to the province. There seems little impetus for change given that studies have shown that privatization of alcohol sales can lead to a net financial loss for governments (Centre for Addiction and Mental Health 2004). However, not only financial reasoning makes the case for a government monopoly. Attentive interest groups maintain that the best mechanism for regulating alcohol consumption and promoting social responsibility is the provincial liquor board (MADD 2012). This social responsibility sits in an uneasy balance with the commercial motivations of public monopolies. Gradually such organizations, including the NLC, have been responding to consumer preferences. The NLC is aware of the issue, and devotes attention to it on its website, emphasizing programs related to responsible consumption, environmental considerations, and corporate citizenship (Newfoundland Labrador Liquor Corporation 2012).

Another important Crown corporation is Nalcor Energy, which conceptualizes, proposes, and implements the energy-related province-building activities of the province. The creation of an energy corporation was a centerpiece of the 2003 Progressive Conservative election document *A Blue Print for the Future*. It was, as well, fundamental to the vision outlined in the provincial government's energy plan of 2007, *Focusing our Energy*. Nalcor Energy is the parent company of Newfoundland & Labrador Hydro, the Churchill Falls (Labrador) Corporation – CF(L)Co. – and the Oil and Gas Corporation of Newfoundland &

Labrador (see chapter 12 in this book, by James Feehan). It also at that time assumed ownership of the Bull Arm Site Corporation, the entity entrusted with building the gravity-based structure for the Hibernia offshore site.

Nalcor's core business is the generation and transmission of electrical power. Beyond this, it has entered the broader energy sector, with interests in oil and gas, wind, research and development, and industrial fabrication. It has five lines of business: hydro, Churchill Falls, oil and gas, the Lower Churchill Project, and, Bull Arm Fabrication (Newfoundland and Labrador 2010b). Hydro controls most of the generation and high voltage transmission lines on the Island portion of the province and sells the power to Newfoundland Power, owned by Fortis Inc. Newfoundland Power owns and controls the distribution lines and services households and industries on the Island. However, in the Labrador portion of the province, Hydro generates, transmits, and sells power itself. Brinco, a private company, developed the Upper Churchill, but the province bought Brinco's shares in 1974, along with the downstream water rights necessary to develop the Lower Churchill.

The province-building rationale for the entity was made clear by official comments and by specific policies. Announcing the Nalcor Energy brand, Premier Williams said that "no longer will we be passive players in the development of our resources; rather we are now fully engaged partners ... Nalcor Energy will ... ensure that we get the most out of our energy resources" (Nalcor Energy 2010). To help with that goal, the province's energy plan established the aim of "a 10 percent equity position in future offshore petroleum projects that require Development Plan approval, where it fits our strategic long-term objectives" (Newfoundland and Labrador 2007a, 20). As well, the province would also continue to pursue the transfer to the province by the federal government of its 8.5 percent ownership in the Hibernia project. Whereas in some cases the 10 percent aim was unachievable (Hebron Development, 2008), in others it was (expansion of Hibernia South, 2009). The energy plan also viewed the ultimate aim as "long-term self-reliance" (Newfoundland and Labrador 2007a; see also Marland 2010).

Nalcor, however, is just the tail end of a series of nation- and province-building episodes in Newfoundland & Labrador history. Space does not permit a review of the complete picture. However, the most notable ones are the Come by Chance refinery, the frequent attempts at co-management of the fishery, and co-management as exemplified by the Canada-Newfoundland & Labrador Offshore Petroleum Board.

AGENCIES, BOARDS AND COMMISSIONS

Agencies, boards, and commissions are state-building institutions that stand apart from the general administration and are vital to the state's operation. They balance private influence with a regulatory "countervailing power" (Galbraith 1993) and provide the capacity-building that is necessary for the state to exercise some of its higher-order roles. The Cabinet Secretariat of the government of Newfoundland & Labrador in 2012 listed a total of 214 agencies, boards, and commissions.[4]

Agencies, boards, and commissions are sometimes simply called Crown agencies. They may also be called committees, tribunals, and corporations. (There may in fact be an overlap with some other categories in this chapter, such as Crown corporations.) In short, to use the language of J.E. Hodgetts, they are "structural heretics" that go under a variety of names. Despite the fact that they are all different, they are all alike in significant ways.

Crown agencies, or ABCs, tend to have a number of common identifying characteristics: non-departmental status, some autonomy from government, a public policy purpose, and a reporting relationship to a minister limited to general policy and not operating matters. They may also in some instances involve a quasi-judicial status. However, there is one major difference that overshadows all others: unlike a government department, a Crown agency carries out duties on its own (Molot 2010).

The state-building activities of entities in this sector in Newfoundland & Labrador are apparent in table 2.5 of this chapter's appendix. To the Crown agency sector are confided the major health and education tasks of the state; its major public economic ventures in shipbuilding, hydro development, and offshore exploration and development; and the varied forms of consumer protection. It is a formidable list. However, it also includes the more ordinary matters under its aegis as well.[5]

The reasons for recourse to the non-departmental form are many and various. One of at least eight rationales has been the alleged inability of departments to undertake business functions or analogous activities and the need for the organizational flexibility that the Crown agency provides. A second reason is the need for removal of some functions from the controversial political arena: some functions would presumably be prone to inefficiency if too much political interference was allowed. A third and related justification is the need to withdraw quasi-judicial functions from the political realm. A fourth justification is that governmental functions of the financial or "business" type are best carried out by agencies that resemble the institutions of private enterprise with which they deal. A fifth rationale is that of easing the co-optation of leaders and experts from the private sector.

A sixth reason may be the regional or trans-jurisdictional nature of the function. Because of the "spill-over effect" of a single jurisdiction's involvement with some services, an "umbrella organization" providing the integration of multi-jurisdictional involvement may be instituted (as in the case of the Atlantic Lotteries Corporation). It may further be given semi-independent status in order to promote local participation in its operation. A seventh rationale for the semi-independent form is the professional nature of the body being regulated; control of access to the profession and certain intra-disciplinary actions by professional corporations is necessary if the "public-interest" is to be protected. Finally, an eighth argument for non-departmental status is that of the relative ease with which legal actions may be brought against agencies as contrasted with departments.

As much as they are valuable tools in the public policy arsenal, the extensive use of ABCs has created problems for governments. One problem is that they tend to proliferate in number, as the following section will demonstrate, and are said by fiscal conservatives to exemplify "big government." As well, the statutory power to set general policy can blunted by confusion over the meanings of general and specific policy. Rather than issuing the mandatory reports that are an important element in a system of responsible government, agencies tend to publish reports that stress technical matters as opposed to accounting for policies adhered to or created. Moreover, standing or special committees tend to provide no meaningful surveillance of Crown agencies – or departments in this province, for that matter. Legislatures in general do not have committees specializing in agency matters; Newfoundland & Labrador has none.

More attention is paid to the ABC sector during government efforts to "streamline," or simplify, the delivery of government services. Such was the case with the 1996 provincial budget. Proclaiming the elimination of twenty-six agencies, boards, and commissions as part of a plan to "right size" government, the Executive Council noted that "of these twenty-six (26), approximately sixteen (16) are inactive, seven (7) are in the process of being eliminated; and three (3) are currently operating."[6] Often an agency is the chosen policy instrument of a predecessor administration, and a newer government will see different routes to policy effectiveness.

It may be time to be more systematic about this sector. Instead of long periods of neglect followed by periodic purges, it may be time to establish agency governance frameworks. In the middle of the previous decade, the government of Alberta set up a task force to examine board governance (McCrank, Hohol, and Tupper 2007), and in 2008 it established a Public Agencies Governance Framework (Alberta 2008) and a procedure for regular review of public agencies covering such matters as recruitment and appointment, term lengths, government representation on boards, orientation and continuing education, ethics and conflict of interest, evaluation, and remuneration. The government even set up an agency governance secretariat. Such an example bears examination.

CONCLUSION

This chapter has presented an overview of the provincial public sector and the factors that animate it. Each component of the public sector tends to be linked with one set of imperatives in particular, if not exclusively. In constitutional imperatives, the departmental executive is particularly affected by responsible government and the prerogative power. First ministers and even the British authorities had the freedom to design government the way they wanted, and the results were often diametric. The legislative bureaucracy must be attentive to the separation of powers, parliamentary supremacy, and parliamentary privilege. At times, this principle has led to different interpretations of what the administration of the legislature should be and sometimes inappropriate use of parliamentary privilege as a shield. Judicial administration is marked by judicial independence and associated concepts, which indicate the need for administrative independence. The implications of these concepts have not been sufficiently explored in this province. Of the political imperatives, province-building is the dominant consideration in the case of resource Crowns and regulators. Nation building drives the health and post-secondary education sectors and is manifested in the drive for national standards and the power of professional groups. State-building is the reason for the existence of the ABC sector, composed of agencies, boards, and commissions.

This chapter has not had time to explore an associated set of considerations. For example, how are we to judge the work of the design corps? Is the executive government too centralized? Has legislative administrative regulation overlooked "politics as a vocation," as Weber would call it? Are judges too influenced by their political masters? Have professionals in health and education hindered nation-building? Lastly, where are the boundaries of province-building and nation-building? These, of necessity, are questions for another day.

Table 2.2
Size of the departmental public service, Newfoundland & Labrador (1985–2010)

Year	Gender		Total
	Male	Female	
1985	5,100	2,100	7,200
1986	5,100	2,100	7,200
1987	5,100	2,300	7,400
1988	5,550	2,450	8,000
1989	5,000	2,900	7,900
1990	5,400	2,700	8,100
1991	4,900	2,400	7,300
1992	5,000	2,600	7,600
1993	4,900	2,700	7,600
1994	4,600	3,000	7,600
1995	5,000	3,000	8,000
1996	4,600	2,900	7,500
1997	4,400	2,900	7,300
1998	4,300	2,600	6,900
1999	4,400	2,700	7,100
2000	4,400	2,700	7,100
2001	4,400	2,800	7,200
2002	4,200	2,800	7,000
2003	4,200	2,800	7,000
2004	4,100	2,700	6,800
2005	4,000	2,800	6,800
2006	4,100	3,000	7,100
2007	4,300	3,200	7,500
2008	4,400	3,500	7,900
2009	4,500	3,600	8,100
2010	4,600	3,800	8,400

Source: Personal correspondence with Executive Council, Newfoundland and Labrador, 2011.

Note: The data provided measures the core public service, which is comprised of government departments and central agencies. As such, it does not include the broader public sector such as health care; education; or other government agencies, boards, and commissions. The numbers shown are approximate and include employees active on the last pay period in December of each year, excluding MHAs, political support staff, and students.

Table 2.3
Regional health authorities employment in Newfoundland & Labrador (2011)

Occupation category	Occupation	EH 2011	CH 2011	LGH 2011	WH 2011	Total 2011
Primary occupations	Audiologist	9	4	1	3	17
	Behaviour management specialist	66	17	9	21	113
	Cardiology technologist	25	6	1	8	40
	Cardio-pulmonary technologist	2				2
	Combined LX technologist	7	3		6	16
	Dentist	–		5		5
	Dietitian/nutritionist	54	13	6	16	89
	Dosimetrist	5				5
	Electroneurophysiology technologist	8	3		2	13
	Genetic counsellor	10				10
	Licensed practical nurse	1,230	489	147	405	2,271
	Manager	692	185	81	163	1,121
	Medical laboratory technologist	284	77	38	53	452
	Medical flight specialists (EH only)	11				11
	Medical physicist	5				5
	Medical radiation technologist	184	57	17	55	313
	Nuclear medicine technologist	12	3		3	18
	Occupational therapist	104	11	4	13	132
	Orthopedic technologist	8	3		1	12
	Pharmacist	65	13	6	14	98
	Physiotherapist	89	19	7	11	126
	Prosthetist-orthotist	9				9
	Psychologist (clinical)	44	6	2	9	61
	Radiation therapist	25				25
	Recreation/development specialist	25	7	2	3	37
	Registered nurse	3,339	736	365	811	5,251
	Respiratory therapist	63	13	3	7	86
	Social worker	514	120	73	77	784
	Speech language pathologist	32	8	3	9	52
	Other (primary)	31	17	5	10	63
Primary occupations total		6,952	1,810	775	1,700	11,237
Ancillary occupations – clinical total*		1,409	352	206	397	2,364
Ancillary occupations – system total**		3,860	1,042	474	1,008	6,384
Grand total		12,221	3,204	1,455	3,105	19,985

Note: Regional Health Authorities employment as of May 1 2011. Employee counts (people paid at least once in preceding three months) vary significantly and should be used with caution. Physicians are excluded from these employee counts. Revision 15 June 2011.
* Ancillary occupations, clinical total, includes audiology technician, cardiology technician, combined LX technician, community service worker, dental technician, medical laboratory technician, medical radiation technician, nuclear medicine technician, occupational therapy support worker, paramedic, personal care attendant, pharmacy technician, physiotherapy assistant, prosthetist/othodontist technician, psychology assistant, recreation therapy worker, social service worker, other. Personal care assistants made up half this total.
**Ancillary occupations, system total, includes administrative/clerical support, biomedical engineering, dietary, facilities, housekeeping, information systems, laundry, materials, records, other. Administrative/clerical made up about 40 percent of this total. The next largest numbers were composed of housekeeping and dietary.

Table 2.4
Full-time enrollments in public elementary and secondary schools (2001–02 to 2008–09)

	Canada	NL	PE	NS	NB	QC	ON	MB	SK	AB	BC	YK	NT	NU
2001–02	5,035,949	84,236	22,843	153,450	122,792	1,088,869	2,046,333	182,448	177,051	529,758	605,049	5,397	9,337e	8,389
2002–03	5,024,286r	81,707	23,242r	150,599	120,600	1,083,082	2,049,535	180,723	178,510r	536,035r	596,858r	5,412	9,422e	8,564
2003–04	4,963,209r	78,967	22,905r	148,514	118,869	1,075,140	2,015,627	180,132	175,897r	533,834r	589,854r	5,327	9,346	8,799
2004–05	4,926,376r	76,903	22,393	145,396	117,145	1,065,214	2,012,093	178,256	172,452r	532,063	580,965r	5,272	9,220	9,005
2005–06	4,889,303r	74,328	21,948	142,304	114,820	1,053,200	2,006,732	176,350	169,302r	532,876	574,428	5,148	9,090	8,779
2006–07	4,836,484r	71,945	21,365	138,661	112,013	1,033,868	1,991,157r	174,107	165,590r	540,880	563,939	5,040	9,198	8,723
2007–08	4,781,704r	69,733	20,813r	135,303	110,288	1,015,195r	1,976,773	173,392	162,182r	538,611	556,779	5,015	8,928	8,694
2008–09	4,735,867	68,255	20,324	133,134	108,407	998,251	1,958,840	172,045	160,362	542,581	551,321	4,804	8,628	8,917
Percentage change, 2001–02 to 2008–09	–6	–19	–11	–13	–12	–8	–4	–6	–9	2	–9	–11	–8	6

Source: Statistics Canada (2011a).

Note: r – revised; e – estimate.

Table 2.5
Examples of agencies, boards, and commissions (2012)

Type of agency	Examples and date created
Regulatory/adjudicative: Make rules for a sector or ensure its operational viability. Make arm's-length quasi-judicial decisions for a sector. Or both.	Board of Commissioners of Public Utilities, 1978
	Landlord Tenancies Board
	Student Financial Assistance Appeals Board, 2006
	Newfoundland and Labrador Legal Aid Commission, 1986
	Canada Newfoundland and Labrador Offshore Petroleum Board, 1985
	Labour Relations Board, 1989
	Board of Commissioners of Public Utilities, 1978
	Multi-Materials Stewardship Board, 1996
	Council of the College of Physicians and Surgeons of Newfoundland and Labrador, 1995
	Newfoundland and Labrador Pharmacy Board, 2005
	Human Rights Commission, 1989
	Law Foundation of Newfoundland and Labrador, 1994
Public trusts: Administer financial assets in the public interest.	C.A. Pippy Park Commission, 1991
	Newfoundland and Labrador Arts Council, 1988
	The Rooms Corporation of Newfoundland and Labrador Inc., 2003
Corporate enterprises: Engage in commercial enterprises.	Churchill Falls (Labrador) Corporation Limited, 1989
	Newfoundland and Labrador Hydro-Electric Corporation, 1989
	Marble Mountain Development Corporation – Board of Directors, 1988
	Newfoundland and Labrador Liquor Corporation, 1990
	Atlantic Lottery Corporation, 1996
	Newfoundland and Labrador Industrial Development Corporation, 1986
	Newfoundland and Labrador Ocean Enterprises Ltd, 1989
	Nalcor Energy 2007
	Nalcor Energy – Bull Arm Fabrication Inc., 1995
	Nalcor Energy – Oil & Gas Inc.
Service delivery agencies: Provide public services or direct how others shall provide them.	Health Boards (various)
	Memorial University Board of Regents
	Board of Governors College of the North Atlantic
	School Boards
	Newfoundland and Labrador Arts Council 1988
	Newfoundland and Labrador Housing Corporation 1990
	Newfoundland and Labrador Municipal Financing Corporation 1979
	Provincial Information and Library Resources Board 1989
	Newfoundland and Labrador Public Service Commission 1989
	Various regional and international airport authorities
Advisory agencies: Provide policy advice to government.	Pension Investment Committee 1981
	Newfoundland and Labrador Government Sinking Fund – Board of Trustees
	Newfoundland Government Fund Limited – Board of Directors 1999
	Order of Newfoundland and Labrador Advisory Council 2002
	Occupational Health and Safety Advisory Council 1991
	Provincial Advisory Council on the Status of Women 1990

NOTES

1   A 1761 statute provided that commissions of judges would remain in effect notwithstanding the demise of His Majesty (1 Geo III, c. 23).
2   A Canadian Judicial Council report revealed as many as six alternate models (Canadian Juducial Council 2006).
3   This explains the significant increase in data-gathering organizations in Canada in past decades (Canadian Institute of Health Information (CIHI), 1994; Canadian Health Services Research Foundation (CHSRF), 1996; Canadian Institutes of Health (CIHR), 2000; Canada Health Infoway (CHI), 2001; and the Health Council of Canada (HCC), 2003), and their activities and analogue organizations in the province.
4   Correspondence between the Cabinet Secretariat and the author, January 2012.
5   The curious will discover, upon examination, that the number of libraries in the province has gone from 104 in 1980, to 96 in 2010, and from 118 full- and part-time employees to 163, and from a budget of $3.2 million to $11.9 million in the same time span (personal correspondence from Newfoundland and Labrador Public Libraries, February 2012).
6   The 26 agencies were (1) the Economic Recovery Commission, (2) the Enterprise Newfoundland & Labrador Corporation, (3) the Farm Development Loan Board, (4) the Fisheries Loan Board, (5) the Newfoundland & Labrador Education Communication Corporation, (6) the Newfoundland & Labrador Roundtable on the Environment and the Economy, (7) the Newfoundland & Labrador Advisory Council on the Economy, (8) the Mining Tax Review Board, (9) the Province of Newfoundland Pooled Pension Fund Board, (10) the Timber Users Appeals Advisory Board, (11) the Automobile Dealers Advisory Committee, (12) the Consumer Protection Advisory Committee, (13) the Consumer Reporting Agencies Advisory Committee, (14) the Financial Disclosure Advisory Board, (15) the Highway Safety Advisory Board, (16) the Insurance Adjusters, Agents and Brokers Advisory Board, (17) the Lotteries Licensing Review Board Panels, (18) the Private Investigations and Security Services Advisory Board, (19) the Board of Directors – Newfoundland Hardwoods Limited, (20) the Newfoundland & Labrador Science and Technology Advisory Council, (21) the Newfoundland & Labrador Petroleum Corporation, (22) the Offshore Petroleum Advisory Committee, (23) the Fire Prevention Act Advisory Committee, (24) the Child Welfare Board, (25) the Day Care and Homemaker Sciences Licensing Board, and (26) the Pesticides Advisory Board.

3

Nationalism in Newfoundland and Labrador

VALÉRIE VÉZINA AND KARLO BASTA

COMPARATIVE THEORY

It would be difficult to understand politics and policy-making in New-foundland & Labrador without keeping in mind the specific culture and identity of that province's population (see Bannister 2003; Hiller 1987; O'Dea 1994; Overton 1980, 1985, 1988; Thomsen 2001, 2010). In their dealings with the federal government in Ottawa, provincial political elites have periodically invoked the separate identity of New-foundlanders and have voiced economic and political demands on their behalf. What is the best way to characterize these claims? Are they akin to regional grievances that have been the staple of politics in much of Western Canada for decades (Gebel 2005, 7)? Or are they an indicator of a particular brand of Newfoundland nationalism,[1] a political phe-nomenon that has more in common with what has been going on in Quebec since the 1960s?

In this chapter, we argue that the articulation of Newfoundland-based demands is best understood as a case of non-separatist nationalism. While there are similarities between these arguments and, for example, resource-based grievances and claims of political marginalization that one can observe in the West or in the Maritimes, we argue that a differ-ent identity dynamic is at work in Newfoundland. Both as a matter of values and preferences and of political discourses, most Newfoundland-ers see themselves as a people apart from other Canadians. Indeed, we will note that this self-conceptualization constitutes a critical difference between regionalism and nationalism. As our chapter demonstrates, this difference has also found its way into the statements of key provincial decision makers.

If we are right and if the claims of Newfoundland's political elites are representative of non-separatist nationalism, what are the broader political implications of this insight? In terms of provincial-federal relations, Newfoundland nationalism may have few short-term implications. However, if it remains one of the few options that the provincial political elites in Newfoundland can use in order to gain leverage with the federal government, such discourse may evolve into a qualitatively different brand of nationalism, possibly with secessionist overtones. While this prognosis may strike one as too alarmist, our scepticism may be tempered if we recall that Scottish and Catalan "regionalisms" (in the 1960s and 1980s, respectively) grew from protest movements to current full-blown demands for independence. More broadly, the case of Newfoundland nationalism may shed more light on other instances of non-separatist nationalism, in conceptual and theoretical terms. The following section examines the conceptual differences between regionalism and nationalism. We then turn to the empirical examination and assessment of Newfoundland nationalism.

"Regionalism" and "nationalism" are closely related terms, given that the political ideology of nationalism has traditionally been linked to territoriality and thus to regions. As we will discuss, nationalism has been defined as encompassing group claims to statehood (Gellner 1983, 1), and the modern state has, in turn, developed according to principles of exclusive territoriality (Ruggie 1993). The conceptual closeness of nationalism and regionalism makes it difficult to distinguish between the two, even as scholars tend to view regionalism as a political phenomenon that is qualitatively different from nationalism. In the Canadian context, political scientists have attempted to explain the stubborn persistence of regionalist sentiments and their political expression. However, a cursory examination of the literature suggests that it is based on an under-theorized understanding of regionalism.

In most major studies of Canada's territorial politics, regionalism is a product of (and is often conflated with) the dissimilar economic and political endowments of different provinces and, at times, trans-provincial regions. Furthermore, except in the case of Quebec and Ontario, the awareness on the part of regional populations that such differences exist has tended to result in collective resentment. As a consequence of these factors, there are important differences in the political behaviour of different populations in Canada, most of which involve identities and political cultures that are clustered within a geographic area. These differences are usually expressed in voting preferences.

As Ross (2009) points out, political culture can be conceptualized in two ways: as a matter of aggregated individual preferences (in the tradition of Almond and Verba) or as a matter of intersubjectively produced and "consumed" discourses (as in Geertz 1973). The seminal work by Elkins and Simeon (1980), for example, includes the economic, social, and political differences between Canada's ten provinces with an emphasis on diverse political cultures. Although they differentiate their approach to political culture from the one pioneered by Almond and Verba (1963), they employ a similarly variable-centred approach in their study. Mildred Schwartz also suggests that regionalism is, in essence, an awareness of a politically relevant territorial cleavage on any number of dimensions, although she foregrounds the economic and cultural ones (Schwartz 1974, 5). Roger Gibbins, for his part, wishes to replace the term "regionalism" itself with an alternative – "territorial politics." Either way, he defines the phenomenon as "an intrusion of territorial-provincial interests in national politics" (1982, 4). Of course, this definition is not particularly useful if we wish to differentiate regional from national political movements, because it does not tell us anything about the philosophical basis on which provincial claims are made. According to Gibbins' definition, there is really no difference between claims of governments in Quebec or Manitoba, since both can be understood as regionalist claims, although he implicitly recognizes the difference between these claims when mentioning "independence movements" as distinct from regionalist ones (1982, 6).

Territorially rooted collective resentment features very prominently in all Canadian scholarship on regionalist politics. In defining regionalism, David Bell adds to a sense of separate regional identity an attachment to one's region (1992, 128). There is also the sense that the population of the region has been wronged, either by other regions or by the central government. Such a sense of grievance characterizes regionalism in Canada's West, as well as in the Atlantic provinces (Bell 1992, 142–5). For Gibbins and Berdahl, a sense of grievance is the central feature and indicator of "western alienation" (2003, 27). Philip Resnick (2000) explores the issue in the case of British Columbia and finds the dimension of victimization integral to regionalism. However, adding the sense of group grievance to our definition cannot by itself draw the line between regional and national political claims. After all, nationalist movements emanating from geographic clusters are steeped in narratives of victimhood at the hands of either the majority group or the state.

Several scholars of Canadian regionalism, including those already referenced, have attempted to distinguish between regionalism and nationalism more explicitly. Gibbins argues that the regionalism of Canada's
Western or Atlantic provinces is, in essence, a response to the perceived
exclusion from power at the centre, whereas in Quebec what is at work
is the rejection of attempts at integration by the centre (1982, 179–81).
In this formulation, regionalism is a response to the central government
that is qualitatively different from its minority (or sub-state) nationalist
variant. In a more recent contribution, Eagles addresses the dichotomy
from a different angle. Whereas Gibbins looks at the underlying motiva-
tion for the two kinds of movements, Eagles examines their goals. While
both are predicated on a recognition of territorially rooted and politically relevant difference, nationalists seek self-government for a group,
either through autonomy or independence (Eagles 2002, 21–2). Yet
Eagles recognizes that regionalist movements might also claim greater
autonomy or even independence (11).

Scholars of European regionalism have faced similar conceptual quan-
daries. For Thomas Hueglin, for instance, regionalism and minority
nationalism are often mentioned in the same breath (1986). Regionalism
takes the form of "a protest movement against political-administrative
and socioeconomic centrality," and can take any number of forms,
including separatist and non-separatist ones (Hueglin 1986, 448).
Michael Keating has even titled one of his works *State and Regional
Nationalism*, merging the two concepts of regionalism and nationalism
and often using them interchangeably (1988, 239). He recognizes that
some scholars distinguish between minority nationalism, which is separatist, and "mere" regionalism, which seeks autonomy within existing
states (9). But in both this and his later works, Keating notes that minority nationalism is compatible with commitment to the current state and
need not be secessionist (1996, 53–4; 2008, 71).

Keating's conceptualization of minority nationalism and regionalism, then, does not resolve the conundrum. However, both Hueglin and
Keating suggest some important possibilities that will be taken up in our
discussion below. The first is that regionalism and minority nationalism
are overlapping categories and that regionalism might be the broader
of the two, subsuming not only nationalist movements, but also non-
nationalist regionalist claims. The second possibility is that they are
simply different points on a continuum between full integration into a
nation-state and complete failure of such integration.

Examining the concept of nationalism may shed more light on the issue and permit us to come up with a theoretically more satisfying distinction. According to some of the leading scholars of the subject, nationalism is, first and foremost, a political principle, one "which holds that the political and the national unit should be congruent" (Gellner 1983, 1; see also Hechter 2000, 7; Hobsbawm 1990, 9). In other words, this political principle holds that every nation should have its own state. Unfortunately, Gellner refrains from providing a definition of nationhood, which makes his conceptualization of nationalism incomplete.

A survey of other scholars' work on the issue points us to an interesting conclusion. For scholars such as Benedict Anderson and Anthony Smith, it seems that what makes a group a nation is the claim to self-government. In Anderson's famous formulation, a nation is an imagined community, one that imagines itself as inherently limited and sovereign (1991, 6). In other words, what makes a territorially concentrated group a nation is its self-perception as a *demos* apart from the rest of the population inhabiting a given polity. For Smith, the transition from cultural self-awareness to politicization of culture through a claim to self-government is what transforms a mere ethnic group into a nation, as does the existence of common legal rights and responsibilities for the group (1987, 154). Both scholars therefore agree that a community that imagines itself not only as culturally different from the rest of the population but as possessing a collective right to self-government is a nation. They do, however, indicate that a sense of cultural separateness is an important prerequisite of such collective self-identification.

Thus, what makes a group a nation is not the demand for autonomy (or limited self-rule), since many regional groups make the same demand. Rather, the key difference is in the political and philosophical principle upon which this claim is made. Where a territorially concentrated group continues to see itself as part of a larger political community, but sees its position in that community in need of improvement, its territorially based claims can be called regionalism. However, if such a group conceives of itself as a demos apart, its demands for self-rule can be called nationalism.

How can one observe these differences in the field? We believe that what is needed is a two-pronged strategy – one that examines the self-identification of the population in question to see where their identity allegiances lie and one that examines the discourses prevailing among the population and their political elites. As we shall discuss later in this chapter, quantitative studies since the 1960s have demonstrated that Newfoundlanders tend to identify significantly less with Canada than almost any other provincially based group, with the partial exception of the Québécois (depending on the period in question). The examination of political discourse suggests that there is at least a partial sense among the provincial political and intellectual elites that Newfoundlanders constitute a group different from most other provincial populations. Whereas Western alienation seems to be a matter of wanting more favourable inclusion at the centre (Gibbins 1982, 181), the emphasis on the political basis of cultural self-preservation in Newfoundland seems to have more resonance with the experience of Quebec. The main difference is that Newfoundland nationalism has not developed in the direction of political secessionism.

We now turn to the empirical identification of these patterns in polling results and an analysis of key official documents, such as party platforms.

BACKGROUND

A strong sense of local identity was an important reason why Newfoundland rebuffed opportunities to join Canada until 1949. Two Newfoundland observers attended the 1864 Quebec Conference,[2] but the fiscal arrangements and the centralized character of early Canadian federalism made Newfoundlanders sceptical of union with Canada. In the divisive Newfoundland election of 1869 the topic of Confederation crossed party lines, and anti-Confederates won a majority of seats (Penney 1981, 12). Initiatives for a union with Canada were shelved for decades, but in 1894–95, owing to a financial crisis in Newfoundland, the Confederation option came back to the table. As a precondition to joining Canada, the government of Newfoundland demanded the assumption of its debts by the Canadian government, but Canada refused. Because of a lack of agreement on financial terms, the political leadership of Newfoundland decided once again against Confederation (Penney 1981, 12).

Newfoundland's political autonomy grew in 1907 when it became a semi-autonomous Dominion (see Penney 1981). However, after World War I and the decline of the fishing industry during the subsequent global economic crisis, the Dominion entered a precarious financial position. Unable to pay the interest on its loans, Newfoundland turned to Great Britain for help. In response to requests from Newfoundland MHAs, the British suspended responsible government and established a Commission of Government, which was an unelected de facto government of the Dominion from 1934 until 1949. Two referenda on Newfoundland's political future were held in the summer of 1948.

In the first, held on 3 June, voters were presented with three options: the continuation of the Commission of Government, responsible government, or Confederation with Canada. When the ballots had been counted, although responsible government had won (with 44 percent of the votes), it had failed to obtain the support of a clear majority. Hence, a second referendum was to take place with two options on the ballot: responsible government or Confederation (the Commission of Government option was dropped, since it had received only about 14 percent of support in the first referendum). On 22 July 1948, Newfoundlanders voted to join Confederation with a margin of only seven thousand votes, and on 31 March 1949 Newfoundland officially became the tenth Canadian province.

In part, as a consequence of the late accession of Newfoundland to Canada as well as a long period of separate political existence, Newfoundlanders have traditionally demonstrated weak attachment to the idea of the Canadian nation, as we will demonstrate later. Moreover, the population has tended to identify with their province over their country to a significantly greater degree than have the residents of most other provinces. For instance, in a 1968 Canada-wide survey, Newfoundland had the lowest mean score on the national identity index, lower even than the francophone population of Quebec (Elkins 1980, table 1). Only 4.2 percent of the population scored "high" on their identification with Canada (compared with 22.1 percent in Alberta, for instance), and 52.1 percent scored low. The next lowest scoring province apart from Quebec was British Columbia, with 37.7 percent of respondents proclaiming "low" but with 27.9 percent declaring a "high" degree of identification with Canada. This is not entirely surprising given that at the time very few Newfoundland respondents would have been born as Canadians. A 1978 survey showed that among the residents of the Atlantic provinces, Newfoundlanders again demonstrated the lowest level of identification with the common state (Gibbins 1982, table 7). Among residents of Newfoundland, 55 percent expressed greater identification with their province than with Canada, while the population of the next province with high provincial identification, Prince Edward Island, scored at 34 percent.

Recent polls suggest that this difference persists. As figure 3.1 demonstrates, over the past decade and a half, residents of Newfoundland have continued to feel greater allegiance to their province than have most

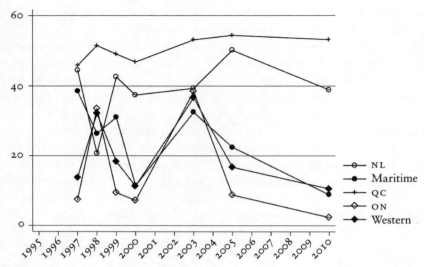

Figure 3.1
Percentage identifying with province more than with Canada, national sample.

Source: Portraits of Canada, 1997-2000 Series, 2003–2005. *Canadian Attitudes toward the Federation.*
Made available by the Canadian Opinion Research Archive, Queen's University at Kingston, ON

other provincial populations, with the predictable exception of Quebec, as well as the partial exception of Prince Edward Island. It is interesting to note that, notwithstanding one year (for reasons that are not
clear), provincial identification is significantly stronger in Newfoundland than in any of the Western provinces, including Alberta and British
Columbia. In other words, Western alienation does not seem to entail a
strong weakening of Canadian identity in the Western provinces.

These data set an important context which allows us to better understand the nationalist discourse periodically deployed by Newfoundland's
political classes. All of its premiers have employed varying degrees of a
nationalist rhetoric that dates back to the nineteenth century (Cadigan
2009, 293). Cadigan argues that "[s]ince Confederation, politicians have
used a particular form of neo-nationalist Ottawa-bashing to distract the
people of Newfoundland & Labrador from the failures of provincial
policies and to co-opt their support" (2009, 296). While this conception
limits the use of Newfoundland nationalism as a means to an end, one
cannot dismiss the impact of nationalism in the creation, fabrication,
and construction of nationalist-based public policies in Newfoundland.
Although there may be cleavages or differences within the nationalist

discourse, it has nonetheless affected leaders' and governments' decision making and policy priorities since Confederation (e.g., Bannister 2003; Cadigan 2009; Lambert 2008).

Examples of such "Ottawa-bashing" can be found among leaders from various political allegiances. For example, in 1959, following disagreements with Prime Minister Diefenbaker on Term 29 of the Terms of Union of Newfoundland with Canada, 1949, which stipulated that a royal commission would advise on additional financial assistance for the province, Newfoundland Liberal premier Joey Smallwood proclaimed three days of national mourning during which all flags were flown at half-mast and the doors of provincial government buildings were draped in black. Smallwood was convinced that Newfoundland's exceptionalism with respect to federal fiscal arrangements had to be maintained, whereas the Progressive Conservative Diefenbaker government was opposed to individual deals with provinces and was inclined to a regional approach to economic development or disparity (e.g., Cadigan 2009). Brian Peckford, a Progressive Conservative, took similar actions in 1982: when negotiations with Prime Minister Trudeau's Liberal administration over offshore oil ownership broke down, he asked all members of the legislature to wear black as a sign of mourning.

CASE STUDY

An analysis of party election manifestos is a necessary first step in determining how nationalism was used under the Danny Williams administration. Such an analysis entails an examination of the "detailed program of measures that it [the party] will put in place if elected" (our translation from Manin 1996, 248). Here, discourse analysis is first used to evaluate the Progressive Conservative Party platforms from the 2003, 2007, and 2011 elections. Then an examination of key events during these time frames is made in order to give context to the discourse used in the election platforms. Particular words are identified as key indicators of nationalism. The words "nation," "pride" (and the adjective "proud"), "destiny," "master," and "giveaways" (as well as the verb "give/gave away") were chosen, since previous research puts considerable emphasis on the nationalistic messages conveyed through their use in Newfoundland (see Marland 2007b, 2010). Furthermore, since we argue that Newfoundland exhibits a non-separatist nationalism, we identified words that reflect a separate cultural group, i.e., Newfoundlanders. Their absolute number of appearances is indicated in table 3.1.

Table 3.1
Nationalist content in PC election platforms (2003–2011)

Words	2003	2007	2011
Pride	0	5	2
Proud	0	5*	2
Destiny	3	0	1
Master	0	1	0
Give/gave away	4	0	0
Giveaway(s)	3	1	0

Source: PC Party (2003, 2007, 2011).
Note: Numbers in the table are absolute numbers and refer to the number of times that the word was found in the document.
* The 2007 PC platform is titled "Proud. Strong. Determined. The Future is Ours." In the discourse analysis, the word "proud" was counted only in the main text (cover, title page, pages 2, 3, 5, and 15). "Proud" occurs much more frequently. As the "motto" of the party, it appears on every page in the footer. Those occurences were excluded from the calculation because they are not part of the main text.

While the first two words appear natural in the analysis, the last three are less obvious. However, as we will demonstrate, controlling one's destiny was a dominant message used by the PC Party in the 2003 election. We note, however, that the word "master" was replaced by "destiny" in the 2007 platform.

The 2003 election, which brought the PCs to power for the first time in almost fifteen years, was preceded by the party's "no more giveaways" campaign. As opposition leader, Danny Williams emphasized the need to stop giving away Newfoundland's natural resources to others. This terminology was used seven times in the party platform. And as soon as he became premier, Williams was emphatic that his administration would not allow any more "giveaways." He refused to sign accords with anyone (the federal government, oil companies, other provincial governments, etc.) if the agreements were not satisfactory and beneficial for Newfoundland. Perhaps the most memorable example was Williams' renegotiation of the 1985 Atlantic Accord. His strategy made him infamous outside his province (Marland 2010), while he was regarded as a "Sun King" (Köhler 2006) among Newfoundlanders. Canadians across the country remember Williams' willingness to remove all Canadian flags from provincial buildings until the federal government negotiated a favourable deal with Newfoundland. In announcing his course of action, the premier said, "I'm not lowering the flags, I'm removing the flags ... down goes the flag" (Antle 2004), and he employed nationalist vocabulary. Furthermore, the act of removing the Canadian flags suggested a symbolic rejection of the Canadian nation. Hence, not only did Williams use nationalist language, but he also acted in a nationalist way. Even though this event exposed existing tension in provincial-federal relations (Baldacchino 2010), it also demonstrated that Newfoundland, or more correctly, Danny Williams' Newfoundland, would not be taken for granted by Ottawa. Once the province had secured the 2005 Atlantic Accord with the federal government, we then find that the 2007 PC Party platform used the term "giveaway" only in the past tense – as something now behind Newfoundlanders; indeed, the expression "giveaways" appeared only once in the 2007 PC platform: "The days of resource giveaways are gone" (PC Party 2007, 10).

Along similar lines to the "no more giveaways" message, the 2003 PC platform urged Newfoundlanders to control their destiny. The word "destiny" appears three times in the platform, and in each instance it is accompanied by the verb "control." In absolute terms, three is not a sizable number, but the context and the references made in each instance reveal considerable passion and enthusiasm for Newfoundland. Furthermore, "controlling one's own destiny" draws a direct analogy to Jean Lesage's "Maîtres chez nous" speech during the 1962 Quebec provincial election campaign. When Lesage used this slogan, he was seeking a mandate to nationalize private electrical power companies. Like Williams, he was trying to convince his people that controlling one's natural resources was essential to the ability to govern oneself.

With respect to Newfoundland, the 2003 PC party platform presents its first reference to control on the first page, where Williams stipulates, "I've spent the last two years growing a team and formulating policies that I believe will help Newfoundland and Labrador so that we can begin to control our own destiny and achieve our true potential" (PC Party 2003, 1). The statement is phrased in general terms and can be applied to all policies and facets of Newfoundland. However, controlling one's destiny is very much linked to controlling natural resources, as this second example shows: "The time has long since passed to forge a new partnership with the Government of Canada in which we have a greater role in controlling our own destiny. We need to work together in a cooperative manner with an emphasis on putting the people of Newfoundland and Labrador on an equal footing with the rest of Canada" (PC Party 2003, 15).

In this instance, the PC Party is appealing to the "people of Newfoundland" as a category, as a group that has not been treated as fairly as it might have been by the federal government. Here, the party's leader is not a separatist; he is proud "to be part of Canada" (CBC News 2009e). However, he uses nationalist rhetoric to rally the people of Newfoundland to a cause through an appeal to existing nationalist sentiments among Newfoundlanders. In several instances (the "Anything But Conservative" campaign or negotiations over offshore revenues), Premier Williams and the PC Party use an "Ottawa-bashing" rhetoric, but this is tempered by the fact that the majority of Newfoundlanders do not support independence. The most recent data available indicate that while 12 percent of the population support independence, 75 percent of the population believe Confederation has been a good thing for Newfoundland (Ryan Research 2003).

The final example of the words "destiny" and "control" can be found is on page 29 of the PC *Blueprint*: "It was a major step towards controlling our own destiny, a right to which any group of people should be entitled" (PC Party 2003). "Major step" refers to a protest against a "bad deal" regarding the development of the Lower Churchill. What is most interesting in this sentence is its connection with self-determination. Here the PC Party and its leader are appealing to Newfoundlanders by saying that under their stewardship no more giveaways will happen, which will allow the people of Newfoundland to control their own destiny. This message and mindset influenced the political decision-making process and policy-making throughout the period.

In 2007, the PC discourse became even more nationalistic; it moved from Newfoundland's control of its own destiny, to seeking to become "masters of our own house" (PC Party 2007, 3). This language resonates with the phrase "Maîtres chez nous" of the Québécois. As Marland explains, from that point forward, Newfoundland "would henceforth claim ownership of its resources on the road to 'becoming masters of our own house.' The use of this nationalist phrase and its association with natural resource ownership would be a continued theme throughout the 2007 election" (2010, 165). During his tenure, the premier and his party's rhetoric often fell back on economic nationalism, which emphasizes ownership and autonomy over the management and exploitation of natural resources.

The Family Growth Policy also contained nationalist rhetoric of the PC administration. Promised in the 2007 election campaign, the policy aimed to promote higher birth rates through an economic incentive: a $1,000 tax-free benefit for each new child born or adopted within the province. Premier Williams' rationale for the policy evokes a nationalist discourse: "We can't be a dying race" (CBC News 2007c). This one-time reference to race generated considerable discussion in the province, since it went beyond the mere imagined community: Williams was suggesting that Newfoundlanders and Labradorians belong to a different group. This type of language is often associated with ethnic nationalism, a nationalism based on an ascriptive identity (Keating 1996, 5). The PC Party's actions are also important here: adopting a "baby bonus" program (Quebec has taken a similar approach) is as much a means to promote one's "heritage" as it is a mechanism to increase the number of Newfoundlanders who identify with that heritage.

Following the absence of the words "pride" and "proud" in the 2003 election platform (even the word "culture" is barely used), we find that these words are used five times each in the 2007 PC platform, mainly in reference to culture. As Marland explains, this type of discourse was a means through which the PC Party could pursue its own ends: "By the time the party sought re-election, its platform was crooning about how the province's 'distinctive culture' was its most valuable natural resource and that the cultural sector would generate economic opportunity while fostering a strong sense of identity, pride and self-confidence ... Culture had therefore become a means of differentiation within the Canadian federation and a tool for claiming special status" (Marland 2010, 167).

The PC Party's emphasis on culture is an indication both of cultural nationalism and of brokerage politics (see chapter 4, by Royce Koop, in this volume). Keating (1996) and Hobsbawm (1983) note the importance of the cultivation of traditions by nationalists. Resuscitating old traditions or creating new ones is an integral part of the nation-building process, and we have observed it in Newfoundland since the nineteenth century. The task of building a separate culture for Newfoundland nationalists is made easier by a pre-existing rich heritage. In his analysis of pre-Confederation Newfoundland, Colton shows how music and identity are intrinsically linked. Through various songs, Newfoundlanders exhibit a strong sense of unique cultural and national identity. Colton explains: "'The Banks of Newfoundland' [a song written circa 1820] has achieved iconic status within a collective national consciousness" (2007, 9). But the pivotal moment in the evolution of Newfoundland musical nationalism took place when the "Ode to Newfoundland" was first performed in 1902. In 1979 it was officially adopted as Newfoundland's provincial anthem, and its familiar refrain of "we love thee, smiling land" continues to be sung by Newfoundlanders at public gatherings.

In a well-known article in *Saturday Night* in 1976, Sandra Gwyn wrote about the "Newfoundland Renaissance," describing the cultural and social revolution that took place in the aftermath of Smallwood's departure from the premier's office in 1972. The 1970s were a period of profound social and cultural change in Newfoundland. Artists, poets, and singers tried to express the true Newfoundland identity through their arts. However, and as Paul Chafe (2008) observes, this identity was invented: "Sandra Gwyn's 1976 article ... did much to establish the trope of the mythical and nature-loving Newfoundlander whose Eden-esque existence was being threatened by modernization."

Other prominent traditions today include the Pink-White-Green (pwg) flag, which is often (erroneously) associated with the so-called Republic of Newfoundland (Chafe 2007; Lambert 2008). The pwg has come to symbolize pre-Confederation Newfoundland, when it was a Dominion, and the mythos of a strong independent nation. That both locals (O'Neill 2005) and politicians (Radio-Canada 2012) display the pwg is an indication of a strong local identity, romanticized notions of political autonomy, and a detachment towards Ottawa and the Canadian nation. As well, in response to local consumer demand, one can buy "Newfoundland Liberation Army" t-shirts and other products that are representative of cultural nationalism (Chafe 2007). Furthermore, the media, even in Quebec, talk about the distinct character of New-foundland (Tremblay 2008, A-1 and A-10; Corbeil 2006, 3).

In 2007 Danny Williams and the PC Party used culture to emphasize the distinct character of Newfoundland, but by the time of the 2011 election, when Kathy Dunderdale was leading the party, the words "pride/proud" appeared sparingly and only in connection with "herit-age," as part of a section in the party's election platform titled "Cele-brating our Proud Heritage" (PC Party 2011). Despite the appearance of a shift away from overt nationalist rhetoric, perhaps as a consequence of a more conciliatory relationship that Dunderdale struck with Prime Minister Harper, it is still interesting to see how culture was used to pro-mote a distinct identity and how Newfoundlanders were encouraged to be "taking pride" (39) in their heritage and culture. For example, Williams and Dunderdale differed in their use of nationalist rhetoric to promote certain policies and justify political demands. Whereas in 2003, and even more so in 2007, the Williams PCs emphasized the need for Newfoundland and Newfoundlanders to control their destiny and to become masters of their own house, the 2011 Dunderdale election plat-form noted that by "[r]ejecting pessimism, we have taken responsibility for our destiny and charted our own course" (PC Party 2011, 1). This type of discourse suggests that for the PC Party in the post-Williams era, Newfoundland's destiny was settled and the people no longer had to fight for control over their natural resources.

A final point needs to be raised regarding the word "nation": it did not generate the anticipated results in the discourse analysis. If one were to do the same analysis for Quebec's political programs, one would see the phrase "nation québécoise" used by all parties, but in Newfoundland "nation" was used in the PC election platforms only to refer to First Nations (the Innu nation, the Métis nation, etc.). The "Newfoundland nation" is not mentioned in any of the platforms. However, as the preceding analysis suggests, nationalism in Newfoundland is expressed in other words, with less explicit – but still very strong – references to the "imagined community" of Newfoundland.

Danny Williams' leadership style helped to affirm Newfoundland's presence and weight at the federal level. As a journalist from Quebec said in the days following Williams' resignation, he was the "René Lévesque of Newfoundland" (Pratte 2010) who by his actions and rhetoric shaped his province's national identity and gave hope and pride to his people. Another Quebec journalist stated that it was hard to blame the premier for what he did: fight for his province's economic resources against a powerful neighbour (Marissal 2010). Premier Williams' political strategy was possible because of the exceptional economic circumstances at the time, characterized by the increasing value of the province's oil resources. As Marland reminds us, "the Williams effect should not be overstated given that much is due to global economic forces" (2010, 177). Claiming autonomy from the central government within the federal structure is one way to affirm distinctiveness. Since it joined Confederation, Newfoundland elites have promoted this agenda both through claims for greater political and economic control and through an emphasis on Newfoundland's unique culture.

POLITICAL DECISION MAKING IN NEWFOUNDLAND & LABRADOR

Is nationalism really on the rise in Newfoundland, and if so, will it last? If we analyze nationalism, not on a temporal continuum, but as a gradual trend, it is possible to understand why it appears to be strong at certain times and not as strong at others, despite similar circumstances. Critical events and circumstances, such as extracting the revenues from offshore oil, make the success of a political leader much more likely:

they facilitate political decision making, and the decisions that are made are generally supported by a population that also reaps the rewards and spinoffs associated with economic growth. Renewed confidence can make nationalist claims much more evident.

However, nationalism may at times remain latent, as is the case in the early stages of the Dunderdale administration. What remains unexplained is how nationalism can continue to exist between the primary incidents that cause nationalism to peak. Michael Billig's concept of "banal nationalism" is useful here. For Billig, nationalism continues to exist on a daily basis: "Daily, the nation is indicated, or 'flagged,' in the lives of its citizenry" (1995, 6), mostly through the use of language in the media but also through political discourse. Bannister writes:

> [Nationalist rhetoric]'s essential logic has remained basically the same for almost two centuries: Newfoundland has a poor economy but is rich in natural resources; its poverty is due to incompetent resource management by state agencies based outside the island; local authorities have superior technical expertise, moral commitment, and popular legitimacy; the absence of proper policies and administration is caused by the lack of sufficient local control over resource exploitation and allocation; thus the key to prosperity is the transference of power to local political institutions. (2003, 147)

As the preceding analysis has shown, the language used by Premier Williams and his predecessors is in line with Billig's banal nationalism and Bannister's argument.

Peaks of nationalism have occurred in Newfoundland throughout its history, most recently during Williams' tenure. In between those moments of "collective effervescence" (Brubaker 2004, 4), the nation of Newfoundland continues to exist and is perpetuated through various symbols (flags, anthems, songs, t-shirts, and so on) and a particular way of life, a unique culture with its own traditions, and an "imagined community."

Nationalism is an underlying feature of Newfoundland politics (Marland 2010) and will likely remain so. At times, its nationalist claims have been more prominent because of economic circumstances, strong leadership, or the unique practices of its political leaders. During other periods, it has remained latent, buried in the daily lives and the survival of the people of the Island. Nationalism in Newfoundland has been an integral part of its politics and public policy process. While Newfoundland's nationalism is distinctly non-separatist, the Newfoundland identity and the way in which it is expressed politically changes and evolves over time. We cannot dismiss the possibility that at some point, depending on the political and economic circumstances (Summers 2001), there might be a turn for a more separatist nationalism.

NOTES

The authors wish to thank the Canadian Opinion Research Archive at Queen's University, Kingston, and particularly Scott Matthews and Randy Besco for providing us with crucial data for this study.

1   Our focus is on the insular part of the province of Newfoundland & Labrador. Although the province also includes the continental part, Labrador, the island of Newfoundland has had a distinct history, and the arguments developed in this chapter refer to the identities that characterize the population of the Island, rather than the entire province.
2   The second meeting between the Province of Canada, Prince Edward Island, Nova Scotia, and New Brunswick to discuss Canadian Confederation.

4

Parties and Brokerage Politics in Newfoundland and Labrador

ROYCE KOOP

COMPARATIVE THEORY

How can the premiers of Newfoundland & Labrador be understood as both government and party leaders, and what are the implications of this understanding for public policy-making in the province? The behaviours of Newfoundland premiers tend to resemble those of brokerage leaders, and the parties that they lead also tend to accord with the expectations of brokerage parties. The brokerage behaviours of premiers result in part from several institutional features of Canada's system of governance and federalism. A case study of the governing styles of Danny Williams and Kathy Dunderdale reveals that policy-making and politics in the province is deeply affected by the brokerage orientations of those leaders. In making such an argument, this chapter's emphasis on brokerage complements traditional accounts of Newfoundland political leaders that emphasize their nationalism, populism, and appeals to Newfoundland regionalism (e.g., Marland 2010).

This chapter, therefore, is situated at the intersection of two approaches to the study of public policy. First, elite theory points to the influence of small groups of powerful individuals over the policy agenda (e.g., Adams 2007). This approach has been persuasively applied to provincial politics given the power of the provinces' premiers and the small groups of advisors that surround them (e.g., Dunn 2005a). Second, institutionalist theory points to the roles of institutions in shaping the behaviours of political actors and, as a result, altering policy outcomes (e.g., Peters 2005). The observation that provincial party leaders act as brokers fits squarely within the elite theory of public policy. But this then begs the question of why party leaders take on brokerage roles. To address that question, I turn to institutionalist theory and point to three institutional features of Canadian government and federalism that incentivize brokerage behaviours at the provincial level: parliamentary institutions that facilitate strong party discipline, a tendency towards asymmetrical federalism (particularly side deals between the federal government and individual provincial governments), and federal institutions that have contributed to the formal organizational separation of national and provincial parties.

The notion of a brokerage party is a distinctively Canadian innovation. In its earliest formulation, the brokerage party was defined on the basis of its expressive appeals and approaches to sociological cleavages within society (see Carty 1992). Brokerage parties make no distinction between societal groups and indeed invite any citizen within the bounds of their big tents. These parties therefore transcend rather than articulate cleavages within society (Dawson 1948, 508).

Recognizing the lack of conceptual clarity surrounding the notion of brokerage parties and leaders, Carty (2013) sets out to define them. Speaking to the importance of the leaders of brokerage parties, all five defining characteristics presented by Carty relate to the behaviours of these brokerage leaders. First, whereas other parties are in fact constrained in the groups of voters they can appeal to, the leaders of brokerage parties are truly free to embrace as many groups as possible. Second, brokerage leaders tend to expand their expressive functions by presenting their parties as "the natural, national governing part[ies]" (Carty 2013, 14). In practice, such presentations are likely to accord with nationalistic sentiments, as has been the case, for example, with the Liberal Party of Canada. Third, whereas many other parties are the product of long evolutionary dynamics, brokerage parties tend to be either created or recreated by enterprising party leaders. Fourth, loyalty to the leader is a crucial prerequisite for involvement in brokerage parties. Finally, the power of brokerage party leaders exceeds that of leaders of other parties, since brokerage leaders come to be seen to personify the party to the public. As brokerage parties' "chief brokers," leaders are not bound by past policy commitments and so can be expected to shift course without regret or apology. Furthermore, the great value placed on leaders means that brokerage parties will be fiercely protective of them.

Carty's criteria remind us of the crucial importance of leaders to the defining of brokerage parties. Brokerage leaders make wide appeals across societal groups in election campaigns, they claim to speak for their provinces as wholes, they remake parties in their own images, they demand complete loyalty, and they are free to shape campaign appeals and government policy largely as they please. Brokerage parties are dominated by and tend to take on the characteristics of their leaders, for better or worse.

Brokerage theory has been applied to Canadian provincial politics (e.g., Wesley 2009). The roots of brokerage in the provinces lie in three aspects of national and provincial political institutions. One is party discipline, which is particularly pronounced in Canada compared to other Westminster-derived systems (Malloy 2003, 117–20). This extends to the provinces, where discipline allows executives to dominate both their governments and parties (Bakvis and Wolinetz 2005).

Strong party discipline empowers leaders to engage in brokerage behaviours. Without such discipline, leaders might expect the policy shifts and inconsistencies that necessarily accompany brokerage behaviours to eventually provoke rebellion from the party's caucus, as caucus members would struggle to explain policy inconsistencies to constituents and supporters. This consideration may cause party leaders to rethink their brokerage approaches; however, strong party discipline erases this imperative for party leaders and provides them with the freedom necessary to act as brokers.

"Asymmetrical federalism" refers to federal systems where individual subnational units are treated differently from one another, either in terms of their relations with the national government or of their powers under the constitution (see Watts 1999). Because Canada's constitution treats the provinces in a broadly symmetrical manner, uniformity characterizes most policy areas in which national and provincial governments must work together. Nevertheless, asymmetry has developed in part as a result of side agreements between the federal government and individual provincial governments. The Atlantic Offshore Accords, negotiated between the federal government and the governments of Newfoundland & Labrador and Nova Scotia, interfering with the calculation of equalization payments provides one example of such asymmetrical side deals (Richards 2008, 75).

The effect of such special arrangements is that premiers, consistent with Cairns' (1977) expectation that provincial governments will continually attempt to enlarge their jurisdictions, know that they can consistently expand their powers by pressing for such agreements themselves. As Brock (2008, 147) puts it, "asymmetry becomes raw self-interest" on the part of premiers. The result is that asymmetry incentivizes one-on-one conflicts between premiers and the federal government. The us-versus-them frame of such conflicts is conducive to brokerage behaviours on the part of premiers, since the prospect of an outside threat (the federal government) allows premiers to speak on behalf of their entire provinces as the natural expression of the provincial will.

Finally, the organizations of Canada's national and provincial parties tend to be formally separate from one another (e.g., Franks 2007, 26). This separation results in part from several characteristics of Canada's federal and electoral institutions, including a decentralized federal system, non-concurrent national and provincial elections, distinctive national and provincial constituency boundaries, and party finance requirements at the national and provincial levels that require disentanglement as a condition of fiscal transparency (see Koop 2011, chapter 1). While there are informal and personnel linkages between national and provincial parties (e.g., Esselment 2010), these parties are nevertheless *formally* separated from one another.

Integrated parties – those with important formal linkages between the national and provincial levels – must maintain some semblance of policy consistency between the two levels, which necessarily makes it difficult for party leaders to pick and choose policies as they see fit. This means that the leaders of integrated parties confront severe obstacles to engaging in brokerage behaviours. In contrast, the formal separation of national and provincial parties removes a crucial obstacle to brokerage on the part of party leaders in the provinces, as these leaders are free to pick and choose the policies that suit them.

Furthermore, the lack of linkages between levels means that federal party leaders cannot invoke party loyalty at the provincial level. Premiers can therefore act as defenders of their provinces and engage in policy disagreements and battles with their counterparts in the federal government even if they are ostensibly members of the same party. The result is that premiers sacrifice party for province (see Cairns 1977) and engage in the brokerage behaviour of speaking out as the natural defenders of the provinces as wholes.

BACKGROUND

Several institutional characteristics of the Newfoundland & Labrador government incentivize the adoption of brokerage techniques and strategies on the part of premiers of the province. This suggests that the

Table 4.1
Newfoundland & Labrador election results, 1949–2011 (percentages)

		Conservative		Liberal		NDP		Other	
Election	Government	Vote share	Seat share	Vote share	Seat share	Vote share	Seat share	Vote share	Seat share
1949	Liberal	32.9	17.9	65.5	78.6	–	–	1.6	3.6
1951	Liberal	35.6	14.3	63.6	85.7	–	–	0.8	0.0
1956	Liberal	32.0	11.1	66.3	88.9	–	–	1.7	0.0
1959	Liberal	25.3	8.3	58.0	86.1	7.2	0.0	9.5	5.6
1962	Liberal	36.6	16.7	58.7	81.0	3.6	0.0	1.1	2.4
1966	Liberal	34.0	7.1	61.8	92.9	1.8	0.0	2.4	0.0
1971	Conservative	51.3	50.0	44.4	47.6	1.8	0.0	2.5	2.4
1972	Conservative	60.5	78.6	37.2	21.4	<1.0	0.0	2.7	0.0
1975	Conservative	45.5	58.8	37.1	31.4	4.0	0.0	13.4	9.8
1979	Conservative	50.4	63.5	40.6	36.5	7.8	0.0	1.2	0.0
1982	Conservative	61.2	84.6	34.9	15.4	3.7	0.0	0.2	0.0
1985	Conservative	48.6	69.2	36.7	28.8	14.4	1.9	0.3	0.0
1989	Liberal	47.6	40.4	47.2	59.6	4.4	0.0	0.8	0.0
1993	Liberal	42.1	30.8	49.1	67.3	7.4	1.9	1.4	0.0
1996	Liberal	38.7	18.8	55.1	77.1	4.5	2.1	1.7	2.1
1999	Liberal	40.6	29.2	49.5	66.7	8.2	4.2	1.4	0.0
2003	Conservative	58.7	70.8	33.2	25.0	6.9	4.2	1.2	0.0
2007	Conservative	69.6	91.7	22.0	6.3	8.2	2.1	0.2	0.0
2011	Conservative	56.1	77.1	19.1	12.5	24.6	10.4	0.2	0.0

Source: Data in this table were collected from reports on the website maintained by Elections Newfoundland and Labrador (http://www.elections.gov.nl.ca/elections/) and from the *Telegram* archives.

brokerage styles employed by Danny Williams and Kathy Dunderdale in recent years are in fact nothing new in Newfoundland politics. Indeed, a historical-comparative analysis of the province's election results demonstrates that the province has, since joining Confederation, been characterized by strong party leaders, lopsided majority governments, and lengthy periods of one-party rule.

Table 4.1 summarizes the vote and seat shares for all major parties in every Newfoundland election held since 1949. Seat shares over 50 percent are bolded to highlight the legislative dominance of each government. The table reveals two features that are crucial to understanding electoral politics in Newfoundland: (1) the presence of four historical party systems where one of the province's major parties remained in power for several terms and (2) the presence of very large majority governments and lopsided legislatures in each of those systems. Brokerage leaders are a crucial aspect of the story of the province's alternating dominant parties.

Four discernible party systems that have existed since Newfoundland joined Confederation in 1949 can be identified; each system has been characterized by a single dominant governing party. Liberal premier Joey Smallwood dominated the first party system, winning six majority governments between 1949 and 1966. Smallwood's long period in office was dominated by both province-building (see Tomblin 1990) and what Overton (2000, 166) argues were revolutions in terms of infrastructure, government relief, and optimism about the future of the province. The 1971 election ushered in a new provincial party system, this one characterized by Progressive Conservative (PC) governance. Frank Moores and his successor, Brian Peckford, won six majority governments between 1971 and 1985. Peckford was notable for his conflicts with the federal government for greater constitutional autonomy and provincial control over natural resources (Cadigan 2009, 260). Liberal Premiers Clyde Wells and Brian Tobin dominated the third system, from 1989 to 1999. While Wells continued the tradition of butting heads with the federal government, most notably over the Meech Lake Accord that would have recognized Quebec as a "distinct society" in Canada's constitution, Tobin's prior experience as a federal cabinet minister and his strong personal relationship with Prime Minister Jean Chrétien led to a calmer period in federal-provincial relations. The following section picks up on the fourth provincial party system, which appeared to arrive in 2003 with the election of Danny Williams and has continued on through the election of Kathy Dunderdale in 2011.

While the Progressive Conservative and Liberal parties have switched positions as dominant parties throughout Newfoundland history, it is important to illuminate the similarities between these systems. Most importantly, there is a clear tendency towards oversized majority governments and lopsided legislatures in the province. Indeed, Siaroff's (2009, table 2) comparative analysis demonstrates that Newfoundland & Labrador has a notable tendency amongst the provinces towards dominant majority governments. Winning parties since 1949 have received on average 75.2 percent of seats in the House of Assembly. Indeed, only once since 1949 has the winning party not received a majority of seats in the provincial legislature (in the 1971 election).

Single-member plurality electoral systems tend to provide a seat bonus to winning parties. However, large majority governments in Newfoundland are not solely a product of electoral system distortions. Siaroff (2009, 83) notes that Newfoundland & Labrador and Prince Edward Island are unique among the provinces in producing very high vote shares for parties. Winning parties have since the 1949 election won an average of 56.7 percent of the vote. The electoral system certainly assists winning parties in Newfoundland, but oversized majority governments are generally the products of very popular leaders and parties winning very high proportions of the popular vote.

This comparative-historical analysis of electoral outcomes reminds us that Danny Williams was unique neither in his popularity nor in his dominance over the House of Assembly. Instead, he followed in the footsteps of a long line of premiers who dominated the legislatures and the governments of Newfoundland. This finding directs our attention to the question of how leaders and parties have consistently produced such high vote shares, and brokerage is an important part of the answer. This perspective contributes to the usefulness of the 2003–11 period as a case study, since this exploration of the use of brokerage techniques by Williams and Dunderdale may shed light on the successful governing approaches of past premiers.

CASE STUDY

The PC Party of Newfoundland & Labrador had languished on the opposition benches in St John's for over a decade before the selection of Danny Williams as leader in 2001, when the previous leader, Ed Byrne, voluntarily stepped aside (Barron 2001). Williams was a high-profile lawyer and cable television executive and thus had a significant public profile in the province before his selection as leader (Marland 2010, 163). It was widely anticipated that he would seek the PC Party leadership. Owing to his profile and strength as a candidate, Williams was uncontested and acclaimed as leader, which allowed the party (and Williams) to avoid a divisive leadership contest.

While the PC Party was not moribund during its eleven years in opposition, it was in the political wilderness and lacked a distinctive identity. Williams assumed the leadership of the party as an outsider; while from a well-known Tory family, he was not a member of the party caucus and entered the House of Assembly only in a June 2001 by-election. Both these factors – a directionless party and a new outsider leader – produced a situation where Williams would be relatively free to shape the party in the manner of his own choosing. Furthermore, Williams' immediate successes as leader – the PC Party won four by-elections in traditionally Liberal districts and a Liberal member of the House of Assembly (MHA) crossed the floor – strengthened both his own position as leader and his ability to give the party a new identity and focus (e.g., *Chronicle Herald* 2001).

Williams worked to shape the PC Party in his own image. In 2002, for example, he unleashed criticism of Liberal premier Roger Grimes' Voisey's Bay Agreement and a plan to commence development of the Lower Churchill Falls. The theme of his criticisms – "No More Give-aways" – was consistent with his later outward-looking brokerage approach (Marland 2010, 163).

Williams continued to shape the PC Party in the 2003 provincial election campaign. By this point, the province's Liberal Party had been in power for fourteen years. The PC campaign was distinguished by three themes. First, it focused on 'change in government. Thus, the party's 2003 election platform emphasized "The New Approach" of Williams. And the campaign capitalized on the feeling that the Liberal Party had grown comfortable in office by promising new rules concerning transparency in issuing public contracts and reducing the power of money and special interests through legislation governing the behaviours of lobbyists (PC Party 2003, 62).

Second, the campaign focused on Williams himself. He featured prominently in the party's platform, for example, which also drew attention to the new leader's skills and history as a lawyer and businessman. "These solutions are not pie in the sky proposals," wrote Williams in that platform. "They are solid fundamentals that I have acquired over my 30 years in the private sector. And just as they worked in the private sector, they will work in government" (PC Party 2003, 1). The party's platform therefore presented not just policies but also the argument that these policies derived from Williams' own experience and could be implemented only with him in the premier's office.

Finally, the PC campaign, while bringing some of the party's and Williams' concerns for private sector solutions to government problems, was consensual rather than conflictual, emphasizing issues that appealed to a broad range of citizens. Thus, while Williams did promise to address the province's fiscal problems by cutting costs and streamlining the civil service, he focused primarily on broadly popular themes related to healthcare, jobs, education, seniors, and poverty.

The 2003 PC Party campaign strongly emphasized and reflected the influence of Williams: he was a new leader, he brought new and valuable skills, and he was concerned with a range of issues that were of interest to Newfoundland society as a whole. Williams was widely expected to win that election – his leadership rating just before the election stood at

51 percent (Corporate Research Associates 2012) – and did so handily. The PC Party won a solid percentage of the popular vote (58.7 percent) and formed a majority government. The leader-oriented campaign had paid off for the PC Party.

As a new premier, however, Williams appeared to struggle to develop a style of governing, beginning with a neoliberal approach to governance but eventually finding his feet with a clearly defined brokerage approach. Williams first emphasized the neoliberal aspect of his program, announcing a broad range of spending cuts, wage freezes, and public service layoffs. Marland (2007b, 76) describes this as "mild fiscal conservatism" leading to "internal strife." The result was a period of friction between the government and the provincial civil service culminating in a strike in April 2004, swiftly followed by back-to-work legislation. A May 2004 poll revealed that a majority of citizens were dissatisfied with Williams and his government (Corporate Research Associates 2012).

In his first term, however, Williams also embraced two issues that appealed to a broader range of Newfoundlanders and Labradorians, and he began to develop a clear, outward-looking brokerage style to governance. The first related to a dispute with Prime Minister Paul Martin over his promised changes to the Atlantic Accord. Williams publicly feuded with Martin over the issue (e.g., Dunn 2005b).

Second, Williams defended the provincial seal hunt from international scrutiny applied by environmental and animal rights advocacy groups. In 2006, Williams appeared on *The Larry King Show* opposite Paul McCartney and Heather Mills to defend the hunt. His position as defender of provincial interests was popular amongst Newfoundlanders and Labradorians. One enthusiastic journalist from the *Telegram* summarized the "overwhelming" response: "People around the world ... lauded Danny Williams for his performance." The comments of a Newfoundland expatriate were also printed: "Keep up the good work back there. You make us all proud" (Gillingham 2006).

In both of these cases, Williams was staking out popular positions that appealed to a wide range of citizens, allowing them to support his party even while disagreeing on issues that divided them, such as the need to streamline the provincial civil service. Furthermore, with his outward-looking brokerage style Williams focused attention on outside threats and trumpeted his battle to fend them off for the good of the province as a whole. In this period, Williams also concluded a deal with several oil companies for the development of the Hebron offshore oilfield, an outcome with widespread support across the province, given concerns over unemployment and underdevelopment (Dunn 2007).

Power helped to discipline an already acquiescent PC caucus. However, the case of Fabian Manning, an outspoken PC MHA and parliamentary secretary, provides an illustration of the authority of brokerage leaders within their parties. In 2005 Manning openly criticized his government's proposals to alter crab processing rules in the province, reporting that his constituents felt that the rules provided processors with too much power over independent fishers (e.g., Roberts 2005). Following his criticisms, Williams announced that he could no longer work with Manning, and the party caucus accordingly moved to eject him (CBC News 2005). It was clear from the episode not only that Williams would not brook dissent but also that the party saw its leader as valuable and was fully willing to circle the wagons around him when it was necessary to do so.

Having refined his brokerage techniques following his tumultuous first two years in office, Williams returned in the 2007 provincial election to a platform with wide appeal across the province, one that addressed a number of social and fiscal concerns in a positive manner (by, for example, emphasizing "prosperity") in its attempt to reach out to a wide range of citizens. Crucially, the general nature of the platform would ultimately allow Williams to engage in brokerage behaviours as premier by picking and choosing which policies he would implement following the election.

The party also emphasized Newfoundland & Labrador's conflicts with outside interests more prominently in this campaign. Williams voiced public outrage over a broken pledge by Prime Minister Stephen Harper to stand by the Atlantic Accords' exemption of nonrenewable resource revenues from the calculation of equalization payments received by the province (e.g., Marland 2007b, 76). Although intergovernmental relations were not a major topic of discussion in the 2007 provincial election campaign, the federal Conservative Party's slight was mentioned in the PC Party's election manifesto: "Prior to the last federal election, Stephen Harper made a solemn written promise to the people of Newfoundland & Labrador to remove nonrenewable resource revenues from equalization calculations. He also promised to honour the Atlantic Accord. Had he honoured his promises, the positive impact on Newfoundland & Labrador would have been enormous. However, he did not honour those commitments" (PC Party 2007, 2). By emphasizing this dispute, the party communicated that it saw such conflicts as transcending divisions within

the province. It also presented itself as the natural carrier of Newfoundland & Labrador values. "We are Newfoundlanders and Labradorians,"
wrote Williams. "Proud. Strong. Determined. We know what it means
to stand on our own" (PC Party 2007, 2). In these ways, the party cut
across divisions in Newfoundland society and focused on unifying issues
in order to appeal to as many citizens as possible. Partly as a result,
Williams improved both his party's vote and seat shares in the 2007 election. The party won 69.6 percent of the popular vote and a stunning 92
percent of seats.

Williams' broad appeal in the 2007 election entrenched his outward-
looking brokerage style. The result provided him with a mandate to
aggressively criticize Stephen Harper's Conservative government, a tactic made possible by the formal separation of the Conservative parties at
the national and provincial levels. Thus, the premier launched his ABC –
Anything But Conservative – campaign during the 2008 federal election,
in which he encouraged Newfoundlanders and Labradorians to punish
the federal Conservatives. Williams focused on Harper's broken promise
on the 2006 Atlantic Accord and framed this as a betrayal of all Newfoundlanders and Labradorians. Williams also dispatched PC MHAS to
campaign against Fabian Manning, by now a federal Conservative MP
who was seeking re-election. The effect of the popular premier's ABC
campaign was clear: Manning was defeated and Harper's Conservatives
failed to win a single seat in the province in 2008.

Back in power, Williams returned to his outward-looking brokerage
style. In particular, he lashed out at the Quebec government over Hydro-
Quebec's attempt to purchase NB Power from the government of New
Brunswick (CBC News 2009k). The deal, according to Williams, was an
attempt by Hydro-Quebec to hamper the development of Labrador's
Lower Churchill hydro-electric project in order to protect its own dominance in the energy sector. And Williams maintained his very high popularity: for example, his personal approval rating in February 2008 stood
at a stunning 85 percent (Corporate Research Associates 2012).

The premier also continued to oppose attempts to highlight divisions
within the province, viewing them as efforts to foil his brokerage efforts
to unite Newfoundland society behind him. In June 2009, for example,
Williams called an open-line radio show to complain after the host questioned the effectiveness of government programs in place to assist fishery
and forestry workers in the province. "We don't need that kind of crap
and pessimism coming out of your mouth," thundered the premier. "I
refuse to listen to pessimists like you" (CBC News 2009j). This was one

of many instances of Williams berating his critics and was in line with his earlier actions against Fabian Manning. Just as Manning articulated divisions within Newfoundland & Labrador, either as a PC MHA who pitted crab fishers against crab processors or as an MP who sided with the federal Conservatives over the provincial Progressive Conservatives, so too did the radio host by pointing out that the government was helping some citizens but not others. Such talk threatened Williams' ability to speak on behalf of the province as a whole, and so he responded.

In 2008, the PC Party demonstrated its willingness to close ranks around its leader in the face of threats, even when the threat appeared to be minute. Following a private dispute with Williams, his deputy premier Tom Rideout was subjected to an "aggressive and coordinated public counterattack" from the premier and the party, including the claim that Rideout had "strong-armed" a minister to secure additional funds for roads in his constituency (CBC News 2008d; Marland 2010, 171). The pattern was repeated in 2010. A member of the Rural Secretariat Advisory Board, Pamela Pardy Ghent, posted an insulting comment about Williams' anatomy on Facebook. On learning of the insult, the minister responsible for the board immediately removed Ghent from her volunteer position (CBC News 2010k). The punishment seemed disproportionate to the crime. The episode therefore illustrates the extent to which the party would go to protect the image and reputation of its leader.

Williams' resignation in 2010 resulted in Deputy Premier Kathy Dunderdale assuming the leadership of the party. After a period in which she claimed not to be interested in it permanently, Dunderdale changed course and announced her intentions to contest the position. Partly because she was seen as Williams' preferred successor, prospective challengers dropped out of the race, paving Dunderdale's way to success.

Premier Dunderdale had promised to step down as interim leader only if she was contested for the leadership; the withdrawal of all candidates therefore led to a smooth transition from interim leader to permanent leader (MacEachern 2010). However, late in the race a fringe candidate announced his intention to run, presumably to force Dunderdale to honour her promise to step down as interim leader and premier. The party executive responded by rejecting his application to run on a technicality, claiming that the candidate, Brad Cabana, had not collected enough valid signatures to contest the leadership (McLeod 2011b). This, together with the spectacle of the entire party caucus lining up to support Dunderdale's bid, projected the image of a party that once again was rallying around its leader. Like Williams several years earlier, Dunderdale would not have to endure an intra-party challenge. The party had become accustomed to a dominant brokerage leader, and it appeared to be conferring the role on Dunderdale.

In her time as premier, Dunderdale has followed the Williams broker-age formula in some ways but diverged in others. Confronted with a potential doctors' strike, she moved quickly to keep doctors on the job, avoiding conflict between well-paid doctors and other Newfound-landers and Labradorians. And the new premier continued to empha-size development of the Lower Churchill Project, drawing attention to it in her first throne speech. On the other hand, Dunderdale has taken a more consensual approach to her dealings with the federal govern-ment, even campaigning with Stephen Harper in the 2011 federal elec-tion campaign and publicly accepting a spoken promise from the prime minister regarding a loan guarantee for the Muskrat Falls development (CBC News 2011c).

POLITICAL DECISION MAKING IN NEWFOUNDLAND & LABRADOR

To what extent can Danny Williams and Kathy Dunderdale be thought of as brokerage party leaders? What are the consequences for decision making and the types of policies adopted in Newfoundland & Labra-dor? And finally, do elite and institutionalist theories help to explain public policy-making in the province?

Carty's first defining characteristic of brokerage parties is that they attempt to subsume as many groups and citizens as possible within the bounds of their broad tents. Williams, with his constant efforts to draw all citizens into his grand efforts, fulfills this requirement. This can be seen in Williams' emphasis, after a small number of false starts, on issues that unified rather than divided the citizens of Newfoundland. Many of his priorities as premier were positions on issues that attracted wide-spread public support throughout the province. Above all they were uni-fying issues. Williams did not publicly distinguish between groups of Newfoundlanders and Labradorians; instead, he emphasized the com-monalities of all citizens in the province and stoked a sense of common grievance by arguing that they deserved special treatment in the federal system. His style of brokerage, however, was outward-looking: he uni-fied provincial citizens in part by turning their attention to threats out-side the province.

It is important to note that Williams fought back whenever local, national, or international actors – whether opposition politicians, members of his own party, open-line radio hosts, or Paul McCartney – threatened his appeal across all sectors of Newfoundland society by pointing to divisions between groups within the province. Williams constantly sought to maintain a unifying appeal and withstand others' attempts to illuminate divisions within Newfoundland.

Second, brokerage parties tend to present themselves as the natural governing parties of their provinces. In this sense, brokerage is linked to provincial nationalism in Newfoundland. Williams attempted to present himself in this manner. By projecting an image of a strong leader that could protect citizens from outside threats, he sought to cast himself in the role of the province's natural governing leader. These attempts can also be seen in the party's election platforms, in which Williams explicitly presents himself as a carrier (and protector) of Newfoundland values. Nationalistic themes may appear in the speeches of party leaders in other provinces, but Williams was particularly consistent in his appeals to a distinctive Newfoundland & Labrador nationalism. Like other brokerage leaders, Williams weaved these themes into his own personal appeal as the natural leader of the province.

Third, unlike other party types, brokerage parties tend to be created or recreated by strong leaders. This is certainly the case for Williams and the PC Party. While the party dates back to Newfoundland's entry into Confederation, by 2003 it had been out of power for over a decade and was lacking an identity. As an outsider, Williams was able to shape the party to his own needs and his own style. In doing so, he displayed the tendency of brokerage party leaders to create or recreate parties that they then use to win and maintain power. Kathy Dunderdale continued the tradition of brokerage leaders who recreate the identities of their parties, for example, by constructing a more congenial relationship with Prime Minister Harper.

Fourth, in brokerage parties, requirements for party loyalty are very high, since party leaders occupy important and highly valued positions as the parties' chief brokers and communicators and so are strongly protected by the parties. Both of these tendencies can be seen in Williams' and the PC Party's reaction to dissenters. The tendency to protect the leader was also seen in the leadership race that eventually saw Dunderdale replace Williams as permanent party leader.

Both Williams and Dunderdale have engaged in behaviours that are typical of brokerage politicians, even though their overall styles have differed somewhat. What are the consequences of brokerage for public policy in the province? Two in particular can be identified: first, the types of policies adopted and, second, the nature of decision making in the province.

First, policies that were prioritized under "chief broker" Williams were those with wide public approval, particularly those that stirred sentiments of provincial citizenship. After a false start with his neoliberal economic approach following the 2003 provincial election, Williams adopted a brokerage approach that emphasized commonalities rather than divisions within Newfoundland & Labrador society. Negative outcomes were inevitably placed at the feet of interests outside Newfoundland & Labrador. This is especially true for the federal government. After Prime Minister Martin opened the door to asymmetrical side deals by renegotiating the terms of the Atlantic Accord, which allowed Williams to triumphantly return home from Ottawa with a $2 billion deal, any unwillingness of the federal government to do so again and again would be met with outrage from Williams, as Stephen Harper found out.

It is not yet clear whether similar policies will be prioritized under Dunderdale, but her willingness to quickly head off a doctors' strike in the province suggests that she has learned about brokerage from Williams. Brokerage has therefore been important in shaping public policy in the province.

Second, decision making under brokerage politicians such as Williams and Dunderdale is inevitably elitist, with the premiers and their small groups of advisors maintaining strict control over the policy process; indeed, this case study offers crucial substantiation of the elite theory of public policy-making. Brokerage parties provide their leaders with wide leeway to pick and choose policies, since this power is necessary for leaders to fulfill their roles as chief brokers. Indeed, the PC Party allowed itself to be shaped in the image of Williams upon his accession to the leadership. And, as with other brokerage parties, the PC Party was and is highly disciplined, empowering Williams to punish anyone who raises questions about policies prioritized or decisions taken. The result is an elitist style of decision making that inevitably leaves the party caucus, the House of Assembly, and the wider party membership out of the policy-making process.

Although the case study demonstrates that both Premier Williams and Premier Dunderdale exhibit brokerage tendencies in their governing styles, it does not, however, mean that all premiers of Newfoundland & Labrador have been or will similarly be brokers. Institutions, including the three examined here, shape elites' attitudes and incentivize certain behaviours over others, but they are not determinative. Leaders bring their own backgrounds, attitudes, and habits to office. Some leaders will enthusiastically embrace brokerage; others will not.

This case study of Premiers Williams and Dunderdale draws on both elite and institutionalist theories of public policy to richly illustrate relationships between institutions, political brokerage, and policy outcomes in Newfoundland & Labrador. Governing institutions have empowered Williams and Dunderdale to assume roles as the province's chief brokers, since many of their behaviours as premier have accorded with the expectations of brokerage leaders. To observe that these premiers have tended to be brokers is not to criticize them or their governing styles. Rather, it is to note that brokerage behaviours have had important consequences for policy-making, particularly in terms of the policies prioritized, and ultimately implemented, in Newfoundland & Labrador.

5

The Brand Image of Governing Parties and Leaders

ALEX MARLAND

COMPARATIVE THEORY

An emerging area of practice and study looks at political parties as "brands" (Lock and Harris 1996; Smith 2001; Smith and French 2009). Branding is concerned with the overall psychological impression conveyed through the sum of all communications. The idea is that synonymous and interconnected messages repeated across a variety of media platforms are much more likely to cause people to recall the overall desired brand positioning and to forget other details. Branding is about communicating symbolism rather than substance, since most audiences do not engage in a deep scrutiny of available information.

The application of branding theory and practice to politics is not seamless, because the commercial sphere is not analogous to the political arena (e.g., Baines and Egan 2001). Nevertheless, political parties seek to manage their brand images across a variety of mass communications. They control unfiltered media such as their advertising and websites, which are the best indicators of what they want to communicate. They cannot, however, control what or how journalists report, so they employ media management techniques such as spin, key messaging, and photo ops (e.g., Grabe and Bucy 2009). Public servants also partake in branding. Central agencies maintain internal guidelines for a common "look and feel" in government communications (e.g., Canada 2012b), which ensures that text and visuals such as photos, videos, colours, props, and logos are unified to project a desired visual identity. Increasingly, the "personal brand" of a party leader is managed too (Needham 2005; Scammell 2007; Smith 2001). For instance, political image handlers seek to create a public persona of a leader that is similar to how citizens in that jurisdiction perceive themselves (Caprara et al. 2007). Collectively, this is a sign that political communication is moving from a mass media model to a consumer model (Scammell 2007).

The democratic implications of leaders becoming commodified celebrities have contributed to the "presidentialization" of the parliamentary system of government whereby the political executive becomes less accountable to the legislature, the head of government is popularly elected, and one person has executive authority (Poguntke and Webb 2005). Another problem is that the public sphere equates brand personality with policy discussion, and citizens evaluate leadership on the basis of image rather than issue management (e.g., Budesheim and DePaola 1994; Verser and Wicks 2006). The personalization of politics "slip[s] into hyperreality" where style is prioritized over substance, where electors judge leaders not on actual skills but on how they are packaged (Zavattaro 2010, 124), and where political actors conceptualize citizens as audiences (Mullins 2008). Further, to strengthen the governing party's brands, there is increasing pressure on public servants to synchronize government messages, images, and public policies with those of the governing party (Chiu 2007).

BACKGROUND

The obvious place to look for information about the branding of provincial parties and premiers is in studies of sub-national elections in Canada. However, empirical research has emphasized voter behaviour, which finds that Canadians tend to have stronger attachments to provincial parties than to federal ones (Studlar 2001) and that incumbents have significant electoral advantages (Krashinsky and Milne 1986). Comparing provincial leaders across Canada is rare, and most of the published work is behaviouralist, journalistic, and reflective.

If there is no available research about the use of branding in provincial politics, then we are resigned to identifying nuggets of information that can provide some foundation of knowledge. A half dozen themes run through the literature. The first theme in studies of provincial politics is that, as we would expect, components of political marketing have become more sophisticated over time. In Newfoundland, opinion polls were used to inform the Progressive Conservative (PC) Party's decision to emphasize their leader in the 1975 campaign, and the news media paid little attention to policy issues, while professional advertising featured

Premier Frank Moores touring the province (Paine 1981, 16). Campaign ads in 1979, including ads sponsored by local candidates, emphasized what Robert Paine (88) called the "brand name" by referring to "a Peckford government." However, the cost of mass media techniques combined with the sense of community in Newfoundland has meant that old-style tactics such as touring, speeches, rallies, debates, and motorcades with vehicles broadcasting music over loudspeakers have an entrenched place in its politics (Gwyn 1972; Paine 1981; Marland 2007b). Newfoundland politicians have also developed a reputation for soundbites and photo-ops, such as Brian Tobin's quip to international media, while standing in front of a fishing net and RCMP officers in New York City, about the need to protect "the last lonely, unloved, unattractive little turbot clinging by its fingernails to the Grand Banks" (Tobin 2002, 132). By necessity, Newfoundland leaders learn to master inexpensive communication techniques, and while they are aware of their public images, they do not appear to think of themselves as brands.

Second, provincial parties seek to play up or play down their relationship with the federal brand. Premier Joey Smallwood routinely promoted his connections to the governing federal Liberal government, especially to Minister Jack Pickersgill, and even ran the federal party's campaigns in Newfoundland. In Nova Scotia, PC premier John Buchanan called a snap election in 1984 to ride off the coattails of new Prime Minister Brian Mulroney, whose PC Party of Canada had just won a landslide. Conversely, if the national brand is seriously damaged, then provincial parties keep their distance. After the collapse of the PC Party in the 1993 federal election, it was sensible for the Manitoba PCs to bring attention to Gary Filmon's leadership and not the party label in the 1995 provincial campaign.

The brand linkage between national and provincial parties is further illustrated by the similarities between party names at both levels of government. One notable exception is the current continuance of provincial *Progressive* Conservative parties in the absence of a national counterpart. Nevertheless, as Anna Esselment has shown, there is considerable electoral collaboration between federal and provincial parties, though she does note that the "bitter feud" between Newfoundland premier Danny Williams and Prime Minister Stephen Harper was a "striking exception" (2010, 873–4).

A third theme in provincial literature is that a governing party readily uses public resources as part of a permanent campaign to reinforce its brand. Traditional pork-barrel politics is now complemented by

Figure 5.1
Government of NL brand signature. Colour scheme used: blue text, green pitcher plant stems, red/orange leaves

government funds being used for political marketing. In the 1970s, the Frank Moores government spent $56,000 on opinion polls to inform its communications decisions (Wells 2008, 240), and in the late 1990s, the British Columbia NDP government used polling and advertising to generate support for the Nisga'a Treaty and by extension for the party (Ponting 2006). Tourism advertising is a common way to build and sustain a positive mythos about the place and a provincial identity. In Alberta, governments and politicians have communicated a theme of freedom, in Saskatchewan it has been security, and in Manitoba moderation has been promoted (Wesley 2011). In 2006, the Manitoba Image Project was launched to develop a positive new image for the province in a manner that was similar to the governing NDP's brand values (Wesley 2010). That same year, a new "brand signature" was unveiled in Newfoundland which was designed to coincide with Premier Williams' efforts to project "a renewed sense of pride and optimism" (Newfoundland and Labrador 2006b; see also figure 5.1). By comparison, in 2007 the Manitoba PCs, the Newfoundland Liberals, and the Newfoundland NDP could not finance effective election campaigns (Adams 2010; Marland 2007b).

A fourth theme is that party leaders increasingly use image management techniques to project and maintain a desired public persona. Appealing to a local identity and cultivating a personal brand as a commoner is a universal tactic. PEI premiers have often evoked their connections to the family farm, including John Walter Jones, who wanted to be known as "Farmer Jones" (Milne 2001, 113), and Alex Campbell, who hired a Toronto advertising agency to film him mingling with Islanders throughout the province (MacKinnon 2005, 33). In Nova

Scotia, Premier Buchanan would "wrap himself in the tartan" (Bickerton 2000, 55), and in Quebec the leader of the Parti Québécois is positioned as the guardian of a national identity. Joey Smallwood so embodied the Newfoundland persona that his portrait could be found in kitchens and bedrooms throughout the province (Gwyn 1972, 154).

Conversely, in an attempt to communicate a message of economic growth, a party leader may be positioned as a business person. New Brunswick Liberal leader Frank McKenna's handlers made sure that he wore "only dark suits, white shirts, striped ties and black knee socks" (Lee 2001, 125), and in 2003 the Newfoundland PC Party promoted "The New Approach" of a government led by businessman Danny Williams (figure 5.2). Alberta politics suggests that leaders' personal brands may ebb and flow. In advertising during the 1971 election, Premier Peter Lougheed was carefully projected as a modern educated businessman (Savage-Hughes and Taras 1992; Tupper 2004). His successor, Don Getty, is thought to have failed to be seen as a common man because of "his strong aversion to political marketing" (Lisac 2004, 252). In contrast, Premier Ralph Klein's handlers conducted surveys, polling, and roundtables when constructing a personal brand of humble beginnings, which was sustained by advertising, brochures, and slogans coordinated through the government's Public Affairs Bureau (Barrie 2006, 66; Sampert 2005; Taft 1997). Likewise, in Newfoundland the apolitical, moral, and conservative image of Liberal Clyde Wells contrasted with the more entertaining style of his predecessors, Brian Peckford and Tom Rideout, and with his successor, Brian Tobin.

A fifth observation is that recent descriptions of provincial contests highlight the role of the Internet in personal and party branding. In 2008 provincial elections, the leader of Québec Solidaire answered questions on her party's website when she was not invited to participate in the televised leaders debate (Bélanger 2009), and the Alberta PCs purchased online advertising to promote their video spots (Chen and Smith 2010). However, as recently as the 2007 election, the Internet had a minuscule presence in Newfoundland politics, where electioneering tends to be "traditional, localized, and frugal" rather than innovative (Marland 2007b, 78). Yet within one electoral cycle the Internet, in particular Kathy Dunderdale's use of Twitter, played a significant role in shaping Newfoundland's political discourse (Marland 2012b).

One common tactic among governing parties when they assume power is to order a change in official colour schemes to match their own, most noticeably on government websites. A high-profile example occurred

Figure 5.2
PC party of NL election manifesto cover (2003). Colour scheme used: blue background and logo, white text, red outlines

when the federal Conservatives overruled Treasury Board guidelines and required that party colours be used on government websites as part of what the prime minister's chief of staff called "strategic brand building" (Cheadle 2011b). Likewise, a blue colour scheme was evident throughout the Government of Newfoundland's website while the provincial Tories were in power. Indeed, all the figures presented in this chapter predominantly used blue colours, including party election platforms, the party election website, the government's logo, and budget materials. However, unlike in the federal sphere, such visual partisan subtleties have not been controversial in Newfoundland.

Finally, election summaries remind us that negativity has a long-standing place in provincial politics. Accounts of provincial elections are filled with stories of religious divisions and hotly contested issues such as public schooling. In the 1870s, party leaders in Nova Scotia wrote letters to the editor condemning their opponents (Beck 1985, 179), a practice that a century later, in 1979, had evolved into the BC Social Credit party coordinating letters signed with fictitious names (Mitchell 1987, 35). In New Brunswick in the 1880s, Liberal leader Andrew George Blair sought to consolidate the support of Acadians and Catholics by smearing his opponent as a Protestant (Doyle 1983, 17), and in 1917, Liberal leader Peter Veniot engaged in fear mongering in Acadian communities that were opposed to conscription (Doyle 1983, 48). Negative messages have gravitated to television as advertising has become more affordable, for example, in the 1986 British Columbia campaign (Mitchell 1987, 152) and in Ontario in the 1990s (MacDermid 1997). More recently, in 2007 the Saskatchewan NDP ran pre-election advertising warning electors that the Saskatchewan Party had a hidden agenda (Tayner and Beaudry-Mellor 2009, 18).

In Newfoundland, negativity is confined mostly to rhetoric and barbs. The exacerbation of religious, class, and identity divisions inhibited the development of a democratic system of government. But since Newfoundland joined Canada, successful leaders have tended to unify the electorate and be rewarded with lopsided majority governments (Marland 2011). However, Newfoundland's politicking is not immune to dirty tricks, such as the alleged case in 1989 of the Liberal Party inventing a favourable poll whose results were reported by the *Telegram* just before election day (Hoy 1992, 148). The most important role of negativity in Newfoundland may be the fear that results from citizens' perceptions of the premier's authority. The literature about Newfoundland politics, particularly in the Smallwood era, is filled with accounts of citizens worrying about their livelihoods and reputations if they speak out and are targeted by the governing party (e.g., Crosbie 1997; Gwyn 1972; Wells 2008).

Before I proceed to a case study of the 2011 elections, a brief summary is warranted about Danny Williams' masterful command of his personal brand image. For much of his tenure Premier Williams' popularity occupied the political stratosphere (for instance see figure 10.1). The remarks of NDP leader Lorraine Michael in 2010 indicate that the opposition was concerned about the corresponding personalization and presidentialization of Newfoundland politics: "Why do people put so much hope in one person? We do have a personality cult here in Newfoundland & Labrador and a lot of it is based on his personality ... It seems to be part of the Newfoundland psyche" (Bailey 2010b).

Christopher Dunn (2007) attributes Williams' popularity to the government's resource policies that sought maximum financial return to the province. But four image management secrets are worth mentioning. First, after two years in office, opinion polls indicated that when Williams sought financial concessions from Newfoundlanders his popularity decreased and when he placed demands on outsiders his support levels soared (Marland 2010). Hence, the PC leader learned to engage in "an unsustainable level of conflict with large enemies" (Dunn 2007, 41). Second, the premier's office timed good news announcements and coordinated supportive calls to open line radio during Corporate Research Associates polling periods in an attempt to influence the survey results (Marland and Kerby 2010). Third, to maintain control of the public agenda, Williams imposed strict party discipline on caucus MHAS, chastised his critics, and ensured that the legislature did not sit often. He did not go out of his way to placate ministers who disagreed with his policy agenda or management style, as Matthew Kerby discusses in chapter 6 of this book, though Kerby does not examine how Williams used the media to reinforce his executive authority over the PC caucus. For example, when Deputy Premier Tom Rideout left cabinet, PC MHAS complied with orders to "chew him up publicly on open-line radio," and supported messaging that labelled other opponents as "traitors" (Wangersky 2011, 73). Fourth, Williams' combination of business acumen, street smarts, and natural charisma resonated deeply with most Newfoundlanders, and they identified with his resolve to improve the province's finances. His personal brand was one of success and winning. When the self-made millionaire who wore "tailored, crisp white shirts, perfect-pressed wide cuffs always" (Wangersky 2011, 11) and drove expensive cars proclaimed that under a Williams government there would be "no more [resource] giveaways" – a sharp contrast with Joey Smallwood's "develop or perish" mantra – people trusted him to make sensible policy decisions.

Danny Williams' personal magnetism meant that he could do no wrong. For instance, in the month when Corporate Research Associates (2012) recorded his highest rating as the leader that Newfoundlanders preferred as premier (85 percent of respondents in February 2008), public controversy had erupted over Williams breaking the law by driving while talking on a cellphone. When the PC Party's support climaxed (the preferred party of 82 percent of respondents in November 2007), Williams was busy denouncing Prime Minister Harper in the national media. In the period when the provincial government achieved its highest recorded satisfaction level (93 percent satisfied in February 2010), Williams opted against using Canada's public health care and paid for private heart surgery in the United States. More significant policy examples include his mass popularity weathering the House of Assembly spending scandal and Eastern Health's mishandling of breast cancer testing (see chapters 7 and 8). When looking at personal brands, it is important to note that to achieve maximum political benefit, even a charismatic leader must make diligent use of image management techniques.

CASE STUDY

Brands are difficult to measure, and various communication outputs must be reviewed to indicate the sponsor's desired image (e.g., Scammell 2007). By considering some aspects of government budget and party election media materials, I provide a comparative basis for interpreting the brand image of the PC Party of Newfoundland & Labrador up to the 2011 provincial election. This includes discussion of the personal brand of Premier Kathy Dunderdale, who on 11 October 2011 became the first woman in Newfoundland history to lead a party to election victory. Selected indicators are compared with the brands of the five other premiers[1] who led their parties into fall 2011 elections and all of whom were re-elected: Liberal premier of Prince Edward Island Robert Ghiz (3 October), Liberal premier of Ontario Dalton McGuinty (6 October), NDP premier of Manitoba Greg Selinger (4 October), Saskatchewan Party premier Brad Wall (7 November), and Yukon Party premier Darrell Pasloski (11 October). For added context, the 2011 re-election campaign of Conservative prime minister Stephen Harper (2 May) is integrated into the analysis.

Government Media Relations

Before the 2011 elections, the Prime Minister's Office (PMO) directed federal public servants to assist with the promotion of Stephen Harper's personal brand by referring to the "Harper government" in government news releases (Cheadle 2011a). Beginning with his first budget in 2004 and lasting until Williams left office in 2010, the Newfoundland Premier's Office demanded the same rhetorical device from the province's bureaucrats. So instead of "Government of Newfoundland & Labrador," the expression "the Williams government" routinely appeared in the titles of government news releases and in ministers' quotes (e.g.,

Table 5.1
Intersection of political brands in budget materials

	NL (PC)	PEI (LIB)	ON (LIB)	MB (NDP)	SK (SP)	YK (YP)	CAN (CON)
Did the main budget news release refer to the government by the premier's name?	No	No	Yes	Yes	No	No	No
How many times was the premier's name mentioned in the budget speech?	0	0	2	0	0	0	0
Did the budget document cover use the same colour scheme as the premier's party?	Yes	Somewhat	Yes	No	Yes	No	Yes

Source: Government budget websites for 2011–12 (for Canada fiscal year 2010–11).

Newfoundland and Labrador 2010j). An examination of the main news releases announcing the government budgets before each election in the jurisdictions that held elections in 2011 shows that the same strategy was used in two other provinces (table 5.1). In Manitoba, the "Selinger government" was mentioned in the 2011 budget news release subheading. In Ontario, the subtitle of its budget release contained "McGuinty government," and the opening sentence did so as well (Ontario 2011). Ontario was also the only jurisdiction where the finance minister referred to the government by the premier's name in the budget speech. All of the other administrations, including Dunderdale's, simply mentioned the government in a general manner in budget materials. Regardless of the aforementioned media report about the PMO's directive, Harper's name did not appear in federal budget communications materials before or after the 2011 election.

As mentioned, a consistent colour scheme is another indicator of party branding. In Newfoundland, the colour of license plates fluctuates between red and blue depending on which party is in power, and the Williams administration authorized blue tourism highway signage, the blue government brand signature, and blue windows on the Confederation Building. Were party colours used on government pre-election budget communication materials across Canada? In most cases, yes (table 5.1).[2] The budget cover in Newfoundland was blue (figure 5.3); in

Figure 5.3
NL government budget cover (2011). Colour scheme used: blue
background, blue and green text, white logo

Ontario it was red; and in Saskatchewan it was green, gold, and white.
In Prince Edward Island, a collage of photos was organized on a white
and red backdrop. However, party colours were not used in Manitoba;
instead, a green colour scheme, the same as the government's logo and
not the orange of the governing NDP, was chosen. In Yukon, the materials were simply black and white. At the federal level, the budget communications not only used the same blue and a red maple leaf as the
Conservative Party of Canada's logo, but it took branding a step further
by associating the budget with the Economic Action Plan of government
advertising, which was been used to promote party messages (Cheadle
2011c).

Party Election Materials

During an election campaign, the political parties issue a plethora of communications materials. With a branding philosophy, the text and visual messages should be similar across media platforms. We would expect the governing party to emphasize the premier in government and election communications, because of the importance of leaders in vote choice (Davies and Mian 2010). Indeed, focusing on the leader is common practice in provincial elections, as suggested by all three political parties' advertising in the 1995 Ontario election (MacDermid 1997). Conversely, if a leader is unpopular, we expect that the party brand would be prioritized.

Party manifestos are a natural locus for political branding. The design of a booklet of policy commitments is under the exclusive control of a party and its leader, making it an excellent indicator of their desired brand image (Lock and Harris 1996, 17). For this reason, some political marketing scholars maintain that a manifesto is the best measure of the party's election offering and its brand (Ormrod and Henneberg 2006, 34). In the provinces, this may simply be an extension of the federal party brand image because party staff may collaborate on election platforms, leading to similar styles of presentation at both levels (Esselment 2010, 879).

Given the preponderance of leadership and Danny Williams' astounding popularity, it is surprising to see that he was not mentioned whatsoever on the cover of the PC Party's election manifesto in 2007 (figure 5.4). Instead, the party logo, blue colours, and the campaign slogan were featured prominently. The message "proud, strong, determined" was evidently deemed a sufficient way to personify the leader and the theme of that campaign (see Marland 2007b).

By comparison, in 2011 we see more evidence of branding synergies in the PC Party's election communications materials. The 2011 Policy Blue Book (figure 5.5) promoted a series of interconnected messages. The party slogan "New Energy" referred to the popular perception of Newfoundland as an energy warehouse and was related to the Muskrat Falls deal in particular. As in 2007, this message was subtly reinforced by the party's blue colour scheme, which conveyed the future through water (as in offshore oil and hydroelectricity) and residents' connection to the ocean. What was particularly clever in 2011 was how these visuals tied in with the framing of the leader's personal brand.

Figure 5.4
PC party of NL election manifesto cover (2007). Colour scheme
used: blue background and logo, white text, red outlines

During the period when Premier Williams negotiated a number of
energy deals, Dunderdale had been his minister of natural resources. For
weeks before the start of the official election campaign, in what appears
to indicate that she was aware of the importance of her public image,
Premier Dunderdale talked about how she had taken up running in a bid
to lose weight. The mainstream media ran feature stories about her new
athleticism, the party uploaded video of Dunderdale jogging to its You-
Tube channel, and her Twitter account was used to inform journalists
and followers about her latest runs in communities across the province.
"Great 6K run through Marystown this morning" was a typical tweet
(Dunderdale 2011).[3] The result was a leader with an energetic personal
brand that was strategically synchronized with the party brand during
the campaign.

newenergynl.ca

PROGRESSIVE CONSERVATIVE

Figure 5.5
PC party of NL election manifesto cover (2011). Colour scheme used: blue and white background and logo, blue text

Did other premiers appear on the covers of their parties' election manifestos? In Prince Edward Island, Ontario, and Yukon, the governing parties' platforms used the party colours but, unlike in Newfoundland, made no mention of the premier. The Manitoba NDP's pledges were posted as text within the party website, thereby emphasizing substance over style and continuity with the federal NDP brand. Conversely, in Saskatchewan, the platform featured a giant photo of a smiling Brad Wall against a green backdrop. The cover also included the popular premier's name twice. Months earlier, the federal Conservative Party manifesto had likewise included a large photo of Prime Minister Harper. The campaign slogan "Here for Canada" was accompanied by a Canadian flag and a blue background. The document's title was "Stephen Harper's Low-Tax Plan for Jobs and Economic Growth," which was a

Table 5.2
Leadership in party election materials (2011)

Was the leader emphasized ...	NL	PEI	ON	MB	SK	YK	CAN
...on the party's election manifesto?	somewhat	No	No	No	Yes	No	Yes
...on the party website?	Yes	Yes	Yes	Yes	Yes	No	Yes
...in video advertising?	Yes	sometimes	sometimes	sometimes	Yes	No	Yes

Source: Materials obtained from governing parties' websites during respective election campaigns.

connection to his preferred personal brand image as a competent economic manager.

The efforts to manage a leader's brand image in printed matter such as election documents has gravitated to staging electronic visuals on the Web. Political websites have evolved from presenting mostly textual messages to promoting visual content (Verser and Wicks 2006). For instance, Stephen Harper's handlers upload and circulate strategically selected daily photos of the prime minister (Marland 2012). To present a consistent brand image, we expect heads of government to feature prominently on their party's website, especially if they appeared on the cover of the party manifesto.

In the 2011 election, Premier Dunderdale was highly visible on the PC Party's website. Her photograph was accompanied by the "New Energy" slogan and party colours (figure 5.6). The Prince Edward Island Liberal and Manitoba NDP sites featured their premiers in a manner similar to the way Dunderdale was featured. In Ontario, Premier McGuinty's photo was the central image, but this approach was inconsistent with the party's campaign logo, which included photos of nine electors. This may reflect how campaign strategists change their minds on whether or not to emphasize the leader. Going into the Ontario election, the Liberal logo was designed to illustrate the party's connection with everyday Ontarians as a strategic branding response to a premier who had become unpopular. During the campaign, as opinion polls indicated that Premier McGuinty's personal brand was becoming an asset compared with that of PC opposition leader Tim Hudak (Nanos Research 2011), strategists appear to have shifted their visual focus to frame the election as a contest between a safe incumbent and a risky novice.

The brand of Saskatchewan's premier was most closely intertwined with his party's. Website visitors were greeted by a photo of the leader,

Figure 5.6
PC party of NL website (2011). Colour scheme used: blue background, blue and white text

and a modified party logo proclaimed "Brad Wall and the Saskatchewan Party." During the federal election campaign, the Conservative Party of Canada's website emphasized visuals of Harper, and its increased use of red was designed to reinforce the packaging of the leader as a Canadian patriot. In contrast, the Yukon Party website contained mostly written content and did not have a tab for information about Premier Pasloski.

As for election advertising, it is a "powerful conditioning" form of media that has an effect on public opinion (Palda 1973, 653). Research is beginning to emerge about the different effects of viewing political advertising on television and online, with initial indications that how viewers perceive candidates differs depending on the medium (Kaid and Postelnicu 2005). Nevertheless, it remains unclear why some advertising is more influential than others, and it is difficult to study because there are so many components to assess (Robinson 2010, 452).

In Newfoundland in 2007, PC Party television advertising revolved around Danny Williams, who was depicted mingling with an adoring public. In 2011, a similar strategy was used with Kathy Dunderdale, though this time the PCs projected a warmer and more inviting tone that contrasted with Williams' "fighting Newfoundlander" image. There were just a handful of ads,[4] three of which were close-ups of Dunderdale talking to an off-camera interviewer interspersed with images of her in the legislature, meeting with citizens around the province, and participating in media pseudo-events. The first ad, "New Energy," began with a blue screen and white text stating, "Kathy Dunderdale: New Energy All Around Us." She talked about the "energizing" potential of the province and said that Newfoundlanders were excited about the future. In "Drive and Determination," Dunderdale talked about how strongly she felt about the province and her responsibility to advocate on behalf of Newfoundlanders. In the third ad of the series, "Experience and Leadership," the premier began by naming the energy deals that she had been a part of during the Williams era, told the interviewer that she was hardworking, and that she was mindful that it was a privilege to be in her position. A fourth spot, "Feel the Energy," was slightly different. It showed visuals of Dunderdale mingling with ordinary people as an original campaign song played in the background. Images of the leader meeting with smiling citizens were interspersed with photos of the Hibernia oil platform and Muskrat Falls as a popular local musician sang a chorus of, "I feel new energy around us today." The ads were thus aspirational and nondescript. There was no significant mention of policy, only the implication that the economy was strong owing to the energy deals managed by the PC government. The objective was to engage the public with their new premier.

Did premiers receive the same treatment in other provinces? Not always. In Prince Edward Island, a series of commercials featured Premier Ghiz, but the emphasis was on informing viewers about select details of the Liberal Party platform, namely details concerning the economy, education, health care, and seniors. The voice-overs in these policy ads had the production value of an airplane safety message, which is to say that they were serious and informative, did not grossly use party colours, and were dull. More whimsical ads showed images of the province and some of the premier. In those ads, Ghiz reminded viewers that Prince Edward Island's resilient economy had weathered the recession.

In Ontario, the Liberal Party's video standards were of an international quality. The party maintained a YouTube channel called Ontario Liberal TV, with over fifty videos. The rotation between sometimes emphasizing the premier and sometimes prioritizing the Liberal logo that was seen on the homepage of the party's website persisted in its TV spots. In some,

Premier McGuinty talked directly to the camera in front of a white backdrop about the economy, education, and health care. In others, black and white video profiled smiling Ontarians. A narrator informed viewers, as the screen transitioned to red and white text of factoids with an uplifting jingle, that they had personally benefited from a variety of Liberal government social and economic policies; there was no mention of McGuinty whatsoever. Spots intended only for an online audience included fake news reports featuring either a man or a woman wearing red while playing the role of a journalist reporting on the latest positive events of the Liberal campaign. Unlike in Newfoundland and Prince Edward Island, the party also had negative ads. "Stand Up" began with a photo of Stephen Harper, saying that he was going to restart health care funding negotiations, and asked viewers if they would rather be represented by Tim Hudak or Dalton McGuinty, whose records on health care were contrasted. White text on a black backdrop stated, "Ask yourself: Who will stand up to Stephen Harper on Health Care?" before turning to a white background with the aforementioned logo comprised of nine Ontarians.

Manitoba NDP videos called attention to leadership in three ways. An uplifting spot titled "Pride" played like a political tourism ad. Factoids about the successful economy, better health care and education, and hydro-electric deals were flashed over images of people working, socializing, and celebrating. The narrator urged viewers not to risk the alternative of PC leader Hugh McFadyen's "plans to cancel projects, privatize and cut." The video quickly concluded with a smiling Premier Selinger wearing business attire but did not mention his name. Other ads similar to the Newfoundland PCs' showed Selinger talking to an off-camera interviewer, but in this case about specific policy issues. A series of negative ads sought to scare Manitobans away from McFadyen, who was painted as a conservative who would cut health care spending, cancel a sewage treatment upgrade, and privatize Manitoba Hydro. "Why would we risk McFadyen?" the narrator asked while a closing screen directed audiences to McFadyenFacts.ca. In another ad, citizens discussed McFadyen's "nice suit" but a track record of supporting cuts; and in another, viewers were informed that with hydro privatization, "rates will go up. We'll never get it back." In the final frame, Selinger assured viewers that "working together we'll [the NDP] make health care better for everyone."

In Saskatchewan, Premier Wall was portrayed as the province's chief executive officer. He cooed about how the smart policy decisions under his government had led to economic achievements, including low unemployment, a large income tax cut, major debt reduction, and investments in infrastructure. A spot titled "On the Right Path" was of Wall, wearing jeans and a casual shirt, talking to viewers while standing on the edge of a prairie field. He remarked that he had delivered on his previous election commitments to strengthen Saskatchewan, including a pledge to "bring families back home," and that he wanted to keep building the province as an economic leader. The high quality of these spots contrasted sharply with the Yukon Party's homemade text-only policy ads.

The Saskatchewan Party also created negative ads using an ominous black and white colour scheme with a sinister voice-over. Just as the NDP in Manitoba had tried to link the leader of the opposition with policy blights taking place when the PCs had been in government, audiences in Saskatchewan were warned about NDP leader Dwain Lingenfelter, who was associated with the previous NDP government, presiding over a "have not" province with a shrinking population. Instead of policy, some of these spots sought to damage Lingenfelter's personal brand by drawing attention to insults he had allegedly made, including referring to Wall as a "loser." The style of the ads had production values on par with the plethora of negative ads created by the federal Conservative Party that seriously damaged the personal brand of federal Liberal leader Michael Ignatieff by focusing on his person rather than his policy.[5]

These cases of negative advertising all appear to have irreparably harmed the opposition leaders' personal brand. After presiding over disappointing election results, McFadyen, Lingenfelter, and Ignatieff all announced their resignations as leaders, and the latter two even lost their own seats. The negativity directed at people seeking to dethrone a premier stands in contrast to the incumbent parties' messages that they were leading the government in the right direction. This is epitomized by the similarity of slogans in campaign advertisements regardless of jurisdiction or party. In Prince Edward Island, the Liberal Party was "Moving Forward Together" and their counterparts in Ontario were going "Forward. Together." Next door, the NDP was "Building a Better Future"; one province over, the Saskatchewan Party was "Moving Saskatchewan Forward"; and to the northwest, the Yukon Party was also "Moving Forward Together." In 2007, the Newfoundland PCs had similarly expressed the idea that "The Future Is Ours"; in the campaign before that, they had released a policy manifesto for "the Future" (figures 5.2 and 5.4). This theme of progress transcends time and place, given that "Step Forward with Peckford" and "Solid New Leadership for the Future" were PC slogans in the 1979 Newfoundland election campaign (Paine 1981, 90), while "Forward" was Barack Obama's slogan in the 2012 US presidential campaign. This puts the 2011 Newfoundland "New Energy" mantra in perspective as a smart twist on a common refrain of governing parties seeking re-election because they claim to have improved their constituents' quality of life. All of this was a sharp contrast with the federal Conservative Party's "Here for Canada" slogan, which was designed to divide the personal brands of Harper and Ignatieff, whom the party's advertising had framed as a Canadian nationalist and an American opportunist, respectively.

POLITICAL DECISION MAKING IN NEWFOUNDLAND & LABRADOR

The integration of business marketing into politics means that parties and leaders are being viewed as products, governments as service providers, and voters as consumers and clients. Political marketers are treating political products and services as brands that are anchored by key components, such as colour, names, and values that can be designed to work in unison with each other. This communications unity guards against the public image of a party brand and a leader's personal brand being in a state of flux or defined by others. To cultivate a desired image, parties need to ensure that all their daily communications are consistent with their brand anchors while simultaneously damaging their opponents' brands. This adds to our understanding of why party discipline is important to maintaining the supremacy of the leader. It explains why a governing party directs public servants to enforce communications synergies with the government, why political opponents are vilified, and why power is perceived to be concentrated in the leader's office.

The governing parties' re-election campaigns in 2011 indicate that the increasing convergence of party, leader, and government communications has democratic repercussions. As the public sphere pays more attention to visual communications and personalities, there is less interest in policy minutiae. The parliamentary system is designed for the citizens' elected representatives to hold the governing party to account in the legislature. This function is eroding as the media reports on the public's impressions of leaders as measured in opinion polls and as power is centralized in the leader of the governing party. The information in this chapter provides a snapshot in time of a number of indicators that can provide the basis for further research. Nevertheless, we can conclude that there is evidence of branding at the provincial level of politics. This has significant implications for the design, communication, and implementation of government policy, especially if society's emphasis on leaders' personal brands increases.

Looking at the case of Newfoundland & Labrador, we can see that the communications expertise of the PC Party was not proprietary to Danny Williams. The party's strategic use of advertising and media relations to position new leader Kathy Dunderdale's personal brand as "new energy" was smart and connected her visually to the party's preferred policy theme. Unlike in past campaigns, the Internet now plays a significant role in Newfoundland politics, and its affordability will present a communications opportunity for underfunded opposition parties in the future. Leadership will continue to be emphasized in political communication and policy debate. It remains to be seen whether Newfoundland political strategists can continue to avoid the damage that negative advertising does to a leader's personal brand.

NOTES

The author wishes to acknowledge the assistance of Victoria Hynes with the background research for this chapter and funding from the Social Science and Humanities Research Council of Canada through a Standard Research Grant for the Comparative Provincial Election Project (Jared Wesley, lead investigator).

1 The Northwest Territories (NWT) went to the polls on 3 October, but Premier Floyd Roland opted not to seek re-election. There are no political parties in the NWT, and the premier is elected by members of the Legislative Assembly. Owing to the absence of party brands, the NWT is not included in the analysis.

2 Note that political parties may have adopted the colours of a jurisdiction's flag, rather than imposing them on government communications.

3 Premier Dunderdale deleted her Twitter account in April 2013 after it fell into disuse and the media reported that she was following a pornographic account. In October 2013 she activated @PremierOfNL and stated that it would be used for information updates.

4 These spots aired on television and were housed on the party's website. The spots analyzed for other provinces were obtained from the parties' websites but did not necessarily air on television.

5 The Harper Conservatives' use of pre-campaign and campaign advertising is too voluminous to describe here, but see Pammett and Dornan (2011).

6

Hatching, Matching, and Dispatching: Cabinet Management and Ministerial Duration under Danny Williams

MATTHEW KERBY

COMPARATIVE THEORY

"Provincial government is premier's government ... the extent of his authority is significantly greater than that of his federal counterpart" (Morley and Young 1983). This is quite a statement. Indeed, while the debate over the extent to which Canadian prime ministers are *supra* rather than *primus inter pares* has consumed some Canadian political scientists, few, if any, argue that Canadian prime ministers are not among the most powerful political actors listed on the Western parliamentary playbill (Bakvis 2001; Savoie 1999, 2005; White 2005). Although limited in scope and scale by sections 91 and 92 of the Constitution Act, 1867, Morley and Young's assertion sets out the heads of Canada's subnational political executives as some of the most powerful big fish in small ponds in the world – although the size, capacity, and importance of the pond is capable of changing, subject to the transformative nature of international and domestic political economies.

By its nature, the Canadian variant of Westminster parliamentary democracy at the subnational level lends itself to a de facto analysis of power relationships through the lens of elite theory. However, and with respect to the study of cabinet relationships, this lens reflects not the iron law of oligarchy à la Michels (1915) or the unbalanced influence of unelected technocrats (Putnam 1977) but, rather, an institutional dynamic akin to a principal-agent relationship whereby cabinet ministers are the agents of the premier while (and paradoxically) the premier and the cabinet as a whole are the agents of the legislature, whose members in turn are the agents of the citizenry.

Müller (2000) and Strøm (2000) describe this as the chain of delegation. With respect to elite theory, the test then is to determine the extent to which the principals are able to respond to moral hazard or adverse selection problems that arise through the democratic and institutional delegation of authority and responsibility. In the cabinet setting, the appointment and dismissal of ministers reflects the premier's ability to manage and control the threats and consequences of moral hazard and adverse selection. While this may involve the promotion and retention of so-called elites to the top of the political hierarchy, at the same time the premier cannot come off as too heavy-handed or unresponsive without losing the confidence or support of his own principals – the members of the legislature whose confidence is needed for the premier to remain in government, as well as the electorate whose votes and public support are also required.

Provincial premiers' power stems from a number of sources, some of which are shared with the Canadian prime minister: premiers are the central figures of the government and their political parties; they control the cabinet agenda; political institutions such as legislative committees are traditionally weak at the provincial level of government, and often they are unable to challenge the authority of the premier; party rules typically do not contain mechanisms to dethrone a sitting premier; provinces are unicameral; and finally and importantly for the purpose of this chapter, provincial premiers have the exclusive authority to appoint and dismiss the very people who are most likely to challenge their power and authority – the ministers in their cabinets.

The study of government survival has become an impressive part of the comparative politics canon in recent years. However, most of the research that examines the institutional and political-environmental determinants of government duration and durability typically centres on national-level governments; research that focuses on the subnational or regional level of analysis lacks visibility, if it even exists at all. This neglect of the subnational level of analysis in the government survival literature is reproduced in its offspring, the literature on comparative political elites, which is a well-established area of scholarly inquiry in the field of comparative politics (Best and Cotta 2000; Norris 1997). However, only lately have political scientists started to systematically examine the patterns that characterize the career paths of political leaders (Dowding and Dumont 2009). Moreover, as Fischer and Stolz (2010) note, even this recent scholarship has failed to address the important role that regional, territorial, or provincial levels of governments play in shaping elite circulation and mobility. This major lacuna needs to be filled given that both subnational and supranational levels of governments have become increasingly important arenas and targets of elite career choice because of their professionalization (e.g., Canada, Germany, and the United States); the devolution of sovereignty (e.g., the United Kingdom, Spain); Europeanization; and the federalization of party systems (e.g., India). Furthermore, and as Stoltz (2001) and Moncrief (1994) argue, as the professionalization of regional political careers has deepened, typically we have seen a parallel increase in the use of political resources and an increased attachment to regional political identity. Finally, and as Poguntke and Webb (2005) observe, the recent change in political and economic conditions (e.g., devolution or the discovery and exploitation of valuable natural resources) and opportunities that exist at the regional or subnational level of government may have altered or reversed what has traditionally been seen as an asymmetrical power relationship between the subnational and national levels of government in certain cases.

Both professionalization and the access to an effective use of political and economic resources and conditions are related to government and ministerial stability insofar as they enhance or detract from political actors' ability to perform their professional functions and remain in office. By extension, ministerial stability is equally important for political functions, such as policy coordination and the design and implementation of public policy (Alderman 1995; Huber and Lupia 2001; Huber and Martinez-Gallardo 2008; Indridason and Kam 2008). Further, the stability of a ministerial elite at the subnational level may directly or indirectly affect the federal-subnational balance of power with respect to the competition and coordination over the provision and distribution of political and public goods, particularly in systems that are characterized by long-serving party governments or dynasties.

Naturally, this topic is of particular interest to Canadian political scientists given the country's status both as an archetypal federal state and as a state that has seen changes in the levels of power and capacity among a number of its subnational units. While the systematic analysis of Canadian political elite career paths at the federal level has begun in earnest (Kerby 2009b, 2011; Kerby and Blidook 2011), the study of provincial-level career paths, with few exceptions, remains largely descriptive and not necessarily focused on cabinet-level elites (Docherty

2011; Kerby forthcoming; Moncrief 1994, 1998; Studlar and Moncrief 1996, 1997, 1999; White 1994). Only recently have political scientists commenced the intensive data-gathering process needed to conduct the kind of research that exists at the national level. Indeed, the absence of reliable or available data on subnational elites is the primary reason why such studies are in their infancy.

Research on the German, Spanish, and Belgian subnational cases has started to surface as a consequence of a concerted effort among teams of scholars in these countries to collect and code data on ministerial careers. However, and as is often the case in Canada and in all areas of political science, the study of subnational elites is typically character-ized as overshadowed and overwhelmed by the corresponding study of political elites at the federal level. This federal-level chauvinism stems in part from the difficulty that comes with prescribing generalizations about what is otherwise a disparate and *sui generis* collective of polit-ical entities distributed across a particularly large and diverse landscape with respect to both culture and geography – "small worlds," as Elkins and Simeon (1980) like to call them. It also stems, in part, from benign neglect. Consequently, and with few exceptions, Canadian political sci-entists and comparativists who study political elites in Westminster par-liamentary systems know very little about Canadian provincial elites.[1] As it stands, there is no systematic comparison of provincial cabinet ministers between provinces or between ministers at the provincial and federal levels of government in Canada.

BACKGROUND

The contemporary study of ministerial elites emerged out of the govern-ment survival debates in the 1990s.[2] Central to these debates was a dis-agreement over the causal determinants of government duration. On one side, advocates of the endogenous-elements approach argued that insti-tutional characteristics that exist "within" governments enhanced gov-ernment durability. On the other side, scholars argued that what really mattered were the exogenous shocks that threatened to terminate a gov-ernment at any particular time. Both sides were effectively reconciled by the publication of the seminal article by King et al. (1990), "A Uni-fied Model of Cabinet Dissolution in Parliamentary Democracies." The authors were able to combine the approaches by using an event his-tory analysis that considered the static institutional government char-acteristics as well as the impact of random shocks on the instantaneous

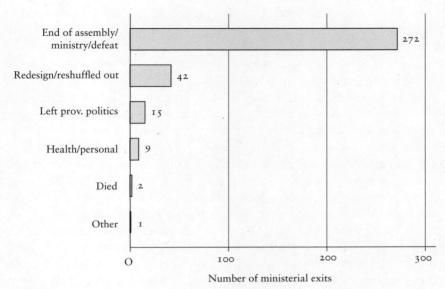

Figure 6.1
Ministerial exits by exit type

probability of government turnover on any given day. Drawing inspiration from King et al., a number of scholars (Berlinski, Dewan, and Dowding 2007; Dewan and Dowding 2005; Dowding and Kang 1998; Huber and Martinez-Gallardo 2008; Indridason and Kam 2008; Kerby 2011) subsequently opened up the government box and applied the same technique to the study of individual ministerial duration by examining the effects of different biographical, institutional, and political-environmental characteristics on individual ministerial duration and durability. Today, this approach is regarded as one of the more common methods for studying elite career paths.

Key to the study of ministerial survival is the focus on individual ministers and their environment rather than the decision criteria employed by the government leaders who decide to sack or retain them. So, rather than asking "why did the leader send the minister to the backbenches?" the question is rephrased as "what personal, institutional, and political-environmental conditions allow an individual minister to continue serving in cabinet until a particular point in time?" The models that explore this question emphasize a variety of factors such as the minister's age and personal history as well as the changing institutional environment in which he serves (see figure 6.1).

If the comparative literature on provincial political elites can be described as spartan, then the equivalent study of elites in Newfoundland & Labrador is best described as virtually nonexistent.[3] True, there is a rich tradition and a library of biographies of Newfoundland party leaders and premiers, but a systematic, comprehensive, and replicable study of Newfoundland political elites has yet to be published. The province is an ideal case to begin such an analysis; its late entry into Canadian Confederation in 1949 naturally restricts the analysis to the contemporary period of Canadian postwar subnational political history and excludes some of the pre-war institutional peculiarities that are found in other provinces as well as at the federal level. Furthermore, Newfoundland has an anecdotal reputation for electing governing parties that are led by charismatic, powerful, and at times domineering leaders. Christopher Dunn, in one of the few academic treatments of the provincial cabinet in Newfoundland, certainly highlights the authoritarian streak in Smallwood's cabinet; he describes it as an "unaided premier in an unaided cabinet" (Dunn 2005a, 48). However, as the cabinet has become more institutionalized over the course of successive ministries, cabinet ministers have been granted greater autonomy (with the support of the permanent and professional bureaucracy) and accountability over their portfolios. With this change comes the higher risk of turnover on the grounds of individual and/or collective ministerial responsibility.

CASE STUDY

In this chapter, I seek to assess the personal as well as the political-institutional factors that make provincial cabinet ministers "durable" with respect to their cabinet tenureship (see Laver 2003). Put another way, I am interested in ascertaining which conditions make it easier or more difficult for provincial premiers to sack their ministers, despite the considerable amount of power and leverage at their disposal. By extension, I am also interested in determining the degree to which the Danny Williams cabinet resembled or differed from previous Newfoundland cabinets with respect to ministerial tenureship.

In order to explore these conditions further, an original dataset consisting of the complete careers of the population of provincial cabinet ministers in Newfoundland & Labrador was assembled. A closer look at Newfoundland ministerial duration and durability generally allows us to take stock of the patterns associated with executive careers in the province; it also sets the foundation for a larger comparative analysis of the remaining provinces and other subnational polities at a later date. The chapter also provides a more detailed examination of Premier Williams, who was an exceptionally charismatic and popular leader. However, his cabinet management style has been described as lacking subtlety and at times as authoritarian (Wangersky 2009). One small way to assess the validity of these criticisms is to examine not the actions of the man himself – indeed, this would be difficult given the secretive nature cabinet proceedings and the tight-lipped former and currently serving ministers – but rather the reflection of his actions through the duration and durability of the ministers who served under him.

Before I turn to the comparison of ministerial duration and durability across ministries, I will highlight some of the major events in cabinet personnel management during the Williams ministry, which began on 6 November 2003, when Danny Williams and his cabinet were sworn into office following the Progressive Conservative (PC) Party's general election victory on 21 October 2003. Seven years later, the ministry ended when Williams announced on 25 November 2010 that he was stepping down effective 3 December. In accordance with Canadian constitutional convention, all the ministers' cabinet memberships terminated with the end of the Williams premiership. Over the course of the ministry, twenty-nine individuals held and managed thirteen different portfolios, as well as various specific responsibilities. Williams' first cabinet in 2003 consisted of fourteen individuals (including the premier) who managed a total of twenty-four portfolios. In addition to the Office of the Premier, Williams initially appointed himself minister of intergovernmental affairs and minister responsible for business. At the time of investiture, four of the ministers were women, and eight represented constituencies on the Avalon Peninsula.[4] Only one minister, former premier Tom Rideout, had served as a minister in a previous provincial government. By the time Williams resigned as premier, the cabinet consisted of seventeen individual ministers who managed eight portfolios and nine named responsibilities. The number of female ministers remained the same: four. Of the seventeen ministers who were serving on the day the premier resigned, three had served as ministers throughout the entire ministry: Joan Burke, Kathy Dunderdale (who subsequently succeeded Williams as party leader and premier), and Tom Marshall.

Over the course of the ministry, Williams reshuffled his cabinet on ten occasions: 23 February 2004, 8 November 2005, 14 March 2006, 5 June 2006, 29 December 2006, 30 October 2007, 21 May 2008, 31 October 2008, 9 July 2009, and 7 October 2009.[5] In addition to these formal reshuffles, there were nineteen independent ministerial movements. A number of cursory observations can be made. First, there were three, possibly four, major cabinet reshuffles over the course of the Williams ministry. The first took place on 8 November 2005 and did not involve removing anyone from cabinet or drawing anyone up from the backbenches. The second major reshuffle followed the emergence of allegations of the improper use of constituency-allowance funding by Minister of Natural Resources Ed Byrne. He was quickly dismissed from cabinet pending an investigation by the auditor general; some minor internal reshuffling took place to fill the vacancy left by him, and Williams also took the opportunity to promote two backbenchers from rural Newfoundland (one from Labrador) to cabinet.

The 30 October 2007 reshuffle followed the 9 October provincial election and exemplifies a classic post-election shuffle: five new ministers (Dave Denine, Charlene Johnson, Jerome Kennedy, Paul Oram, and Patty Pottle) were added to cabinet, while two ministers were dropped (Jack Byrne and Tom Osborne). Williams conducted another major reshuffle one year later on 31 October 2008, which saw a number of ministers move portfolios as well as the addition of Susan Sullivan from central Newfoundland to the cabinet table. Notable in this cabinet reshuffle was the retention of two ministers, Joan Burke (Education) and Ross Wiseman (Health), who both faced considerable public criticism over their respective handling of the search for a new president at Memorial University of Newfoundland and the ongoing breast cancer testing scandal. A final reshuffle took place following the resignations of Paul Oram (Health) and Trevor Taylor (Transportation), both of whom resigned for personal reasons.

Ministerial movements and portfolio reshuffling are common occurrences in parliamentary democracies. Government leaders need to reshuffle in order to satisfy ministerial ambitions inside and outside cabinet, to prepare and put a good face forward for upcoming elections, to deal with natural attrition, and to remove poor performers at a convenient time (Alderman and Cross 1987; Indridason and Kam 2008; Kam and Indridason 2005). For the most part, cabinet reshuffles are routine and fairly predictable in their timing. In this respect, Williams has remained true to the mould. More interesting are the unexpected ministerial exits, which take place as a result of an exogenous shock, a scandal, or an unexpected crisis. All things being equal, government leaders prefer that ministers, even difficult ones, stay put until a routine cabinet reshuffle. A consequence of the considerable power that Canadian

Table 6.1
Ministerial exits from the Danny Williams cabinet

Minister	Portfolio	Date exited cabinet	Reason
Elizabeth Marshall	Health and Community Services	27 Sep 04	Resigned following dispute over Williams' management style
Ed Byrne	Natural Resources	21 Jun 06	Following allegations of fraud
Loyola Sullivan	Finance	29 Dec 06	Retired from provincial politics
Paul Shelley	Human Resources & Labour & Housing	19 Jan 07	Family reasons (did not run in 2007 election)
Jack Byrne	Provincial Affairs	09 Oct 07	Dropped from cabinet, appointed deputy speaker, died in office 4 June 2008.
Tom Osborne	Justice	30 Oct 07	Dropped from cabinet (following accelerating cancer testing scandal)
John Ottenheimer	Municipal Affairs	30 Oct 07	Retired from provincial politics
Tom Rideout	Fisheries and Aquaculture	21 May 08	Resigned following dispute over road funding in constituency
Trevor Taylor	Minister of Transportation and Works	24 Sep 09	Family reasons
Paul Oram	Health and Community Service	07 Oct 09	Health reasons
Dianne Whalen	Registrar Gen., minimal responsibility for Emergency Preparedness	03 Oct 10	Died in office

prime ministers and premiers wield, combined with the focal point of their office, is that when problems arise that result in a ministerial dismissal or exit, attention naturally turns to the premier or prime minister, who has the exclusive authority to appoint or dismiss a minister. Or in many cases, they possess the necessary resources to retain a minister should they desire to leave on their own accord. Nevertheless, and as Sutherland notes, "the public manifestation of trouble in cabinet is exit" (1991, 101).

Table 6.1 notes that while Williams was premier, eleven cabinet resignations occurred outside the context of a routine cabinet reshuffle. One exit was tragic but not contentious: Dianne Whalen died in office. Two ministers resigned from cabinet citing family reasons. Minister of Human Resources, Labour and Employment Paul Shelley resigned in January 2007. Minister of Transportation and Works Trevor Taylor resigned his portfolio on 24 September 2009 also citing family reasons. He subsequently resigned his seat in the House of Assembly one week later. At the time of his resignation, there was speculation that Taylor was in a conflict with cabinet over the decision to relocate an x-ray machine from a small town in his rural constituency to a larger, more populated centre. Paul Oram resigned from cabinet and the House of Assembly citing health (high blood pressure) as the reason for his departure. However, in the period immediately before his exit, Oram faced public criticism for his handling of the ongoing crisis in the Department of Health over breast cancer testing and the cancellation of x-ray services in Trevor Taylor's constituency, as well as accusations of conflict of interest over his ownership of two personal-care homes while simultaneously serving as the health minister. It is worth noting that the high blood pressure was allegedly caused by the significant burdens associated with serving as the minister of health.

Two ministers retired from provincial politics. John Ottenheimer retired and was appointed the chairman of Newfoundland & Labrador Hydro. He subsequently ran, and lost, as a federal Conservative Party candidate in the 2011 federal election. Loyola Sullivan retired from provincial politics at the end of 2006 and was immediately appointed by the federal government to serve as an ambassador for fisheries conservation. Like Ottenheimer, he ran as a federal Conservative for a seat in the House of Commons in the 2011 election and lost, as did Taylor.

In addition to the "personal" and "retirement" justifications for ministerial resignation, two ministers were dropped from cabinet and took on House of Assembly roles. Jack Byrne was reshuffled out of cabinet following the 2007 election and became deputy speaker of the House; he died eight months later following a sudden illness. Tom Osborne left cabinet following his tenure as minister of health and minister of justice to become the deputy chair of committees in the House of Assembly.

Two ministers resigned amidst open conflicts with the premier. Health Minister Elizabeth Marshall resigned in 2004 claiming that Williams had gone over her head and made decisions in the Department of Health without consulting her first. In May 2008, Deputy Premier, Government House Leader, and Minister of Fisheries Tom Rideout resigned from cabinet following a conflict with the Premier's Office over funding for roads in his constituency. He subsequently resigned his seat in the House of Assembly one month later. Marshall resigned her seat in 2010 when Prime Minister Stephen Harper appointed her to the Senate.

Finally, one minister, Ed Byrne, was dismissed following allegations of improper constituency allowance spending. Williams also initiated the Green Commission to investigate (see chapter 7 of this book, by Kate Puddister and James Kelly). Byrne was subsequently convicted of defrauding the Crown and influence peddling.

It is often difficult to make sense of official reasons for ministerial resignations. Politologues sometimes point to exits to "spend more time with family" or for "health" reasons as code for dissent, dissatisfaction, or a dismal performance in cabinet. On the other hand, the demands of public service can be and often are trying on ministers' attempts to maintain a family or private life. The big explosions, such as the Beth Marshall or Tom Rideout resignations, are self-evident with respect to cause. But others, such as Tom Osborne's unexplained demotion or Trevor Taylor's or Paul Oram's exit from both cabinet and the House of Assembly, are not as obvious. For this reason, it is necessary to move beyond the official but sometimes inaccurate accounts of ministerial exits and look to the conditions that enhance or detract from ministerial durability and survival in cabinet, rather than hunt for some kind of elusive smoking gun.

Data and Methods

The analysis of ministerial duration and durability that follows is informed by an original dataset that consists of the population of ministers who have served in the Newfoundland & Labrador provincial cabinet for the period from 8 April 1949, the investiture date of Joseph Smallwood's first cabinet following Newfoundland's entrance to Canadian confederation, until 3 December 2010, the day that Danny Williams resigned as premier.[6] In total, the dataset consists of 341 ministerial spans. Figure 6.1 shows that of the 341 spans, 272 ended when the premier resigned, thus terminating the ministry, at the end of a general assembly, or when a minister was defeated in a general election thus ending both the minister's legislative and ministerial careers simultaneously. Fifteen ministers resigned from their portfolios to retire or to pursue other opportunities outside elected provincial politics. Relatedly, nine ministers who "voluntarily" exited from the cabinet cited health and/ or personal reasons for their departure. Only two ministers died while

Table 6.2
Ministerial movements by ministry (years in parentheses)

	Combined		Involuntary		Voluntary	
	Number	per year	Number	per year	Number	per year
Smallwood (22.8)	24	1.08	17	0.77	7	0.32
Moores (7.19)	10	1.44	8	1.15	2	0.29
Peckford (10)	9	0.93	8	0.82	2	0.21
Wells (6.73)	9	1.34	3	0.45	5	0.74
Tobin (4.73)	3	0.65	1	0.22	2	0.44
Grimes (2.73)	4	1.52	2	0.76	2	0.76
Williams (7.08)	7	0.99	3	0.42	4	0.57
Total/Mean	66	1.14	42	0.66	24	0.47

serving as a minister, although several more gave up their cabinet seats and died shortly after; one minister resigned his seat to contest the party leadership. This leaves forty-two ministers who were forcibly moved out of their cabinet positions and who returned to the backbenches.

When broken down by ministry, table 6.2 shows that Joey Smallwood's ministry contains the highest frequency of ministerial exits (unsurprising given its duration), although when re-examined as exits per year, he holds the median position on the table. Frank Moores' administration holds the record for the highest overall minister turnover per year; Brian Tobin presided over the ministry with the lowest turnover. Here we find Williams situated closer to the bottom of the table with nearly one ministerial exit per year. When the ministerial exits are broken down into voluntary and involuntary exits, we find that Moores' position at the top of the "combined" table is largely bolstered by the above average number of involuntary ministerial exits (1.15 per year). Wells (0.45 per year), Williams (0.42 per year), and Tobin (0.22 per year) hold down the bottom of the table as the premiers who do not "sack" their ministers. Indeed, over the course of contemporary Newfoundland political history, it appears that there is a decreasing trend in the frequency of involuntary ministerial exits. Conversely, and with respect to involuntary exits, the opposite appears to be the case, although the trend is not perfectly linear. Here we find Williams straddling the median position, slightly above the mean frequency per year.

Looking instead at actual ministerial durations rather than the cabinet exits advances another story. The box plot in figure 6.2 reveals quite a

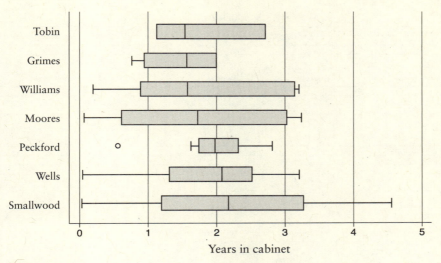

Figure 6.2
Ministerial duration. Sorted by median duration, uncensored exits only

bit of variation between premier-assemblies and within them. Looking only at those cases of ministers who prematurely exited the cabinet, the median duration by premier-assembly for a minister remaining in cabinet is between 1.54 years (Tobin) and 2.17 years (Smallwood). The skew varies between premier-assemblies; there is no distinctly obvious trend, although once again the Williams ministry sets itself as being remarkably "average" with respect to ministerial duration.

A somewhat clearer picture emerges when ministerial duration is represented in the form of Kaplan-Meier survival curves, which show the rate of ministerial survival for each premier-assembly and for each of the three general exit categories: combined, voluntary, and involuntary.[7] Figure 6.3a demonstrates that the overall rate of turnover varies quite a bit between premiers and even within their own ministries. For example, Brian Tobin presided over a particularly stable ministry. The same cannot be said of Smallwood's sixth term in office (1966–71), which marked the beginning of the end of his tenure as premier. Other general assemblies that experienced higher rates of turnover include Moores' third term in office, Wells' first term, and, to a lesser degree, Williams' first term.

When ministerial turnover is broken down into voluntary and involuntary exit categories, the data indicate that Newfoundland premiers, like federal prime ministers, avoid forcibly sacking their ministers. We see

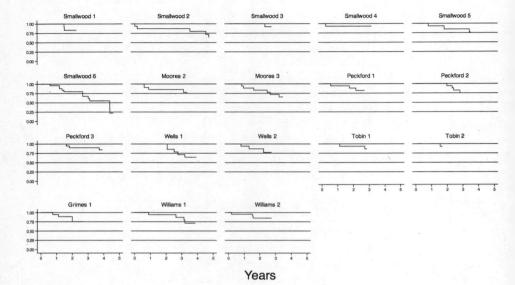

Figure 6.3a
Ministerial survival functions by government, voluntary and involuntary exits combined

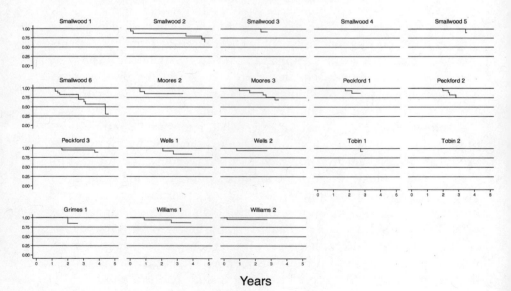

Figure 6.3b
Ministerial survival functions by government, involuntary exits

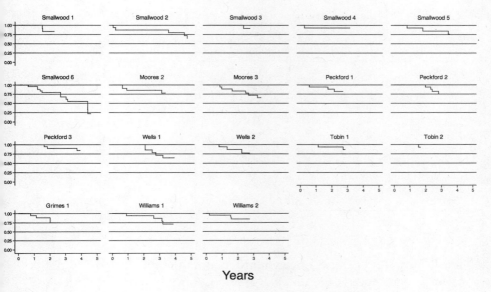

Figure 6.3c
Ministerial survival functions by government, voluntary exits

that survival estimates for involuntary exit (figure 6.3b) are largely flat, suggesting that ministerial removals to the backbenches are relatively rare occurrences. Indeed, the outliers are linked to specific general assemblies (Smallwood 6, Moores 3, and Peckford 2). Generally speaking, voluntary exits (figure 6.3c) to retire or return to private life are also largely "slow" when considered in isolation; given the opportunity, and like their federal counterparts, ministers in Newfoundland opt to stick it out and wait to step down at the end of a legislative term or when a premier resigns.

On their own, the Kaplan-Meier survival curves paint a picture of ministerial movement in Newfoundland & Labrador that is idiosyncratic and rather *sui generis* with respect to each premier and the individual cabinets over which they preside. Consequently, generalizations based on these data are difficult to make. For this reason, in addition to the ministerial durations, data on individual ministerial characteristics were collected, as were time varying institutional data that pertain to the political environments in which these ministers reside. Table 6.3 presents the summary statistics for these data. Overall, we find that women constitute 10 percent of the total number of ministers; 42 percent of ministers represent constituencies on the more-populated Ava-

Table 6.3
Summary statistics

Variable	Obs	Mean	Std. Dev.	Min	Max
Female = 1	341	0.1	0.3	0	1
Avalon = 1	341	0.42	0.49	0	1
Finance minister = 1	341 ·	0.07	0.25	0	1
Williams	341	0.12	0.33	0	1
Majority size	341	76.12	11.11	58.8	92.8
Leadership challenger = 1	341	0.14	0.35	0	1
Lawyer = 1	341	0.12	0.33	0	1
Age at exit (all)	341	50.54	8.94	29	74
Age at exit (uncensored)	66	52.16	10.12	31	74
Years experience at exit (all)	341	4.26	4.02	0.01	21.76
Years experience at exit (uncensored)	66	3.48	3	0.06	11.49

lon Peninsula; 6 percent of the ministers hold the finance portfolio; the average percentage of seats held by the governing party in the House of Assembly is 76;[8] party leadership challengers make up 14 percent of all cabinet ministers; and 12 percent of ministers are lawyers. The average age of ministers who exit cabinet is 50.1; when only those ministers who exit by way of a voluntary or involuntary exit are considered, the average age increases slightly to 52.1. Ministers who prematurely exit the cabinet have, on average, 3.48 years of previous cabinet experience, compared to the 4.26 years of experience when all ministers are considered.

These additional data are used to inform an event history model of ministerial duration. Event history analysis is an established and popular econometric approach commonly used by social scientists interested in the relationship between duration and the occurrence of an "event." Event history models are well-matched with temporal data because of their ability to accommodate censored time series and the violation of the assumption of normally distributed errors, which typically arise when working with time-to-event data (Box-Steffensmeier and Jones 1997). This class of econometric model has been used to study a variety of political phenomena, including government duration (Ferris and Voia 2009; King et al. 1990), leadership duration (Bienen and van de Walle 1989), ministerial duration (Berlinski, Dewan, and Dowding 2007), and ministerial appointment (Kerby 2009b, 2011). This chapter employs a particular class of event history model: a semi-parametric Cox proportional hazard model. The Cox model is adopted because its flexibility with respect to the parameterization of the hazard function is particularly well suited when there are no *ex ante* assumptions about the shape of the distribution of time of an individual's risk of experiencing a terminal event. Once specified, the event history model is able to relate cabinet ministers' individual and political characteristics, as well as the characteristics of the political environment in which they serve, to the time it takes to exit the cabinet. Duration is recorded as the span that elapses from cabinet appointment until cabinet exit. Ministers who die in office, are defeated in a general election, or exit the cabinet when the premier ceases to be the leader of the governing party or when the general assembly comes to an end are treated as censored. In order to simultaneously consider both the voluntary and involuntary modes of ministerial exit, a competing risks specification is adopted here. The competing risk approach is used because this class of model allows for the independent consideration of the explanatory variables that increase the hazard of experiencing a terminating event via different modes of exit (see Diermeier and Stevenson 1999; Huber and Martinez-Gallardo 2008).

The primary statistic of interest when using event history analysis is the hazard rate, which refers to the instantaneous probability that an individual will experience an event at a point in time given that the individual has "survived" until that point.[9] By focusing on the hazard rate, one is able to ask, "What is the likelihood that a cabinet minister will exit the cabinet at any point in time since becoming a minister, given how long he has served in cabinet, conditional on a series of covariates?"

Results

Table 6.4 presents the Cox proportional hazards competing risk model of ministerial turnover in Newfoundland & Labrador for the period of 1949 to 2010. Column 1 presents the hazard ratios for the covariates included in the "combined" model, in which voluntary and involuntary exits are pooled. Here we find that the previous ministerial-experience variable is highly significant statistically. The hazard ratio of 0.96 tells us that for each year of cabinet experience that a minister possesses, the hazard of exiting the cabinet decreases by four percent. Two other variables are statistically significant at the .10 level: party leadership challengers experience a hazard of cabinet exit that is almost 80 percent higher than non-leadership contenders. This result contrasts with research on federal-level ministerial turnover, which shows that party leadership contender status is negatively related with cabinet exit (Kerby 2011). On

Table 6.4
Competing risks Cox proportional hazards model

	Combined hr/se	Involuntary hr/se	Voluntary hr/se
Age (years)	0.941	0.929+	0.991
	(−0.05)	(−0.04)	(−0.14)
Age2	1.001	1.001+	1.00
	0.00	0.00	0.00
Female = 1	0.923	1.412	0.396
	(−0.44)	(−0.76)	(−0.44)
Avalon = 1	0.849	1.009	0.584
	(−.2)	(−0.24)	(−0.22)
Finance minister = 1	1.269	0.828	1.998
	(−0.51)	(−0.67)	(−1.19)
Williams = 1	0.882	0.470*	1.962+
	(−0.16)	(−0.17)	(−0.7)
Majority size	1.006	1.022	0.979
	(−0.01)	(−0.02)	(−0.01)
Leadership challenger = 1	1.789+	1.599	1.961
	(−0.62)	(−0.95)	(−0.92)
Lawyer	0.374+	0.417	0.258
	(−0.21)	(−0.28)	(−0.29)
Prev. ministerial experience	0.960***	0.964***	0.944*
	−0.01	−0.01	−0.02
Failures	66	42	24
Ministers	351	351	351

Note: Standard errors adjusted for clustering on assembly.
+ p< 0.10, * p, < 0.05 ** p < 0.01, *** p < 0.001

the other hand, the hazard associated with the lawyer variable parallels federal-level research: ministers with a legal background experience a decreasing hazard that is associated with their occupation.

The next two columns present the competing risks models for involuntary and voluntary ministerial turnover. Column 2 confirms the expectation that ministers, for the most part, did not really need to worry about being moved to the backbenches. The hazard ratio of 0.47 for the Williams variable indicates that ministers who served under Williams had a hazard of being sacked from cabinet that was 53 percent lower than the hazard of ministers who served under all other Newfoundland premiers. This variable is statistically significant at the .10 level. The other control variables that proved to be statistically significant in this model include age. Ministers could expect the hazard of involuntary exit to decrease by about seven percent for each year that they added to their birthday calendar; however, the quadratic effect introduced by age reveals that the decreasing hazard levels off at the age of fifty-five. Additionally, and like the combined model, each additional year of cabinet experience reduces the hazard of involuntary exit by 4 percent.

Finally, column 3, which presents the voluntary exit model, also reveals that the Williams variable is statistically significant at the 0.10 level. However, this time the Williams variable is positively related to the hazard of involuntary exit: ministers who served under Williams experienced a hazard of voluntary exit that was almost two times that of ministers who served under previous premiers. Once again, previous ministerial experience reduces the hazard of involuntary exit, as it did for the other models.

This last result is quite interesting since it reframes the Danny Williams ministry in a novel way. Williams may have been highly protective of his ministers, much more so than his predecessors, even to the extent that he did not dismiss ministers from cabinet unless they engaged in criminal activity or challenged his authority in a public manner – something that, at best, was a rare occurrence. The reluctance to dismiss ministers may also stem from Williams' strong standing in the public opinion polls and the sizable majorities that his party commanded in the House of Assembly, especially during his second mandate. Other research on ministerial turnover at the federal level suggests that prime ministers hold back from sacking ministers unless they absolutely have to. This may stem from ego or an unwillingness to let on that there may be a problem in cabinet. Indeed, even in the face of continuous calls for a minister's resignation or criticism, either in the legislature or in the media, the hazard of involuntary exit typically increases only when the calls for resignation are accompanied by a drop in government popularity (see Dewan and Dowding 2005; Kerby 2009a).

On the other hand, ministers in the Williams cabinet were much more "at risk" of leaving the cabinet on their own accord, whether to pursue other options outside the House of Assembly, to spend more time with family, or for health reasons, than those ministers who served in previous cabinets under different premiers. What explains this unusually high risk of voluntary exit? A definitive answer is difficult to put forward. Ministers are bound by convention not to discuss what happens in cabinet. The possibility of post-ministerial political opportunities or rewards bestowed by the premier or her successor only solidifies this principle, particularly for those individuals who are still active in provincial politics. Williams may not have had to sack his ministers.

His charisma, public popularity, and the authority granted to him by his majority governments meant that in the event of an incident that may have warranted a ministerial sacrifice under other circumstances (for example, the cancer testing scandal), Williams could turn a blind eye or even afford to give a wayward minister the opportunity to simply resign from politics without any serious consequence. The depth of the selection pool of potential ministers was sufficiently large and the willingness of ambitious or willing MHAs to fill the void and reside close to the top of the greasy pole at a time of unprecedented growth and government popularity was certainly enough to not cause the premier great pain.

Alternatively, Williams' intense personal popularity could not have rested well with some ambitious ministers. Ministers typically thrive on moving their way upwards on the political food chain – this is at the core of what political scientists refer to as progressive ambition theory. However, Williams' reluctance to shake the cabinet up combined with a tendency for micromanagement, a tendency that led to Elizabeth Marshall's exit from cabinet, surely meant that ministers with higher expectations with respect to their political careers may have decided to move on. Williams, the only person with the power to offer the carrots that might have convinced these ministers to remain, was clearly willing to let them go.

POLITICAL DECISION MAKING IN NEWFOUNDLAND & LABRADOR

A study of ministerial turnover provides a unique lens with which to examine the decision making capabilities of individual cabinet ministers, as well as the premier, with respect to career paths. Two cases of what I refer to as "involuntary" cabinet exit took place as a consequence of decisions. In the case of Tom Rideout, his resignation as deputy premier followed Williams' refusal to increase funding for road works and road repairs in Rideout's constituency, after Rideout believed he had secured the funding and agreement with the minister of transport. Thwarted expectations are not uncommon in politics; what is unusual is to see former premiers, like Rideout, who possess considerable ministerial and legislative experience, exit in such a tizzy.

Ordinarily, one expects leaders or senior members within the governing party to possess some kind of protected-species status in the cabinet hierarchy that shields them from incidental resignation threats. For example, at the federal level, prime ministers prefer to keep their former challengers or rivals bounded by collective ministerial responsibility and cabinet secrecy rather than leave them to their own devices (and supporters) in the backbenches. We know that former leader/challenger status is negatively associated with involuntary exit at the federal level. This does not appear to be the case in Newfoundland & Labrador, where Premier Williams could afford to let a minister with Rideout's credentials go without taking a hit to his popularity among the public or to his authority in cabinet and the legislature. In fact, Rideout's departure from cabinet elicited only a short-term shockwave that faded as quickly as the resignation issue emerged – to the extent that Rideout resigned his seat in the House of Assembly without any consternation, only two months after his departure from cabinet.

Minister of Health Elizabeth Marshall's departure stemmed from her unwillingness to abide by the premier's decision to manage certain matters in her portfolio, in particular labour negotiations with striking nurses. Marshall's resignation was accepted without hesitation and without the pressing need to immediately draw a backbencher with similar qualifications or gender into cabinet. Coincidentally, it was Tom Rideout who took over the health portfolio on an interim basis following Marshall's exit.

The voluntary exits that took place during the Williams ministry may also shed some light on decision making with respect to appointment and dismissal. The general labels associated with most of the exits in fact cloud what may be secondary, or primary but not evident, reasons for departure. Both Loyola Sullivan and John Ottenheimer explicitly left cabinet to retire from the rough and tumble of provincial politics (Ottenheimer, to deal with personal health matters), only to take up the mantle again by running for seats at the federal level under Stephen Harper's Conservative Party label following brief stints in federal and provincial Tory sinecures. Trevor Taylor, who voluntarily resigned from cabinet in 2009 for family reasons, also ran as a Conservative for a federal seat in the 2011 election; all three ex-ministers lost their election bids. The point here is simply that the combination of these ministers' willingness to voluntarily leave what are commanding positions in provincial government and then subsequently to pursue and accept the nomination to run federally as part of a team led by their former leader's nemesis, suggests that Williams' approach to federal-provincial relations and perhaps cabinet management may not have sat well with all those who served under him. Voluntary exit to retire or for health and/or family reasons may in fact be a more subtle way to express one's discontent with the premier's management style.

Finally, and also of significance, are instances of non-resignation: cases where one might expect a minister to resign (for example, in the face of calls for resignation) but where resignation never takes place. Education minister Joan Burke's handling of the search for a new president for Memorial University attracted condemnation from the international academic community and the national and provincial media, as well as a threat by the Canadian Association of University Teachers to censure Memorial University, the province's only university. Minister of Health Ross Wiseman came under fire from opposition parties and the media, who called for his resignation when the Cameron Inquiry report on inaccurate breast cancer testing results found him "lacking in due diligence." In both cases, Premier Williams decided to afford them the protection covered by collective ministerial responsibility. Ultimately, neither minister was reshuffled and both served until the end of the Williams ministry and continued to serve in cabinet under Premier Dunderdale, with Wiseman becoming speaker after the 2011 election. It is worth noting as well that neither minister publicly offered to resign.

This chapter has presented a first systematic look at the patterns of ministerial turnover in Newfoundland & Labrador for the period of 1949 to 2010. A competing risk Cox proportional event history model of voluntary and involuntary ministerial exit indicates that the Danny Williams ministry, which lasted from 2003 until 2010, was indeed unique in contemporary Newfoundland political history. The findings of the model suggest that while Williams' ministers were comparatively safe in their jobs – that is, Williams was not trigger-happy about dismissing his ministers to the backbenches – they were much more at risk of leaving of their own volition than ministers who served under previous Newfoundland premiers. This suggests a more self-censoring approach to ministerial accountability or, alternatively, an unwillingness to abide by the authority of a highly charismatic and powerful premier in a system already known for bestowing considerable power on its leaders.

NOTES

1   Graham White's work on provincial and territorial cabinets is a welcome exception to the norm.
2   For a more detailed review of the government survival debates, see Warwick (1994) and Laver (2003).
3   See the bibliography in Dunn (2005).

4   Indeed, one of the first criticisms Williams faced in the media resulted from not appointing a minister from Labrador.

5   Following from the comparative literature on ministerial elites, a cabinet reshuffle is defined as any instance when two or more ministers experience a ministerial transformation at the same time. The transformation can take the form of a move to a new responsibility or portfolio, or it may entail an exit from cabinet.

6   Because of the lack of variation, the short-lived 35th General Assembly, which ended in a hung parliament, was not included in this analysis.

7   Kaplan-Meier curves are the graphical representation of the Kaplan-Meier estimator, which is a non-parametric estimate of the survivor function – the probability that an observation will survive beyond time t. For the purpose of this research, the Kaplan-Meier estimator is used to estimate how long ministers remain in cabinet prior to exit. The Kaplan-Meier estimate is particularly useful when examining career path data, because it is able to accommodate right-censored exits whereby a minister leaves the cabinet for a reason other than the one under investigation.

8   Recall that the short-lived 35th General Assembly (1971–72) is not included in this analysis.

9   The hazard rate is expressed as

$$h(t) = \lim_{\Delta t \to 0} \frac{\Pr(t \leq T \leq t + \Delta t \,|\, T \leq t}{\Delta t}$$

which is the probability that an individual will fail at a time that is conditional on having survived until that time.

7

The Judicialization of (Past) Politics:
The Cameron Inquiry and the Green Commission

KATE PUDDISTER AND JAMES B. KELLY

COMPARATIVE THEORY

The judicialization of politics in Canada has generally been associated with the introduction of the Charter of Rights and Freedoms, since it has allowed the judiciary greater influence in shaping public policy outcomes. In this chapter, we consider the unique approach to this phenomenon in Newfoundland & Labrador: the use of commissions and judicial inquiries as a response to public policy failures of past governments that rose to public attention during the Williams ministry. Focusing on the Cameron Inquiry, which investigated testing errors in cancer screening, and the Green Commission, which involved a spending and expenditure scandal by members of the House of Assembly, this chapter argues that Danny Williams successfully managed both public opinion and criticism through arms-length review processes. Neither the Cameron Inquiry nor the Green Commission criticized the Williams ministry for these policy failures, suggesting that the judicialization of politics, when it centres on the policy failures of previous governments or independent actors, may produce significant policy changes by incumbent governments. They occur because incumbent governments are not directly tied to the policy failures or scandals and, as a result, use inquiries and commissions to manage public opinion and as a pretext to establish a new policy status quo.

BACKGROUND

The adoption of the Constitution Act, 1982 and, more importantly, the Charter of Rights and Freedoms serves as a demarcation point for an enhanced role of the judicial branch in Canadian political dialogue and governance. To be sure, courts have always had a political role in Canada, including the various decisions of the Judicial Committee of the Privy Council, such as the declaration of women as "persons" in *Edwards v. Canada (Attorney General)* ([1930] A.C. 124) and the protections provided by the courts to religious minorities in Quebec before the Quiet Revolution (for example, *Roncarelli v. Duplessis* [1959] S.C.R. 121). However, Canada has experienced reinvigorated notions of judicialized politics since the entrenchment of the Charter. The judicialization of politics implies an expansion of judicial methods and decision making outside the traditional sphere of the courts, often invited by politicians and bureaucratic decision makers (Vallinder 1994, 91). As a result, with judicial determination of the constitutionality of public policy, Canada is experiencing a greater involvement of the judiciary in core policy debates (Kelly and Manfredi 2009).

Fundamentally, judicialization involves transforming any traditionally non-legal process into one influenced by judicial determinations and procedures. In some circumstances, bureaucratic decision makers and politicians may turn to the judiciary to achieve a sense of legitimacy and formality of decision making, utilizing the non-partisan branch to achieve political ends, as in the Canadian practice of reference questions. Arguably, this also occurs when politicians call judicial commissions of inquiry to address political scandals and controversies. Commissions of inquiry are often established in an attempt to relieve the government from intense scrutiny from both the opposition and the public, resulting from the surfacing of a controversy or scandal (Courtney 1969, 201). There are both partisan and non-partisan motivations behind calling a commission of inquiry. Commissions may be enacted to achieve educative ends, insofar as they are used to increase public understanding of an event and to foster political compromise, but also to achieve political ends such as shoring up public support, delaying government action, and avoiding blame (Marier 2009, 1206).

The use of this investigatory procedure is not a recent phenomenon; rather, in Canada commissions of inquiry have been used since before Confederation. Several were called shortly after the Act of Union in 1840 and fifteen were enacted after Confederation, between 1870 and 1879 alone (Courtney 1969). As a result, judicial commissions of inquiry have become the institutionalized response to political scandal and controversy. Because of this institutionalization, the public has come to expect inquiries as the appropriate response to political missteps and approves of them as a means of fostering transparency and the disclosure of the internal aspects of government (Gomery 2006, 787).

The province of Newfoundland & Labrador has relied on judicial commissions of inquiry to investigate basic governmental issues such as the minimum wage (Higgins Commission in 1966) and the logging industry (Dunfield Commission in 1960). However, the province also has a history of using judicial inquiries to deal with highly controversial problems, such as the 1989 investigation into sexual abuse at the Mount Cashel Orphanage by the Hughes Commission; the Lamer Inquiry in 2006, which addressed the administration of justice and the wrongful convictions of three men; as well as the Wells Inquiry in 2010, which investigated offshore helicopter safety following a tragic crash.

Relying on commissions of inquiry as a means to deal with political scandal and conflict can be seen as an example of judicialized politics. Since calling a judicial inquiry is an act of the executive that is not part of judicial responsibilities, the justice appointed to head the commission is carrying out a function of the executive branch (O'Connor 2007). Thus, by calling a commission, political decision makers are transferring a portion of their authority to the judicial branch. While it is not a requirement that commissions be led by a judge, justices are selected to provide the credibility of the judiciary and the legitimacy of being separate from political actors (O'Connor 2007). Furthermore, the fact that the ability to initiate an inquiry is a sole power of the executive provides a premier with a wide range of discretion and serves to concentrate the usage of a powerful political tool solely in the hands of the premier and the provincial political elite.

While there are clear benefits from relying on the judiciary to conduct commissions, such as the authority and legitimacy of the bench, doing so can raise serious questions about the proper role for the judiciary and notions of judicial independence. Thus, Courtney (1969) argues that by thrusting a judge into this role, the neutrality of the judicial branch suffers from the controversial and often partisan issues that he or she must investigate. Furthermore, the impartiality and objectivity of the justice may appear to be jeopardized when he or she returns to the bench (O'Connor 2007).

Consequently, judicial commissions of inquiry are preferred to alternatives such as parliamentary committees and executive investigations, since the appearance of neutrality on behalf of the judge will aid in the acceptance of both the findings and the recommendations of the commission (Courtney 1969, 201). Furthermore, the issue being scrutinized may require legal expertise to adequately investigate. In fact, the courts themselves have recognized the educational and investigative benefits of judicial inquiries, contending that they are essential in restoring public confidence (*Canada (Attorney General) v. Canada (Commission of Inquiry on the Blood System)* [1997] 3 s.c.r. 440). Moreover, judicial inquiries are often preferred to legislative committees because they do not expire with the legislative session and do not create additional responsibilities for legislators (Courtney 1969, 209). The latter issue is arguably more pertinent for smaller governments like Newfoundland & Labrador, which lack the infrastructure and bureaucratic support to undertake comprehensive investigations.

CASE STUDY

In the case of Newfoundland & Labrador, during the tenure of Premier Danny Williams two major judicial inquiries or investigations took place – the Green Commission and the Cameron Inquiry. In both of the political and bureaucratic scandals under investigation, the House of Assembly and the Executive Council were implicated to varying degrees. However, the popularity of Danny Williams did not suffer as a result of either investigation's findings. Rather, he emerged from both controversies relatively unscathed and perhaps *more* popular. This effective use of commissions by the Williams administration highlights the populist tendencies of the ministry, insofar as first ministers are able to circumvent traditional government institutions stemming from their ability to dominate their governments (Marland 2010). Furthermore, the following episodes examined emphasize the utility of elite theory in the examination of the Williams ministry, since the control of the government and its response to two scandals emanated from a minority in the executive branch that was accepted by the mass public, as evidenced by the lack of blame placed on Williams and his advisors following the scandals. Williams was able to effectively utilize the judicial inquiry function to serve his own political ends and to remove blame from himself, arguably aiding in the survival of his government and thereby contributing to the judicialization of politics in Newfoundland & Labrador without a concurrent loss of political or policy autonomy – two outcomes generally associated with the increased involvement of judicial actors in legislative decision making.

The Cameron Inquiry and Policy Impacts in the Health Sector

As Maria Mathews also discusses in chapter 8 of this book, news of faulty breast cancer testing in Newfoundland & Labrador first surfaced in the public sphere following a news investigation by the Canadian Broadcasting Corporation regarding the case of Peggy Deane. Deane had tissue retested for estrogen receptors (ER) and progesterone receptors (PR) by an American specialist who found that the original results were incorrect, sparking the review by the Eastern Regional Integrated Health Authority – Eastern Health – not only of Deane's tissue but also of approximately four hundred individuals who had previously been tested by Eastern Health, making Deane the index case for the retesting (Cameron 2009, 2). The retesting gained national media attention, spawning investigative reports into the misdiagnosis by several media outlets.

When the news broke regarding the errors at provincially run Eastern Health, the government, led by Premier Williams, found itself at the centre of negative media attention, widespread public discontent, and the filing of a class action lawsuit by a local attorney. On 16 May 2007, news of the breast cancer testing problems reached the House of Assembly and sparked questions from Opposition House Leader Kelvin Parsons. Questioning the minister of justice, Parsons urged the Williams government to call a judicial inquiry into the testing problems. Opposition calls for an inquiry continued the following day, prompting a confirmation from Williams that his government would undertake a full review (Newfoundland and Labrador 2007c).

Premier Williams called a judicial inquiry from a position of dominance in the House of Assembly, since the Progressive Conservative (PC) party held an overwhelming majority of seats, allowing it to weather the storm during question period. Moreover, the timing of the initiation of the Commission of Inquiry may have been strategic on the part of the Williams ministry, since a fixed election date in October of the same year allowed for the negative media attention to ease and allowed incumbents to emphasize that the issue was currently being resolved by the inquiry when they were questioned on the campaign trail.

The Department of Health and Community Services of Newfoundland & Labrador announced the official order for a judicial commission of inquiry under section 3 of the Public Inquiries Act 2006 on 22 May 2007, and shortly thereafter it announced the appointment of Justice Margaret A. Cameron of the Newfoundland & Labrador Court of

Appeal to lead the commission. Because the initiation of the Commission of Inquiry on Hormone Receptor Testing (the Cameron Commission) was a product of the Public Inquiries Act (unlike the Green Commission), it was granted an operational budget and a wide investigatory scope, with full subpoena powers (Newfoundland and Labrador 2007b). The inquiry's mandate was to investigate how high the ER/PR testing error rate was, to determine causality, and to assess whether responsible authorities communicated the errors to the public within an appropriate time (CBC News 2008f).

Having such a wide scope, the Cameron Inquiry was quite extensive, with 93 witnesses and almost 130 days of testimony; the final report was released almost two years later in March 2009 (Cameron, vii). Witnesses included individuals from high positions within the Premier's Office, including the clerk, the chief of staff, and Danny Williams himself, who apologized during his testimony (Newfoundland and Labrador 2008f) and took the opportunity to speak directly to patients and their families. He expressed his regret for the incident and the miscommunication on behalf of his government and previous governments – an action that garnered a positive response from local media and the public. The premier empathized with the victims by relating the incident to his own mother, explaining that this tragedy could have happened to his own family, which added a personalized tone to his apology (CTV News 2008). This action not only served to increase public respect for the provincial government's handling of the scandal, but it also reinforced Williams' persona as a man of the people, highlighting the populist thread that was often present in his rhetoric. Moreover, the fact that many individuals from high positions within the Premier's Office were implicated and required to testify demonstrates the centralization of executive power during the Williams ministry.

However, the operation of the Cameron Inquiry was not without its own controversy. Premier Williams publicly criticized the operation of the inquiry, likening it to a "witch hunt" and arguing that it was far too adversarial and functioned too much like a prosecution (CBC News 2008k). Williams' comments prompted the opposition parties in the House of Assembly to argue that he was attempting to rein in and undermine the inquiry (Newfoundland and Labrador 2008a), but this public criticism of the Cameron Inquiry – and of those responsible for carrying out its mandate – did not hurt the popularity of Premier Williams. Rather, he successfully conveyed to the public the idea that he was criticizing the inquiry *on their behalf*, in the populist vein of the Williams government, and that this position was a responsible reaction designed to resolve the testing failures that prompted the launching of the Cameron Inquiry (Foot 2009). Thus, Williams' criticism of the inquiry ensured that the public would not personally blame the premier, since he was able to convey that he, like the public, wanted appropriate and timely results. His criticism, therefore, was about the slow process – and not the substantive findings – of the Cameron Inquiry.

The Cameron Inquiry found that the cancer screening problems at Eastern Health were system-wide – there were failures not only in the laboratory but also within the management system which allowed the problem to exist for such an extended period of time without detection (Cameron 2009, 433). The inquiry found that overworked pathologists and the absence of a regulatory body to set and accredit standards were contributing factors to the testing failure (Hede 2008, 836).

The Cameron Inquiry found that the problem with the management of the crisis emerged because Eastern Health lacked a crisis management plan that provided clear guidelines and outlined responsibilities and, more importantly, because it did not require those involved to document their attempts to address the problem (Cameron 2009, 434). Furthermore, it found that the current legislative structure placed the minster of health and community services in an oversight role over regional health authorities such as Eastern Health. In this respect, the Department of Health and Community Services was found negligent in exercising due diligence in the dissemination of the information regarding the problem to the Williams ministry, resulting in a lack of information and appreciation of the cancer testing situation. The inquiry implicated many parties, not only laboratories where testing was found to be incorrect, but also Eastern Health's senior management, the minister of health and community services for inadequate handling of the situation, and the Premier's Office.

The mandate of the Cameron Inquiry was wide-ranging and so were the recommendations resulting from its findings. Some suggestions were aimed at the laboratory, such as the continual monitoring of research on ER/PR testing and the establishment of in-house training for laboratory technicians. Others were aimed at management and government, such as the installation of a provincial director of pathology, the creation of a licensing requirement for regional health laboratories, and the creation of a national accreditation institution in collaboration with other provinces (Cameron 2009, 459–68). Furthermore, the recommendations were also aimed at the inquiry process itself, suggesting changes in the use of evidence and the level of disclosure required for patients and individuals adversely affected (Cameron 2009, 470; see also the discussion in chapter 8 about evidence-based decision making).

The report also addressed the problems of political accountability during the scandal, specifically the unclear relationship between the minister of health and the regional health authorities, such as Eastern Health. However, the inquiry found that the minister, who was accountable to the House of Assembly, needed to exercise an oversight function for the health authorities, which was lacking during the ER/PR testing scandal. The Department of Health and its minister needed to exercise due diligence in reporting all communication from Eastern Health to the public, rather than providing only part of the story (Cameron 2009, 438). However, the inquiry made no recommendations concerning political oversight or accountability either directly or indirectly to the Office of the Premier or concerning the minister of health's reporting to the House of Assembly. This demonstrates that recommendations of the inquiry dealt largely with the operation of health authorities and not with the executive branch of the government, allowing it to emerge largely unscathed from the commission.

Following the release of the Cameron Inquiry Report, Premier Williams faced intense criticism that called for the resignation of the minister of health and community services, Ross Wiseman (see Matthew Kerby's discussion of ministerial resignations in chapter 6). Williams rejected such demands, arguing that Wiseman had been appointed minister of health and community services after the problem first surfaced. However, the premier did concede that his government's communication to the public and the practice of accepting indiscriminately the information regarding testing from the health board could have been handled in a better way (Brautigam 2009), and he did agree to implement many of the recommendations of the inquiry. As of early spring 2010, thirty-nine of the sixty recommendations had been implemented, and the remaining ones were in progress; over $21 million of the 2009 provincial budget had been dedicated to their implementation (Newfoundland and Labrador 2010g).

Following the ER/PR testing scandal and the subsequent Cameron Inquiry, Premier Williams emerged largely unscathed, since he was able to distance himself from the scandal and Eastern Health, owing in part to the settlement of the class action lawsuit and his acknowledgement in his testimony to the inquiry that his government had erred in its handling of the ER/PR scandal. When it surfaced after the release of the Cameron Inquiry Report that Eastern Health was retesting more ER/PR tests and attempting to mislead the public regarding the number of retests, Williams came out on the offensive. He stated, "They [Eastern Health] should be shot over it. They've learned absolutely nothing from the whole process" (Canadian Press 2009c). These cutting remarks helped to situate Williams again on the side of the people, pitted in a struggle against those who wished to defraud the people of Newfoundland & Labrador. These actions served to invigorate the populism often associated with Danny Williams' rhetoric (Marland 2010).

The Green Commission and Policy Impacts in the Legislature

As Christopher Dunn outlines in chapter 2 of this book, long-standing problems have been associated with the question of how member of the House of Assembly (MHA) compensation and expenses should be governed. The sudden resignation of former PC leader Ed Byrne as minister of natural resources on 22 June 2006 unleashed the judicialization of politics that culminated in the Green Commission. In a hastily called news conference, Premier Williams confirmed that Byrne, the MHA for Kilbride since 1993, had stepped aside from cabinet in response to concerns expressed by provincial auditor general John Noseworthy. This complaint centred on misspending and fraudulent expense claims by Byrne during his time as an MHA.

In response to a series of auditor general reports on questionable expenditure and constituency allowance claims by MHAs, in July 2006 Premier Williams established what came to be known as the Green Commission. The Review Commission on Constituency Allowances was headed by the Honourable J. Derek Green, chief justice of the Supreme Court of Newfoundland & Labrador, Trial Division. As such, it had the appearance of the judicialization of politics in response to a spending scandal by the House of Assembly dating back to 1996. For instance, it was headed by a sitting judge who was appointed as a commissioner under the Great Seal of Newfoundland & Labrador by Order in Council "with inquiry subpoena power" (Green 2007, 1–5). In this respect, the commitment of the Williams government was equal to that of former prime minister Paul Martin. Specifically, in 2004 Martin established the Gomery Commission to investigate spending irregularities identified by the auditor general of Canada in relation to the Sponsorship Program enacted by the federal government after the 1995 Quebec referendum on sovereignty-association (Wanna 2006, 15–19).

There is, however, a notable difference between the Green and the Gomery Commission: only Gomery was constituted as a judicial inquiry or commission under its terms of reference. Instead, the Green Commission was tasked with suggesting "best practices" for constituency allowances and expenditures (Green 2007, 1–5). Further, the Royal Canadian Mounted Police (RCMP) and the Royal Newfoundland Constabulary (RNC) handled criminal matters in both cases. As well, the Green Commission could not review the findings of the auditor general's reports in relation to spending irregularities by MHAs, since the premier designated this as a "go-forward" commission. In essence, Danny Williams remained proactive by signalling his commitment to this serious issue by appearing to create an independent judicial inquiry. But instead, he deftly protected the sovereignty of the House of Assembly *as an institution* through terms of reference that saw the Green Commission function simply as an advisory commission reporting to the House of Assembly on possible legislative changes to augment existing expenditure practices (1–6). However, this protection did not extend to members of the House of Assembly or to its public servants, who were found to have engaged in irregular spending and expense practices.

Unlike the background to the Gomery Commission, where the federal opposition parties lobbied for strict terms of reference because only the governing Liberal Party of Canada was implicated, under the Green Commission all Newfoundland's political parties were regarded as affected by the spending and expense scandal in the House of Assembly. At the root of the Green Commission inquiry were irregular practices that allowed generous remuneration to exist without sufficient financial controls or oversight of constituency allowances provided to MHAs, regardless of their party affiliation. Indeed, the Green Commission indicated that the problem lay in the incremental relaxation of expenditure scrutiny by the Internal Economy Commission (IEC), a bipartisan committee of the House of Assembly charged with overseeing the remuneration of sitting MHAs (Marland 2007a, 38). Perhaps more importantly, the IEC had included members of the political executive, including a Liberal minister who was eventually implicated for questionable spending on wine and artwork.

Beginning in 1993, the IEC Act was amended to remove the requirement that an independent commission be appointed immediately after a provincial election to "review and make binding recommendations regarding MHA compensation and expense reimbursement" (Green 2007, 5; see "Executive Summary"). Although the act continued in force, the IEC simply disregarded key safeguards on unregulated compensation to MHAs. In addition to the changes in regard to the independent commission, the IEC "relaxed the rules governing expenditures on furniture and equipment. Severance pay benefits for MHAs were increased; salaries and benefits for parliamentary positions were increased. All of this was done without the appointment of an independent commission as previously required by the IEC Act" (Green 2007, 6; see "Executive Summary").

Most problematic for the Green Commission was the IEC's attitude towards the IEC Act: "Whenever it presented an obstacle to the measures contemplated by the IEC, the IEC Act was changed. Such legislative changes were processed expeditiously by the House of Assembly, usually in the last days of a session and with minimal discussion or debate" (Green 2007, 6; see "Executive Summary"). The composition of the IEC is important, since it blocked the auditor general from investigating the spending practices of MHAs, and then-premier Brian Tobin chose not to interfere. Indeed, it was marginalized as a legislative blockage by the time Danny Williams established the Green Commission. Further, it is an illustration of C.E.S. Franks' remark, *Quis custodiet ipsos Custodes?*, in regard to the fiscal management of the House of Assembly solely by its members without external or internal oversight (2008, 156–8). In 1999, the act was amended to remove reference to the Morgan Report (the only independent commission convened under the IEC Act) and its recommendation regarding processes for establishing salaries and expenditures by MHAs. In the post-Morgan era, the IEC Act was amended to provide the IEC with unlimited ability to establish the rules governing MHA compensation and expenditure allowances without effective oversight (Green 2007, 6; see "Executive Summary").

Although the IEC incrementally freed MHAs from internal scrutiny and auditing by the House of Assembly, it was, like all public bodies, subject to external review by the provincial auditor general. This was also severed in 2000, when the IEC Act was amended. This legislative change prohibited the auditor general from reviewing the spending practices of the legislature and MHA allowances, as well as barring the comptroller general from access to the spending documentation of the House of Assembly (Green 2007, 7, in "Executive Summary"; Franks 2008, 158). In response, the IEC established that the House of Assembly would be subject only to an annual audit by an auditor appointed by the IEC, though it failed to regularly appoint an individual to perform this task (Green 2007, 7; see "Executive Summary").

This lack of effective oversight continued until Premier Williams over-ruled the IEC and invited the provincial auditor general to examine con-stituency allowance expenditures in 2006 (Marland 2007a, 38). After Noseworthy released a series of interim reports in the summer of 2006, which indicated questionable spending practices and limited oversight controls, the premier decided to establish the Green Commission before the auditor general released his final report in 2007 (Franks 2008, 155). That report would cover the period from 1999–2000 to 2005–06, and it indicated that a total expenditure of $25 million had been processed for 115 MHAS across party lines, which averaged out to $216,960 per MHA (Marland 2007a, 37). The auditor general concluded that expenditures of $7.6 million were either an *Inappropriate Expenditure* ($2.2 million) or based on *Inadequate Documentation* ($5.4 million) (Noseworthy 2007, 2–3). Indeed, the fact that all political parties in the House of Assembly were implicated may explain the reluctance of any political leader but Danny Williams – a self-made millionaire who was donating his salary to charity – to confront this issue.

Before the auditor general reported, the Green Commission was cre-ated and released its findings in May 2007, four months before the final report by the provincial auditor general. More than reporting on best practices, the Green Commission included draft legislation, known as the House of Assembly Accountability, Integrity and Administration Act, for consideration by the House of the Assembly (Franks 2008, 155). Indeed, the Green Commission made eighty recommendations in its report, and the draft legislation was accepted by the House of Assem-bly and passed within two weeks of its release (Franks 2008, 156). The legislation received minimal scrutiny by the House of Assembly and was passed without significant debate. In fact, it is more accurately charac-terized as the Green Commission's *legislation* that was simply passed by the House of Assembly as a matter of legislative practice.

Since the Green Commission was established as a result of fraudulent practices by MHAS and an incremental weakening of spending oversights by MHAS, the House of Assembly was unable to resist policy correc-tions in the draft legislation presented by the commission. Indeed, eighty recommendations were accepted without much debate in the House of Assembly. The commission had a significant policy impact for a number of reasons. First, it was necessary for an independent actor to address a pressing public policy issue since the House of Assembly lacked the credibility to resolve it. The involvement of the Williams ministry in the spending scandal was limited, since it had assumed office only in

2003. Danny Williams could therefore fully accept the Green Commission, since it targeted the actions of the House of Assembly and not the Williams ministry.

The draft legislation, which made sweeping reforms to the expenditure practices of MHAS, was passed as the House of Assembly Accountability, Integrity and Administration Act. First, it transformed the clerk of the House of Assembly into an "accounting officer," thus severing the internal review of expenditures from the IEC (Franks 2008, 159). Second, the act accepted the Green Commission's recommendation that the clerk must be nominated by the House of Assembly. Further, the act specified that the Speaker of the House of Assembly bears responsibility for the selection process, and it established an Office of Law Clerk to support the clerk of the House (Franks 2008, 160). In the past, the clerk had relied on legal advice from the Department of Justice, a practice that the Green Commission argued was no longer appropriate.

Third, the IEC was replaced by a Management Commission with responsibility for ensuring that the expenditures of MHAS conformed to the standards of the executive branch.[1] To ensure transparency, section 19 stated that routine meetings of the Management Commission must be open to the public and that it must make its records accessible to the public and the media. Finally, under section 43, the act reestablished that the Management Committee must appoint a yearly auditor. As well, the provincial auditor general may serve as auditor of the House of Assembly, and an Audit Commission must be established by the Management Commission and must include two lay persons appointed by the chief justice of the province.[2]

The Green Commission, therefore, was an important agent of legislative reform in the context of the regulation of public expenditure in Newfoundland & Labrador. The Green Commission's draft legislation was rapidly accepted and implemented because of the diminished ability of the House of Assembly to oppose its findings and policy recommendations. In this respect, the commission allowed the Williams ministry to respond to a damaging political scandal of individual MHAS without suffering political damage as a government. For instance, the commission's terms of reference involved the practices of the House of Assembly and not of the Executive Council. Thus, Williams defused this issue by appearing to judicialize politics but, in the end, agreeing to recommendations that simply brought the practices of the legislature in line with those of the executive. However, judicial inquiries are merely one example of how politics can become judicialized. Political actors not only attempt to seek advantage through the judiciary; their political goals can be influenced or constrained through other interactions with the judicial branch, notably through the function of judicial review. The following section provides an assessment of the greater picture of judicialized politics in Newfoundland & Labrador.

Newfoundland & Labrador and the Supreme Court of Canada

In other provinces, disagreements with the Supreme Court of Canada tend to focus on its Charter jurisprudence and the invalidation of provincial public policies as inconsistent with the Charter's rights and freedoms. For instance, the 2009 declaration by the Supreme Court of Canada that Quebec's prohibition on private English instruction was unconstitutional generated condemnation of this decision among Quebec's political and intellectual elites with the release of *Nguyen v. Quebec* ([2009] 3 S.C.R. 208). Further, Alberta's refusal to extend human rights protections for gays and lesbians under the provincial human rights code, which was a violation of the Charter's equality provisions in *Vriend v. Alberta* ([1998] 1 S.C.R. 493), evoked criticism of the Court by the Alberta government.

Thus, a notable feature of Charter politics in Newfoundland & Labrador is the general absence of provincial statutes invalidated as inconsistent with the Charter of Rights. Indeed, Newfoundland & Labrador has fared rather well before the Supreme Court of Canada under the Charter. The highest-profile challenge to a provincial statute, the Public Sector Restraint Act, which rescinded a pay equity agreement as unsustainable given the province's fiscal situation in the late 1990s, was upheld by the Court in *Newfoundland (Treasury Board) v. N.A.P.E.* ([2004] 3 S.C.R. 381) as a reasonable limitation on equality rights protections. This 2004 decision occurred at the beginning of the Williams era in Newfoundland & Labrador, though it involved a policy decision of a previous Liberal ministry.

The surprise resignation of Supreme Court of Canada Justice Michel Bastarache in 2008 saw the Williams ministry lobby Prime Minister Stephen Harper's government to appoint a Newfoundlander as Bastarache's replacement. Indeed, since Newfoundland & Labrador's entry into Confederation in 1949, the federal minister of justice has never appointed a member of the provincial bar to the Supreme Court of Canada. While this may be simply a symbolic issue, the Court is an important federal institution that is based on the principle of regional representation. By convention, Atlantic Canada is provided with one appointment to the Supreme Court of Canada. As the only Atlantic province never to be represented, Newfoundland & Labrador justice minister Jerome Kennedy viewed this as "a serious oversight" (Tibbets 2008) that needed to be addressed through Justice Bastarache's replacement. Although the appointment of Supreme Court of Canada justices is by order-in-council, the attempt to cast greater transparency on this process began under former prime minister Martin, who created a parliamentary process for the review of selected candidates. Having adopted this appointment process for his first two judicial appointments to the Supreme Court of Canada, it was assumed that Prime Minister Harper's recommended candidate would be questioned before a parliamentary committee. Indeed, it was agreed that the parliamentary committee would be further empowered to produce the short list of three candidates for appointment. From this list, the prime minister and minister of justice would decide which candidate would be appointed and then questioned by the parliamentary committee (Makin 2008).

In this context, in his role as minister of justice, Jerome Kennedy was set to appear before the parliamentary committee tasked with producing the short list of candidates. Kennedy intended to argue that constitutional convention dictated that the next appointment must come from Newfoundland & Labrador. Facing opposition to his desire to appoint a member of cabinet to the parliamentary committee responsible for the short list, the prime minister bypassed the process and simply announced that Justice Cromwell of the Nova Scotia Court of Appeal would replace Justice Bastarache (Makin 2008). This generated tremendous criticism by Minister Kennedy, since it was linked to the Harper government's perceived mistreatment of Newfoundland & Labrador in federal-provincial relations, though Premier Williams chose not to make this a major grievance as part of his well-publicized political battle with Harper (see Royce Koop's contribution in chapter 4 of this book).

The unilateral appointment of Justice Cromwell denied Newfoundland & Labrador an important opportunity to lobby for the inclusion of a qualified member of the provincial bar as a shortlisted candidate. Indeed, Minister Kennedy argued that "Stephen Harper continues to treat this province with disdain and disrespect" and "in effect is saying we don't have qualified candidates" (Makin 2008). Since Justice Cromwell is not required to retire until 2027 at age seventy-five, the appointment of the first Newfoundlander to the Court may not occur for many years.

POLITICAL DECISION MAKING IN NEWFOUNDLAND & LABRADOR

The judicialization of policy failures through the establishment of commissions and inquiries occurred over two pressing public issues during the Williams era: systemic failure in cancer screening and problematic spending practices by MHAs that led to significant public outrage. In both cases, independent review processes were necessary, since the House of Assembly and its members were responsible, to varying degrees, for these policy failures. However, in a demonstration of the vast power of the Office of the Premier, Williams was able to call the inquiries solely at his own discretion, allowing him to control the timing and circumstances. The use of independent commissions and their findings helped the Williams ministry escape political scandal without suffering any significant political cost in the end. In fact, the popularity of the Williams ministry increased *after* the release of the Cameron and Green Reports. Although other factors undoubtedly contributed to Williams' popularity, rather than causing public concern the reports appear to have reassured citizens of Williams' executive authority. This result is particularly significant, since the judicialization of politics is suggested to result in a loss of political and policy autonomy for democratic actors. The particular manifestation this phenomenon in Newfoundland & Labrador – the judicialization of policy failures committed largely by *previous* and not by *incumbent* governments – can explain the significant policy impact of the reports submitted by Justices Cameron and Green, as well as the rapid implementation of their recommendations by the Williams ministry.

NOTES

1   House of Assembly Accountability, Integrity and Administration Act, 2007, S.N.L., ch H-10.1., s.20, http://assembly.nl.ca/legislation/sr/statutes/h10-1.htm.
2   Ibid., s. 23.

8

Health Policy in Newfoundland and Labrador

MARIA MATHEWS

COMPARATIVE THEORY

According to the "Framework of Understanding the Context of Decision Making," the decision-making world can be divided into three inter-related domains: the institutional structure for decision making, the domain of values, and the domain of information (Lomas 2000). The institutional structure consists of the formal bodies (executive, legislative, bureaucratic) and informal bodies (composed of policy brokers, coalitions, stakeholders, citizens) that formulate policy options and make decisions. The domain of values involves the interplay between ideologies ("views about what ought to be"), beliefs ("casual assumptions about what is"), and interests ("responses to incentives and rewards") (143). The domain of information includes the producers (e.g., researchers, think tanks, pollsters, and so on) and purveyors (e.g., the media, "experts," networks, advocates, etc.) of knowledge.

Lomas compares the institutional structure to a sausage machine and values and information to the ingredients that go into it. With the emergence of evidence-based decision making, there has been a growing expectation that high-quality research evidence should form the basis of the information used to frame and justify policy decisions. Information can come from many sources and different purveyors, and values emerge from a complex interplay of ideologies, interests, and beliefs. Values not only privilege some sources of information over others but also influence the lens through which evidence and purveyors are appraised.

Since the 1990s, evidence-based decision making has been viewed as the optimal approach to decision making in health care (Black 2001; Canadian Health Services Research Foundation 2000). This approach stems from the evidence-based movement within medicine and was strongly endorsed by the National Forum on Health, which defined it as "the systematic application of the best available evidence to the evaluation of options and to decision making in clinical, management and policy settings" (Gainer et al. 1997, 6). Evidence-based decision making is regarded as particularly desirable in health policy as a means to contain costs, improve quality, and promote accountability (Lomas et al. 2005; Gainer et al. 1997).

Evidence-based decision making implicitly judges the type of information and the role of values that should dominate policy-making. Researchers generally view evidence in terms of science: as explicit, derived through rigorous methods, and reproducible by others. Evidence, according to many researchers, is the product of scientific inquiry (largely, although not exclusively, from a positivist stance) that is open to expert scrutiny (e.g., through peer-reviewed studies). In contrast, decision makers view evidence in its colloquial sense, that is, as "anything, that [based on its relevance] establishes a fact or justifies a belief" (Lomas et al. 2005, 7). Policy-makers view other types of information, such as personal experience, anecdotes, expert opinions, and medico-legal reports, as evidence (Black 2001; Lomas 2000). While scientists determine the applicability and relative value of evidence on the basis of its methodological rigour, policy-makers consider its local relevance (Lomas et al. 2005). The Canadian Health Services Research Foundation has cautioned that unlike what happens in medical decision making, evidence plays a less influential role in managerial and public policy decisions:

As the concept of "evidence-based decision-making" expands from evidence-based medicine into the world of managers and policy-makers, we would do well to examine the generalizability from service professionals to this different kind of decision maker. The assumptions underpinning evidence-based medicine may not translate directly to the work of managers and policy makers ... The nature of uncertainty faced by clinicians is different to that faced by managers and policy makers. Assuming that the role of all decision makers is to combine facts and values to determine action, then the weight of uncertainty for clinicians is balanced toward clarifying the facts and less about the values. The uncertainty for managers and policy makers is weighted increasingly toward the [values]. (2000, 2–3)

Although the use of "evidence," and research evidence in particular, has gained traction in health policy circles, it is still only one of many influences on the decision-making process. For research to influence decisions, it must align with the values of the policy-makers (Lomas 1990). The debate over what constitutes evidence and the role that it plays in decisions spurred the Canadian Health Services Research Foundation (2000) to adopt the broader term "evidence-informed" rather than "evidence-based."

What types of evidence form the basis of health policy decisions in Newfoundland & Labrador? What parts of the institutional structure dominate decision making? What values influence decisions and views of evidence? This chapter uses the "Framework of Understanding the Context of Decision Making" to examine health policy decisions taken by the government of Newfoundland & Labrador and compares policy decisions related to the organization and delivery of health care services with decisions related to health promotion. This review and analysis is limited to publicly available materials, such as media articles, government reports and press releases, research papers, and the report on the Commission of Inquiry into Hormone Receptor Testing, as well as the Progressive Conservative (PC) Party of Newfoundland & Labrador platforms from the 2003, 2007, and 2011 elections. By describing the nature of the information used to substantiate decisions, the elements of the institutional structure that dominate the decision-making process, and the values that influence the decisions made, we may hope to gain a better understanding of how the three domains (institutional structures, information, and values) interrelate and how policy decisions were made by the government of Newfoundland & Labrador.

BACKGROUND

Danny Williams and the PC Party swept to power on the heels of the Sudden Acute Respiratory Syndrome (SARS) outbreak in the spring of 2003. A previously unknown disease that was described as atypical pneumonia, SARS presented with flu-like symptoms accompanied by respiratory problems. As a new disease, little was known about its treatment, diagnosis, prevention, or transmission (Health Canada 2004). In Canada, individuals exposed to SARS were quarantined for ten days and instructed to limit contact with others. By the end of 2003, there were 251 SARS cases and forty-three deaths reported in Canada and 8,096 cases and 774 deaths world-wide (World Health Organization n.d.). Roughly one-fifth of SARS patients were health care providers.

By the fall of 2003, most provinces across Canada were implementing the recommendations of the National Advisory Committee on SARS report, *Learning from SARS – Renewal of Public Health in Canada* (also known as the Naylor report). Not surprisingly, given the timing of the report's release and the provincial election in October 2003, there was little mention of public health in the PC Party's platform (2003). Strengthening public health capacity was, however, one of the four strategic directions outlined in the Department of Health and Community Services' 2006–2008 Strategic Plan (Newfoundland and Labrador 2006h). "Public health" refers to the range of programs, services, and policies that are designed to promote health and prevent disability, morbidity, and premature mortality (Canada 2011). Public health initiatives target groups of people or the population as a whole and include activities such as vaccinations, healthy-eating and physical-activity campaigns, health education, disease surveillance, and legislation. In contrast, the term "public *health-care* system" refers to the system of treatment of individuals that usually takes place in institutional settings (e.g., in hospitals, clinics, and health professionals' offices) and is financed through the government-funded health insurance scheme (i.e., "medicare") in Canada.

In 2002, the Royal Commission on the Future of Health Care in Canada (the Romanow Commission) released its final report. In addition to endorsing the five principles of the Canada Health Act (universality, comprehensiveness, public administration, portability, and accessibility), the report called for increased accountability and review of health system performance; increased federal health funding through dedicated cash transfers, particularly targeting a number of key areas (including wait times, health human resources, home care, primary health care, "pharmacare," population and public health, aboriginal health, and electronic health records); and improving accessibility to services, drugs, and technology. The federal and provincial governments responded to the Romanow report with the 2003 First Ministers' Accord, which largely foreshadowed the Ten-Year Plan to Strengthen Health Care of 2004 (Health Canada 2003). Many promises in the PCs' 2003 election platform concerning the delivery of health services largely relate to the themes identified in the Romanow report and the 2003 First Ministers' Accord. For example, the bulk of the platform's promises in a section about health care featured subheadings concerning "a shared

responsibility," "predictable long-term funding," "[expanding] medicare to include home care and pharmacare," a "focus on patient care,"
"timely access to health services," "access to quality care," and "access to
technology." These promises largely echoed the sentiments and funding
conditions made in the report, the accord, and related federal/provincial/
territorial discussions.

CASE STUDY

Policy Decisions regarding Health Care Organization and Delivery

The Commission of Inquiry on Hormone Receptor Testing marks a
pivotal period during which decision making in health policy was transformed in Newfoundland & Labrador. The Williams government's
efforts to reorganize health services in the province, manage the HINI
immunization campaign, and negotiate physician wages illustrate the
shifts in the types of evidence, the roles of the institutional structures,
and the dominant values that influenced policy decisions.

In September 2004, the provincial government announced the consolidation of the health authorities from fourteen health and community
services boards into four regional integrated health authorities (Newfoundland and Labrador 2004b). The amalgamation of health regions,
preceded by regional operational reviews, had fulfilled a 2003 PC platform promise to re-examine and streamline the regional organization of
health services in the province (PC Party 2003). Despite the reorganization, during the first term of the Williams government there was generally
little controversy related to the government's health reforms and policy
decisions, until the media began reporting problems with tests used in
the treatment of breast cancer. Problems with the estrogen (ER) and progesterone (PR) hormone receptor tests conducted in the province were
first detected by Eastern Health's staff in May 2005 (Cameron 2009).
Following an informal internal investigation, Eastern Health decided to
retest all breast cancer patients who had been tested between 1997 and
2005 and whose initial ER/PR status was clinically negative. The ER/PR
test helps determine whether a breast cancer patient would benefit from
anti-hormonal therapy. Eastern Health had identified a number of false
negative cases who, on the basis of their incorrect tests, would not have
been offered Tamoxifen or an aromatase inhibitor (Cameron 2009).
Despite its decision to retest patients, Eastern Health had not established

a protocol for communicating with patients. It had also decided against disclosing concerns about the ER/PR tests to the public.

Internal and external reviews found that the problems with ER/PR testing stemmed from improper techniques in the handling of tissue and the testing of slides, as well as inadequate quality control and quality assurance practices. The first review was conducted by a local pathologist before the ER/PR problems came to light. Two additional reviews were done by Canadian experts in pathology and immunohistochemistry at the request of Eastern Health after the ER/PR problems were detected. Despite these reviews, Eastern Health personnel continued to suggest to government officials in the Department of Health and Community Services and cabinet that a change in testing equipment was the cause of the incorrect test results (Cameron 2009).

The media first broke the story about ER/PR testing problems in October 2005 (Cameron 2009). The reporter had incorrectly heard that there were problems with mammography tests and was informed by Eastern Health that the problems were instead related to ER/PR tests. Eastern Health then hastily began to contact patients after the problems were reported by the press. Eastern Health and the Department of Health and Community Services provided little other public comment until August 2006, when Eastern Health declared that it had contacted all patients who had been affected by the retesting. In December 2006, as part of a technical briefing to local media, Eastern Health reported an error rate of 12 percent among the retested cases. It continued to suggest that the testing problems were due to equipment changes.

In May 2007, a news story reported that the retesting had produced an actual error rate of 42 percent (Cameron 2009). It also stated that the number of patients whose test results had changed was higher than the number Eastern Health had reported at its technical briefing. The story was based on an affidavit sworn by an Eastern Health employee as part of a class action suit. The story renewed concerns about whether all patients who had been retested had been contacted. Assurances from Eastern Health led Ross Wiseman, the minister of health and community services, to declare in the House of Assembly that all patients had been contacted. The minister also directed Eastern Health to place advertisements in provincial newspapers stating that it had contacted all retested patients and had notified patients and their doctors of test results. Nonetheless, reports by patients that they had not been contacted continued to swirl.

Closer scrutiny of the information Eastern Health had provided to the Department of Health and Community Services, as well as the ongoing public outcry, led the provincial government to question Eastern Health's handling of the ER/PR retesting. With less than six months before the October 2007 provincial election, the government established the Commission of Inquiry on Hormone Receptor Testing. In addition, Premier Williams announced the creation of the Task Force on Adverse Health Events and appointed "the province's most senior public servant," Robert Thompson, as its chair (Newfoundland and Labrador 2007d). In June, Justice Margaret Cameron was appointed to lead the Commission of Inquiry.

The PC party's 2007 election platform made relatively little mention of the ER/PR testing scandal, promising only to follow through on the recommendation of the Task Force and the Commission of Inquiry (PC Party 2007). In fact, in comparison to the 2003 platform, few pages are dedicated to the delivery of health services in the province. The 2007 platform made promises related to the acquisition and upgrading of capital equipment and infrastructure, the implementation of health human resource management, the provision of timely access to care, the development and implementation of chronic disease and mental health strategies, the removal of financial barriers, the continued implementation of electronic health records, and the strengthening of public health capacity. During the campaign, when asked about the ER/PR scandal Williams would respond by saying that the inquiry had been struck to uncover answers.

As Kate Puddister and James Kelly describe in chapter 7 of this book, the Commission of Inquiry heard from witnesses between March and October 2008 (Cameron 2009). The witnesses included patients and family members of patients who had been affected by testing errors; health care providers (physicians, nurses, etc.); administrators from regional health authorities; bureaucrats and elected officials, including the premier; cancer care advocates; researchers from the Newfoundland & Labrador Centre for Health Information; and experts in pathology, cancer care, ethics, and patient communication. The proceedings were webcast and televised on a local community channel, and developments were regularly the topic of news articles and call-in shows.

Testimony from health authority administrators decried the budget cuts and confusion that followed the amalgamation of health regions in 2004. The chair of the Eastern Health board, appointed by the minister, refused to apologize to patients. By May, Premier Williams was attacking the very commission he had established to restore confidence in the health system (CBC News 2008j). He accused the commissioner of taking an inquisitorial approach and focusing on assigning blame rather than suggesting solutions.

The impact of the inquiry on the Williams administration reached beyond cancer care: it changed the government's approach to re-organizing the health care system. In late August 2009, the new health minister, Paul Oram, announced that the government would be cutting laboratory and x-ray services in the communities of Lewisporte and Flower's cove (CBC News 2009c). The announcements were met with protests in both communities, where crowds "booed Premier Danny Williams" (CBC News 2009d). The government reversed its decision in Flower's Cove – the minister denied any connection to an upcoming by-election in the community (CBC News 2009d). The following week, Jerome Kennedy took over the Health and Community Services port-folio Oram, who resigned from politics citing health problems stemming from the demanding nature of the health portfolio. While mulling can-cellation of the cuts in Lewisporte, Kennedy noted that the government was re-evaluating its decision to review laboratory and x-ray services in the province: "[We're] reviewing whether or not the review is even necessary at this point ... [s]o, we are going to play it by ear right now and really see where we go with Lewisporte and Flower's Cove" (CBC News 2009g).

This would not be the only time the minister of health and commun-ity services reversed his position in response to public pressure. The next challenge to the government's handling of a major health issue came amidst the HINI swine flu immunization campaign in November 2009. The response to the pandemic was one of the first serious challenges to the public health system, which had been strengthened following the SARS outbreak. On the advice of medical experts and the Public Health Agency of Canada, the government identified priority groups to be vac-cinated first, with additional groups announced as supplies became avail-able (CBC News 2009a). However, following a public backlash, Minster Kennedy abandoned expert advice and expanded the criteria to include all children (as opposed to children in grade 3 and younger). He cited the emails he had received from parents as the justification for his policy change (CBC News 2009h). A week later, on his decision to vaccinate seniors, Kennedy noted, "I will not blindly follow the medical advice" (CBC News 2009f). Health officials had advised that seniors were at lower risk of HINI infection than other groups of the population.

The inquiry – or more correctly, Williams' actions during the inquiry – had a lasting impact on salary negotiations between the government and the province's physicians. In May 2008, during the inquiry, Premier Williams and Ross Wiseman (minister of health and community services) met privately with pathologists and oncologists, who identified their demanding workloads, poor remuneration, and high turnover as contributors to the ER/PR problems (CBC News 2008b, 2008g). Two weeks after the meeting, Minister Wiseman announced an increase in the salary for pathologists in the province (Newfoundland and Labrador 2008c). The new wage package represented an increase of $73,000, or roughly 35 percent of their base pay rate. Similar remuneration packages were offered to medical and radiation oncologists. The wage increase was described by the minister as a one-time offer in response to an exceptional situation (Newfoundland and Labrador 2008c).

While the agreement was received favourably by oncologists and pathologists, the Newfoundland & Labrador Medical Association (NLMA) and many of its members saw it as a divisive decision that privileged some physicians over others (CBC News 2008e). The NLMA had not been involved in the negotiations and had heard of the agreement only after being informed by individual oncologists and pathologists who had been approached personally by the minister. The NLMA did not receive information from the government about the agreement until much later. In a letter to the NLMA membership, President Joe Tumilty wrote that the decision was "entirely unilateral with absolutely no consultation whatsoever" (Tumilty 2008). While he did not oppose the increase, he warned that the government's decision would be divisive if not applied to members of the entire medical community who faced similar working conditions and hardships. He noted that the tactics ran contrary to the spirit of the provincial Medical Care Act, which states that the association may "act on behalf of its members or a group or section or division of its members, and negotiate for, and on their behalf, with other persons or agencies, including government agencies."[1] Premier Williams argued that the pay increases were necessary to attract and keep physicians in the province (CBC News 2008c).

In July 2008 three gynecological oncologists threatened to resign if they too did not receive the salary increase awarded to the oncologists and pathologists (CBC News 2008a). In addition, the three physicians demanded several improvements to their workplace. After initially refusing their demands and insisting that the province could cope without the three physicians (CBC News 2008b), the government reversed its initial stance and granted the same wage increase given to oncologists and pathologists (CBC News 2008c). It was also extended to seven other specialists who treated hematological and pediatric cancers. In its news release, the government detailed its agreement to a number of additional demands made by the physicians, including demands for reclassification of their services; additional office space; secretarial, research, and clinical support for the services; and operating time (Newfoundland and Labrador 2008d). Williams noted to the media that making amendments outside the collective bargaining agreement set a dangerous precedent (CBC News 2008c). The government's concession highlights another example of how public outcry and media coverage influenced policy decisions.

In September 2009 the existing contract between physicians and the province expired (CBC News 2010e). The contract, negotiated by the NLMA, covered remuneration for all salaried and fee-for-service family physicians, general practitioners, and specialists. Fee-for-service physicians receive a standard, negotiated fee for providing a specific service (Léger 2011). The physician's remuneration depends on the number of services provided. Fee-for-service physicians submit invoices to their provincial or territorial health insurance plan – in Newfoundland & Labrador, the Medical Care Plan (MCP). Fee-for-service physicians are independent small business operators; they act as their own employers and are responsible for running their own medical clinics (managing staff, equipment, etc.) and arranging their own employment benefits (including parental, disability, and annual leaves, insurance plans, pensions, etc.). The majority of doctors in Canada receive most of their income through fee-for-service payments (Canadian Institute for Health Information 2005).

Salaried physicians in Canada are generally employees of hospitals or regional health authorities (Léger 2011). They are remunerated a set amount based on the number of hours worked and receive employment benefits. Since the physician is an employee, the physician is not responsible for overhead. Salaries are a means of attracting and retaining physicians to smaller markets (such as rural communities) where there is unlikely to be a sufficient number of patients to generate high income through fee-for-service billings.

The number and proportion of physicians paid by fee-for-service and salary vary by province; Newfoundland & Labrador at the time had the highest proportion of salaried physicians in Canada (excluding the territories). An estimated 42 percent of physicians in the province derived the majority of their earnings from salary (Canadian Institute for Health Information 2005). The government's decision to augment the wages of pathologists and cancer-treating physicians created a "two-tiered system" among the salaried specialists (Stokes Sullivan 2010a). By September 2009, when the existing contract between the NLMA and the government expired, roughly sixty (40 percent) of the province's 150 salaried specialist physicians received the higher salary rates (Stokes Sullivan 2010a).

Negotiations for a new contract began on 13 April 2009 (Newfoundland and Labrador Medical Association 2010). In March 2010, Premier Williams publicly declared the NLMA contract demands to be excessive, and the provincial government withdrew its negotiating team from bargaining (CBC News 2010g). The government also suggested that there would be no additional increases for physicians who had received wage increases in 2008. In November, fourteen salaried specialists, most of them located in St John's, resigned to protest the government's contract offer. They demanded that all salaried specialists receive the same increase in pay that had been awarded to pathologists and physicians who treated patients with cancer (CBC News 2010b). The resignations were met with a dismissive response from the minister, and Premier Williams took to the airwaves to comment on the ongoing negotiations on local television and call-in radio programs (Stokes Sullivan 2010a).

The NLMA held a well-coordinated publicity campaign that included a series of media briefings featuring the resigning physicians and the patients who would be affected by the withdrawal of their services (McLeod 2010). A series of news reports praising the individual physicians and highlighting the patients they helped ran in the media over the course of the following weeks (CBC News 2010d, 2010f; Stokes Sullivan 2010b, 2010c, 2010d; Sweet 2010). The government refused to renegotiate. Eighty-six percent of physicians voted to reject the government's offer (Canadian Press 2010a).

Following Danny Williams' resignation on 3 December 2010, the government, under the direction of Premier Kathy Dunderdale, took a softer, more conciliatory tone towards the doctors (CBC News 2010c). Health Minister Kennedy noted that he had received many emails from patients and parents who wanted the province to reach a deal with the physicians (CBC News 2010j; McLeod 2010). In a complete reversal of their stance in the previous contract offer (CBC News 2010a), Kennedy acceded to the demands of the fourteen specialists, and all salaried specialists were given the same increase in their base salary as the pathologists and cancer-treating physicians. All salaried specialists also received wage increases over the duration of the contract (CBC News 2010b).

Health Promotion Policy Decisions

The Williams government released a number of health promotion strategies aimed at improving the health and well-being of the population. Unlike decisions relating to health care organization and delivery, the approach to formulating policy related to health promotion remained stable over time.

In 2005, it released *Working Together for Mental Health: A Policy Framework for Mental Health and Addiction Services in Newfoundland and Labrador* (Newfoundland and Labrador 2005g). The framework, which had been developed in consultation with consumers, their families, and service providers, proposed the improvement and integration of mental health *with* addiction services. The call for integration recognized the "co-occurring" and interdependent nature of mental health and addictions issues and the need for a coordinated treatment approach. In addition to strengthening the mental health and addiction services provided by primary health care teams, the framework proposed developing and disseminating indicators to measure the quality of those services. These indicators would be used to promote system accountability and quality improvement.

The plan of 2006, *Achieving Health and Wellness: Provincial Wellness Plan for Newfoundland and Labrador* (Newfoundland and Labrador 2006a), built on and continued the work of the Provincial Wellness Council established under the previous Liberal administration. It proposed initiatives to foster healthy lifestyles, improve nutrition, reduce tobacco consumption, and prevent injuries; it highlighted priorities derived through broad-based consultation and emphasized collaboration across many government departments and with non-government organizations.

The *Provincial Healthy Aging Policy Framework* recognized the growing number of seniors in the province (Newfoundland and Labrador 2007e). By 2017, an estimated one in five residents of the province would be over the age of sixty-five. Between 2007 and 2017, the proportion of the population over the age of seventy-five would double from 6 to 12 percent. Like the other health promotion strategies announced by the Williams government, the *Provincial Healthy Aging Policy Framework* was developed through a series of consultations with government departments, the public, and local, regional, and provincial organizations. Among the priorities identified in the framework was the need for more research on issues of aging to support and inform policy and planning. The framework listed key areas for further research and allocated $200,000 per year to fund projects.

The initial consultations for developing a cancer control strategy for the province began in 2004 as a collaborative effort between the Department of Health and Community Services, the regional health authorities, and the Canadian Cancer Society – Newfoundland & Labrador Division. The final document, *Gaining Ground: A Provincial Cancer Control Policy Framework for Newfoundland and Labrador*, outlined nine policy directions that spanned the cancer care continuum (i.e., the various phases of possible intervention: prevention, screening, diagnosis, treatment, supportive care, and palliation) (Newfoundland and Labrador 2010d). It also proposed establishing the Provincial Cancer Control Advisory Committee to identify priorities, monitor progress, and create an evaluation strategy. The document highlights the need for evidence-based clinical and policy approaches.

POLITICAL DECISION MAKING IN NEWFOUNDLAND & LABRADOR

Although policy decisions related both to the organization and the delivery of health care services and to health promotion fall within the mandate of the Department of Health and Community Services, a comparison of policy decisions in these two areas during the Williams administration reveals striking differences. It is also revealing to consider the attributes of the policy issues. Soroka (2002) notes that an issue may vary in terms of obtrusiveness (the likelihood that individuals directly experience the effects of the issue), its concrete or abstract nature, and the drama and/or conflict associated with it. Although the style of decision making may have been similar at the start of the Williams era, the Commission of Inquiry on Hormone Receptor Testing marks a pivotal period during which decision making related to the organization and delivery of health care services appears to change. Notably, these decisions relate to issues that are obtrusive, concrete, and dramatic. After May 2007 (hereafter, post-inquiry), decision making was centralized in the executive, political expediency was highly valued, and colloquial knowledge was emphasized. In contrast, the inquiry had comparatively little effect on decision making related to health-promotion policies. These issues were unobtrusive, largely abstract, and involved little drama or conflict.

Policy options continued to be developed by the bureaucracy with input from a wide variety of government and non-government agencies. The decisions showed a growing reliance on scientific evidence and emphasized the values of equity, quality, and accountability.

Types and Sources of Information

In its handling of ER/PR hormone testing, the government relied on the information provided by Eastern Health and its medical experts. In her findings, Justice Cameron noted that "Eastern Health certainly failed in its duty to be forthright with Government, as on a number of occasions it withheld relevant information as to the extent and the cause of the problem from those charged with the responsibility for the quality of health care in the province" (2009, 456–7). However, she concluded that by blindly accepting the information provided by Eastern Health with little scrutiny, the department failed in its responsibility to ensure the quality of health service delivered in the province:

> The current legislative structure clearly establishes a relationship between the regional health authorities and the Minister and it is, in my view, the Minister who must exercise the oversight role. In the context of the ER/PR problem, it was the failure of the Department on behalf of the Minister to exercise due diligence in respect to the information provided that contributed to the Government's lack of appreciation of the problem ... had due diligence been exercised, departmental officials would have realized that there was a difference in their understanding of what was to be publicly communicated and what was in fact communicated and that certain figures relating to the number of patients affected by ER/PR which were being provided to the Department just did not add up. (Cameron 2009, 438)

The Department of Health and Community Services had failed to scrutinize the information provided by Eastern Health and, as a result, had not taken adequate actions to correct the testing problems or the decisions made by Eastern Health.

Given the rebuke, the reluctance of the government to rely on expert advice and evidence provided by bureaucrats in the health system is not unexpected. Post-inquiry, the minister reversed policy decisions that had been based on system reviews and scientific evidence. In defending his decision to cancel cuts to laboratory and x-ray services in two rural communities, Minster Kennedy noted at a debate during the 2011 election campaign that "there was an external review done in 2004 and if we had followed the recommendations at that time then there would be no rural health care left" (Quinn 2011).

Premier Williams and Minister Kennedy used direct media communications to frame policy decisions and shape public opinion. While this strategy may have proven effective in other policy areas, it appears to have had mixed success in health policy decisions, notwithstanding the premier's public apology (see chapter 7 in this book). Williams' negative comments about the Cameron Inquiry proved fruitless in squelching criticism of his government's handling of the ER/PR testing issue. Likewise, his attacks on physicians did little to sway public opinion during the physician contract negotiations. His affinity for using the media to frame issues and vet policy options suggests a desire to promote emotion-based policies over rational decision making (Marland and Kerby 2010).

In policy decisions made post-inquiry, the government appears to have placed greater emphasis on first-hand anecdotal information provided by individuals. For example, the decision to increase oncologists' wages came after a meeting between the physicians, the premier, and the minster of health and community services. Likewise, in justifying his position on HINI immunization priority groups and his reversal on remuneration for salaried specialists, Minister Kennedy cited personal emails from individual patients. The emphasis on the opinions of the "common man," or front-line worker, agrees with previous assessments of Premier Williams' decision-making style. In their study of the use of talk radio by political parties in Newfoundland, Marland and Kerby concluded that "public feedback on existing or newly implemented policy may prompt political actors to take action or speed up a process" (2010, 1012). The willingness to assuage the public backlash stirred by revelations at the Commission of Inquiry or by the rationing of flu vaccinations bolsters depictions of Williams as a leader with a "diminished appetite for confrontation with his people" (Marland 2010, 164).

In contrast, the four health promotion frameworks released by government cite extensive statistics and research studies to justify priorities and policy options. Both the *Provincial Healthy Aging Policy Framework* and *Gaining Ground: A Provincial Cancer Control Policy Framework for Newfoundland and Labrador* highlight the need for more local research (e.g., literature, performance, and health service utilization reviews; audits of available resources; program and outcome evaluations, etc.) to inform policy and program planning. They facilitate research through grant funding or investment in surveillance and research infrastructure. They also call for the creation and release of quality indicators to provide regular assessment of system performance in relation to population health and well-being, healthy aging, mental health and addiction services, and cancer control.

The Role of Institutional Structures

The negative publicity from the handling of the ER/PR testing issue was the first public backlash against the government's handling of health system matters and appears to have triggered more public, direct, and urgent intervention by the executive into health policy decisions. Post-inquiry, the premier and the minister appear to be *more* directly involved in policy decisions, often overriding the bureaucracy and its senior officials. The premier's interference in ministerial policy decisions was not unprecedented. Elizabeth Marshall, the minister of health and community services from October 2003 to October 2004, quit the cabinet because Premier Williams made decisions relating to the department without consulting or informing her (CBC News 2004). Likewise, testimony at the Inquiry on Hormone Receptor Testing revealed that senior bureaucrats had provided information to Williams about Eastern Health's progress with ER/PR retesting without informing Minister Tom Osborne (Cameron 2009). Marland (2010) suggests that the usurping of ministerial authority by the premier's office and the negative view of institutions are characteristics of a populist leader. Likewise, Williams' penchant for decisive action in the face of perceived crisis, such as his short-sighted decision to increase oncologists' wages, reinforces his reputation as a "leader who is willing to bypass elite power structures" (Marland 2010, 165). The involvement of the premier is viewed as integral in bringing about policy change in the Williams government (Marland and Kerby 2010).

The development of health promotion policies seems to have provided a greater role for the bureaucracy. There have been no reversals of health promotion policy, and the wide consultation of stakeholders and the generally uncontroversial health promotion positions adopted by government have not engendered organized public protests and negative backlash. Moreover, like most health promotion activities, a drastic improvement in outcomes (such as health status or cancer control) is not expected within an election cycle, and there is relatively little media scrutiny of reported progress to create controversy or a political appetite for greater executive involvement.

Dominant Values

While the reviews of the health system conducted in the pre-inquiry period suggest that cost-effectiveness was one of the values that shaped decisions related to health care organization and delivery, accessibility appears to dominate policy decisions in this area in the post-inquiry period, at the expense of values of quality or cost containment. For example, the decisions to continue to operate laboratories in two rural communities run counter to the growing number of studies that have shown that better quality in health care is positively correlated with higher volumes. Even the Cameron Report noted that the small number of cases seen in rural hospitals contributed to errors in hormone receptor testing (Cameron 2009).

In contrast, the health promotion frameworks announced by the Williams government emphasized equity, quality, and accountability, as well as accessibility. For example, high-risk and vulnerable groups were prioritized to promote equity, the development of indicators and evaluation frameworks was proposed as a means to demonstrate quality of services and accountability of strategy partners, and the proposed health promotion strategies did not suggest limiting access to services for any group. Given the alignment of the scientific evidence with the values that appear to shape policy-making in health promotion, it is not surprising that policy decisions were based on scientific rather than colloquial evidence. Lomas notes that "where there was consensus on values, the research was permitted to justify them and to draw out the beliefs and assumptions for the policy" (1990, 533).

This review of policy decisions highlights the evidence, institutions, and values that shaped health policy decisions during the Williams era. Decision making and the policy-making process evolved over the seven years of PC government under the leadership of Danny Williams. The Commission of Inquiry on Hormone Receptor Testing has had a substantial impact on the policy decision-making process as it has related to the provision of health services. Ultimately, the type of evidence, the prevailing values, and the role of the institutional structures have varied depending on the attributes of the issues. Obstructive, concrete, or dramatic issues drew more direct involvement of the premier or his minsters and often led to decisions supported by anecdotal evidence, embracing populist sentiments and overruling bureaucratic structures and pro-cesses. Post-inquiry decision making reinforced the power of the pre-mier while eroding the authority of institutional structures and blurring the boundaries between legislative and administrative decision making. Throughout the post-inquiry period, satisfaction ratings – those who were completely or mostly satisfied with "the overall performance of the provincial government led by Premier Danny Williams" – never dipped below 85 percent (Corporate Research Associates 2012), suggesting strong public support for Williams' approach. The direct and prevailing involvement of the premier in ministerial issues, as well as the continued public support for this approach, highlight the premier's powerful and dominating influence in government policy decisions.

NOTE

1   Medical Act, 2011, S.N.L., ch. M-4.02, s. 5(2)b. http://www.assembly.nl.ca/legislation/sr/statutes/m04-02.htm#5.

9

Educational Governance and Policy in Newfoundland and Labrador

GERALD GALWAY

COMPARATIVE THEORY

Although the study of politics has a long history, the field of policy studies is relatively new; most of the classic literature has emerged since the 1950s. Traditional theories of policy development have their roots in a positivist epistemology in which certainty, rationality, and impartiality are valued as guiding constructs and where it believed that economic and social costs and benefits can be assessed and policy decisions identified in a surgical, unbiased manner, independent of political ideology, personal beliefs, and other forms of ambiguity (Stone 1988). Over the past quarter century, however, a number of authors have questioned the usefulness and validity of the dominant policy development theories (Lindblom and Woodhouse 1993; Majone 1989; Stone 2002; Taylor et al. 1997).

Economic-rationalist theories have been widely criticized because they fail to account for individual values, fears, and personal beliefs; political interests; advocacy; and anecdotal influences. The work of policy theorists such as Beck (1994, 1997), Kingdon (1995), Levin (2004), and Stone (2002) has recognized the interplay of rationalism with other influences such as personal bias, advocacy, and political exigency in the policy process. As Levin comments, "The political world is ... shaped by beliefs more than facts" (2001, 14). Kingdon's work is important because it expands the policy development process beyond rational choice to include a role for the active intervention of ideas and policy options that go beyond efficiency or personal or group benefits to include considerations such as equity, altruism, advocacy, and the public interest.

Furthermore, this framework opens space in the literature for less tangible policy evidence, including argument, persuasion, reasoning, interpretation, and the influence of political considerations – key elements of policy formation described by Lindblom and Woodhouse (1993), Majone (1989), and Stone (2002).

Part of the reason for such diversity in how policy theorists understand policy development/analysis relates to larger societal changes – a more impatient and critical public, a lessening of faith in traditional structures (government, churches, schools, and industry), global and demographic changes that have affected individual communities, and the rise of individualism and the market-state (Bobbit 2002; Fleming 1997; Glass and Rud 2012). Beck (1997) argues that with the general erosion of industrial modernity in all realms of social activity, faith in basic certainties about the nature of progress is undergoing a gradual collapse. According to Taylor et al., many policy definitions emanating from economic-rationalist discourse are misleading because they give the impression that there is a general consensus about the values underpinning policy and because they do not address "the political nature of policy as a compromise which is struggled over at all stages by competing interests" (1997, 24).

If we have learned anything about education policy through sixty years of study, it is that policy-making is complex. It involves multiple actors across time and space; it is argued, debated, and disputed by almost everyone from teachers and academics to politicians, industry leaders, advocacy groups, and parents. Many issues in Canadian society are cast as educational problems requiring immediate intervention by policymakers and creating an unstable and risky political environment. Public expectations for education have never been higher, and there are many competing interests for how schools should function and how education should be structured. In this chapter I consider one of those contested areas: educational governance.

In the following case studies I examine two significant educational governance changes in Newfoundland & Labrador: the replacement of the denominationally based system with a public system of education in 1997 by the Liberal government of Brian Tobin and the subsequent consolidation and centralization of public educational governance by the Progressive Conservative (PC) government of Danny Williams in 2004. Both are examples of governance change, but the two cases are fundamentally different. The social and economic antecedents to the 1997 changes pushed the government to establish a public education system, but even then required a royal commission and two public referenda. In the resulting system, with eleven non-denominational districts, governance still rested predominantly with regionally representative elected school boards. The 2004 consolidation of English school boards from nine to three on the island portion of the province and the appointment of interim "transitional committees" to replace elected school boards, had the result of diminishing regional authority for education and accumulating that governance power within the Williams government and a few "super boards."

BACKGROUND

The influence of the Christian churches is engraved in the social and economic fabric of Newfoundland & Labrador, but perhaps it is most evident in the province's system of education. The first Education Act of 1836 envisioned publicly funded schools open to children of all denominations; however, early attempts to reach agreement on how such schools would be organized failed. Funding for education was instead divided on a proportional basis among the Christian churches, inscribing in the Newfoundland way of life a denominationally based system that lasted for more than a century and a half (McCann 1988). By the turn of the century, there were separate publicly funded schools for adherents to the four major Christian faiths – Roman Catholic, Anglican, Methodist, and Salvation Army – creating the conditions for a long legacy of separation and underfunding.

The problems inherent in providing adequate funding for duplicate school systems came to light early and persisted until the end of the twentieth century. In the 1860s, politicians and the public complained of "widespread illiteracy, uneducated teachers, and deprivation arising from grants apportioned per head of denominational population, rather than on the basis of need" (Rowe 1964, 47). Almost a century later, when Newfoundland entered Canada as its tenth province, general educational conditions were still quite backward – underdeveloped, poorly resourced, regionally disparate, and inaccessible to many citizens (Rowe 1964). Annual expenditure per student for elementary and secondary education was approximately $35, about one third of the $104 Canadian average (Crocker and Riggs 1979; Wisenthal 2008). After Confederation, the new provincial government had a difficult time making up for lost ground. Teacher qualifications remained low, and the system was in dire need of expansion and upgrading. However, an unprecedented

63 percent rise in student enrollment (approximately fifty thousand students) between 1950 and 1960 stifled any real progress towards meeting the government's goal of advancing education to Canadian norms. Even though $70 million had been spent on education over the ten-year period, Premier Joey Smallwood admitted that in relative terms the situation in the late 1950s was worse than it had been in 1949 (Andrews 1985). When Philip Warren released the findings of the report of the Royal Commission on Education and Youth in 1967, he confirmed that many schools in the province still had only outdoor washroom facilities or no washrooms at all; few had gymnasiums, libraries, or science labs; most teachers had not completed university degrees; and few rural students made it to high school. The impact of these conditions was reflected in the achievement outcomes of the province's students. In the 1960s, grade 9 pass rates typically fell in the range of 50 to 55 percent (Newfoundland and Labrador 1967). By the 1970s, there had been some improvement, but more than a third of students still failed to reach grade eleven (Galway 2011).

As the 1980s approached, the education budget was nearing $300 million (Crocker and Riggs 1979), but the province was struggling to keep pace with school construction and maintenance, teacher salaries, pupil transportation costs, and an expensive and geographically isolated duplicative infrastructure. Enrollment, which climbed to 163,000 in 1971–72, had begun its dramatic forty-year decline, and as the 1980s progressed, the gravity of the enrollment crisis was apparent. By the early 1990s, the number of school-aged children had dropped to approximately 125,000, creating more than 130 low-enrollment[1] schools (Newfoundland and Labrador 1992c). In the dying days of the Peckford government, there was considerable public discussion over the future of the denominational school system. Funding issues, inefficiency, low achievement, and a perceived mismatch between the school curriculum and the demands of a changing economy led to several policy studies (McCann 2002). In 1986, the Royal Commission on Employment and Unemployment charged that few changes had been made in the system since the implementation of some of the recommendations from the Warren Commission two decades earlier (Warren 2012). That same year, the Newfoundland Teachers' Association released a report, *Exploring New Pathways,* in which they argued that the system was isolationist, over-administered, and underfunded (Hancock 2012). Then, in 1989 the report of a government-appointed task force found that the system suffered from a "crisis of low expectations," and it called for better instruction, improvements to schools, and sweeping curricular changes (Newfoundland and Labrador 1989).

During the last two decades, each provincial government – sometimes with the involvement of the courts – has restructured its governance model for education with the stated goal of improving operational efficiency (Galway et al. 2012). One of the most publicly visible reforms has been a reduction in the number of school boards, largely through district consolidation (Canadian School Boards Association 1995; Dibbon, Sheppard, and Brown 2012; Fleming 1997; Lessard and Brassard 2005; Watson et al. 2004; Williams 2003). The changes to education in Newfoundland & Labrador have been notable in that the government centralized governance, first with the move to a public system in 1997 and second in 2004 by combining nine of its public school districts on the island portion of the province into three.

Consolidation of 1997

Philip Warren, education minister in the Wells government and one of the architects of the reforms of 1997, recently recounted the state of the education system when the Wells government came to power and the reasons why a review of the denominational system was inevitable:

> Declining enrollments, fiscal restraint, and demands for improved programs, facilities, and services had highlighted the problems of duplication inherent in the system ... Some claimed that education had become a major impediment to our competitiveness in the information-based economy, nationally and internationally, and a threat to our place in the world and our standard of living ... Such developments brought unprecedented pressure on policymakers and politicians to improve educational performance and reform our system. (Warren 2012, 43)

Although some of the contributing factors to school reform – such as enrollment decline and duplication of infrastructure – were already well recognized, the economic currents that pushed the reform of the system in 1997 were hard to ignore. In 1991, Canada's inflation rate had risen to 5.9 percent, and by 1995, the debt-to-GDP ratio peaked at a staggering 71 percent before trending downwards by the end of the decade (Canada 2001). The federal government under Prime Minister Jean Chretien made deep cuts to federal spending, including reductions in government-to-government transfers (Egan and Palmer 2011). In Newfoundland & Labrador, federal transfers for post-secondary education decreased by 49 percent between 1991 and 1996 (Newfoundland and Labrador 1999). At the same time, the closure of the $700 million northern cod fishery displaced some thirty-one thousand fish harvesters and processors, the vast majority of whom lived in Newfoundland & Labrador (Newfoundland and Labrador 1999). A resulting wave of unemployment, out-migration, and urbanization dominated the social and political agenda of the provincial government for the remainder of Premier Wells' term in office and beyond. Accordingly, when the royal commission brought forward its call in 1992 to restructure the education system, much of its case was based on addressing issues of fiscal accountability. While acknowledging the significant role that the churches had played in the development of education in Newfoundland, the royal commission would not endorse their continued involvement, taking instead the position that the existing administrative structure was no longer reasonable or viable.

The ten-year period between 1990 and 2000 was punctuated by numerous restructuring debates, referenda, senate hearings, constitutional amendments, and legislative changes. When Premier Wells stepped down in 1996, four years after the report of the commission, the provincial government had still not reached agreement with the churches on a model for a restructured school system. After further attempts to reach a compromise failed, Premier Brian Tobin took a much harder line and aggressively pursued a different policy option – a fully non-denominational system. The premier charged that discussions with the denominational authorities had been a never-ending debate, with the provincial government, the school boards, the teachers' association, parents, and students on one side and the churches on the other.

Was the negotiation between government and the churches a genuine attempt to reach a settlement compromise, or was it just a public relations exercise? The question is still contested (Fagan 2012). Warren claims that the denominational authorities and their advisors underestimated the resolve of the government to push forward the reform agenda and misread the public mood, "not realizing that many citizens of all denominations no longer supported the system, and were prepared to vote accordingly" (2012, 69). The choice of the churches to prolong the process by contesting, through the courts, key aspects of how schools would be designated under a new governance system served only to frustrate government negotiators. For their part, the Roman Catholic Church and the Pentecostal Assemblies regarded the centralization of governance (and the appropriation of school property without compensation) as a grave injustice. Fagan implies that government acted in bad faith and "failed to seize the opportunity to provide a fair and balanced resolution that would meet the stated goals of all parties" (129). Either way, after such a protracted period of public discourse, many people had grown tired of the continued uncertainty; a 1997 referendum on the question of school governance resulted in 73 percent of voters opting for a public school system. The scope of the subsequent system reform was unprecedented; between 1997 and 2000, in the name of efficiency and modernization, twenty-seven school boards were merged into eleven, and more than 150 schools were closed.

In terms of governance, Premier Tobin accomplished more than a transfer of power from the denominational school boards to the new public school boards. Among the significant changes that were obscured in the tangle of school and district closures, teacher transfers, and student reassignments was a new governance relationship between the public school boards and the government. The new system imposed a model with significantly greater accountability requirements. A new Schools Act stipulated an enhanced role for the Department of Education (DOE), included provisions for more accountability to government, and gave additional power to the minister. Among these changes were requirements for written approval before hiring a school board's director of education and for written approval of employment contracts.[2]

Consolidation of 2004

I have noted elsewhere (Galway 2012) that in a contracting education system, the relationship between enrollment and staffing does not follow a linear model. For a host of reasons, there are limits to how far efficiency measures may be extended. Enrollment decline is not uniformly distributed; as such, reductions in teacher allocations and operational funding are usually not scalable. There are also political risks. In her book *Policy Research in Educational Settings: Contested Terrain* (2000), Jenny Ozga observes that these are uncertain and risky times and that decisions about education must be negotiated with a diverse and impatient public.

Such was the case in the aftermath of the newly restructured education system. Facing growing pressure from school boards and the public, in 1999 – just two years after reforming the system – the provincial government decided to appoint another task force: the Ministerial Panel on Educational Delivery in the Classroom. The Sparkes-Williams commission, as it became known, was struck to take on the job of resolving a mounting list of system-level grievances, but the vexing problem facing the panel was how to manage the allocation of teachers during a period of enrollment decline while recognizing the needs of small, rural schools.

The panel's recommendations, which included equipping schools, increasing the allocation of teachers, and hiring teachers for more online learning, were welcomed by school boards. A new approach to apportioning teachers recognized and accounted for factors like multi-grading, school size, and grade level in determining appropriate staffing allocations. However, the recommendations were expensive and cost government more than $20 million in the first year of implementation alone (Newfoundland and Labrador 2000). Moreover, public satisfaction with the changes was short-lived. In 2003, just three years after the new funding model was implemented, the Newfoundland and Labrador Teachers' Association (NLTA) presented to government and school boards a brief titled *Putting the Teacher Back in Teaching* (2003). In the brief, the NLTA called for increases in teaching and school board positions, more school-based secretarial and technical staff, and teacher assistants to help with non-teaching duties in schools. Such was the educational landscape in Newfoundland & Labrador when the PC government, led by Danny Williams, came to power in 2003.

Armed with a consultant's report showing a large current account deficit, the new government wasted little time in moving forward on its own centralization agenda. In a surprise move, as part of the 2004–05 budget, the education minister announced plans to further consolidate school districts in an effort to achieve $6 million in administrative savings. The plan called for a reduction in the number of school districts on the island portion of the province from nine to three – eliminating five central offices – with the remaining boards covering significantly larger geographic regions. More surprising was the schedule for consolidation: the government's plan was slated to come into effect in September 2004 – allowing just four months to reorganize the system in time for schools to reopen under the new structure. In a 2004 press release justifying the change, the government made this argument:

With enrolment forecasts projecting just over 60,000 students by 2011, further consolidation of school boards is warranted ... Just four years after the 1996–97 reorganization, the Sparkes-Williams Report of the Ministerial Panel on Educational Delivery in the Classroom (2000) ... considered recommending further school board consolidation. It stated: *"that some $13.8 million is dedicated to the operation of school board offices, and efforts to achieve efficiencies through future board consolidation would seem achievable and necessary within the next several years."* (Newfoundland and Labrador 2004f; italics in the original)

Although the Sparkes-Williams Commission commented on the challenges of resourcing an education system under sustained enrollment decline, it is doubtful that it envisioned such a sweeping change to school system governance. The commission actually rejected the idea of any further centralization of school boards, instead proffering the idea of partnerships and shared services within the school board structure as it existed at the time (Newfoundland and Labrador 2000). Most of the "savings" referenced in the 2004 budget speech would come from reductions in personnel, including senior district management, professional staff, and support staff. In a document titled *School Board Restructuring Transitional Committee Orientation Document* (Transition Document) sent to newly appointed "interim boards," government stipulated a pared-down staffing model with a significantly reduced complement of district administrators and program specialists (Newfoundland and Labrador 2004g).

Several researchers who have examined the centralization of school governance in Newfoundland & Labrador agree that the economic circumstances and other policy evidence on which the 1997 reforms were based are hard to refute (e.g., Austin and Hunter 2012; Dibbon, Sheppard, and Brown 2012; Galway and Dibbon 2012; Hancock 2012; Hodder 2012; Sheppard 2012; Warren 2012), but the justification for the consolidation of 2004 is far less apparent. One obvious problem is that the financial evidence does not support the government's position, expressed in the budget speech and in news releases, that the changes were motivated by a need to reduce administrative costs. The centralization of school governance undertaken by the Williams government initially achieved its projected budget reduction, but its public commitment to reining in administrative costs was short-lived, raising questions about the possibility of different, more strategic motives for the changes. In the year before school boards were consolidated, public spending on school district administration was $17.6 million. After districts were centralized in 2005–06, these expenditures fell to $12.2 million (Newfoundland and Labrador 2004a, 2005f). However, by 2010–11, administrative costs had climbed to a staggering $22.0 million – an increase of 80 percent in just five years (Newfoundland and Labrador 2010c).

Dibbon, Sheppard, and Brown imply that the restructuring exercise in 2004 was actually a pretext for a broader centralization agenda intended to gain more direct influence over school board decision making. Their research, based on interviews with former school board members and senior school district and DOE personnel, characterizes the 2004 consolidation of school boards as "an attempt by government to gain greater control over school boards" (2012, 229). They cite several post-reform actions taken by the DOE that affected school board autonomy and the arm's-length relationship of government to its elected boards. Among the changes outlined in the Transition Documents were changes to hiring practices whereby the recruitment of school district directors was handled through the Public Service Commission and the DOE. In addition, there were changes in contract language, including a more robust role for the minister in approving and renewing appointments of district directors and other requirements intended to align school board operations with the strategic plan of the DOE.

In another study, Sheppard interviewed a large sample of senior educational administrators, analyzed relevant district and provincial documents, and drew the following conclusions: "The general view of most senior district officials is that since the 2004 legislated restructuring of school districts, government and its officials have assumed near total control over school boards ... Whether or not it was the government's intent to assume more control over the public education system, from the perspective of the vast majority of our interviewees inside and outside of school districts, this has become a reality" (2012, 212–13).

Sheppard's (2012) work also raises questions about how these changes in government-school board relations have the potential to politicize local decision making. As the government becomes more influential in the daily operations of school boards, there are far fewer independent voices in policy discussions, and the potential for those in the system to contest the direction of the DOE is diminished. While the primary focus of this discussion has been on the influence of elected school boards, public officials in the district administration, and those whom they represent, other interests, such as those of the teacher's union, are also affected. The existence of fewer governance structures means that there are fewer opportunities for teacher's organizations, such as local branches and special interest groups, to be engaged and consulted, thereby limiting their ability to influence the educational agenda. In one of Sheppard's interviews, a senior official of the NLTA expressed concerns that school boards have become too large to manage and too weak to challenge the government on education matters: "In the current structure no single district director, school board chair, or provincial school boards association challenges the government any more. The current climate stifles independent thought. The word controlling comes to mind ... The more the Department of Education and the Minister takes a top-down approach in directing the districts, the more things (programs) become politically driven" (2012, 212).

There have also been other, more public demonstrations of intervention in school board decision making. As noted in chapter 1 of this book, during a 2005 by-election campaign, Premier Williams circumvented the Nova Central School Board, which had adopted a motion to close a school in Bishop's Falls as part of its plan to reorganize the schools in that community. In expressing his views on the school board's intentions, the premier stated publicly that the government felt the school in question should remain open: "We're satisfied ... the school is viable" (Jackson 2005, 4). The premier went on to indicate that "this was not a sign that government is prepared to overrule school boards but if boards ... make decisions that are wrong decisions, then we have a responsibility to make the right ones" (Jackson 2005, 4). Subsequent to that public statement, in a special school board meeting held in April 2006, the Nova Central School District rescinded their earlier motion to close the school in question and introduced another motion to keep the school open (Nova Central School District 2006).

Historically, school boards have been free to make educational decisions independently from the daily machinations of provincial politics, provided that they act within boundaries specified in the legislation that governs them. However, after the 2004 education reform in Newfoundland & Labrador, there seems to have been a fundamental shift in the power relationships between the ministry, schools boards, and directors of education. It is only now, in the wake of educational reform, that researchers have been able to deconstruct and understand how such changes expose the apparent contradiction between strict government oversight of school district operations at one level and the political claim made by governmental authorities that school boards operate independently. Several researchers (e.g., Dibbon, Sheppard, and Brown 2012; Green 2012; Sheppard 2012) assert that in the aftermath of the reforms, boards became less autonomous, more bureaucratic, and more distanced from the constituencies they were elected to serve. They describe a post-reform education system that is more centralized and more sensitive to provincial politics and the government agenda in its day-to-day operations. While this shift may be evident to those closely connected to the governance and administration of education, these researchers assert that the gradual and subtle centralization of school governance has not been as clear to parents or to members of the general public. They argue that fewer districts, new contractual demands for district directors, different recruitment practices, and interference in board decisions signified government's intention to manage school districts from the centre.

POLITICAL DECISION MAKING IN NEWFOUNDLAND & LABRADOR

The centralization of the education system during the late 1990s represented a period of profound change for all those associated with education and was a defining chapter in the history of Newfoundland & Labrador. On balance, both the first and second wave of reforms accomplished the government's stated goals. However, the arguments for restructuring education in 1997 are far more compelling and must be conceptualized differently from the changes undertaken in 2004.

Elsewhere I have argued that a confluence of factors – demographic, social, political, and economic – created a "perfect storm" of policy influences, giving the Tobin government enough public support to reform the school system and centralize administration with ten elected public school boards (Galway and Dibbon 2012). This conceptualization draws on the work of Kingdon (1995), who explains policy formation in terms of agenda setting and decision making under conditions of ambiguity. Kingdon's multiple-stream model (problems, policies/solutions, and politics) implies that a cascade of real-life contextual factors – political events, interest groups, fiscal pressures, bureaucratic procedures, catastrophic events, and feedback on existing policies and programs, etc. – converge to shape the future of a public policy.

In the context of the Newfoundland education system, the "problems" stream emerged in the form of a radically contracting enrollment base, continued low achievement in the face of an increasingly global economy, fiscal shortfalls, poor-quality infrastructure, and a general loss of faith in the denominational structure. The "policies" stream identifies policy issues arising from ideas and concepts generated by political ideology or by formal policy actors such as networks of academics, the justice system, legislators and bureaucrats with common interests, commissions, or the recommendations of major studies. According to Kingdon's theory, in order to survive and be adopted, these policy proposals/solutions must be reinforced through the identification of the same policy option at about the same critical moment by another stream – a process described as coupling. By 1992, when the Williams Commission reported, the proposal to consolidate three separate school systems into a single public system had gained widespread approval. The government, the teachers' union, certain academic voices, the business sector, and a large segment of the population of parents were all calling for change, and it seemed that the only way to resolve some of the persistent problems affecting the system would be through major restructuring.

The "politics" stream refers to the identification of policy issues based on the national or regional mood, special interests, and public officials. The attractiveness of policy options emerging from any one, or from a combination of one or more of these streams, is thought depend on the robustness of the mood, power, and resources of special interest groups and the degree of change or turnover within the political arena. Coupling occurs when the streams come together – that is, when two or more streams simultaneously highlight the same problem and generally converge on a desired policy option and when that option is favoured or accepted by policy-makers and the public. In this situation, Kingdon uses the metaphor of an "open policy window" to describe a fertile opportunity to effect policy change. Although the opportunity may occur serendipitously, in many instances the so-called "dots" are connected by policy entrepreneurs. Kingdon (1995) suggests that even when conditions are favourable for a policy shift, the intervention of a policy entrepreneur is required to ensure that the opportunity to initiate action is not lost. Policy entrepreneurs may also work to deliberately connect streams or to "interpret" the messages emerging from different streams as being connected and to bring these connections to the fore. In applying Kingdon's model to this case study, the actions of Premier Wells and Premier Tobin position them as policy entrepreneurs who were instrumental in carrying through significant reforms.

Some of the same education policy problems – namely enrollment and finance – that existed in the 1990s still nagged the Williams government after it came to office in 2003. However, it is difficult to apply the same theoretical lens (multiple streams) to the centralization policy of that administration. The 2004 centralization policy is more consistent with the components of risk theory – the ways that decisions are made in an unsettled socio-political environment (Beck 1997). According to Beck, all forms of government operate as a form of authority in which an individual or group of individuals exercise power over the citizenry. In order for any government to perform effectively and sustain itself, there must be "legitimation of authority"; that is, the government must have the confidence of the electorate that it deserves the authority it has.

Several educational researchers have described the educational landscape in Canada over the past quarter century as turbulent, unsettled, and risky (Galway 2006; Levin 2003; Levin and Riffel 1997; Ungerleider 2003a) as policy-makers have tried to negotiate the problems of fewer students, unstable budgets, and new expectations for schools. There is widespread agreement that policy-making in education now occurs under a microscope: it has become highly politicized and subject to intense media attention (Levin 2004; Lingard and Rawolle 2004; Thomson 2004; Ungerleider 2003b). Public expectations for schools have never been greater, and these expectations are constantly changing and being redefined, creating a chaotic and uncertain political policy context where change has replaced stability as the norm.

Beck says that in risk societies, "certain features of industrial society become socially and politically problematic" (1997, 5), and the problems, fears, and conflicts of modern society begin to overtake political and public debate, creating a lessening of confidence in government authorities or a "crisis of legitimation." Within this social context, policies and government initiatives frequently encounter the resistance of duly affected groups, which creates political risk. Dibbon, Sheppard, and Brown (2012) cite numerous recent examples of incidents where the political and ideological interests of provincial governments have run counter to the perceived mandates of school boards and the governance roles of elected trustees. In several notable cases, government authorities have intervened to influence or overturn school board decisions. These interventions have ranged from public statements by ministers or premiers criticizing the policy decisions of school boards to more extreme measures, such as the outright dismissal of board members. Governments have also frequently used commissioned studies and other policy instruments to set in motion significant structural and governance reforms, such as the decision to centralize school boards in 2004.

In terms of risk theory, we can conceptualize these actions both as a public demonstration of government legitimation and as a means of mitigating political risk. Following Beck (1997), it might be theorized that in a politicized environment, the values, reward systems, and accountabilities against which school board trustees and superintendents operate are likely to differ substantively from those of politicians and senior bureaucrats, thereby creating a policy environment that might be antagonistic to local governance. Accordingly, greater centralization and greater control over local districts would improve the risk environment.

For policy-makers, the challenges posed by declining enrollments are daunting. Since enrollments in some regions of Canada are likely to continue to decline, it seems inevitable that ministries and school boards will turn to various forms of consolidation to achieve efficiencies. Canadian and American research has already provided enough evidence to cause us to re-conceptualize educational restructuring in purely economic terms (Galway et al. 2012). The logic of consolidation, which seems self-evident – create economies of scale and redirect savings to improve and expand educational programs (or to fund other priorities) – is flawed. Claims about the financial benefits of consolidation are problematic in that they are often mired in political rhetoric. Furthermore, the assumptions behind such claims tend to oversimplify the complexity of structural reform. At the conceptual stage, it is difficult, if not impossible, to accurately predict the administrative, human resource, transportation, and construction costs associated with consolidation. Even when savings are realized, as in the case of the 1997 and 2004 reforms in Newfoundland & Labrador, such economies tend to be short-lived and come at the expense of considerable system-level upheaval. Regrettably, some consolidation proposals may serve little purpose beyond their usefulness as signals to the public that governments are looking for ways to deliver services more efficiently or perhaps as means of maintaining tighter controls over the public agenda.

Many of the arguments for educational consolidation are difficult to counter, but achieving efficiency and fiscal accountability by centralizing decision making has major implications for democratic discourse. Given that they are already a vanishing species, if there is to be meaningful local educational governance in Newfoundland & Labrador and throughout Canada, elected school boards may wish to consider how they are situated in relation to the governments who create and fund them and the public who elect them. School boards have the authority to begin a public discourse on local governance. It might be preferable to take action now while school districts still cling to a public profile than to wait until they are no longer recognizable.

NOTES

The author gratefully acknowledges funding support for this work from Memorial University's Harris Center for Regional Policy Development and Memorial University's Faculty of Education.

1   Fewer than one hundred students.
2   Schools Act, 1997, S.N.L., ch. S-12.2. http://www.assembly.nl.ca/legislation/sr/statutes/s12-2.htm.

10

Fishing for Change: Fisheries Policy in Newfoundland and Labrador

MARIO LEVESQUE

COMPARATIVE THEORY

Fisheries are notoriously difficult to manage sustainably. The traditional thinking, popularized by Garrett Hardin (1968), was that a tragedy of the commons would be the end result because the lack of ownership rights in the resource would make it extremely difficult to overcome the problem of getting harvesters to contribute to its management (the problem of free riding) and address issues of overharvesting. The solutions put forth involved direct government management or resource privatization (e.g., quotas), yet such solutions have proven to be problematic because of political considerations, bureaucratic incentives, and market difficulties, including failures (see Finlayson 1994; Pinkerton and Edwards 2009; Sproule-Jones 2008).

We now know that a tragedy of the commons is but one possible outcome. Fisheries and other common pool resources continue to be sustainably managed in many locales, including in the Japanese coastal fisheries (Ruddle 1989), in other traditional Pacific fisheries (see Agrawal 2002), and in communal land tenure in Switzerland (Ostrom 1990). The study of such locales has found that bottom-up solutions, solutions generated by harvesters or appropriators themselves, are often more effective than direct government control or privatization. In other words, formal organization to address problems of collective action can be achieved endogenously. This method is grounded in the public choice approach to public policy decision making, in which individuals (attributes of the community), institutional arrangements (rules and their configurations), and the nature of the goods (characteristics of goods, biophysical conditions) interact to create acceptable and economically efficient public policies that place the least number of limitations on individual choice.

The study of how these elements interact has yielded thirty-three institutional design principles for the sustainable management of common pool resources (see Agrawal 2002).[1] Of these, eight institutional design principles advanced by Elinor Ostrom have dominated the literature to form the core of common pool resource (CPR) theory. They are as follows:

1 Clearly defined boundaries for both appropriators and the resource;
2 Congruence between appropriation and provision rules and local conditions;
3 An assurance that those affected by the rules can participate in their modification;
4 An active monitoring system that is accountable to the appropriators or is managed by the appropriators themselves;
5 A system of graduated sanctions;
6 Access to rapid, low-cost, and local conflict resolution mechanisms;
7 A minimal recognition of the rights of appropriators to organize that is recognized by external government authorities; and
8 For larger resource systems, an assurance that principles 1 to 7 are organized in multiple governance layers or nested enterprises (see Ostrom 1990, 90–102 for a full discussion).

Trying to achieve institutional change to better align with what CPR theory suggests is required for sustainable resources management is no easy task. It involves a cost-benefit analysis by those involved to determine whether it is worth their effort to change the rules. This calls into question attributes of the resource and appropriators that either lower costs or increase benefits, thereby increasing the likelihood that self-organization will occur. Four main resource attributes have been found to be associated with an increased likelihood of self-organization (see Ostrom 2000 for an extended discussion). First, there must be a feasible chance for improvement in the resource. Without it, participants will not expend the effort needed to address policy changes or, at best, they will contribute minimally to such efforts given the negligible benefits that will ensue. The second attribute relates to indicators. Accurate information is imperative, hence the need for reliable, valid, and low-cost indicators to provide frequent assessments of the condition of the resource and to reduce uncertainty surrounding decision making. The resource must also have a relatively predictable flow, the third key attribute. An uncertain resource flow decreases the expected benefits, thereby decreasing the incentive for appropriators to contribute to self-organization. Finally, a spatial element exists in relation to the resource system. It needs to be of sufficient size, given available technology, for participants to develop a precise understanding of its boundaries while simultaneously developing an intimate knowledge of its microenvironments.

Taken collectively, the likelihood of self-organization is increased if a feasible chance for improvement in the resource exists. This possibility is based on having accurate information about the resource, which increases the emphasis on the indicators used in its assessments, predictable resource flows (e.g., seasonally, yearly), and an accurate understanding of the resource system's boundaries and microenvironments. A particular combination thereof – for example, a feasible chance of improvement, poor indicators, moderate predictability, poor resource system understanding – decreases the likelihood of self-organization but does not eliminate it, depending on individual appropriators' cost-benefits and their attributes, to which we now turn.

Six appropriator attributes are associated with an increased likelihood of self-organization: salience, a common understanding, a low discount rate, trust and reciprocity, autonomy, and previous organizational experience and leadership. The greater the share of his or her livelihood an appropriator derives from the resource, the more he or she will be willing to contribute to the costs of organizing and maintaining a governance system. This also applies to the level of understanding appropriators have about the resource itself. The greater the common understanding about the resource system and about how one's actions affect others, as well as the resource, the more likely self-organization becomes. Appropriators also need to have few viable and attractive alternative options, thus creating an incentive for them to manage the resource sustainably. A high level of trust and reciprocity among appropriators reduces costs such as monitoring, while having the autonomy to locally develop rules for access and harvesting lowers the associated bargaining costs. Finally, previous organizational experience and local leadership breeds familiarity with rules and their formation and greatly increases the "buy-in" from appropriators. The above variables and their interaction greatly affect an appropriator's cost/benefit analysis in determining whether and the degree to which he or she will be committed to organize and maintain a management system to ensure a sustainable fishery.

The question examined in this chapter is how the government of New-foundland & Labrador has changed fisheries policy to better align with long-identified sustainable-resources management principles. Various reports, media coverage, and press releases are combed to construct an overview of fisheries policy changes from 2003 to 2012. The congru-ence of the provincial situation with the attributes of both the resource and the appropriators that increase the likelihood of a self-governing system is then assessed. The greater the congruence, the more likely it is that desired changes will be facilitated; the less the congruence, the less likely it is that desired changes can occur, making it harder for the Williams and Dunderdale administrations to place the fishery on a sus-tainable footing.

Such an investigation underscores the responsibility for fisheries man-agement in Canada, which lies principally with the federal government. Under section 91 of the Canadian Constitution, the federal government retains exclusive legislative power over sea coast and inland fisheries, as well as over navigation and shipping. The powers afforded to the fed-eral Minister of Fisheries and Oceans under the Fisheries Act are far-reaching in the for-capture fishery, including powers over conservation and management of fisheries and habitats, licensing, and enforcement (Rose 2003). Little room is apparently left for provincial marine fish-eries management, which is shortsighted given the potentially signifi-cant contributions of the provinces to generating scientific information, fish processing, and aquaculture. As CPR theory suggests, all stakehold-ers need to be actively engaged for sustainable resources management which facilitates an examination of the efforts of the government of Newfoundland & Labrador. It also suggests the need for willing part-ners to address changes, calling into question the antecedent conditions which shape their cost-benefit analysis – resource and appropriator attributes.

BACKGROUND

Instability is perhaps the only stable thing in the fishing industry (Jentoft 1993), and events preceding the Williams administration reflect this. Efforts to assume greater control of coastal stocks and address foreign overfishing led Canada to ratify the United Nations Law of the Seas Convention in 1977, which expanded coastal states' jurisdiction to two hundred nautical miles. A sense of optimism permeated the industry, in that it could finally control its own destiny. A larger fishing area meant more fish to catch, and prices generally increased. New investment and expansion of the fishery ensued to replace foreign fishing vessels within Canada's expanded territory.

Overcapacity issues soon cropped up, and governments played a central role in the problem. In their pursuit of employment policies, governments embraced the Kirby Report's (1982) recommendations to increase the Total Allowable Catch (TAC) as a solution to industry overcapacity, and they also encouraged offshore trawlers to fish in the inshore regions when their supplies were dwindling. This strategy solved nothing. In 1990, there were 60 percent more fishermen than in the 1970s, fish plants had doubled in size and increased in number, and there were 50 percent more plant workers. The industry was ready for larger harvests, yet harvest projections never materialized (Canada 1993).

Part of the problem arose from overly optimistic and poorly designed harvest prediction models (Harris 1989). Moreover, scientists assumed that they could accurately predict fish stocks and that they understood the ecosystem (Bavington 2010). These were significant assumptions given that data for fish stock estimations did not include data from inshore fishermen, which was considered too "primitive" and unscientific (Finlayson 1994, 110). In fact, it was the inability of scientists to devise a model that incorporated inshore and offshore data that was the problem and not the inshore fishermen themselves, who were long predicting a collapse of the fishery. It did not help matters that decision makers were ignoring their own data (Tobin 2002, 82) and that some fishermen had long been under-reporting catches, thus contributing to overfishing.

By 1992, the federal government had realized too late that the fishery had collapsed, and it announced a moratorium on cod fishing. The effect was devastating: 90 percent of the Newfoundland groundfish fishery disappeared and has yet to recover; twelve thousand inshore fishermen and fifteen thousand plant workers lost their jobs (Canada 1993). While these job losses were substantial, other sectors of the fishery (e.g., lobster, crab) were unaffected, although they involved significantly smaller employment activity. Overfishing by foreign vessels of straddling stocks continues, although to a lesser degree. Industry rationalization and restructuring, stock assessments, joint management, and overfishing have dominated discussions since the collapse. Moreover, federal fisheries science and management has been discredited, which left the fishery in a precarious state at the time Williams became premier.

CASE STUDY

Under successive Williams-led administrations, the government of New-foundland & Labrador focused on three main fisheries issues. Tran-sitioning the traditional fishery into a leaner yet sustainable industry through rationalization and restructuring[2] initiatives remained para-mount, given problems of overcapacity and the state of the resource. Efforts were also directed at addressing foreign overfishing to protect traditional fishing stocks. These efforts went beyond increased enforce-ment within Canada's jurisdiction to joint and custodial fisheries management initiatives with the federal government, for which New-foundland & Labrador continues to advocate. Custodial initiatives would mean that Canada, as the coastal state, would assume manage-ment responsibility on behalf of the international community for fish stocks beyond the two-hundred-mile limit to cover the full continental shelf, thereby including cod stocks that straddled the boundary. Under-pinning these changes was the establishment of an extensive provincial fisheries research agenda to complement and challenge federal fisheries research.

The provincial government had limited success in transitioning the traditional fishery into a leaner yet sustainable industry. The policy chal-lenge surrounded what to do about issues such as overcapacity (e.g., harvesting and processing). This was especially important for rural New-foundland since it involved balancing the needs of the inshore fishermen located in the many outports with those of the offshore trawler fleet.

Early commitments were modest. For instance, the 2003 Progressive Conservative (PC) election platform largely focused on value-added pro-cessing and a quality assurance and marketing program, but it mini-mized restructuring efforts (PC Party 2003, 35–6). This was perhaps the result of Danny Williams' political acumen. He probably calculated that restructuring efforts would be contentious with stakeholders and their representatives, the Fish, Food and Allied Workers (FFAW) union and the Association of Seafood Processors (ASP), and would make it difficult to get elected. Time would prove Williams correct.

Efforts to transition the traditional fishery surround the 2003 Dunne Report and the 2007 Fishery Industry Renewal (FIR) Strategy. Shortly after assuming office, the Williams administration approved the Dunne Report in principle, and the premier entrusted Fisheries Minister Trevor Taylor – an MHA from the Northern Peninsula with a fishing background – to oversee its implementation, which included creating a new operational structure for the processing sector, enhancing the quality assurance program, and developing a pilot project for raw-material sharing (Dunne 2003). The FFAW provided mixed approval for the Dunne Report, approving of most recommendations but opposing production limits (i.e., quotas) for processing plants (FFAW 2004). The processors, on the other hand, saw the Dunne Report's recommendations as "significant and important steps" (Association of Seafood Producers 2004), and the government proceeded to implement a number of them.

The changes implemented for the processing sector were significant. As the Dunne Report outlined, concern surrounded the number of fish-processing licenses and how they had been issued by the provincial government. Previously, too many licenses had been issued in an ad hoc manner, thus contributing to processing overcapacity, under circumstances that were less than transparent, with ministers exercising much discretion. Following the Dunne Report's recommendation, a Fish Processing Licensing Board was established to handle licensing applications. However, unlike Dunne's recommendation of a fully independent board, the licensing board that was created had the ability only to advise the minister, who then made the final decision. In determining its advice, the board was charged with clear criteria to be used in assessing the viability of applications relating to the sources and quantity of raw material; production, marketing, and plant infrastructure plans; and labour availability and financial feasibility. Provisions for both board and plant reporting mechanisms were also established. In sum, these changes represented the Williams administration's attempt to establish a more open, transparent, and accountable licensing decision-making process while retaining the final decision-making authority (see Newfoundland and Labrador 2005d).

Yet such changes did little to quell concerns from inshore fisherman. To them the issue was one of increased corporatization of the crab fishery by processors who indirectly controlled and potentially owned crab licenses to ensure plant viability. This threatened the very existence of inshore fishermen, who were also facing higher operating and licensing costs, among other things (Davis and Korneski 2012). As a result, one notable recommendation that had been implemented was terminated. The pilot project for raw material sharing was terminated in 2006 upon a review brought about after significant and sustained opposition, which included legislative protests involving more than five thousand harvesters and plant workers at Confederation Building in St John's, as well as flotilla blockades of St John's harbour (FFAW 2005). A renewed focus on collective bargaining ensued as one mechanism to address industry restructuring (see Cashin 2005).

The above efforts led to the development of the Fisheries Industry Renewal (FIR) Strategy. Beginning in 2006, Premier Williams met with new provincial fisheries minister Tom Rideout and federal Department of Fisheries and Oceans officials and stakeholders to plot a course of action. A federal-provincial working group was formed to work on a renewal strategy, and trips to Iceland and Norway were also made by the premier and Minister Rideout to learn from their experiences with fishery renewal (Newfoundland and Labrador 2006f, 2006g). Note the close involvement of Williams throughout this period, which is perhaps a response to the negative outcome of his hands-off approach with Taylor, who had been shuffled to another department.

In early October 2006, a discussion paper on fishery renewal was distributed for review, and industry consultations began. In April 2007, the province announced the FIR Strategy and committed to implementing a processing policy renewal, an enhanced fisheries loan guarantee, enhanced market research and promotion, a fishing industry workforce adjustment program, and various health and safety initiatives. Similarly, the federal government committed to fleet rationalization, vessel size flexibility, and various capital gains adjustments to aid the industry, though no funds were offered for license buybacks to reduce harvesting capacity, a key harvester demand (Newfoundland and Labrador 2007f).

The province's FIR Strategy commitments were repeated in the 2007 PC election platform (PC Party 2007). Yet progress stalled by late 2008, much to the chagrin of the FFAW and owing in part to the lack of commitment by both provincial and federal governments to licensing changes, because of associated costs (Baker 2008). The global financial crisis of 2008, which caused seafood demand to drop and strengthened the Canadian dollar against the US dollar, only complicated matters. New provincial fisheries minister Clyde Jackman responded that "money was not the only solution" and that concrete answers needed to come from the industry (FFAW 2009). New discussions ensued to address changing market conditions, and a memorandum of understanding (MOU) was reached in 2009 to address key areas for long-term development of the industry. The MOU stressed the need for rationalization before industry restructuring and demanded significant provincial government funding ($450 million) for its implementation. To date, the Dunderdale administration has refused to move forward on the recommendations until a restructuring plan has been developed, a point Dunderdale herself reiterated after the 2011 provincial election, noting that government could not be continually relied on to financially address industry problems.

Even less progress was made on issues of overfishing and the policing of the illegal fishing of straddling stocks ("custodial management"). The challenge for fisheries management is that Canada's two-hundred-mile limit does not extend to the full limits of the continental shelf; the nose and tail of the Grand Banks remain outside this area. Fish that are within Canada's jurisdiction swim into international waters only to be caught with relative impunity. This is significant for the sustainability of the cod stocks and the fishing industry, since those areas remain prime fishing grounds; foreign vessels routinely overfish these locations and undermine Canada's efforts to manage the cod fishery. This brings into question issues of enforcement and efforts to extend Canada's management into international waters, both areas of federal jurisdiction.

Newfoundland & Labrador's position was to press the federal government to pursue custodial management – unilaterally if necessary. To the province's dismay, no progress was made on these issues owing to the federal government's preference for diplomatic solutions, which was consistent with the recommendations of the Saunders Report (2003). It stated that a unilateral assertion of custodial management by the federal government would be a breach of international law and would lead to other difficulties, and it therefore concluded that Canada would be better to pursue change from within the Northwest Atlantic Fisheries Organization (NAFO). Many discussions were held, including prime ministerial meetings with the Russian and French presidents in 2004, and Canada hosted an international conference on overfishing (Conference on the Governance of High Seas Fisheries and the United Nations Fish Agreement: Moving from Words to Action) in St John's in May 2005, yet progress was stunted given the lack of interest from the international community. In the end, Minister Taylor reaffirmed Newfoundland's position of custodial management to federal fisheries officials (Newfoundland and Labrador 2005c), no doubt ceding to local political pressure and perhaps in the hope of gains on other issues. Soon thereafter, Taylor supported the May Report (2005) on straddling stocks, which recommended that the federal government move to replace NAFO with a new Regional Fisheries Management Organization (RFMO) which would deal with overfishing in tangible ways and which would recognize custodial management (see May, Russell, and Rowe 2005).

Ottawa disagreed. It rejected the May Report's recommendations, reiterating its preference to work for NAFO reform from within (Canada 2005). With minimal progress by October 2008, questions arose about whether the federal Conservatives understood the concept of custodial management, which alarmed Minister Taylor, who by then had returned to the fisheries portfolio in an acting capacity (Newfoundland and Labrador 2008e). His concerns were realized in 2009 when NAFO amendments, which provided for enhanced management on the Grand Banks, involved some foreign management of stocks *within* Canada's two-hundred-mile limit. Despite Premier Williams' loud objections emphasizing that "the giveaways must stop" and asserting that Canada was trading away its sovereignty, the amendments were ratified (PC Party 2003, 8; Canadian Press 2009a).

More success was to greet the Williams and Dunderdale administrations in establishing a provincial fisheries research agenda. Following the Dunne Report's recommendation, a significant research agenda was established to complement and challenge federal fisheries research. As the 2003 PC platform stated, a sustainable fishery requires "fisheries policies based on the best available scientific evidence" (PC Party 2003, 34). This agenda was pursued in conjunction with other stakeholders, such as the FFAW and federal fisheries scientists. Of note was the 2003 PC platform pledge for a Fisheries Science and Management Research Institute to be established at Memorial University, which morphed into the Centre for Fisheries Ecosystem Research as part of Memorial University's Marine Institute and which received multi-year, multi-million dollar funding. Similar significant investments have been made in other fisheries development initiatives since 2007, and funds have been provided for numerous other smaller and more routine initiatives (e.g., sea cucumber research and fisheries scholarships; Newfoundland and Labrador 2010e).

Considerable investments were also made in the aquaculture industry. As the PC 2003 platform stated and as was reiterated in the 2007 campaign, aquaculture remained "the best prospect" for a fishery of the future (PC Party 2003, 36). To this end, other multi-million dollar investments were made through the Capital Investment Program, industry support for cod commercialization, and to help establish salmon production farms (Newfoundland and Labrador 2006i, 2009b). Overall, aquaculture investment increased by a factor of six to ten times during the 2003–04 to the 2009–10 budget years, while investment in fisheries development approximately doubled over the same period (Newfoundland and Labrador, DFA Annual Reports, 2003–04 to 2008–09).

In contrast, federal government investment in fisheries research was sporadic. While the federal government supported various initiatives with the province, such as the Cod Recovery Strategy and aquaculture initiatives, it also reduced core scientific research (Newfoundland and Labrador 2005c). Such cuts were termed short-sighted and quickly denounced by the FFAW and the province, but to no avail (FFAW 2006). Since then, significant cuts to federal fisheries research and enforcement have continued as the recent federal government budget outlines, yet such cuts, among other things, have contributed to an erosion of support for the federal Conservative government, as recent public opinion polls have indicated (Canada 2012a; "Time to Flip" 2012).

What can we make of these developments? Looking at the situation from a CPR theory perspective, we see a poor fit with what theory informs us is required for sustainable fisheries management. Clearly defined boundaries for appropriators and the resource do not exist given the situation of the cod fishery off the Grand Banks – the boundary does not encompass the cod's habitat, nor does the management regime include all fishermen. This has undermined attempts to ensure congruence between local conditions and appropriation and provision rules. Only limited direct participation of appropriators in crafting rules exists given their representation by union leaders and government officials, though increased opportunities exist for participation through the Fish Processing Licensing Board. The monitoring system is accountable to higher levels of government only and does not include appropriators themselves. While graduated sanctions exist, conflict resolution mechanisms are drawn out over a long period. The resource system is organized in multiple layers, yet appropriators are devoid of important rule-making powers (e.g., provision and appropriation), which are concentrated in the federal government. In essence, we observe a top-down management system that is contrary to what is required by CPR theory to ensure a sustainable fishery. This suggests that overlapping fisheries jurisdictions are dysfunctional for common pool resources management, but such an interpretation minimizes the importance of a cooperative intergovernmental culture to broker solutions for sustainable resources management.

Yet should we be surprised with this poor fit between theory and practice? The short answer is no if we closely examine attributes of the resource and appropriators. There are four key attributes of the resource:

a feasible chance for improvement, indicators (valid, low-cost, frequent assessments), a predictable resource flow, and spatial understanding (boundaries, microenvironments). A feasible chance for improvement in the fishery appears questionable in view of the lack of management control of stocks in the nose and tail of the Grand Banks. No progress has been made on this issue, since custodial management has not been pursued by the federal government. The end result has proven less than desirable, with Canada ceding some management rights to the international community *within* its two-hundred-mile jurisdiction. It appears that a step backwards has been taken, which has had a negative effect on appropriators. The lack of trust in federal science that the collapse of the cod fishery generated eroded confidence in federal resource indicators and led the province to invest heavily in its own fisheries science in order to challenge federal data.

A high level of uncertainty also exists in the predictability of the resource flow. It remains unknown whether the traditional fishery will recover, and much depends on being able to effectively manage fish stocks, including straddling stocks. Moreover, our knowledge of the stocks' boundaries and microenvironments remains poor and leads to blanket decisions on quotas. The healthy status of stocks along the Labrador coast but not surrounding the island portion of the province has frustrated harvesters in Labrador, who desire larger catch quotas (Interview with official from the Torngat Fish Producer's Association, November 2011). Collectively, government actions have decreased the outlook for improvement in stocks and have contributed to contested indicators, unpredictability in stock flows, and insufficient resource-system knowledge, all of which has worked against appropriator efforts to organize and maintain a self-governing system for a sustainable fishery.

Government actions have also affected appropriator attributes associated with an increased likelihood to self-organize: salience, common understanding, a low discount rate, trust and reciprocity, autonomy, and prior organizational experience and leadership. The fisheries' lack of importance in comparison to other issues facing the federal government (e.g., trade) is evident given that they have considered ceding management control to the international community. This action has fuelled a deeper mistrust in the federal government by appropriators and the provincial government. It has also underscored the lack of common understanding surrounding management of the resource. Perhaps worse still is the lack of autonomy that appropriators possess given the concentration of power over the fisheries in the federal government.

Most appropriator-desired changes need to be reviewed, approved, and enacted by the federal government, which seriously undermines their incentives (increases costs) to participate in devising their own solutions. In essence, appropriators and the province are largely pawns in a larger federal game, with little federal leadership on the issue (contrast the current lack of federal leadership with Canada's successful efforts to address overfishing during the mid-1990s; see Tobin 2002).

Matters are increasingly complex when one considers appropriator attributes in regard to industry rationalization and restructuring efforts. For appropriators, fisheries issues remain paramount, yet one questions the importance of the fishery for the Williams and Dunderdale administrations. Fisheries issues have not played a major role in recent provincial elections. The 2011 election, for example, was dominated by health care issues, and Dunderdale largely refused to discuss fisheries issues even when confronted by fisheries workers in Marystown (CBC News 2011d). No doubt this was done to help former fisheries minister Clyde Jackman win re-election (he won by forty votes). Appropriators' lack of trust in government has heightened with the retreat of both levels of government from the FIR strategy in late 2007 and in response to provincial demands for a restructuring plan before industry rationalization can move forward. This has left appropriators in want of better solutions and processes. Current cutbacks to federal fisheries research have only deepened mistrust of the federal government, as did cuts to FFAW research by the provincial government in 2012 (CBC News 2012b).

The result is that appropriators face increased costs and decreased benefits for participating in organizing and maintaining a self-governing system for the fishery. Hence we should not be surprised by the poor fit between CPR theory and practice.

POLITICAL DECISION MAKING IN NEWFOUNDLAND & LABRADOR

Despite the significant popular approval for Williams himself and his government (see figure 10.1) the government of Newfoundland & Labrador made little progress on the fisheries file (see also Feehan 2011) and appears to be in a precarious position in regard to fisheries management. On the one hand, it is and wants to continue to be supportive of the industry and desires to broker a solution between two powerful interest groups – the FFAW and the ASP. Since these interests are equally powerful, the result is often a circular exercise that results in stalemate (as evidenced by the dispute over shrimp pricing that jump-started the

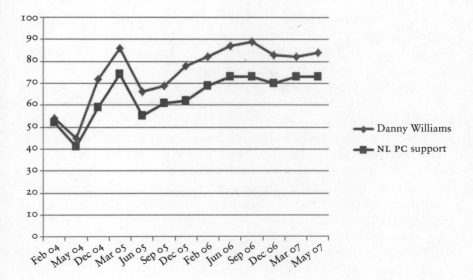

Figure 10.1
Satisfaction with Danny Williams and support for NL PC Party, 2004–07. *Source*: Angus Reid (2007). *Note*: These polls stopped in 2007.

MOU process). On the other hand, the government of Newfoundland & Labrador operates within a framework of limited constitutional authority on the file, which limits the range of actions it may pursue and contributes to its frustration (see CBC News 2012a). Yet the province is an equally powerful player with motives of its own in this process, and it continues to make equal contributions to continued industry challenges. This fragmented fisheries policy community challenges decision making for which Canadians have expressed concerns, as revealed in public opinion polls (Coffen-Smout 1998).

This situation also questions the applicability of elite theory and its relationship to agenda setting in Newfoundland & Labrador fisheries policy. For elite theory to hold, significant control of the agenda is required by elites. In this case, if by elites we mean political elites, then sufficient evidence exists, as shown in Williams' inability to shape the fisheries policy agenda and to broker solutions, to dismiss elite theory. On the other hand, if we broaden our conception of "elites" to mean governing elites, that is, to include the broader range of fisheries policy actors in and out of government, then while the evidence suggests support for elite theory's existence, given the cadre of prominent actors, including Williams, Dunderdale, and various federal and provincial fisheries ministers, as well as leaders of the FFAW and ASP unions (with the exclusion of the small fishermen in various negotiation processes), the theory nonetheless fails given the inability of the governing elites to significantly control the agenda. Rather, each member of the *governing* elites wanted something different regarding policy and used the institutional structures to ensure minimal or disjointed policy changes resulted.

From the perspective of sustainable resources theory, the actions of the Williams-Dunderdale administrations have worsened prospects for successful industry rationalization and restructuring, since the province's actions have heightened mistrust among stakeholders. Both the FFAW and the ASP were caught by surprise, for instance, when the province rejected the MOU, since they had followed the parameters with which they were provided. The fact that small fishermen and rural communities were not part of the MOU negotiations has only further alienated the government (Hunt 2011). The result was an MOU that focused on creating vertically integrated enterprises with significant costs to rural communities since a fleet reduction of 50 to 80 percent was recommended (Clift 2011). In other words, the process was top-down, ignored small stakeholders, and put forth an industry vision of sustaining economically efficient aquabusinesses, rather than having a sustainable fishery (see Walsh 2011 for a broader discussion). This approach was inconsistent with long-held public opinion concerns with the health of fish stocks, rather than with fishing enterprises per se, and the lack of recognition of biodiversity and community-based management solutions in current fisheries policies (Environics Research Group Limited 2007; Kellert, Gibbs and Wohlgenant 1995; Coffen-Smout 1998). It also worked against the progress made through the establishment of the Fish Processing Licensing Board.

Perhaps of greater concern is the bullish approach taken by the province in rejecting the MOU. Fisheries Minister Clyde Jackman was clear in stating that industry change is naturally occurring given socio-economic conditions and that when combined with the high cost of the recommended changes, there was no rush to initiate them. He responded by citing the need for a restructuring plan (Hunt 2011). This response was misleading, since rationalization and restructuring came to mean the same thing for the government given that a significant industry downsizing (up to 80 percent) was recommended, which necessitated restructuring (Walsh 2011). One interpretation offered here is that the province came to realize the detrimental effect this would have on rural

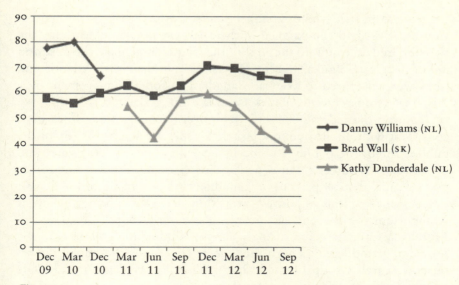

Figure 10.2
Canada's most popular premier, 2009–2012. *Source:* Angus Reid (2007)

communities, a cost that it has chosen not to impose on them, and has stalled for time. The fact that no action on the MOU was taken in the Dunderdale administration's first year, when politically unpopular decisions are typically undertaken by a new government, is tentative support for this interpretation. That support for Dunderdale significantly eroded during this period, as shown in figure 10.2, suggests that rationalization and restructuring will continue indefinitely, while in the interim, natural attrition will perform the government's work.

Matters have also worsened in regard to custodial management of straddling stocks. However, this interpretation is less a reflection of the actions of the provincial government than a denunciation of the federal government's actions. The federal government's credibility in fisheries management has further eroded, given that it ratified NAFO changes that weakened Canada's ability to manage its fishing resources. The changes included more stringent voting formulas (e.g., requiring two-thirds majorities), making future changes harder to achieve, and potentially providing international interests with management functions *within* Canada's two-hundred-mile limit, which makes pursuance of custodial management in the future very difficult, if possible at all (see Rowat et al. 2007 for an overview; also Beswick 2010). The result has been to increase mistrust among stakeholders, especially since the federal Conservatives had campaigned in the 2006 election on extending "the two hundred mile limit to the edge of the Continental Shelf, the nose and tail of the Grand Banks, and the Flemish Cap in the North Atlantic and [they were] prepared to exercise Canadian custodial management over this area" (Conservative Party of Canada 2006, 20).

However, the federal Conservative government's actions have been consistent with public opinion. Fisheries issues are not at the top of the public's mind; the public is preoccupied with issues of freshwater and oil and gas resources (Nanos 2009). For example, a 2007 Environics poll revealed that 78 percent of Canadians are not aware of the federal government's actions to address overfishing even though they believe it is important (95 percent) (Environics Research Group Limited 2007). Moreover, Canadians increasingly support diplomatic solutions to the problem, giving legitimacy to the federal government's actions (Environics Research Group Limited 2007). While the Williams/Dunderdale administrations may have made little progress and even complicated the fisheries file, they appear to be working against the current or swimming upstream in relation to custodial management.

One positive change has been the development of a significant provincial fisheries research agenda. No longer must appropriators rely solely on federal fisheries science, which has long been discredited (Dunn 2005b). Consistent with CPR theory, provincial fisheries research has been pursued in collaboration with other stakeholders at various levels of governance, including the FFAW and the federal government. However, any progress must be tempered by subsequent cuts to fisheries research by both levels of government (see CBC News 2011e; 2012b).

Collectively, these developments suggest a move that is inconsistent with what CPR theory requires for a sustainable fishery. Mistrust among stakeholders has been heightened, while industry management has increasingly become top-heavy, allowing for international actors and minimizing the role of local appropriators in the process. Issues of power concerning who can do what, when, and where permeate proceedings, calling into question the workings of Canadian federalism. Federalism constitutionally divides sovereignty between two or more levels of government. In Canada, management authority over fisheries remains within the purview of the federal government. Simply put, fish in the water are a federal responsibility (i.e., with respect to harvesting), while fish on the docks (i.e., with respect to processing) are a provincial responsibility. This suggests that clear jurisdictional responsibility vested in *one* government (i.e., federal or provincial) is required for sustainable resources management, with public opinion polling revealing a preference for the federal government (Léger Marketing 2007).

In the current situation, appropriators and the government of Newfoundland & Labrador remain in a subservient position with a limited ability to effect policy changes given the need for federal government approval. However, such a solution remains blind to fish and fisheries ecosystems, which do not respect artificially imposed man-made boundaries. Rather, a willingness to cooperate and a culture for intergovernmental cooperation is required to address issues, even though it may increase the complexity and timelines for decisions to be made, as is evidenced with the ongoing efforts at industry rationalization and restructuring. It is important to note that the federal government has to date not signed the MOU, though it participated in the process. This suggests that the federal government may have different priorities, and its reluctance may have contributed to the decision of the government of Newfoundland & Labrador to back away from the MOU: it realizes that it cannot move forward on its own. It also brings into question the need to consider political incentives when pursuing policy changes. For example, successive federal minority governments may have led to false hopes on custodial management. While it is easy to promise many things during an election campaign, such as the federal Conservatives' pledge to exercise custodial management over straddling stocks as it sought to form a government, it is nonetheless much harder to deliver, especially in a minority Parliament (Rowat et al. 2007).

Federalism has also allowed each level of government to blame the other for the disarray in fisheries management. Both fishermen and the province have long blamed the federal government for the collapse of the cod fishery (Feehan 2011; Dunn 2005b; Young 2003a). Poor federal science has been cited as a factor, which is why Rose (2003) advocated a significant provincial fisheries research agenda, which the government of Newfoundland & Labrador has successfully established. Each level of government also blamed the other for backing away from the FIR commitments in 2008, while the province has recently criticized the federal government's lack of commitment to fisheries research given its announced cutbacks.

The question that remains is whether the developments in the fisheries during the Williams-Dunderdale tenure suggest the existence of a "benevolent dictatorship." Both have assumed what appears to be an autocratic approach to decision making, with policy decisions directed from the top. This is contrary to what CPR theory suggests is required for a sustainable fishery. Yet given limitations posed by power differentials introduced by federalism (i.e., overlapping jurisdictional issues), limitations that are not considered by CPR theory, the limited progress on the fisheries file by Williams-Dunderdale is not surprising. Given this situation, the short-term outlook of the fishery looks bleak, with appropriators hoping that benevolence will soon come in the form of transitional aid from a renewed and enhanced commitment to intergovernmental cooperation.

NOTES

1   Common pool resources are valued natural or human-made resources that are available to more than one person and are subject to overuse and degradation. They include fisheries, groundwater basins, irrigation systems, and common grazing land. The difficulty in their management arises from their two defining characteristics – excludability and subtractability.

2   Rationalization (downsizing) and restructuring (reorganization) are closely intertwined. See Walsh (2011) for a full discussion.

11

A Brighter Future for Whom? Rural and Regional Development in Newfoundland and Labrador

KELLY VODDEN, RYAN GIBSON, AND MICHELLE PORTER

COMPARATIVE THEORY

Situated in one of Canada's most rural provinces, Newfoundland & Labrador's more than six hundred communities are dispersed over a land base of 406,000 square kilometres. The majority of these communities have less than five hundred residents. According to the 2011 census, more than half (52 percent) of the provincial population resides in rural and small-town communities, compared to a rate of 18 percent in Canada (Statistics Canada 2012a). Residents in rural and small-town communities in Newfoundland & Labrador experience lower incomes and formal-education levels, and higher rates of unemployment and dependency on seasonal employment and government transfers than do their urban counterparts (de Peuter and Sorensen 2005). These characteristics present challenges for policy-makers and rural residents alike.

Rural and small-town communities are of cultural as well as economic and environmental stewardship significance for the province and for Canada as a whole. Rural workers and the natural resources located in rural areas make important contributions to the provincial economy and are integral to the province's culture and identity. Yet both the effectiveness of the provincial government's role and its level of engagement in rural and regional development have been areas of controversy, contestation, and debate for many years, and past policies of successive provincial governments have resulted in less than favourable outcomes.

More than forty years ago, the provincial government under long-time Liberal premier Joey Smallwood was criticized for having little interest in rural planning and development. As McCrorie noted, "One should not be surprised if 'planning' in Newfoundland amounts to nothing more than a disjointed series of handout programs, designed to integrate the rural population in this manner with the commercial, semi-industrial, urban-based community, or keep the rural community content and indebted" (1969, 86). Nearly two decades and three premiers later, Simms advised the Royal Commission on Employment and Unemployment that "despite the interest and intent of numerous programs, there is a strong feeling that there has been no real effort made towards adopting an effective integrated approach for the long-term development of the province's rural sector" (Newfoundland and Labrador 1986, 1).

"Rural" as a unit of analysis and policy focus has multiple and often contested definitions; however, this chapter uses Statistics Canada's definition of "Rural and Small Town" (communities with a population of less than ten thousand and beyond the regular commuting zone of an urban agglomeration of ten thousand or more.)[1] Hereafter, "rural" therefore refers to communities beyond the St John's Census Metropolitan Area (within the Northeast Avalon region) and the Bay Roberts, Corner Brook, and Grand Falls-Windsor Census Agglomerations.

Beginning with staples theory, this chapter draws from systems, corporatist, and elite theories of policy-making, together with the Organisation for Economic Cooperation and Development's (OECD's) new rural paradigm to assess the Williams and, since 2010, Dunderdale administrations' interactions with rural communities. Initially developed by Mackintosh (1923) and Innis (1930) nearly a century ago, staples theory remains a useful framework for exploring social-ecological conditions and political economy in Canada and in rural Newfoundland & Labrador. European exploration in North America initiated patterns of rural dependency on natural resources and external actors that have continued to affect conditions in rural Newfoundland to the present day (Ommer et al. 2007). Resource extraction and the marginalization of rural as "periphery" and "hinterland" in relation to centres of political and financial capital characterized these founding relationships.

In the staples model, core-periphery relationships are developed as rural and northern communities become sites of staple extraction and urban centres sites of processing, trade, and finance. Continued research has furthered the understanding of staples dependency in light of current conditions and political and economic complexities (Barnes, Hayter, and Hay 2001; Gunton 2003; Ommer et al. 2007).

Many authors, including Innis, have described Newfoundland as an example of a staples-driven, export-dependent jurisdiction, its social and economic relations shaped by its natural-resource base and controlled from its inception by colonial officials and a powerful merchant class (Brodie 1990; Cadigan 1992; Innis 1954). Of particular relevance for rural Newfoundland is the notion of a "staples trap," which refers to conditions that entrench resource extraction in a community or region (Kassam 2001). While more optimistic versions of staples theory emphasize opportunities to diversify staples economies through linkages and reinvestment of resource rents (Gunton 2003), economies caught in the staples trap find that one staple simply succeeds another when the original demand (and/or the resource) decreases. This creates an economic system with greater susceptibility to restructuring and boom-bust cycles; lack of diversification, research and development, and innovation; and a tendency towards overexploitation and depletion of renewable resources (Clapp 1998; Hayter and Barnes 1990; Storey 2008).

As Lawson (2005) points out, staples are a medium for economic and political power gained through resource exploitation. The dependency stream of staples theory highlights the development of corporatist coalitions between the state, organized labour, and industry, relationships that lead to the establishment of subsidies, supportive regulations, the provision of transportation infrastructure, and health and social services by provincial governments. This development also results in patterns of top-down, centralized models of decision making dominated by foreign and domestic elites (who are often based in urban centres) and a focus on large-scale industrial development facilitated by capital, political power, and technology (Albo 2005; Barnes, Hayter, and Hay 2001). In Newfoundland & Labrador this has resulted in a legacy of dependency not only on natural resources but also on government and top-down leadership, often from popular charismatic leaders accused of monopolizing power yet regarded as provincial heroes (Vodden 2009; Webb 2001).

The new rural paradigm concept offers another way of thinking about rural Newfoundland & Labrador. Over the past twenty years, economic development and growth have focused on economies of scale and agglomeration (Amborsio-Albalá and Bastiaensen 2010). In the 2000s, the OECD initiated a Working Party on Territorial Policy in Rural Areas to evaluate rural policy and economies. The working party noted that

Table 11.1
Comparison of new and old rural paradigms

	Old approach to rural policy	New approach to rural policy
Objectives of policy	Equalization, natural resource-based income	Competitiveness of rural areas, valorization of local assets
Key target sector	Natural resources	Various sectors of rural economies (ex: tourism, manufacturing, ICT)
Main tools	Subsidies	Investments
Key actors	National government, workers in natural resource-based industries	All levels of government, various local stakeholders (public, private, NGOs)

Source: OECD (2006)

rural economies throughout the OECD lagged behind national averages, but noted also that "rural" should not be interpreted as "declining," pointing to rural economies that were in fact thriving. The output of the working party was the creation of the "new rural paradigm," focusing on two principles: place and investments (Ward and Brown 2009).

The new rural paradigm suggests that the policies best suited to assist rural regions should encourage critical mass through partnerships, prioritize investments in public goods and services, and advance innovation (OECD 2006). This policy reorientation concerns changes in two key areas: policy focus and governance structure (see table 11.1).

In particular, under the new rural paradigm, rural policy moves from government subsidization of declining economic sectors to more strategic investments designed to increase productivity and competitiveness. The paradigm focuses on identifying local/regional assets that can be utilized to generate competitive advantages and emphasizes new forms of collaboration and partnership between government and communities/regions for policy construction, implementation, and evaluation. The paradigm thus calls for a cross-cutting and multi-level governance approach (OECD 2006). There is a concerted shift from sectoral to more holistic and territorial policy approaches that recognize the importance of locally based strategies (Trapasso 2010).

Together, the contrasting approaches of staples-driven development, with its associated corporatist structures and centralized decision making, and the new rural paradigm offer a framework to evaluate the influence and direction of the Williams administration in rural and regional development.

BACKGROUND

It was not until 1961 that the majority of Newfoundland & Labrador's population was living in centres with populations of one thousand or more – thirty years later than in Canada as a whole (Bollman and Clemenson 2008). The province's census rural population has experienced fluctuations of growth and decline since 1951 and now lies just slightly above 1951 levels,[2] while the urban population has nearly doubled over the same period. The census rural population has been in steady decline since reaching a peak in 1991 (Statistics Canada 2006b). While rural population declines were also experienced elsewhere in Canada, declines in this period were greater in Newfoundland than in any other province or territory. Most rural and small-town communities lost 20 to 40 percent of their population from 1991 to 2006, while the Northeast Avalon region grew by 5 percent (Community Accounts 2006b). Population declines in the province as a whole levelled off from 2001 to 2006 (−1.5 percent) and reversed in 2011, but as Census Metropolitan Areas (CMAs) and Census Agglomerations (CAs) grew over the past decade, the rural and small-town population shrank by 3 percent (Statistics Canada 2006a, 2007, 2012a).

Out-migration coupled with low birth rates and population aging has contributed to population losses. Census figures show a continued trend of population aging in rural areas: decreases in age cohorts under forty-five years and increases in cohorts over forty-five years between 2001 and 2006. These trends can be seen in rural areas across Canada and internationally but are particularly pronounced in Newfoundland & Labrador, which as of 2006 had the lowest fertility rate in the country and high rates of youth out-migration. Fishery-dependent rural areas have been most affected by these trends (Newfoundland and Labrador 2006c).

Rural communities remain heavily reliant on the natural resource sectors. The percentage of rural residents engaged in both "agriculture and other resource-based industries" and "construction and manufacturing," often tied to primary sectors, is higher than the provincial average (see figure 11.1). Employment in primary sectors is more than three times higher than in urban centres. Thus, policies related to resource industries typically have the greatest impacts on rural workers and their communities, which are also subject to the pressures of resource economies, including job losses owing to technological change, resource depletion, increasing international competition, and volatility in prices and demand

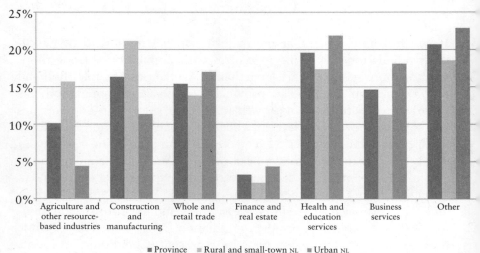

Figure 11.1
Percentage of population by industry, 2006

(Freshwater, Simms, and Vodden 2011). According to Community Accounts (2006a), primary sector dependence increased from 2001 to 2006 in the province, highlighting the relevance of concerns related to the impacts of resource dependency.

It is important to note that rural Newfoundland & Labrador is diverse. The socio-economic changes of the past two decades have been experienced differently in each community and region: as some communities have struggled with the changes, others have flourished. As of May 2006, for example, unemployment rates were lowest in the Northeast Avalon metropolitan area (10 percent, compared to the provincial average of 18.6 percent), but also in the mining communities of western Labrador (8.6 percent), while the fishing-dependent regions of southeastern Labrador and the southwest coast of Newfoundland experienced unemployment rates exceeding 50 percent (Community Accounts 2006a). Finally, despite the province's "rural-urban divide," there is also a growing rural-urban interconnectedness as family members move to urban areas, commuting becomes more common, rural manufacturers seek to serve urban markets, and urban residents continue to look to rural areas for their natural resource wealth and amenities.

CASE STUDY

From a rural development perspective three key aspects emerged across the Progressive Conservative (PC) election platforms of 2003, 2007, and 2011: (1) economic and natural resource development, (2) service provision and infrastructure, and (3) rural governance and decision making. Case studies emerged from several rural and regional development research initiatives undertaken from 2003 to 2011, drawing from more than 570 mail-out and internet surveys and 200 in-depth interviews with rural government, non-government, and business leaders, together with extensive dialogue through workshop and focus group sessions and secondary documentation review (Freshwater, Simms, and Vodden 2011; Gibson and Dominaux 2010; Porter and Vodden 2012; Tucker et al. 2011; Vodden 2009; Woodrow et al. 2011; and others).

Economic and Natural Resource Development

The 2003 and 2007 PC platforms committed to initiatives that added value to natural resources and diversified economies in rural communities and regions. Attempts to encourage secondary manufacturing and other ventures in the province have had a long history plagued by small domestic markets, competitive challenges, and the relative ease of large-scale resource development.

Most provincial governments have attempted rural diversification (cf. Affaires municipales et Régions 2007; Manitoba 2003). Premier Williams' approach was to create a new Regional Diversification Strategy, which identified nine regions (overlaid on twenty existing economic zones, as discussed further below). At the local level, community residents and municipalities are concerned that in many cases rural diversification has meant little more than countless trails, museums, and other tourism-related projects that complement but will not sustain rural economies. Further, despite a commitment to diversification, the primary resource sectors of fisheries and aquaculture, agri-foods, forestry, mining, and energy have been emphasized in party platforms. Developments in two resource sectors that featured prominently in the research initiatives described earlier and play a dominant role in the provincial economy and policy discourse are discussed next.

As Mario Levesque outlines in chapter 10 of this book, the Williams and Dunderdale administrations have made a series of stated commitments to fisheries investments and have undertaken, commissioned, and responded to a variety of reports about the fishery. This includes documents such as the *Fishing Industry Renewal Strategy (2007), the Seafood Marketing Review Panel Report* (2008), and the Memorandum of Understanding (2009–11), which represent significant provincial efforts to explore the challenges and opportunities associated with the fishery. While this attention to the industry has been viewed favourably overall, community leaders and fisherpeople from fishing-dependent regions remain skeptical that the changes recommended will contribute to more sustainable, viable rural communities. In fact, many fear they will be the targets of efforts to downsize the industry, as outlined in the *Fishing Industry Rationalization and Restructuring* report ("the MOU report"). The report recommended a reduction in the inshore fleet (vessels of less than forty feet) by 30 to 80 percent, with the greatest reductions concentrated on the northeast and west coasts of Newfoundland and southern Labrador (Clift 2011; Woodrow et al. 2011). The implication is a reduction in employment opportunities in these fishing-dependent regions.

Experiences on Change Islands, a northeast coast community, suggest that an announcement of rationalization or restructuring of the fishing industry is rarely a positive one for local fisherpeople. Research highlights community concerns about a top-down regulatory regime that often pays little attention to local solutions and recommendations on both the provincial (processing) and federal (harvesting) levels or to the future of the fishery as the community's mainstay. Island residents have called for the inclusion of considerations such as equity, environmental stewardship, and opportunities for small-scale innovation in discussions on fisheries restructuring. A disproportionate reduction in the number of inshore fisherpeople without measures to restrict increased fishing capacity and capitalization among those remaining may have significant impacts on the viability of fishery-dependent coastal communities without corresponding reductions in industry capacity or enhancements in fisheries sustainability and viability. Commitments to "regional balance" in fisheries restructuring require further elaboration and dialogue that addresses considerations of both intergenerational and geographic equity considerations.

Residents express frustration with provincial and federal policies that do not take into account the specific needs, experiences, and contexts of their communities not only in fisheries but also in regulations pertaining to small business, as well as a need for increased funding opportunities to support diversification efforts that build on local assets and aspirations (Fürst et al. 2011).

In the 2000s public attention to the apparently declining relevance of the fishery to the overall provincial economy has been often overshadowed by increases in the province's oil revenues. The provincial government negotiates and secures benefits from offshore oil development on behalf of the whole province. The commitments of the Williams administration moved from a 2003 platform that included providing industrial benefits for adjacent communities to a 2011 position, under the Dunderdale administration, where no particular priority was given to the area of immediate impact in the distribution of these benefits.

Provincial governments over the past three decades have promoted offshore oil and gas as the "new" staples. The Williams administration insisted on greater benefits and equity, but benefits on a provincial level (e.g., royalties to the province or employment across the province) have been prioritized over benefits for individual communities (e.g., royalties allocated to municipalities or employment of workers from adjacent communities). This dichotomy between benefits at the provincial and community levels was explored in the Isthmus of the Avalon region.

Interviews in the Isthmus of Avalon reveal the tensions experienced when local benefits are no longer prioritized. To many rural communities, the Isthmus region is in an enviable position because of its industrial development. Yet interviews with Isthmus community members, particularly leaders in business, local government, and community organizations, uncover a complex and at times uneven distribution of industrial benefits.

The development of the Hibernia oilfield began in 1990 and has been followed by further developments related to the Terra Nova, White Rose, and, most recently, the Hebron field. Direct employment in oil and gas extraction is limited relative to the scale of the industry (1,800 jobs, 0.7 percent of total employment in 2005; Community Accounts 2006a), but the province has benefited greatly from associated opportunities for supply firms, spending on research and development and infrastructure and in other sectors, and royalties (Storey and Shrimpton 2008). Curran et al. (2009), House (2006), and others point out, however, that the benefits of oil development have been concentrated in the greater St John's capital region.

The Isthmus region is a site of intense, primary-sector-driven industrial activity, home to facilities such as the North Atlantic oil refinery, still-operating fish-processing plants, the Bull Arm drydock and fabrication site (operated by Nalcor, a Crown corporation), and the Whiffen Head transshipment terminal. Residents in the Isthmus region feel that because requirements for local jobs have been defined at a provincial level, not enough jobs have been given to people living in the communities most affected by the oil industry, and they resent the continued high rates of unemployment and ongoing out-migration in the region. Additionally, while some municipalities have been able to benefit from tax arrangements with adjacent industry, others have not, which has resulted in dramatic inequalities between neighbouring communities. These issues have led to the interpretation that benefits from nearby industrial, and particularly oil-driven development, have largely passed them by and that local leaders have limited influence over provincial-level decisions affecting their communities (Curran et al. 2009; Porter and Vodden 2012).

Rural Services and Infrastructure

As the Williams administration took the reins of power, municipalities in the province were experiencing significant difficulty maintaining many aspects of their basic operations, facing issues such as shrinking municipal revenues because of out-migration, decreasing financial transfers from the provincial government, increasing debt (Kitchen 2002; Locke 2011), service delivery and infrastructure gaps, inability to fund preventative maintenance (Quinton and Lane 2009), and inadequate human resource and financial capacity (Feehan et al. 2009). The absence of legislation allowing for the collection of grants in lieu of taxes for provincially owned properties exacerbates financial pressures in the municipal sector (Locke 2011). *What's the Plan?*, a 2011 provincial election campaign by the municipal association Municipalities Newfoundland & Labrador (MNL), declared that "towns are struggling," estimating that the province has a $3.5 billion infrastructure gap (MNL 2011a, 1).

Rural communities across the province identify infrastructure and service challenges that hinder both economic development opportunities and quality of life, which are essential for attracting and maintaining residents, including youth and skilled workers. Illustrative challenges raised by interview and survey respondents include:

· access to health and childcare services;
· inadequate local infrastructure, such as local business development centres, industrial parks, and wharves;

- aging municipal infrastructure (buildings, roads, equipment, and so on);
- a lack of cell phone coverage and/or broadband Internet access;
- an increasing concern about affordable housing;
- the ability to sustain recreational facilities; and
- the lack of locally available professional development and adult education programs.

While many communities face the challenges noted above and conditions, such as the availability of affordable housing, have worsened in some areas, investments made over the past decade are also acknowledged. The province's ferry replacement strategy has been seen as a signal to the coastal and island communities of the northeast coast that their development needs have not been entirely overlooked (Fürst et al. 2011). Broadband access has been expanded since 2003, and further investments are planned through the Rural Broadband Initiative. In Budget 2011, the Dunderdale government provided the first increase in Municipal Operating Grants in over a decade (Reid 2011). Spending on the provincial roads program has resulted in highway improvements in some areas, but in others local leaders continue to call for improvements along with a greater say in transportation spending.

Underlying problems such as the need for new and increased revenue sources remain unresolved. Municipal leaders suggest the current tax system does not provide sufficient revenue to support even basic services (MNL 2011b; Locke 2011). Through MNL they have called for a new fiscal framework throughout the Williams and Dunderdale eras, heightening their efforts in 2011–12 (MNL 2005, 2011b, 2012).

Amidst these developments there has been a gradual movement towards regional services and collaboration. As a tool to increase sustainability and address service and infrastructure challenges, regional cooperation has shown promise. Recent service-sharing arrangements, restructuring initiatives, and the creation of a Community Cooperation Office by the provincial municipal association are the result of this focus.

Senior government, municipality, and community leaders have explored, and continue to explore, avenues for regional collaboration. Three recent examples are illustrated to demonstrate the breadth of these initiatives. In the Northern Peninsula region, the NorPen Waste Management Authority, created in 2001 and formalized as an authority under the Regional Service Board Act in 2005, is responsible for residential, municipal, commercial, and industrial waste collection for approximately ten thousand residents. In the Isthmus of the Avalon region, four towns have formed a joint committee, bringing these municipalities together to work collaboratively on industrial benefits planning, tourism, and recreation initiatives. On Change Islands and Fogo Island, multi-community collaboration is taking place in the form of an agricultural cooperative, joint socio-economic development planning, and ferry consultations, among other initiatives. These illustrations of regional collaboration have facilitated planning and service delivery in rural areas that individual communities would have had limited capacity to deliver otherwise.

The provincial government has offered support and financial incentives for regional efforts, but because regions are only as strong as their member municipalities, regions experience similar challenges.

Rural Governance and Decision Making

The Williams administration put its stamp on rural development early on with the establishment of the Rural Secretariat in 2004. The secretariat was created to build on the strengths of the former Strategic Social Plan (SSP), with its vision of healthy vibrant communities built on local strengths and capacities and SSP regional steering committees (House and Earle 2004). The Rural Secretariat is mandated to promote regional economic, social, cultural, and environmental well-being; work with partners to build strong regions; bring regional concerns to the province; enable research; and foster identified growth opportunities (Newfoundland and Labrador 2010f).

Positioned within the Executive Council, the new entity was housed at the centre of government. In addition to the secretariat, nine regional councils and a provincial council were created. Regional councils were tasked with developing a holistic and comprehensive understanding of their regions, reviewing regional economic and social measures, facilitating regional collaboration, and providing policy and program advice related to important issues for their regions (Newfoundland and Labrador 2010f). The Provincial Council, which includes representatives of each regional council as well as post-secondary institutions and other community appointees, meets with cabinet and deputy ministers twice annually to discuss problems and priorities (Close, Rowe, and Wheaton 2007).

The creation of the Rural Secretariat introduced a new player into the rural governance system and created uncertainty regarding previously existing organizations and initiatives and the ongoing roles and responsibilities of the parties involved. Since the 1960s, community-based economic development has seen the grassroots initiation of economic development boards in communities throughout the province. In response to charges concerning the ineffectiveness of existing development associations and "a plethora of non-integrated, largely uncoordinated programs and projects" (Monitoring and Evaluation Subcommittee 1997, 5; Newfoundland and Labrador 1995), twenty (later nineteen) Regional Economic Development Boards (REDBs) were formed in 1995 under Liberal premier Clyde Wells. The REDBs were to provide a stronger institutional framework for rural and regional development, led by local stakeholders with provincial and federal support. Members of each REDB were to be locally elected, in contrast to the Rural Secretariat Regional Councils, which are made up of provincially appointed citizen representatives.

Although the Williams government committed to continued financial contributions for REDBs, signals regarding political support for the boards were mixed.[3] REDBs had no representation on the new councils and were left uncertain about their relationship with this latest form of regionalization. In 2007 the PC Party committed to following through on its Regional Diversification Strategy through the Rural Secretariat and its partners (PC Party 2007). The strategy was originally designed with input from REDBs in 2003; however, the 2007 election platform item did refer specifically to the involvement of REDBs. Eight years after the formation of the Rural Secretariat, those involved in these two types of regional development structures continue to negotiate and learn about their respective roles, areas of overlapping interest, and opportunities to work together to pursue common goals.

The councils, together with regional partnership planners, have worked to better understand issues in their regions, foster collaboration, and submit policy recommendations to the provincial government. Councils receive responses to their policy advice from relevant departmental officials, but there is little available evidence to suggest that their recommendations have been incorporated into provincial decision making. While this can in part be attributed to the difficulty of clearly identifying factors that contribute to policy change, despite the councils' stated mandate, according to some members "government is really not interested in seeking regional input" (Kearley 2008, 29). Close, Rowe, and Wheaton (2007, 16) refer to the Rural Secretariat as "a return to a familiar model that makes the provincial and federal governments, not communities and their citizens, the principal agents of change in rural areas."

In 2009, the Newfoundland Speech from the Throne committed the provincial government to exploring a new model of regional collaboration with communities to advance regional sustainability (Crosbie 2009). The Northern Peninsula Regional Collaboration Pilot Initiative promised a new approach to government-community shared decision making in the province. The initiative involves fifty-five communities in the St Anthony–Port au Choix Rural Secretariat region, and it was asked to provide advice regarding regional investments, to facilitate regional discussion of issues, and to communicate local knowledge about ways to support regional collaboration (Case 2009). However, preliminary assessment based on ongoing research indicates that the initiative is involved primarily in consultation and advocacy and that decision making remains centralized in St John's. Further evaluation is required in order to offer additional insights into the impact of the model and its potential for replication.

Another model of community engagement is for municipalities to act as a voice for rural Newfoundland & Labrador. Since the mid-1900s, there has been a drive towards incorporating communities under the Municipal Act; there were thirty incorporated municipalities in the late 1940s, and today there are 276 rural and urban municipalities. The vast majority of these are rural. Although the democratic and local governance role of municipalities is pivotal, most are focused on "keeping the lights on" because of issues discussed above.

As the expectations of local governments grow within the province but also nationally and internationally, many municipalities are struggling to meet these growing demands. This is particularly true for small towns. A 2011 municipal census indicated, for example, that 59 percent of small towns with fewer than one thousand residents did not have a contested election in 2009, in contrast to 12.5 percent of towns with over four thousand residents. Planning capacity is also weak; just over half of small municipalities had an emergency preparedness plan (55 percent) and only 48 percent had a land use/zoning plan in place, compared to 94 and 100 percent respectively for communities with over four thousand residents (Keenan 2011). In a 2008 municipal self-assessment, only 40 to 65 percent of municipalities fared well with regard to governance indicators such as the presence of council standing committees and participation in councillor training (Quinton and Lane 2009). Further, many small communities depend on government financial assistance for survival (Locke 2011).

Here also, regionalism is offered as a response. A relatively weak but growing number of joint councils exist as a forum for municipalities to discuss common issues and collaboration opportunities, and while there is a push by MNL to examine the potential for regional government to strengthen the municipal sector, significant barriers to regional governance remain. In the case of this much-debated and politically volatile issue,[4] both Liberal and PC governments have chosen a "hands-off" approach, facilitating and encouraging regional cooperation and amalgamations rather than initiating mandatory restructuring. The Department of Municipal Affairs has invested in developing municipal capacity through the Municipal Training Program and partnerships with the Municipal Training and Development Corporation but has been criticized for its level of engagement in assisting municipalities to strengthen their planning capacity and thus to play a more effective role in local governance and decision making.

POLITICAL DECISION MAKING IN NEWFOUNDLAND & LABRADOR

The new rural paradigm calls for a shift from natural-resource-based to more diverse rural economies that build on local assets and focus on enhanced competitiveness. Policies that support continued staples dependency are thus consistent with the "old rural paradigm." However, in a province where 33 percent of provincial revenues come from offshore oil, mining, and forestry royalties, the incentives for continued focus on staples extraction are great. Premier Williams and his successor have played central roles in setting an agenda for rural policy that is focused on natural-resource development.

The story is not one-dimensional, however. Williams' administration made positive policy and program contributions in rural development through initiatives such as the Rural Secretariat's "rural lens" on government policy (Newfoundland and Labrador 2013c) and instruments such as cabinet papers, poverty reduction and youth retention measures, investments in rural infrastructure, and tourism marketing. But investments in diversification have been dwarfed by those in the resource sectors. Research and development spending through the Research and Development Corporation of Newfoundland and Labrador (RDC) has been focused on geosciences and ocean industries (RDC 2012), activities that are concentrated in urban centres and support the lucrative mining and oil and gas sectors while further increasing the provincial government's economic and political power.

Conditions in the province suggest that the influences of early resource extraction patterns and the staples trap are ongoing, with the current government's sights set on Labrador, for example, as a "superwarehouse" of energy and resources ripe for development (PC Party 2011). Rural and regional development under the Williams administration can be understood by drawing from elitist and neocorporatist theories of public policy, as well as insights from staples theory and political economy. Decision making on policy and programs has been concentrated in the provincial capital and dominated by a powerful central executive, particularly the Office of the Premier and the Executive Council. In some instances, organizations representing major interests, particularly business and labour but also provincial, municipal, and economic development associations, engage in political exchanges that influence policy. The involvement of major seafood processors as represented by the Association of Seafood Producers (ASP), fisheries workers as represented by the Fish, Food and Allied Workers (FFAW), and the government of Newfoundland & Labrador in the Memorandum of Understanding (MOU) to explore options for fisheries rationalization and restructuring provides a cogent example of the continued presence of the state-business-labour triad observed in staples economies (Markey, Pierce, and Vodden 2000; Markey et al. 2005).

A shift to the new rural paradigm requires a more collaborative, multi-level governance and systems-oriented approach to public policy. Although elitism and corporatism have been dominant, there have also been illustrations of experimentation with more open approaches to public policy development during the Williams era, such as the Rural Secretariat Regional Councils and the development of poverty reduction and youth retention and attraction strategies, both of which have had implications for rural communities.

The Williams administration's Rural Secretariat has provided opportunities for rural community engagement, regional advocacy, and review of government policy from a rural perspective, but its impact on provincial policy is uncertain. How the provincial government responds to the lessons learned from the regional collaboration pilot initiative under way in the Northern Peninsula also remains to be seen. Case studies in the fishery and oil and gas sectors provide limited and sporadic evidence of power sharing and meaningful community-government collaboration. These cases suggest that the province has not witnessed a significant shift in rural governance since the PC Party formed the government in 2003. With the loss of REDB funding in 2012–13 and thus one of the key agencies responsible for rural and regional development at the local level, the balance of any shift that has occurred has surely been in the direction of more centralized control. Little evidence exists in the cases presented above that rural development players have been provided with a direct role in decision making, such as budget allocation or program design, or that a political and bureaucratic culture in Newfoundland & Labrador described as clientelistic and highly centralized has been altered (Close 2007; House 1992).

Building on the OECD's series of territorial reviews at the national level, the new rural paradigm was put forth with an explicit message focused on place-based as opposed to sector-based development. Yet under the Williams administration, the province has not seen a comprehensive reorientation away from sector-based policies, and the local level remains a weak, dependent player in multi-level governance.

Although the Williams administration's 2003 election platform proposed a plan for social and economic development, to date there has been no comprehensive plan, strategy, or policy for the province and, in particular, for the province's rural regions. The province might look to the provincial rural policy in Quebec for what is described as one of the most advanced examples of rural policies in the OECD, one that is place-based, bottom-up, multi-sectoral, and committed to building social and community capacity to facilitate the participation of rural communities in the new economy (Affaires municipales et Régions 2007; OECD 2010).

The Progressive Conservative government has made and continues to make efforts to enhance rural communities throughout the province; however, its effectiveness and the level of priority given to rural regions remain unclear. The case studies presented illustrate a continuation of many of the characteristics of resource regions posited under staples theory and limited adherence to the principles of the new rural paradigm. Future administrations will need to address notions of decentralization and power sharing, coherent plans (and plan implementation) for rural sustainability, and recognition of the important role of regional and economic development organizations existing in the province, as well as local governments, to tackle head-on the many challenges faced by rural communities and to provide hope for a brighter future in the province's rural and remote regions.

NOTES

1   "Rural and Small Town" (RST) Canada refers to areas outside either a census metropolitan area (CMA) or a census agglomeration (CA) (du Plesis, Beshiri, and Bollman 2001). The term "census rural population" for 1981

to 2006 refers to persons living outside centres with a population of 1,000 and outside areas with 400 persons per square kilometre. Before 1981, the definitions differed slightly but consistently referred to populations outside centres with populations of 1,000 and greater (Bollman and Clemenson 2008). RST areas are further subdivided into no, weak, moderate, and strong metropolitan influence zones (MIZs) according to the level of influence of larger urban centres on an RST area.

2   The 1951 census was the first census of population conducted by Statistics Canada after Newfoundland joined the Canadian confederation.

3   In 2012 both federal and provincial governments announced that core funding for REDBs would cease as 2012–13 funding agreements came to an end.

4   Rooted in sentiments remaining from the resettlement era and subsequent amalgamation attempts, previous efforts to examine regional government as an option for Newfoundland & Labrador have met with resistance. A 1997 report of the Task Force on Municipal Regionalization concluded that there was "very little public support for the concept of either Regional Councils or Regional Service Authorities" but recommended that a Regional County Services Board be established in each of the twenty regional economic zones (Boswell, Faour, and Synard 1997, 2).

12

The Challenge of the Lower Churchill

JAMES P. FEEHAN

COMPARATIVE THEORY

This chapter is about the policy approach of the Williams administration to developing the hydro-electric potential on the lower section of the Churchill River, usually referred to as the Lower Churchill. Whatever form that development takes, several billion dollars will be involved. That is a huge cost for a jurisdiction of half a million people. Beyond that, there are other important policy considerations, such as the long-term security of electricity supply, as well as the socio-economic and environmental impacts. Not only is the approval of the government of Newfoundland & Labrador required for the project; it is also the resource owner, and its Crown corporation, Nalcor, is the project proponent.

Such extensive involvement of provincial governments in the electricity sector is not a new phenomenon in Canada. Only in the late nineteenth and early twentieth century was electricity the purview of private business. During the twentieth century, provincial governments came to dominate that sector. Their main instrument was the Crown corporation, the "hydro corporation." Eventually, in all provinces with the exceptions of Alberta and Prince Edward Island, hydro corporations accounted for practically all the generation – whether water-powered or otherwise – and transmission of electricity within their respective boundaries. Some distribution remained within the private sector or was handled by municipally owned utilities, and some energy-intensive industries retained ownership of their own-use hydro facilities. Still, hydro corporations have been the outstanding feature of the electricity sector since the mid-1960s.

Interestingly, the federal government played practically no role in the development of these province-centric electricity sectors. This reflects the constitutional allocation of responsibilities: provinces have jurisdiction over natural resources and over property rights. The former is important because it establishes authority over hydro-electric sites – an authority that was confirmed in 1982 by the addition of section 92A to the Constitution Act – and the latter is important because it allows the provinces to expropriate land for transmission lines and to take over privately owned electricity assets. The federal government does have jurisdiction over interprovincial and international trade, but the evolution of electricity was largely a within-province phenomenon. Significant interprovincial and international trade in electricity is a fairly recent phenomenon. Indeed, it was only in the late 1950s that the federal government established the National Energy Board (NEB), with a mandate that includes regulation of international trade in electricity. Also, federal environmental policy encompasses electricity generation projects. Otherwise, electricity policy remains solidly under provincial jurisdiction.

Provincial governments have used their authority to impose a high degree of public ownership and regulation. There are several explanations for this (see Jaccard 1995, 579–82; Netherton 2007, 109–12; and Zuker and Pastor 1985, 428–9). One of the early rationales for ownership was to eliminate the monopoly power of privately owned regional utilities. The prices charged by those firms were seen as excessive, and they were criticized for being too slow in extending electrification to rural areas and in investing in additional capacity to support industrial growth.

In 1906, the Hydro-Electric Power Commission of Ontario, the forerunner of Ontario Hydro, became the first provincial hydro corporation. By the mid-1960s, more than two-thirds of the Canadian electricity sector, and an even larger share of its generation assets, was under provincial ownership (Zuker and Pastor 1985, 437). In general, these hydro corporations were guided by a policy of low prices. To that end, they were typically financed at high levels of debt, often subsidized implicitly by provincial government loan guarantees, and exempted from corporate income tax. Little equity was used to finance these corporations' investments, and the returns on that equity were kept low. Electricity prices within various rate classes, e.g., residential, commercial, and industrial, were usually uniform even when the cost of providing electricity was substantially higher for some. Where waterpower was used for generating electricity, little or no water royalties were collected by provincial governments. In some cases, energy-intensive industries were supported by electricity prices that were at or even less than cost, or the prices were less than what could be earned if the electricity had been sold out of province. Cheap electricity was seen as a catalyst for industrial and economic growth. This low-price policy has usually been supported by provincial price regulation, especially when there are private electricity firms operating. Under these arrangements the idea of generating significant returns on government-owned capital and the natural resource for the benefit of taxpayers receives little weight. Thus, low electricity prices can come at a high implicit cost.

The period from the 1960s to the 1980s was the heyday of the hydro corporations. During that time, according to some analysts, provincial governments had practically given those institutions carte blanche on major issues (Vining 1981, 176). Yet the governance and financial results of several of these corporations were less than stellar. Vining implies that the generally poor performance of hydro corporations resulted from those institutions' decision-making processes: "Existing monopoly bureaucracies in the energy field may be strongly biased in favour of centralized, capital-intensive forms of new energy production and distribution" (1981, 182).

Since the 1980s, hydro corporations have had to adapt to increased public-policy sensitivity to the environmental, community, and socioeconomic effects of their activities. This is especially true for large new projects, particularly those that affect isolated or aboriginal communities, that have pronounced localized environmental effects, or that increase greenhouse gases and other emissions. Governments now require environmental assessments of significant projects. In addition to taking on these important social responsibilities, hydro corporations have been challenged by fiscal and financial circumstances. The case of the now-defunct Ontario Hydro is particularly conspicuous. By the 1990s, its extensive investments in non-hydro electricity generation were performing very poorly, and its debt levels had grown alarmingly high. In the mid-1990s, it was re-organized by the Ontario provincial government into distinct units, each associated with different aspects of its activities. That government also attempted to privatize the newly created generation and distribution components. The privatization effort was unsuccessful, but private-sector generators have been allowed greater presence in the province.

It is interesting to note that the privatization of hydro corporations remains generally unpopular in Canada. As of 2012, only one privatization had occurred. In 1992, largely because of its difficult fiscal circumstances and not without controversy, the Nova Scotia government sold Nova Scotia Power to the private sector. Around the same time, the Newfoundland government under Clyde Wells attempted to sell Newfoundland and Labrador Hydro (NLH), exclusive of its Churchill Falls assets, but backed down in the face of massive public opposition.

Still, many policy experts have called for changes to the policy regimes in which provincial hydros operate, whether privatized or not. Some economists have argued that provincial loan guarantees and the acceptance of low returns on equity induce hydros to make too much investment in capacity (Jenkins 1985). In addition, there are challenges to traditional electricity pricing. Economists point out that when prices charged by hydro corporations are lower than marginal cost, which is the cost of producing an additional unit of electricity, there is excessive consumption of electricity (Bernard and Chatel 1985). Along the same lines, it has been estimated that the low prices charged to the aluminum industry by Hydro-Quebec amount to an implicit subsidy of $190,000 per job annually (Bélanger and Bernard 1991, 202), and one critic has calculated that the total cost of Hydro-Quebec's inefficient practices is about $10 billion annually (Garcia 2009). An implication of these sorts of criticisms is that provincial governments should eliminate such losses by changing their policy regimes to allow electricity prices to be brought into line with marginal cost (Bernard and Duclos 2009; Boyer 2005; Feehan 2012; Zuker and Pastor 1985).

Another way to achieve such an outcome is to allow competition in electricity markets. It is an axiom of microeconomics that competition will lead to a price that reflects marginal cost. Some policy researchers argue that the old monopoly characterization of the electricity generation no longer applies (Cairns and Heyes 1993, 54; Jaccard 1995, 584). Competition is now feasible because markets are large enough to support many firms, because technological improvements make relatively small generating plants competitive with large ones, and because there is greater scope for electricity trade across borders, especially where owners of transmission assets are required to provide access to competitors.

This new emphasis on competition has led to some restructuring in Canada. Alberta has introduced a competitive market framework for electricity. Less successfully, so has Ontario (Carr 2010). Developments in the United States have also been influential. Actions by the Federal Energy Regulatory Commission (FERC) in the 1990s support competition by requiring owners of transmission assets to allow others to transmit their electricity on their infrastructure. For Canadian producers to export to the United States, they must comply with FERC policy, allowing any others to use their transmission capabilities on a non-discriminatory basis, according to an open access transmission tariff (OATT) formula. At the same time, some analysts are also calling for actions that facilitate interprovincial trade in electricity to further the scope for more competition (Carr 2010).

In summary, the paradigm of provincial low-price policies and Crown hydros is in a state of flux. New considerations are in play. There are environmental concerns; the waste associated with traditional low-price policy is under attack by policy experts; the scope for competition is increasing; and the North American electricity market is becoming more integrated. Yet the Crown hydro model remains dominant in most provinces, especially in those where water power provides most of the electricity generation, i.e., in British Columbia, Manitoba, Quebec, and Newfoundland & Labrador.

BACKGROUND

Since 1949, Newfoundland premiers have sought the development of the enormous hydro-electric potential on the Churchill River – known as the Hamilton River until it was renamed in honour of Winston Churchill on his death. In the 1960s, during the Smallwood era, the Churchill Falls site, which is one of the largest in the world, was developed by Brinco, a private consortium that Premier Smallwood had attracted in the early 1950s. However, the associated sale agreement between Brinco's subsidiary, the Churchill Falls Labrador Corporation (a NLH subsidiary since 1973), and Hydro-Quebec, which does not expire until 2041, has generated relatively few benefits for Newfoundland (Feehan and Baker 2007). On the other hand, it has been an enormous windfall for Hydro-Quebec. That one-sided outcome and the circumstances that led to it continue to influence political culture in the province and have led to a widespread distrust of Quebec by Newfoundlanders.

It is against this background that successive premiers have attempted to find a plan to develop the two substantial hydro sites downriver from Churchill Falls. Those sites, Gull Island and Muskrat Falls, while smaller than Churchill Falls, are too large for provincial needs. An export market or a new, large energy-intensive industrial consumer is needed for the sale of the surplus. Given the central Labrador location of the Churchill River, the need for an export market brings Quebec, as the only adjacent jurisdiction, into play. It is a potential buyer or, failing that, the route to markets beyond, e.g., Ontario or New England. Attempts over the past decades to reach an accommodation with Quebec for either option have been fruitless.

Before Danny Williams came to office, the most recent attempt to develop the Lower Churchill was made by the Liberal administration of Roger Grimes. The Liberals had been in power since 1989, and Grimes became premier in February 2001 following his election as party leader. Only two months later, Williams was selected as Progressive Conservative (PC) Party leader and in June won a by-election enabling him to face Grimes in the House of Assembly. Grimes had a two-alternative strategy with respect to the Lower Churchill. One was to negotiate a sale agreement between NLH and Hydro-Quebec, the two provinces' respective Crown hydro corporations. The other option involved attracting an energy-intensive aluminum smelter. By the summer of 2002, the latter option was found to be unattractive and dropped. Also by that time, negotiations with Hydro-Quebec were well advanced. They were centred on development of the Gull Island site, with the bulk of its electricity to be sold to Quebec.

The momentum for that deal was lost in late 2002. In November, following a review of the proposed terms, the chair of NLH's board of directors and one other member resigned, while a third voted against it (CTV News 2002). At the same time Williams, who was leader of the official opposition, was a vocal critic and was organizing public protests. Lloyd Matthews, the minister of mines and energy at the time, questioned the merits of Williams' protest, arguing that there was no final deal, that negotiations were still going on, that if a deal were to be reached its terms would be made public, and that Premier Grimes had committed to bring any agreement to the legislature for a full debate and a free vote (Newfoundland and Labrador 2002). However, the negotiations quietly died out by early 2003, several months before that year's provincial election. The following case study is about what happened when Williams succeeded Grimes as premier.

CASE STUDY

The Lower Churchill was not a pivotal issue in the October 2003 election campaign. The PC Party platform did not directly attack Grimes' efforts to reach a deal with Hydro-Quebec. It was no longer in play; the political damage to the Liberals had already been done by the events of late 2002. Still, the PC platform, which emphasized Danny Williams' leadership and an assertive approach to natural resource development and to dealings with the federal government, did have something to say about the Lower Churchill. It reminded voters of the Churchill Falls experience and asserted that the federal government must act by giving the province the right to transmit through Quebec in order to end Quebec's "stranglehold" over the Lower Churchill's future. It ruled out "desperate deals" (PC Party 2003, 30–1).

The PCs won the October 2003 election handily. The first fourteen months or so of Williams' administration were dominated first by the poor state of the provincial government's finances and, later, by an acrimonious dispute with the federal Liberal government over the fiscal benefits from offshore oil production. While these matters made headlines, the Lower Churchill still figured as a priority on Williams' agenda. That was made evident in September 2004 when Premier Williams announced a strategy for the Lower Churchill. The government would issue an invitation for Expressions of Interest (EOI) to develop that hydro resource. Williams indicated that all options would be considered. Also, the process was opened to all interested parties, including Crown entities and the private sector (see chapter 2 of this book, by Christopher Dunn, for more on Crown entities).

Despite this willingness to consider all options and all forms of partnership, the hydro-corporation model eventually prevailed. In August of 2005, Premier Williams, in conjunction with NLH representatives, announced that the evaluation process for the EOI had narrowed the potential candidates to three. At the same time, it was indicated that a 100 percent NLH development remained an option. In a development closely related to that option, in January 2006 the provincial government directed NLH to apply to Hydro-Quebec TransEnergie, the subsidiary of Hydro-Quebec that operates transmission assets in that province, for transmission access to carry Lower Churchill electricity to potential markets in Quebec, Ontario, the Maritimes, and New England.

In May of 2006, Williams announced that, having considered the top EOI proposals, his administration had decided that the best option was the hydro-corporation model. As he stated, "We have the experience, knowledge and capacity to take on a project of this magnitude and we are recognized as world leaders in hydroelectric operations and development. This is about doing it by ourselves, for ourselves. We are on a path to be masters of our own destiny and the successful development of this project will be a significant step forward in reaching that ultimate objective for this province" (Newfoundland and Labrador 2006e). This decision was probably influenced by improving fiscal circumstances following Williams' successful campaign to pressure the federal government under Liberal prime minister Paul Martin to concede more offshore revenues. In this improved situation, both the provincial government and NLH went into action. NLH would consider the possible development options; provincial officials would continue negotiations with the Labrador Innu, a community of about twenty-five hundred people who claimed aboriginal rights in the Lower Churchill area. Also, the groundwork would be laid for the preparation of the Environmental Impact Statement (EIS) as required by both federal and provincial legislation. In December 2006, the project was formally registered for an environmental assessment (Newfoundland and Labrador 2006d).

The next major step came on 11 September 2007 with the release of the provincial Energy Plan (Newfoundland and Labrador 2007a). That document confirmed the intent to develop both Gull Island and Muskrat Falls. The plan also included a transmission link from the Lower Churchill to the island of Newfoundland. Most island energy needs are met by on-island hydro power, but the large oil-fired Holyrood generation station (HGS) must be used to top up generation to match consumption and is critically important during the winter months when electricity demand peaks. The proportion of electricity provided by the HGS varies with hydrological conditions and demand. Following the 2009 closure of the energy-intensive newsprint mill at Grand Falls in central Newfoundland, NLH's annual reliance on the HGS fell to about 15 percent; practically all the rest came from on-island hydro sites (Feehan 2012, 4).

The Energy Plan envisioned the closure of the HGS, thereby eliminating its air pollution and avoiding the purchase of costly fuel oil. Its output would be replaced with electricity from the Lower Churchill. Even with that substitution for the HGS' output, export markets remained pivotal. The capacity of the HGS is 490 megawatts (MW), while the Lower Churchill's capacity is in excess of 3,000 MW: Gull Island is about 2,250 MW and Muskrat Falls about 825 MW. The extra energy has to be sold somewhere in order to make the projects worthwhile investments. To that end, the Energy Plan identified two paths to external markets (Newfoundland and Labrador 2007a, 44):

- the Quebec route: surplus energy would be moved using Quebec's transmission system for possible sales there as well as in Ontario, the Maritimes, New England, and New York; and
- the Maritimes route: all Lower Churchill electricity would be brought to the island of Newfoundland, and the surplus would be further

transmitted by subsea cables into the Maritime Provinces for sale there or beyond.

Just days after the release of the Energy Plan, a provincial election was called. The Lower Churchill did not figure prominently in it. The PC Party platform made only a general reference to Lower Churchill power in a brief statement about the Energy Plan (PC Party 2007), and it did not ignite much debate. This is not surprising. On one hand, it was still at a proposal stage. On the other hand, the previous few years had been dominated by Premier Williams' struggle with the federal government over offshore oil revenue sharing. Through his confrontations with Prime Minister Paul Martin, Williams won substantial concessions, which, combined with rising offshore oil production and, especially, higher oil prices, dramatically improved the province's finances. This improvement allowed Williams to remove fiscal austerity from his agenda and shift to defending the province's natural resources. The image of Williams aggressively confronting the federal government and the subsequent improvement in the provincial economy, which was in part driven by increased provincial government spending and lower taxes, made the premier extraordinarily popular. He led his party to a massive election victory that October.

Perhaps the dominant issue in the year following Williams' election triumph was his ABC – "Anything but Conservative" – campaign during the federal election. As Royce Koop mentions in chapter 4, Williams had launched that aggressive attack campaign against the governing federal Conservative Party, which had won office in 2006, in retaliation for changes to the federal equalization program that could indirectly offset some of the advantages conceded by Paul Martin. Still, despite all the attention about the poor relations with Ottawa, quiet progress was made on the Lower Churchill. Most notably, in September 2008, the provincial government and the Innu leadership reached an agreement on land claims, including a Lower Churchill Impacts and Benefits Agreement.

Another necessary step was the review of the project's EIS. In January 2009, a joint federal-provincial EIS review panel was established. Soon after, Nalcor, the province's newly established parent corporation for NLH, submitted the EIS, and the Joint Review Panel work was under way by March. The EIS covered the Lower Churchill project, defined as the development of both Gull Island and Muskrat Falls. It did not include transmission and undersea cables to the island, which were left to be the subject of a later and separate assessment.

Despite the progress on these fronts, difficulties with Quebec were soon to come to a head. By late 2009, NLH's request to Hydro-Quebec TransEnergie for transmission access remained unresolved, and it lodged complaints about TransEnergie with the Quebec regulator, the Régie de l'énergie. No doubt because of those difficulties, in a speech to the St John's Board of Trade in September 2009, Williams harshly criticized Hydro-Quebec, remarking on the exorbitant profit it makes on the Churchill Falls contract, and he described that Quebec institution as uncooperative, obstructionist, and insistent on having a stranglehold on energy transmission in eastern Canada (Williams 2009). Then in October the premiers of Quebec and New Brunswick announced that they were negotiating an arrangement by which Hydro-Quebec would purchase the poorly performing New Brunswick Power. Williams, who interpreted this as a threat to the Maritimes route option, was quick to enter the New Brunswick debate. As he had done on other occasions, Williams successfully attracted media attention. He was highly critical of the merger as not being in his province's interest, but he also warned New Brunswickers that Hydro-Quebec's motives in their province were suspect. In the end, intense popular opposition from within New Brunswick was so great that the deal was scrapped by the spring of 2010 (CBC News 2010h). Williams' involvement probably helped that opposition. Also, his actions in this case were further evidence of the extent to which he would go to protect the interests of his province.

On the other front, the overland route for the Lower Churchill had become ever more problematic. Since 2007, there had been difficulties in reaching an agreement with TransEnergie on acceptable terms for use of the Quebec transmission system. Indeed, that lack of progress was likely a spur to Williams' quick entry into the New Brunswick debate. In May of 2010, Quebec's Regie d'energie ruled against NLH's formal complaints against TransEnergie's treatment of its application. Williams was quick to denounce and harshly criticize the Regie's ruling. In the subsequent months, Williams lashed out at Quebec. In a speech given to the Economic Club of Ottawa in June, he launched a wide-ranging attack on Quebec, arguing that it was too favourably treated in the Canadian federation. He pointed out that Quebec government maps provocatively show large sections of Labrador to be inside Quebec; he denounced Hydro-Quebec's treatment of his province with respect to the 1969 Churchill Falls contract and its lack of cooperation in providing transmission access for the Lower Churchill project; and he attacked the Regie's recent ruling as being outright unfair (Williams 2010a).

By the summer of 2010, it was clear that there was little prospect of getting a route through Quebec on acceptable terms any time soon. Without that route, Gull Island, which is the larger and more economic site, could not proceed. Its potential output is so large relative to the provincial market that the bulk of its energy would have to be sold out of province in order to realize its economic advantage. Without a route through Quebec and in light of the enormous cost of transmitting so much electricity via a route around Quebec, that was not feasible. And Williams had already rejected Grimes' failed plan to sell Gull Island power to Hydro-Quebec at the border. Therefore, if he was to have a Lower Churchill development during his second term, it would have to be Muskrat Falls.

In November of 2010, Williams, along with Nova Scotia premier Darrel Dexter, Nalcor/NLH officials, Innu leaders, and senior executives of Emera Inc., the owner of privatized Nova Scotia Power, announced an agreement. At this well-organized public event, and with Innu elders in attendance, it was announced that Nalcor and Emera had agreed on a term-sheet as the basis for finalizing a development plan. Initially, the basic elements of that thirty-five-year deal were as follows:

· the Muskrat Falls site would be built and owned by Nalcor;
· transmission lines and a subsea cable would bring the electricity to the island, and Emera would have a minority ownership in this component;
· Emera would build and own a subsea cable link between the island and Nova Scotia and would receive approximately 20 percent of Muskrat Falls' annual energy for doing so (ownership would revert to Nalcor after thirty-five years); and
· Nalcor would have free access to Emera's cable link so it could export Muskrat Falls power that was surplus to provincial needs.

Surprisingly, on 25 November, just days after all the fanfare of the public announcement of the Muskrat Falls deal, with his popularity still extremely high at 76 percent according to a November poll (Corporate Research Associates 2012)and with no pressure from within his party, Danny Williams announced that he would leave politics. He would be returning to active participation in his extensive business interests in Newfoundland & Labrador. His departure was abrupt. His resignation as premier, as PC Party leader, and as a member of the House of Assembly was to take effect just a week later. This fast exit is especially astonishing considering Williams' close interest in the Lower Churchill. Throughout his time in office, this file was a priority for him. He was passionate about it. Now, after seven years of effort, the groundwork for proceeding was finally at hand. Yet, with much remaining to be done, Williams was returning to private life.

Criticism of the Muskrat Falls plan soon followed the initial announcement. The first critics were associated with the provincial Liberal Party, with former premier Grimes and then the leader of the opposition, Yvonne Jones, figuring prominently. Thereafter, doubts were raised by broader and more diverse groups and individuals. At this time, the new premier, Kathy Dunderdale, who was the former minister of natural resources, and her successor minister, Shawn Skinner, were the key respondents to the criticisms. Initially, the minister defended the exemption of the Muskrat Falls development from a review by the province's Public Utilities Board (PUB). However, to allay doubts, in June 2011 the government gave ground and directed the PUB to do a review. The PUB's mandate was limited to a comparison of Muskrat Falls with a single alternative, namely, an isolated-island option developed by NLH that was based on continued reliance on the HGS. Other options such as conservation, the use of wind, and, oddly, the use of natural gas, which is in abundant supply at the operating oil fields in the offshore area east of St John's, were excluded from the PUB's reference question.

During this time, the provincial government and Nalcor continued to defend the project, arguing that the power was needed and that Muskrat Falls was the best option available. On the other hand, criticisms from the opposition parties and many citizens did not let up. They appeared especially in the print media, figuring prominently in the province-wide newspaper, the *Telegram*. Then in August the Joint Review Panel for the Lower Churchill EIS issued its final report. After more than two years of public hearings and study, the panel concluded that "there are outstanding questions for each of Muskrat Falls and Gull Island regarding their ability to deliver the projected long-term financial benefits to the Province ... and Nalcor's analysis that showed Muskrat Falls to be the best and least costly way to meet domestic demand requirements is inadequate" (Joint Review Panel 2011, 25 and 34).

Following this negative assessment, questions about the Muskrat Falls project continued to appear in the media and during the October 2011 provincial election campaign. Also, the Liberal Party's platform committed to ordering Nalcor to restart negotiations with Quebec, Ontario, and the federal government to develop the entire Lower Churchill, and it effectively dismissed the Muskrat Falls project by saying that the Liberal Party would not support subsidizing rates for electricity users in Nova Scotia or any other province or state (Liberal Party 2011, 19). On the other hand, the New Democratic Party (NDP) platform was less critical and made only a general commitment to ensuring that the Lower Churchill would be developed in an economically and environmentally sustainable manner for the benefit of the province (NDP 2011, 17). The PC Party platform did not devote a great deal of space to its Muskrat Falls plan, but it did embrace it. Also, that document pointed out that the PUB had been commissioned to review Nalcor's analysis and stated that an independent consulting firm had confirmed Nalcor's calculations (PC Party 2011, 23). The PCs' campaign was also helped by Prime Minister Harper. With Dunderdale replacing Williams, there has been a rapprochement of sorts with Ottawa. In early April 2011, Harper, in the midst of the federal election campaign, visited St John's and with Dunderdale at his side at a campaign rally, publicly announced that a re-elected Conservative government would provide a loan guarantee, or equivalent financial assistance, for the project.

As it turned out, while it was an issue in the provincial election campaign, Muskrat Falls was not a pivotal one. Of the two opposition parties, the Liberals were the harsher critics. Yet it was the NDP, which had little to say on this matter, that made substantial gains in the popular vote. The Liberals increased their seats by two, but their popular vote fell slightly. So despite the Joint Panel report of only two months earlier, Muskrat Falls in itself did not sway voters. In part, this may have been the result of the government saying less and less about the project and generally leaving it to Nalcor/NLH to respond to the various critics. That was quite a departure from Williams' domination of debate on policy matters in which he was closely involved. In any case, and despite declining by almost fourteen percentage points in the popular vote and losing six seats, the PCs handily won the 2011 election with 56 percent of the vote and thirty-seven of the forty-eight seats.

Still, criticism of Muskrat Falls continued. Even a former chair of the PUB raised doubts (Vardy 2011), as did some individuals associated with the former PC government of Brian Peckford; the former premier himself called for more review in an open letter to Premier Dunderdale in February 2012. Nalcor continued to respond to public criticism, but there would be no immediate prospect of a legislative review. On Election Day Dunderdale indicated to the media that the House of Assembly would not be recalled until the spring of 2012, and she went so far as to suggest that debates there are of little value. Still, she did commit to a Muskrat Falls debate in the spring sitting of 2012, which was subsequently changed to the fall sitting. In the interim, the PUB reported at the end of March 2012 that it had inadequate information to justify endorsing Muskrat Falls. The provincial government was critical of the PUB's report and, along with Nalcor, continued to strongly advocate for the project. It cited previous and newly engaged consultants' reports in support of the project. Future regulatory reviews were ruled out.

POLITICAL DECISION MAKING IN NEWFOUNDLAND & LABRADOR

As is common with provincial elections, Danny Williams had won office with big majorities, which give premiers tremendous latitude for decision making. Williams' determined and competitive personality, his strong leadership style, and his impressive record of accomplishment further enhanced his commanding stature within his cabinet and across the provincial public sector. His first half-year in office was difficult because of the province's poor fiscal condition and his consequent austerity program. As a result, by May 2004 his party was effectively tied with the Liberals at 41 percent versus 39 percent, and his own leadership ranking was at 39 percent (Corporate Research Associates 2012). That would soon change. By the end of 2004, he had won his dispute with the federal government over offshore oil revenues. His aggressiveness in pursuing that goal, his effectiveness in the national and local media, and his ultimate success gained him nearly universal popularity among his constituents.

His other disputes with external parties involving natural resources further added to his appeal amongst voters. Gaining control over and using natural resources for local benefit have long been policy priorities for the people of his province. Indeed, those goals predate the union with Canada, as evidenced by Newfoundland's successful defence in the 1920s against Canadian claims to most of the interior of Labrador and by the nineteenth-century efforts of Newfoundland governments to gain sovereignty over the so-called French shore.[1]

Williams put these natural-resource and territorial matters at the top of his political agenda. Thus, his tough negotiating stance with offshore oil companies over royalties and local benefits, his denunciation of Quebec's Churchill Falls deal, and his decision to expropriate the hydroelectric assets of AbitibiBowater when that Delaware-incorporated company announced the closure of its central Newfoundland newsprint mill were all very popular with the general public. As well, his personal style in communicating these matters both to and through the media, while often irritating to Canadians elsewhere, endeared him to many at home. Indeed, the impressive staging of the Muskrat Falls announcement is an excellent example of Williams' great ability to display support and build momentum for his policy directions.

Also, his success in securing more offshore revenues through his 2005 agreement with the federal government and the good luck of rising oil prices allowed his regime to cut taxes, increase public spending, and run record budget surpluses. Williams' aggressive approach with respect to natural resources was paying off. It is therefore perhaps not surprising that his harsh reactions to any dissent within his caucus and to criticism from local sources were tolerated or overlooked by the general public. In terms of the big picture, Williams was delivering what his people wanted. In return, the people gave him widespread support.

With regard to the Lower Churchill file, the public also had confidence in Williams, who, with Nalcor, followed the approach consistent with the traditional hydro corporate model – big on investment and not overly concerned with economists' notion of efficiency. When Nalcor ran into difficulties in reaching an agreement to transmit electricity through Quebec, Williams denounced Quebec. Given Newfoundland's past experience with its neighbour regarding Churchill Falls, Williams' attack met with wide approval by his compatriots. However, another reason why there had been little opposition to Williams on that file is simply that effectively for all of his time as premier, there had been no specific project. There were only concepts and options.

This changed when the Muskrat Falls agreement was announced in late 2010, but that was only days before Williams chose to leave office. This project is different from the issues that brought Williams to astonishing popularity. It is largely an intraprovincial matter. Emera is involved, but its role is secondary. The project does not involve a struggle between Newfoundland & Labrador and the federal government or Quebec or an external developer. The costs and benefits largely fall on the province's people, which makes decision making more difficult because the winners and losers will be local. With Premier Williams' abrupt departure, his successors in the Dunderdale regime inherited this potentially divisive issue.

It is interesting to consider how the Williams era relates to the elite theory of public policy decision making as discussed in chapter 1 of this book. According to that theory, control of government rests with a powerful minority that is accepted by the public, which remains compliant unless adversely affected. Regarding the Williams administration, that theory could be pushed further by narrowing the elite down to a single person, namely, Danny Williams himself. Some might even put him in the category of benevolent dictator, but that would be unfair and pejorative. His domination of the province was a democratic phenomenon. He won free and fair elections because of his outstanding personal capabilities and his unconventional and aggressive tactics in fighting for the province's natural resource interests. Moreover, he achieved real results.

As an aside, it is worth remarking that the "first-past-the-post" electoral system leads to a seriously underrepresented opposition in the legislature, which enhances any government's position and gives greater latitude to a government headed by a person of outstanding abilities. However, this problem of concentrated power is an institutional failure that should be addressed by reform of the electoral system. It is not a fault of Williams or any other premier.

Still, elite theory has some application here. After all, the provincial electorate gave him extensive leeway in his fights with external opponents. Internal dissent was very muted and isolated. Consistent with the theory, the public were compliant. In this case, it was because Williams was perceived as bringing broad-based gains to the province. Such leeway might not have been extended to him on the question of Muskrat Falls.

As elite theory implies, if people believe that they will be adversely affected, then their support for the elite may wane. As mentioned, Muskrat Falls is an issue where no outside antagonist is involved. The project that would require substantial provincial government spending and would add billions to the provincial debt; people within the province would bear the costs and benefits, and some are unconvinced of the merits of the project. Many have raised doubts about it and argued for alternatives to be examined more thoroughly. Had Danny Williams stayed on as premier, he would have had to deal with serious opposition not experienced since his first six months in office.

NOTE

1   The French Shore refers to rights given to France over most of Newfoundland's west coast under the 1713 Treaty of Utrecht, which lasted until 1904.

13

The Political Economy of the Labour Market in Newfoundland and Labrador

JOHN PETERS, ANGELA CARTER, AND SEAN CADIGAN

COMPARATIVE THEORY

Labour markets in Canada and other rich democracies have been fundamentally transformed over the last twenty years. Deindustrialization has led to a significant decline in relatively well-paid unionized jobs in manufacturing (Emmenger et al. 2012a; Western 1997). The proportion of workers who belong to unions has gone into decline. Collective bargaining systems that once played a role in raising wages and improving the income distribution across economies have been reformed or undermined and replaced by private incentive-pay schemes or by profit-sharing arrangements that subvert negotiated wage scales (Glyn 2006). Public sector service jobs that once ensured wider income equality and job security for lower-skilled workers have seen significant layoffs, contracting out, and privatization (Flecker et al. 2009).

Average unemployment levels have increased between 5 and 15 percent since the 1980s (Lindvall 2010), and the share of atypical employment in the overall Organization for Economic Cooperation and Development (OECD) workforce (part-time and fixed-term combined) has grown from an average of around 10 percent to country-specific levels of 25 to 35 percent (Gautie and Schmitt 2010). Because of these concurrent trends, inequality in advanced industrial societies has increased during the past decades. Labour markets are now strongly "dualized" between "insiders" with good jobs, long-term security, and adequate pensions and "outsiders" facing high risks of atypical employment, unemployment, and limited access to social protection and pension incomes (Emmenger et al. 2012b; Hiesz and LaRochelle-Côté 2006; King and Rueda 2008).

These dramatic changes in labour markets and the growth in inequality have prompted academic analysis of the impact of politics on public policies (Beramendi and Anderson 2008; Emmenger et al. 2012b; Hacker and Pierson 2010; Kelly 2009). This work emphasizes how democratic political institutions and processes, in interaction with organized interests, influence macroeconomic performance through policies on growth, unemployment, employment performance, labour market institutions, and social protection (Emmenger et al. 2012b; Huo 2009; Pontusson 2005).

Three factors are considered central to understanding the recent variations between national labour markets and labour market deregulation policies. The role of political parties and their leaders are the first factor. Left parties are recognized as contributing to widespread unionization, generous social policies, and lessened inequality (Boeri, Brugiavini, and Calmfors 2001; Huber and Stephens 2001; Western 1997). In contrast, right parties are strongly linked to weaker wage-setting institutions (Iversen and Soskice 2008). Labour and social democratic parties have been instrumental in expanding union rights, lowering the cost of unionization, and facilitating public sector expansion aiming to maintain full employment and improve equality. Conservative parties have supported economic growth, free markets, limited social protection, and deregulated labour and product markets to support business productivity and employment performance (Amable 2003).

Trade unions and business interests comprise the second important set of factors affecting labour markets, economic change, and inequality (Korpi 1983). The literature on labour markets and welfare states has underscored how the extent of labour organization and coordinated bargaining across the economy determines how far labour can influence government policy and constrain policies favouring business alone (Boeri, Brugiavini, and Calmfors 2001; Western 1997). At the same time, the analysis notes how business interests and employer associations are also increasingly dominant participants in the policy and legislative process (Mares 2003).

Shifts in the balance of business and labour power have varied widely across countries (Frege and Kelly 2004). Confronted with globalization and neoliberal economic policy, unions in countries with strong labour movements and collective bargaining protection have been strategically innovative (Hamman and Kelly 2011). This has provided some protection to unionized workforces and public sector employment, which has in turn supported higher-quality jobs and greater income equality. At the same time, business organization has surged. Powerful economic interests have poured vast new resources into politics by lobbying on particular bills and funding parties and research institutes to shape political debate (Crouch 2011; Hacker and Pierson 2010). Organized labour has been able to counter the push for wage concessions, greater flexibility, and reductions in social protection only in locales where there are larger unionized workforces, public sectors, and extensive collective bargaining.

Economic shocks that have transformed government macroeconomic policies and public sector services comprise the third important set of factors that explain labour market policy. In the 1990s, in response to the pressure of rising deficits, all governments – left and right – introduced tax cuts to stimulate stronger investment and employment growth and to underpin government revenue (Huo 2009). But the extent and speed at which governments adopted these policies and restructured the public sector depended on the scale of declines in economic growth and the rise in deficits (Glyn 2006). In Germany, Italy, Canada, and Austria, quickly rising deficits were met with dramatic reductions in government spending and widespread privatization, outsourcing, and contracting out of public service employment (Peters 2012). During economic downturns or when facing high deficits, right-wing governments were also generally more aggressive in their efforts to weaken unions, deregulate employment standards, and introduce new "active" labour market or "workfare" measures to enforce wage moderation (Bosch, Lehndorff, and Rubery 2009; Moody 2007).

However, governments (nationally and regionally) that have experienced less-dramatic economic slowdowns or economic crises have enacted fewer policy changes and made fewer changes to public sector collective bargaining and employment. Moreover, during upturns, right-wing governments have adopted strong pro-cyclical budget measures to stimulate growth, including corporate and income tax cuts and increased government spending (Amable 2009). The conclusion that scholars have drawn from this is that the economic contexts of growth or downturns strongly condition the response of governments to tax and public service cuts, the deregulation of public sector collective bargaining, and other public policies.

Together, these three arguments offer a framework for understanding labour market outcomes. A key implication is that partisan policy preferences are shaped less by elections and votes than by current economic conditions and how organized interests are able to influence policy change within existing institutional frameworks. Economic actors – especially when they are capable of sustained collective action on behalf of shared material interests – have a significant and ongoing impact on how political authority is exercised in the labour market and in the economy more broadly. This theoretical framework is now applied to recent labour market developments in Newfoundland & Labrador, situated within the Canadian labour market context. This framework represents a slight departure from other chapters in this volume, since it understands the important power of the premier as embedded in, and strongly influenced by, the broader political and economic context (in Premier Williams' case, the dramatic rise of extractive sector revenues).

BACKGROUND

During the 1980s and 1990s, led by parties promoting a new economic conservatism, liberal market governments across Canada, the United States, and Great Britain sought to weaken unions, deregulate employment standards, and introduce new "active" labour market or "workfare" measures to enforce wage moderation (Moody 2007; Pontusson 2005). Were these trends evident in Newfoundland & Labrador? Many of them were in the 1990s, but then the province became more unique within Canada, as workers and unions avoided many of the negative labour policy and labour market dualization trends common throughout Canada.

Canada currently has one of the most segmented labour forces among affluent countries. It has among the highest proportion of workers in low-paid employment (more than 24 percent of full-time workers) and a labour market that is characterized by high levels of atypical employment (more than 31 percent of total employment) and by limited employment and social protection. These rates are comparable to the United States, often noted as having the most dualized labour market (King and Rueda 2008; LaRochelle-Côté and Dionne 2009). Also, like other liberal market economies such as the United States and Great Britain, Canada has sought to reduce unemployment by focusing on the control of labour costs and shrinking the state in order to achieve economic competitiveness (McBride 2005).

Government reform efforts have focused on cost control, expenditure restraint, and ending passive income security measures to reduce individual "disincentives" to work. The supply of public goods like social assistance and unemployment insurance has also been restricted through the tightening of means and jobs tests, the reduction of benefit levels, and cuts in the duration of benefits (Battle, Torjman, and Mendelson 2006). In the early 1990s, Canada's unemployment insurance system provided income benefits for roughly 80 percent of the unemployed (Mendelson, Battle, and Torjman 2009). By 2005, after a series of flexibility reforms, tightening of qualifying conditions, and decentralizing to economic regions, the renamed Employment Insurance (EI) program was accessible to only 40 percent of the unemployed. And in 2009, after the worst economic crisis in more than sixty years and federal Conservative reforms to limit EI benefits, in cities like Toronto, with its high immigrant workforce and extensive non-standard employment, only 20 percent of the unemployed qualified for benefits (Canadian Labour Congress 2011).

Within the provinces, reduced employment standards allow greater employer flexibility in hiring and firing and allow employers to use part-time, contract, and self-employed workers as needed. Provincial governments have also let the minimum wage languish far below the basic median wage, freezing minimum wages and letting them sink with inflation. In 2010, the minimum wage ranged from a high of 50 percent of the median wage in Ontario to a low of 39 percent in British Columbia – figures even lower than those in the United States, the country most commonly believed to have the lowest minimum wage in North America and Western Europe (Lucifora and Salverda 2009).

Newfoundland & Labrador was a partial exception to these Canada-wide "dualization" trends for several reasons: first, because of the way the province was able to maintain comparably higher EI coverage. With the introduction of reforms in 1996, both the work requirements and the maximum duration of benefits under the EI program varied according to regional unemployment rates. This regional variability created a multi-dimensional labyrinth of individual entitlements that served the province well. For resource industry provinces such as Newfoundland & Labrador and New Brunswick, the regional variation of the EI program (along with special legislation for fisheries workers) provided key means to support more than 90 percent of the rural unemployed. Most distinctively, Newfoundland & Labrador's unionized workers were also able to access EI benefits, both because of union assistance to the unemployed and because of union advocacy and lobbying to maintain income security for their members. In Newfoundland & Labrador, the Fish, Food and Allied Workers (FFAW) union, which is affiliated with the Canadian Auto Workers (CAW) union, provides all its members with extensive education and counselling on how to use the EI system to full effect.

The strength of bipartite bargaining and the strong public sector, construction, and fisheries unions in the province have also had a significant impact in resisting attempts by governments and employers to lower labour costs and make the labour force more flexible. Initially established in the construction industry to deal with major public works in the 1960s, coordinated bargaining frameworks among province-wide employer and labour associations became more common with the extension of collective bargaining rights to fish harvesters and public employees in the 1970s and the consolidation of bargaining institutions in the wake of a series of strikes in the 1980s (Luchak 2003).

One of the key reasons why public sector collective bargaining became more centralized in the 1980s and 1990s was that unions adopted an increasingly militant stance in the face of government attempts to lower costs by laying off workers and undermining public sector compensation and benefits (Cadigan forthcoming). During that time, Newfoundland's weak economy meant that governments regularly demanded concessions, wage freezes, and restrictions on the public sector's right to strike. But province-wide sectoral negotiations resulted when Brian Peckford's Progressive Conservative (PC) government fought with the Newfoundland Association of Public Employees (NAPE) over Bill 59, an Act to Amend the Public Services (Collective Bargaining) Act. This bill permitted the government to designate up to 49 percent of public-sector union members as essential public employees and to limit their right to strike, especially by outlawing rotating strikes (Cadigan forthcoming). Having failed in challenging Bill 59 in the Supreme Court of Newfoundland, fifty-five hundred public sector workers went on strike on 3 March 1986. They returned to work after a month, but five thousand went on strike again in September when the government did not back down from the intentions of Bill 59. Such militancy was instrumental in leading to the first in a series of government policies that enacted wage freezes for public employees, but also in establishing more centralized public sector collective bargaining and the provincial mobilization of public sector employees.

Following further sectoral agreements and government-imposed wage freezes in the 1990s, public sector unions sought to coordinate pattern agreements that exchanged long-term wage restraint, a "pension holiday" (that allowed the provincial government not to contribute to pension benefits), and cuts in public expenditure for a government commitment to maintain the status quo in public sector employment. Under Premier Brian Tobin in the late 1990s, Newfoundland public sector unions bargained job and employment issues with local boards and then negotiated major wage and job commitments with the premier and Treasury Board officials at a central table. This further committed unions to seek the status quo in full-time employment in exchange for the acceptance of wage restraint and limits on their using strikes through centrally negotiated agreements.

In the fisheries, the strength of the FFAW/CAW in representing and mobilizing harvesters and processors across the province accounted for the institutionalization of centralized bargaining and price-setting frameworks in the industry. In the 1980s, the FFAW/CAW was the first fishery local among the affluent democracies to have the government extend collective bargaining rights to all harvesters and processors under government jurisdiction (Cashin 2005). Then, with the government moratorium on cod fishing in the 1990s, rising unemployment, and strikes in the fishing industry, the government moved to create labour stability with central price arbitration for FFAW/CAW workers and for processing companies' producer associations in 1998. In 2003, fish companies sought to break the arrangement and drive down fish costs by illegally locking out workers. But the return of strikes and lockouts with individual negotiations on species led to further negotiations that consolidated province-wide bipartite bargaining.

In the construction trades in the mid-1990s, the International Building Trades Petroleum Development Association, PCL Industrial Constructors, and oil companies agreed to a comprehensive construction agreement that centralized collective bargaining between major employers and building trades. Under government auspices, these ranged from employer associations in construction to a bargaining council for fisheries (Luchak 2003). Accompanying these organizations was an employer's council that provided legal advice, updates on legislation and health and safety, and coordinated discussion on employment-related issues across the province. While employer organizations are common across Western Europe, these Newfoundland employer institutions are unique in North America, especially in regard to their scope and organizational resources (see Boeri, Brugiavini, and Calmfors 2001).

The centralized bargaining frameworks in the industry were first supported and then subsequently formalized by Special Project Order government legislation for the construction of oil and gas projects (Cadigan 2010; Cooper 2001). First used in 1997, this legislation put in place special labour legislation that ratified both oil and construction employer organizations and bargaining frameworks for construction unions. In doing so, it ensured that employer organizations consented to central-ized sectoral unionized bargaining and in turn that unions agreed to restrictions on strikes and arbitrated settlements in return for closed-shop arrangements and coordination with government to ensure train-ing and apprenticeships. Unique in the Canadian oil and gas industry, which has often – as in Alberta – been strongly opposed to collective bar-gaining and extensive unionized worksites, these Special Order Projects ensured that the majority of construction work would be undertaken by unionized workers agreeing to binding arbitration arrangements (rather than strikes) throughout the projects' lifetime.

While Newfoundland & Labrador's labour markets were unique in these ways, there were similarities to changes in other provinces during the 1990s. The recession in the early 1990s, one of the worst since the 1930s, combined with the cod moratorium, contributed to an unemploy-ment rate of 20 percent, the highest in Canada (Newfoundland and Lab-rador Statistics Agency 2012). The recession hit the resource industries, concentrated in rural areas, hardest (see chapter 11 of this volume). In forestry, international competition led to falling demand for newsprint, and firms responded by laying off thousands of workers, contracting out, and using more unorganized workers in logging (Cadigan forth-coming). Mechanized harvesting eliminated jobs while stressing wood supplies. In the fisheries, overfishing, overcapacity, and the economic downturn led to a moratorium on the cod fishery and put approximately thirty thousand people out of work (Higgins 2008). Fish plants closed, boats remained docked, and hundreds of coastal communities experi-enced record levels of out-migration, with the province's population declining by a record 10 percent.

The recession similarly affected public services and public sector employment. With record deficits, the Liberal governments of Clyde Wells and Brian Tobin passed provincial budgets with dramatic cutbacks in government spending and wage freezes for public employees. In some cases of collective bargaining, the government reneged on existing union contracts and cancelled pay equity settlements to more than fifty-three hundred women in the health care sector. At other times, the province enacted back-to-work legislation, a trend common to provincial govern-ments throughout 1980s and 1990s (Panitch and Swartz 2003).

By the early 2000s, workers in Newfoundland & Labrador were faced with one of the most difficult regional labour markets in North America. With the rapid decline of employment in resource industries, unemploy-ment across the province was widespread, particularly in rural areas. In

1987, for example, the fishery, forestry, and paper industries employed more than thirty-one thousand workers. By 2001, only thirteen thousand workers remained employed in these sectors. Poverty, always high in the province, had risen to over 21 percent, and labour market participation and the activity rates of men hit a new low at 55 percent.

CASE STUDY

During the Williams era the province experienced a dramatic economic turnaround that resulted in some important but also limited labour market improvements, most notably in employment growth in the oil and mining sectors, as well as in the public sector. In less than ten years, the expansion of global resource industries and a global resource market alongside high prices for oil, nickel, and iron transformed Newfoundland & Labrador into a "have" province.

Since 1997, over one billion barrels of oil have been produced in off-shore Newfoundland. In 1999, the oil and gas (and related construction and manufacturing) industries accounted for 14.3 percent of Newfoundland's GDP. By 2010, this figure had more than doubled to 39 percent (Newfoundland and Labrador 2010i). Overall, oil and gas accounted for 58 percent of total output growth between 1997 and 2010 (Atlantic Provinces Economic Council 2011). Direct revenues from oil accruing to the provincial government from 1997–98 to 2008–09 amounted to $6.22 billion.

The gains from oil production were paired with a booming mining industry: the growth of global demand for, and therefore rising prices of, nickel and iron resulted in a more than four-fold increase in returns (Peters 2010). In 1999, mining contributed $972 million to the provincial economy. By 2010, it was a $3.7 billion industry, directly accounting for more than 7 percent of GDP.

The growth of these resource industries created employment. The resource boom contributed an average of 5.1 percent of total employment with the growth of oil and gas as well as construction jobs (figure 13.1). The indirect and induced impacts of the resource and construction industries meant an average of 10,600 new jobs per year, ranging from 3,500 jobs to 15,600 at the respective lowest and highest job years. In addition, more workers not employed in the oil and gas, mining, and construction industries began to hold jobs supporting those sectors. Over the course of ten years (1999–2009), new jobs in retail, accommodation, food, transport, and business services accounted for 35 percent of all employment

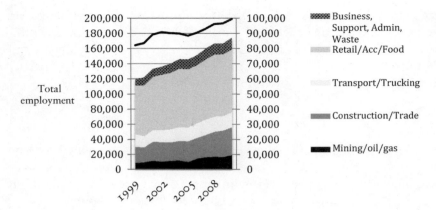

Figure 13.1
Newfoundland & Labrador employment and private sector employment growth, 1999–2009 (thousands). *Sources:* Statistics Canada (2013a, 2013b)

growth from 1999 to 2009 (figure 13.1). Most of this job growth took place in St John's and on the Avalon Peninsula (Cadigan 2012).

However, Danny Williams began his leadership of the PCs with the province in very restrained economic circumstances. Williams first led the party arguing for austerity measures and lower labour costs. He campaigned on getting the province's fiscal house in order, and his initial stance on labour policies – marked by demands for wage and benefit concessions – reflected this, mirroring longstanding trends in liberal market democracies. Most notably, in 2004 the new PC government attempted to restructure the public service by committing to cutting social expenditures, enacting a two-year wage freeze, and posturing to eliminate four thousand public sector jobs. This led to a bitter strike by more than twenty thousand Canadian Union of Public Employees (CUPE) and NAPE workers that ended with the government passing back-to-work legislation that imposed significant wage moderation (a two-year wage freeze and 2 and 3 percent increases) in the next two years.

But by 2005, the economic situation of the province had improved considerably, thanks to significantly growing oil revenues, ongoing economic growth, and a decline in unemployment (although unemployment rates, particularly in rural areas, remained the highest in the country). This improved economic context led to a change in the PCs' labour policy position to one that sought pragmatic accommodation and open negotiations with organized labour.

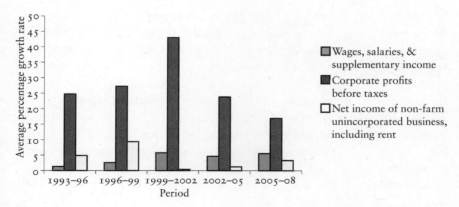

Figure 13.2
Percentage of select contributions to Newfoundland & Labrador GDP (income-based).
Source: Statistics Canada (2011b).

Unlike other Canadian provincial governments that looked to frag-
ment public sector collective bargaining in order to enforce wage
restraint and public sector restructuring, in Newfoundland & Labrador,
the premier, the Treasury Board, and the minister of finance began negotiating one-on-one at a central table with individual public sector leaders
on key wage and benefit issues. This was in contrast to all other Canadian provincial administrations, which had sought to use the Treasury
Board or provincial public boards with new financial powers to deregulate public sector labour relations and enact flexible employment standards frameworks, including the "two-tier[ing]" of wages and benefits
for all new hires as well as temporary and part-time workers (Peters
2012). Moreover, rather than undertake typical measures to facilitate
union decertification and strengthen employer controls on workplaces,
the PC government worked with unions and central employer councils
to maintain existing industrial relations frameworks.

In large part, this accommodating stance on the part of government
resulted from strong profits in the business sector, which helped secure
its support for current labour market frameworks. In Newfoundland
& Labrador, corporate profits escalated dramatically over the previous decade, while wages and other income for working people grew
below productivity rates (figure 13.2). In percentage terms, even with
declines from record levels (1999–2002), profits still grew three times
faster in Newfoundland than in Canada as a whole (Weir 2008). This

boost in returns was strongly supported by the federal and provincial government's cuts to the rate of corporate taxation, which fell by as much as two-thirds during the oil boom, in large measure because of the deals that governments have agreed to with the private sector to secure resource development (Stanford 2008a, 2008b). Consequently, the explosion of resource-industry profits did not translate into correspondingly higher incomes for workers in Newfoundland; profits increased nearly five times as fast as employment earnings (Weir 2008). Such supply-side stimulus to the oil and gas industry as well as other economic interests has helped secure business support for the PCs' economic policies. It has also led to large business interests pragmatically accepting PC labour market policies.

In the fishery sector the Williams government also continued to expand on earlier centralized bargaining frameworks between fishers and plant owners. For example, as Mario Levesque discusses in chapter 10 of this volume, in 2004 the Williams government first attempted to stabilize the industry by imposing a production or "catch" quota in the crab and shrimp fishery that was to be used across all species. But a massive five-week protest by the FFAW/CAW against the quotas – one that threatened to give all bargaining power to the companies and reduce fishing jobs – led the Williams government to appoint Richard Cashin, the former long-serving president of the FFAW/CAW, to a special committee to investigate and make recommendations on the fisheries. In November 2005, Cashin proposed a central bargaining table with the FFAW/CAW and the processor association, the binding extension of agreement provisions on all processors if the largest processors signed on, a binding arbitration price panel, and accreditation of processor organizations before the labour relations board (Cashin 2005). In early 2006, the Williams government amended the Fishing Industry Collective Bargaining Act to formalize centralized bargaining between the parties and introduced all the major recommendations of the Cashin committee.

One of the most notable results has been that, again in contrast to provincial labour market developments elsewhere, union density has remained high. Union density rates in 2009 were the highest in Canada, at more than 37 percent of total employment. In the private sector, union density remained the highest in Canada, above 21 percent, whereas Canadian private sector union density fell to 17 percent (figure 13.3). The rate of union coverage in the construction industry in the province has been particularly high, rising steadily from almost 22 percent in 2003 to

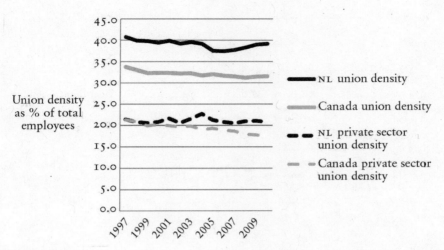

Figure 13.3
Union density rates, Newfoundland & Labrador and Canada, 1997–2009. *Source:* Statistics Canada (2013c)

29 percent in 2008, while the rate in the mining and oil sector has consistently ranged between 55 percent and 44 percent.

Equally distinctive, the PCs made new public investments and continued income-securing labour market policies thanks to the oil boom and resource-generated revenue growth. The Williams administration did so while paying down government debt and underfunded pension liabilities. However, in contrast to other provincial administrations, it did not enact strict policies of fiscal austerity; rather, it undertook a number of pro-cyclical expansionary measures.

As tracked in the auditor general's reports, over the decade from 1999 until 2009, spending increased 51 percent, with a 77 percent increase for health and a 71 percent increase for education (Noseworthy 2009). In total, health, education, and social expenditures (rising by $1.7 billion) made up the majority of new spending initiatives, contributing to more than 60 percent of new spending (figure 13.4). Infrastructure spending was also significant, with 38 percent of the 2009 infrastructure stimulus package going to roads.

Such public spending has prevented welfare and public service retrenchment, and unlike other governments facing debt problems, the Williams government neither reduced nor significantly restructured health, education, and social funding. By 2005 it sought to make investments in

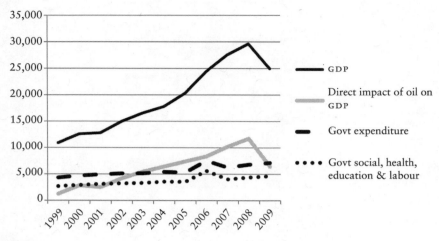

Figure 13.4
Newfoundland & Labrador GDP, oil, and government spending, 1999–2009 (millions)

health care, long-term care, education, and training programs. Since that time, spending increases have grown steadily, with fiscal-year 2009 representing the largest increase in spending: an 8.8 percent increase over the previous year (Noseworthy 2009).

The results for Newfoundland & Labrador's public sector were the growth of public employment as a percentage of total employment and the growth of full-time, unionized jobs – both features unique in North America. As figure 13.5 demonstrates, the province has traditionally had a much larger public sector than the rest of Canada, averaging over 32 percent of total employment during the past decade. In comparison, across Canada the public sector has generally made up no more than 22 percent of total employment. Under the Williams administration, full-time employment in the public sector also grew by more than eight thousand, and that administration also targeted vulnerable labour market groups.

Another key part of social spending was the PCs' attention to the dire problem of the high provincial poverty rate, among the highest in Canada. In 2005, with the return of budget surpluses, the Williams government launched a new Poverty Reduction Initiative to improve the overall contour of means-tested income replacement programs and develop new "active" labour market measures that would assist students and low-income individuals to enter the labour market (Newfoundland and Labrador 2009a). The government also introduced new pharmacare

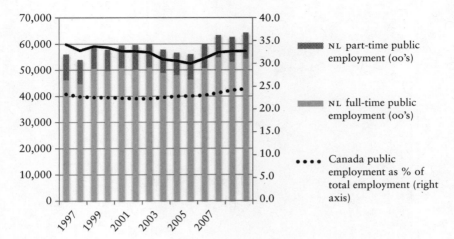

Figure 13.5
Newfoundland & Labrador public employment and growth, 1997–2010. *Source:* Statistics Canada (2013b, 2013c)

programs, functional increases to income support, significant increases to minimum wage rates, and improvements to social housing.

Alongside these policies, the PC administration tried to combat poverty and social exclusion by introducing new transition policies to promote employment, especially in the low-wage sector. It focused attention on the activation of single parents, disadvantaged families, and students leaving post-secondary education. For the longer-term unemployed, the government prioritized reducing benefit enrolment by enabling the unemployed to return to work. Traditional income security programs have been left relatively untouched, and benefit levels have marginally increased. Public assistance recipients may also receive support for work, transportation, training, and placement courses. Women may qualify for rental subsidies and child tax benefits when returning to work. NL Works, a program of the provincial government, has provided employment counselling and wage subsidies for private and not-for-profit employers.

Macro-evidence on poverty rates suggests that while Canada and Newfoundland & Labrador's poverty rates remain among the highest in the industrialized world, the PCs' policies have been significantly more successful than elsewhere in Canada. Canadian poverty rates before taxes and transfers as measured by the standard "low-income-cutoff" ratio (LICO) have remained high. In fact, they are among the highest in the OECD (OECD 2008). In contrast, Newfoundland & Labrador has

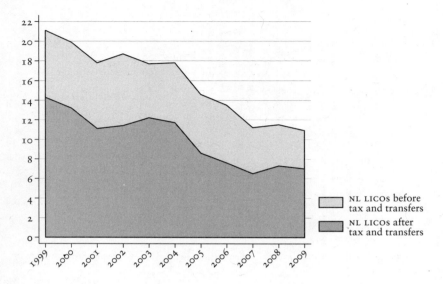

Figure 13.6
Poverty rates in Newfoundland & Labrador, 1999–2009

experienced a decline both before and after tax and transfers (figure 13.6). Economic growth and increased employment is one of the reasons for the decline in poverty; the new policies for reducing poverty appear to be another.

Since 2003, poverty among all low-income persons has decreased by more than 38 percent in the province, compared with a 15 percent decrease in Canada. Poverty after tax and transfers has also declined. Social and fiscal measures were successful in 2003 in reducing income poverty by 31 percent and by 36 percent in 2009. Both reductions were better than those across Canada and well above the 13 percent poverty reduction in the United States (but far below Sweden's poverty reduction rate of 82 percent) (Brandolini and Smeeding 2008). However, poverty rates remain stubbornly high in Newfoundland & Labrador compared to other provinces.

POLITICAL DECISION MAKING IN NEWFOUNDLAND & LABRADOR

Over the past decade, like other provincial and national governments in this period of fiscal contraction, the Williams PC government emphasized debt reduction, economic growth, and business profitability. Certainly, its actions were geared to removing tax, regulatory, and institutional constraints on those with economic clout. Further, both the federal and the provincial Conservative governments made significant efforts to forward rapid, extensive oil development (Carter 2011).

Yet new legislation did not create markets that were only in the interests of a narrow economic or multi-national corporate interest. Even with the enormous influence of Premier Williams and his interest in further economic growth, PC economic, resource, and human capital policy remained committed to improving both business-oriented supply-side conditions and retaining government's role in managing resources and economic development for the interests of the *province*, as well as for developing "self-reliance" (PC Party 2003, 2007).

The elite theory framework helps explain key aspects of the labour policy story in this province. Decision making on labour policy was indeed concentrated among a minority group of actors, including Williams' administration, business organizations, and unions that mobilized and engaged in conflict to forward policy interests. The different labour policy path taken in the province is partly explained by labour's influence and the role of centralized bargaining that brought unions and business organizations to the same table with government. However, extending from elite theory using a comparative political economy framework draws attention to how these elites are not free from larger economic circumstances. Similarly, the power of the premier, while critically important for this period, is greatly influenced by strong – often external – political-economic tides, in this case the influx of resource revenues.

This is most obvious in the dramatic shift in Williams' approach to labour and social investment. He began his tenure as premier issuing threats to labour and warnings of coming fiscal austerity. Yet this stance was transformed, thanks to resource revenues, into a policy approach unique in Canada and North America. Most distinctively, his government continued to facilitate the extension of coordinated labour market negotiations with businesses and unions rather than deregulate wage-setting institutions and employment standards. High union density has been maintained as a result. In addition, the PCs forwarded active labour market polices to assist rather than penalize students, women, and the long-term unemployed to enter the labour market. The provincial government also increased public spending and public sector employment. These labour market and social policies stand in contrast to other Canadian provinces and comparable state cases.

These distinctive policies were possible during Premier Williams' administration thanks to the fiscal room permitted by resource revenues. The rapid shift from austerity and attacks on organized workers to spending and progressive labour policy resulted from the interplay between Williams, business interests, and organized labour *within the context of economic conditions*. A combination of elite theory followed by comparative political economy analysis elucidates policy transformations during the Williams period.

Yet despite the remarkable uniqueness of the labour and social policies of the Williams' administration, a number of labour market and socio-economic problems remain and deepen. Even during this period of unprecedented growth, employment and renewed social investments have not solved the long-standing problem of unemployment and poverty. Newfoundland & Labrador's 16 percent provincial unemployment rate is still the highest in Canada – and even worse in rural areas hit by jobs losses in the fishery and forestry sector. New jobs in the oil and mining sector have not replaced job losses in these traditional, rural sectors (Cadigan 2012).

Further, despite the demand for labour in poorly paid and unorganized service sector work and cyclically available construction, fisheries, and tourism industries, working women, on average, are enjoying fewer of the benefits of the boom than are working men. Instead of a boom, the reality for many workers over the past decade has been a continuing divide or "dualization" between those with good jobs and those with atypical employment who struggle with low-wage work, growing job insecurity, and the simple lack of permanent jobs in the province (Cadigan 2012).

Perhaps the larger problem is how to continue new social spending and proactive labour policies once the resource boom ends. Revenues primarily from oil production allowed the PCs the economic flexibility to address economic and social problems. But estimates of remaining oil reserves indicate that 42 percent of offshore oil has already been produced after just over ten years of production (Canadian Association of Petroleum Producers 2010). If the province's unique labour market and social spending policies have been permitted in great part by oil revenues, the pressing question is, therefore, what happens to government policy when these finite resources are exhausted.

14

Conclusion: Inferiority or Superiority Complex? Leadership and Public Policy in Newfoundland & Labrador

ALEX MARLAND

Some time ago, Kornberg, Mishler, and Clarke remarked that the "policy process holds the key to understanding provincial government" (1982, 203). Decades later, the extent to which a province's first minister shapes public policy is unclear, in part because of temporal, institutional, and personal variables. While a strong public policy and public administration presence exists in the Canadian political science canon, far less attention is paid to public policy as it relates to individual leaders, especially at the provincial level of analysis. The study of Canadian provincial politics tends to be comprised of collections of case studies within edited works, with very few (such as Dunn 2001, 2006a; Elkins and Simeon 1980; Lewis 2012; Wesley 2011) taking a more thematic and comparative approach. The core Canadian contributions to the comparative public policy literature usually addresses the structure of policy-making as well as the institutions, both rules and agencies, in which policy is developed and implemented. The relationship between leadership and public policy output has been far less a priority in Canadian academia and is not well understood at the provincial level.

This is especially true in Newfoundland & Labrador, where the democratic system has some weaknesses and where it is believed that elected officials have little influence unless they are part of the premier's inner circle. Stable one-party dominance and low seat turnover produces non-governing parties that are so dishevelled and partisan that there is often no credible opposition. The House of Assembly is so rarely open that public debate largely occurs on talk radio and in the Kathy Dunderdale era has gravitated to micro-blogging on Twitter (e.g., CBC News 2011i). Powerful interest groups are clustered around unionized labour on the left of the political spectrum and there appears to be little interest in cultivating a more pluralist public sphere. The local media is as much a conveyor of political infotainment that treats the premier as a celebrity as it is a fourth estate watchdog. Finally, as elsewhere, elections and policies tend to be about personalities rather than ideas.

The political actors in any system of government influence and reflect its policy inputs, discussion, outputs, and evaluation. Through an examination of politics and public policy in Newfoundland & Labrador, this book adds to our knowledge about whether a premier has as much power over government policy decisions as is popularly portrayed. The case of the Progressive Conservative (PC) government led by Danny Williams is fascinating because of his populist style during a period of rapid economic growth. By profiling a range of public policy issues, this book's contributors have provided a basis to look at this central research question about executive power in a broad manner, through a multidisciplinary lens anchored in political science.

This chapter arrives at conclusions about the relevance of certain public policy theories identified in chapter 1, namely elite theory and institutionalism, which were hypothesized as being especially applicable to politics and public policy in Newfoundland & Labrador. Collectively the cases point to an alarming centralization of authority in the Office of the Premier, an unsettling willingness of the electorate to trust local elites, and a flawed political system. This book therefore supports the contention that there was a public "feeling" of the premier's control over the provincial government during the Williams era (Wangersky 2011, 136) and, for some, a fear of being on the wrong side of the governing party's agenda. This suggests that the concept of *primus inter pares* is indeed out of touch with the realities of governance. And yet modern government is so complex and the details of policy decision making so invisible that concerns seem justified only when compared with idealist notions of an advanced democracy. Based on this case study, we must question the normative view that the centralization of government authority is both far-reaching and nefarious. In Newfoundland & Labrador, the premier is first among unequals, but normally the authority of the *primus* over the *pares* should not be equated with the despotism that characterized the Joey Smallwood era.

EVIDENCE THAT A PREMIER HAS TOO MUCH POWER

Reflecting on the opportunity for first ministers in small jurisdictions to centralize power in their office, Graham White remarked that "[p]rovincial government is indeed premiers' government" (2005, 77). As with his study, the policy cases profiled in this book provide further evidence of the presidentialization of the parliamentary system of government. They demonstrate that a premier can at times have exclusive decision making authority over public policy. The clout of a governing leader's inner circle is derived from the broad-based internal support that results from party leadership campaigns, from the installation of supporters in key positions, and through the swift expunging of dissidents by means of the parliamentary norm of enforcing party discipline. A leader is the party's public "face" and unless power is delegated, she has the final say over strategies and tactics concerning media positioning, policy decisions, legislative matters, and electioneering. The head of government sets and controls the agenda; has access to considerable institutional resources, including central agencies staffed by skilled and informed civil servants; moulds the government structure; and at times makes decisions without consulting the responsible minister. A leader's supremacy over the party is vast, and the supremacy of a popular head of government is even more so. The authority of a premier in Canada is such that, absent an individual or government election defeat, her forcible removal is rare.

In Newfoundland & Labrador, the desire for a political superhero meant that citizens empowered Premier Williams to set the public agenda, and they generally sided with his framing of policy and personal disputes. The PC Party's active management of their leader's personal brand allowed him and his government to act decisively on their entwined political vision. These values were anchored by the core principle of improving the quality of life in Newfoundland society through a number of policies that were designed to increase the province's capacity for self-reliance. A perception that the premier and his party were motivated by the greater good increased the ability of cabinet to exercise its executive authority and pursue its agenda. This was, of course, facilitated by rising oil revenues.

The power of a premier grows when there are fewer threats to her supremacy. In Newfoundland & Labrador the political marketplace lacks the diversity of competing ideas and sources of power that are found in pluralist democracies (e.g., Bachrach and Baratz 1962; Conn

Table 14.1
Public sector employment in Newfoundland & Labrador (2011)

Public sector employer	Employees
Federal government (14.4% of public employment in NL)	
Federal government: general[1]	7,442
Federal government: business enterprises	2,563
Provincial government (65.6% of public employment in NL)	
Provincial government: general	11,520
Provincial government: health and social service institutions	20,918
Provincial government: universities, colleges, vocational and trade schools	10,918
Provincial government: business enterprises	2,060
Municipal government (20% of public employment in NL)	
Municipal government: general	4,298
Municipal government: school boards	9,565
Total	69,284

Source: Statistics Canada (2012d). Modified from CANSIM table 183-0002.

Note: Number of employees includes full-time and part-time employees and does not denote full-time equivalents.

[1] Includes reservists and full-time military personnel.

1973; Dahl 1961). A history of difficult economic circumstances and a related culture of dependency on government contribute to this situation. There is considerable uptake of federal and provincial government welfare programming; moreover, two-thirds of public sector employment in Newfoundland & Labrador is with the provincial government (table 14.1). The role of government in Newfoundland society is such that with few exceptions, cooperation and accommodation tends to prevail over confrontation and conflict.

All of this predates Williams' premiership, and, rather than change the political system, he leveraged it to support his agenda. This led to a top-down policy vacuum. As Matthew Kerby explains in chapter 6, over time the most independent thinkers left provincial politics. After Dunderdale was installed as interim premier nobody within the PC Party came forward to challenge her for the position. The ensuing absence of a leadership campaign meant that the governing party did not undergo the policy renewal or debate over policy direction that is common elsewhere when party leadership changes hands. In some ways, this violates the core democratic principle that leaders may be installed only after winning a general election, though Dunderdale did go on to win a majority of seats within a year. That MHA Tom Osborne, who crossed the floor to the Liberal party in 2013, was the only PC MHA to subsequently speak out publicly against her leadership when the government's, the party's, and the premier's popularity plunged speaks volumes about partisan loyalties in Newfoundland & Labrador.[1]

The chapters in this book summarize cases whereby Premier Williams ignored democratic norms and exerted executive authority over government policy. The era also demonstrates how leaders can leverage nationalism and cloud the public's assessment of policy options. At times, as Valérie Vézina pointed out, an underlying nationalist philosophy guided policy decisions. The degree to which ethnic nationalism motivated a 2007 policy for a $1,000 baby bonus is unclear. In a flurry of economic nationalism in 2008, all political parties' MHAs supported the hurried expropriation of AbitibiBowater assets in Grand Falls-Windsor, which would cost the province over $100 million for its accidental assumption of responsibility for the environmental cleanup of a mill, while the federal government paid $130 million to settle a NAFTA lawsuit filed by the company (Sweet 2012). Quebec has been a favourite source of regional grievance because of the maligned Churchill Falls deal, which, as Jim Feehan remarked, made it politically unpalatable for Newfoundland to deal with Quebec on Muskrat Falls and instead led to an agreement with Nova Scotia. Premier Williams often took verbal shots at Quebec, climaxing in a comedic turn on CBC TV's *This Hour Has 22 Minutes* in 2010, which reflected his celebrity status and during which he referred to Quebec as "getting away with highway robbery" and "giving Newfoundland & Labrador the shaft" (Gaudreau 2010).

The politics of nationalist policy can indeed be confusing, given that in 2012 Premier Dunderdale maintained that Muskrat Falls "will break Quebec's hold over Newfoundland and Labrador" (CBC News 2012a), whereas former premier Roger Grimes argued that there is no truth to the portrayal of Quebec as "an obstinate group that constantly puts up roadblocks" (Grimes 2012). In all cases of nationalism-inspired policy the presence of heightened political emotion invites questions about the policy's rationality.

Whatever the wisdom of government policies, it is the first minister who is granted the constitutional authority to make strategic decisions, and so it is natural that the system will revolve around her. Policy choices often involve a no-win scenario for which the head of government will foremost be accountable. For instance, collective bargaining with public servants puts the premier in the precarious position of defending the greater interests of the public treasury against the financial demands of labour unions who represent a powerful voting bloc. In such cases, setting public policy is a thankless task; for even if there is initial support for holding the line on the allocation of finite resources, the public soon gets upset with any labour stoppage that reduces or suspends public services or economic activity.

Depending on the situation a premier's executive authority can lead to policy losses or victories. The Upper Churchill deal signed by Premier Smallwood continues to resonate as a costly policy mistake. Conversely, Premier Williams' business, legal, and political acumen was a competitive advantage in natural resource negotiations when he secured public participation in corporate profits rather than settle for job creation. While such hands-on involvement in select policy files emboldens arguments that the provincial government is controlled by the centre, at a cost of broad public engagement, this is of greatest concern when elites benefit at a cost to the masses. This was not the case with the Williams administration, for its policies were widely supported and foremost benefitted the greater good.

EVIDENCE THAT A PREMIER'S POWER OVER PUBLIC POLICY IS OVERSTATED

The policy cases profiled in this book indicate that claims and perceptions that a premier has excessive power are largely media-induced. Premiers benefit from institutional structures such as the electoral and media systems, but there are plenty of other aspects of institutionalism that steer policy development. As the opening chapter established, the process of designing, implementing, communicating, and evaluating public policy is more complex than is popularly presented. It is rarely simple to change an existing policy or introduce a new one, even when the head of government makes a public commitment to do so. As Christopher Dunn has observed: "Provincial government is cabinet government. It has sometimes been called 'premier's government,' but this contention is true only in a limited sense ... Today's institutionalized cabinet has made the dominant premier pattern not necessarily impossible, but harder to achieve. Power and authority are more diffuse than they ever were" (1996, 165).

A governing party is bound by statutes and regulations, some of which can be changed if it controls a majority of seats in the legislature, but it must follow other laws such as the Constitution of Canada. Premier Williams always enjoyed the confidence of a majority of MHAs and followed the principles of responsible government, collective responsibility, and ministerial responsibility. His administration limited a premier's power to control the timing of elections by introducing fixed-date election legislation. The PC Party recognized statutory offices of the legislature, and its leader commissioned the Green Report in response to the auditor general's concerns about improper conduct by some MHAs, including a key minister who was immediately removed from cabinet. Not only did Williams initiate the Cameron Inquiry but he and his senior political staff testified, as well as his ministers.

As Dunn discussed in chapter 2, over time public policy and governance in Newfoundland has evolved from sectarianism and ministers dispensing patronage positions to a modern, professional public service that balances evidence against politicians' preferences. Within the public service, Williams required that deputy ministers be held to account by performance contracts. Increasing emphasis has been placed on strategic planning, annual reporting, policy evaluation, and staff training. Policy instruments such as cabinet papers require that departments communicate with one another and that a "lens" be applied to ensure that diverse issues such as the environment be considered. Furthermore, Dunn and Gerald Galway noted that policy is driven by national standards and that controversial policy reforms imposed by previous Liberal administrations were supported by and extended under the PC government. In short, government policy is far too complex and broad to be micromanaged by the head of government, except in isolated cases.

We must also consider that by demonstrating such intense interest in public opinion polls, the Williams government embodied a certain degree of direct democracy, because, in the main, the PC Party prioritized what the majority of Newfoundlanders and Labradorians wanted. The cabinet stopped demanding internal reforms when opinion polls showed disapproval; their leader's unconventional methods were criticized but often achieved results; government benefits trickled down to people through instruments such as the Poverty Reduction Strategy; and Crown corporations, notably Nalcor, were used for the purpose of building provincial capacity. Premier Williams assumed the public's preferred role of high-profile lobbyist for Newfoundland's interests. He reversed a legacy of bad economic deals (though Williams' deals have yet to stand the test of time), and he was a champion of his citizens' identity while being careful to dismiss separatism.

As with Brian Peckford, the "bad boy of Confederation" act generated some results; however, it also wore thin. After ordering the removal of Canadian flags from provincial buildings in 2005, Williams achieved a policy coup by securing a $2 billion payment from the federal government through a renegotiated Atlantic Accord. Upon returning from Ottawa, he was greeted as a hero as he yelled "We got it!" at the St John's Airport. But his confrontational style with the next federal administration – ranging from his so-called Anything But Conservative campaign in the 2008 federal election to publicly slagging Prime Minister Harper – did not prevent the federal Conservatives from changing the equalization formula in 2009, which reportedly reduced the province's bottom line by $1.6 billion.

Over time, the premier's national influence waned as his demands for preferential policies competed with powerful interests elsewhere in Canada. Even in his own electoral district a *Western Star* editorial suggested that Williams retire following an outburst against the leader of the provincial NDP (CBC News 2010l). This set the stage for his successor, Premier Dunderdale, and PC MHAs to endorse the Harper Conservatives in the 2011 federal election in return for a pledge of financial support for the Muskrat Falls project. A premier of a small province like Newfoundland & Labrador soon recognizes that asymmetrical federalism is unsustainable and residents learn that no matter how powerful they perceive their premier to be her executive authority is localized.

Despite beginning her tenure with an agenda, over time the premier becomes "chief broker," which is a democratic form of elitism. Royce Koop (chapter 4) writes that the PC Party is the latest instance of a dominant political party that brokers policy interests. But as Maria Mathews (chapter 8) observes, the mediation of policy options involves cabinet, not just the premier, because evidence-based decisions must conform to political influences. For instance, when the health minister announced in 2009 that he was overruling medical experts' recommendation that only young children, as opposed to all children, should be immunized against H1N1, this was the communication of a cabinet decision to prioritize populism over policy expertise. While the premier approved, if not initiated, this directive it demonstrates that a leader's decisions must be supported by others. In policy-making many political calculations must be considered.

An agenda to initiate public policy reforms is influenced by the activation of local vested interests. Evidence for elite theory must be counterbalanced with group theory, which plays out daily in private meetings between the political executive, senior public servants, and interest group representatives. As Mario Levesque explained in chapter 10, a major policy initiative to reform the fishery in 2005 failed because the Fish, Food and Allied Workers (FFAW) sustained political pressure by shutting down the legislature, organizing flotillas that blocked St John's harbour, occupying and vandalizing the fisheries building, calling open-line radio to complain, and generally stimulating public unrest. Premier Williams set the agenda early in his government's mandate but backed down and then avoided further use of his political capital on the file. Levesque demonstrates that the Newfoundland fishery is emblematic of the tragedy of the commons and of the unwillingness of an industry with a history of agitation to agree on reforms about the management of a common pool resource. The political pressure applied by special interests on federal, provincial, and municipal governments and the consequent impotence of political leadership means that fisheries policy in Newfoundland will operate in an indefinite state of crisis. People alleging that a premier controls public policy need only look at this topic to recognize her limitations.

Proponents of the head of government as friendly dictator thesis also overlook that in today's society solutions to policy problems are difficult to impose and prone to discussion in a 24/7 media environment. Independent reports, expert advice, and political intuition often produce plans of action that are publicly unpalatable and that cannot be sold by politicians. Moreover, transparency is generally increasing owing to rule changes: in the Smallwood era, legislative debates were not always recorded in *Hansard*, whereas now they are televised and available online. In the past, obtaining data through government websites or access to information procedures was not an option for the opposition or journalists.[2] Those who peek behind the government's curtain stand to learn that instead of the government managing change, policy tends to be driven by events, which places politicians and public servants on a reactive footing.

A premier's authority over public policy is therefore shaped by forces that are beyond the government's control. Kelly Vodden, Ryan Gibson, and Michelle Porter observe (chapter 11) that the Williams administration chose to prioritize increasing economic rents for the benefit of the province as a whole rather than for individual communities. Despite his command of the government system and even with unanticipated oil revenues, Premier Williams was unable to "save" rural Newfoundland. He could not bring back the cod fishery; he was unable to fill under-populated public schools; he could not meet all the public's demands for healthcare; and when he retired from office he left behind a government that still had considerable financial debt. Public policy has an insatiable demand for more resources, and the political executive has limited options that are constrained by a variety of competing pressures, economic forces, unforeseen events, and political structures.

At times, Premier Williams' role as the "face" of the government enabled him to make policy decisions that were democratic and responsible yet added to perceptions of his executive authority. His prompt decisions to appoint independent agents to investigate the House of Assembly spending scandal and government actions surrounding the Eastern Health cancer screening test errors were high-profile cases of the premier using his executive authority to identify solutions to public policy problems in a transparent manner. As Kate Puddister, Jim Kelly, and Maria Mathews have discussed (chapters 7 and 8), when the premier publicly apologized for the cancer test mistakes, which cost lives, he embodied a "l'état, c'est moi" image, albeit one that was empathetic to the need for good government and to his subjects' feelings. All of this contributed to a perception of the premier having more control than is possible in a system that abides by the rule of law.

ASSESSING THE APPLICABILITY OF ELITE THEORY AND INSTITUTIONALISM

No single policy model can characterize decision making in any government. In Newfoundland & Labrador there is evidence of corporate pluralism and laissez-faire pluralism when the provincial government bends to the pressures of powerful labour unions and business interests. This is especially true in the areas of health care and the fishery, with the latter also invoking public pluralism and public choice theory. Conversely, these and other models do not adequately describe Newfoundland politics. This is why we have undertaken to assess the applicability of elite theory and, to a lesser extent, institutionalism.

The information presented in this book does not support a conclusion that the Williams administration was a form of "benevolent dictatorship" (Mayo 1949). It is important to bear in mind the source of allegations of modern Newfoundland government being a one-man show or a dictatorship. Opponents have their own agenda of countering a premier's popularity and authority by seeking to frame her in an unfavourable light. For example, the opposition parties' demands in 2012 for a special debate about the Muskrat Falls hydroelectric project, including the ability to summon witnesses, were understandable, since this is standard parliamentary practice elsewhere. Instead, Premier Dunderdale, citing months of discussion in the public sphere, introduced a private member's motion that allowed a two-hour legislative debate. The media dutifully reported the comments of the leader of the NDP, Lorraine Michael, who charged that the Dunderdale government was arrogant and "as close to dictatorial as one can imagine in a democratic society" (CBC News 2012c). Michael's concerns may have some merit, but they are exaggerations, and such commentary feeds controversy. The media's government watchdog function is juxtaposed with competitive pressures to present conflict and infotainment.

The media includes such exaggerations in their reports because it provides colour. At times journalists themselves are the source of such commentary. In 2010 Premier Williams complained to the CBC's ombudsman about a column authored by the executive producer of CBC News in Newfoundland that appeared in the *National Post*. The premier's complaint centred on the producer's remark that "Trying to get someone to talk openly and freely from the business community, and from inside the government, is tougher than previous times. People have a fear that Danny will find out. That sounds kind of like a Beijing sort of thing, but it's there, and our reporters have come across it" (CBC Ombudsman 2010). These concerns also have some merit, and it is one of the reasons why researching Newfoundland politics and public policy is so difficult. But the journalistic standards of the CBC are among the highest in Canada. The CBC ombudsman cautioned that reporters need to be careful when using hyperbole. He concluded that "it is both unfair and unreasonable to compare [the Williams] government, in the lively world of Newfoundland politics, with that of an autocracy," and yet he defended the producer's view that Newfoundlanders "appeared disinclined to speak publicly." This is another example of an autocratic narrative sustained by the media's participation in it and contributing to perceptions of a leader's power and fears of "unknowable harms" (Furedi 2005, 133).

In a strange way, this is related to a Newfoundland premier's self-appointed quest to improve citizens' collective confidence. This is commonly known as "the old Newfoundland inferiority complex" (Newfoundland and Labrador 1992b), which is a symptom of Newfoundland's lower socio-economic status compared with the Canadian mainland and which was aggravated by the "have not" label. Before Newfoundland joined Canada, Smallwood used his *Barrelman* radio program to energize the Newfoundland ethos, to profile success stories, and to encourage greater self-reliance (Naváez 1986; Webb 1997). Premier Williams likewise sought to build confidence among Newfoundlanders and to generate respect for his people on the Canadian mainland. His speeches and soundbites were filled with references to citizens' optimism, pride, and determination (e.g., Williams 2010b), just as Smallwood championed Newfoundlanders' toughness, resilience, and ingenuity. By using the mass media to communicate positive messages about Newfoundland and Newfoundlanders, both men became celebrities who were proud defenders of the political identity that they shared with their audiences. Ironically, their command of local politics was possible because they took advantage of the very subordination and dependency that they publicly lamented, and their inflated media presence contributed to their audience's perceptions of the speaker's superiority.

These case studies provide a sufficient variety of indications of elite theory that, although we can reject the benevolent dictatorship label, we can notionally confirm the presence of elitism during the Williams era. This elitism includes a small number in power deciding public policy for the masses; elites who were drawn from an upper socio-economic class; power transition that was gradual and orderly; and the elites' support and preservation of the existing social system (Stewart Jr, Hedge, and Lester 2008, 55). An interesting characteristic of elite theory is that those in power design policy that prioritize the elites' interests over the interests of the masses. A condition of the model is that elites set the agenda and influence the apathetic masses so that society exhibits shared preferences. Thus, those in charge derive their power and status from electors, but it is the masses who are subject to elites' policy priorities and decisions.

This component of the model is difficult to assess. There is considerable evidence that the PC Party and the political executive brokered competing policy demands and thus that elites tended to be responsive to the masses. The premier's foremost agenda of negotiating natural resource deals was for the greater benefit of Newfoundland society. Upon becoming premier he pledged that whenever he felt that "his business holdings create[d] a conflict of interest, he [would] not participate in making a government decision" (CBC News 2003). Williams donated his premier's salary to charity and increased the transparency of salary details for premier's office staff (Newfoundland and Labrador 2004h). He dealt swiftly and decisively with a major spending scandal that largely predated his administration. And yet, the PC Party's 2003 pledges of transparency did not fully materialize, and a 2007 election platform commitment to legislate whistleblower protection was not fulfilled. Salaries of staff in the premier's office were increased (CBC News 2007b), the retiring premier sought to appoint his communications director to a patronage position (CBC News 2011b), and after retiring he stated that he had "been working on" a major real estate development project in St John's "for probably close to 20 years" (CBC News 2011a). Elitism also comes through in evidence of group theory when the PC party and interest groups negotiated policy solutions around each other's agenda.

Perhaps the most prominent evidence for the elitist model during the Williams era is related to the observation that "to the extent a person or group – consciously or unconsciously – creates or reinforces barriers to the public airing of policy conflicts, that person or group has power" (Bachrach and Baratz 1962, 949). In this light, the stifling of pluralistic debate by publicly scolding people, by enforcing strict party discipline, and by fuelling nationalist sentiments was the premier's principal power. Verbal outbursts supported his efforts to set and build public agendas. In this way the impression of centralized power was valid.

Woven throughout the applicability of this model is populism. The personal affection that Newfoundlanders attached to their premier was best illustrated when Williams went to the United States for private healthcare. Newfoundlanders had cause to reflect on what this said about Canada's public health care system, about the management of the government during the premier's absence, or even about why their premier's changed hairstyle warranted media coverage (e.g., Canadian Press 2010b). However, their personal concern for the premier's well-being trumped politics. It is interesting that during this period public satisfaction with the provincial government reached 93 percent, the highest number recorded by pollsters during the era, and the 81 percent preferring Williams for premier marked a two-year high (Corporate Research Associates 2012). The rhetoric and style of this administration fits into two of the typologies of populist leaders summarized by Margaret Canovan (1982). Critics' complaints fit a "populist dictatorship" model similar to Smallwood's reign whereby power was derived from the leader's role as a demagogue who was supported by the masses. However in reality Premier Williams operated a "politicians' populism" whereby he led a catch-all party that blurred political divisions in society by uniting Newfoundlanders under a vague notion of "the people" and by eschewing some political norms altogether.

Responsibility for the public legitimacy that Premier Williams enjoyed, as with a number of elites before him, ultimately resides with the Newfoundlanders and Labradorians who empowered him. In his summary of international cases of authoritarian leadership, Seymour Martin Lipset

(1959) identified lower socio-economic class as a core condition for a populace accepting dictatorial regimes. If such circumstances can be loosely applied to Newfoundland, then government policies that have supported increasing levels of formal education, a rising standard of living, and a stronger collective self-confidence may result in citizens being less susceptible to personality politics, less dependent on government, more tolerant of competing points of view and more demanding of democratic ideals. However, Barro's (1999) extension of Lipset's work found that increased per capita GDP owing to oil production is related to slowed democratization, suggesting that such free money is a deterrent to political efficacy.

We have also found evidence of institutionalism. Institutionalism posits that it is the rules, codes, symbols, and norms of political institutions that influence human actors' behaviour, as opposed to citizens and organizations shaping government behaviour (Howlett, Ramesh, and Perl 2009). This pattern begins with an electoral system that suppresses opposition representation in the legislature and a system of government that in many ways fuses the executive and legislative branches. It is evident in the incrementalism of sequential policy decisions, such as the government's sometimes token attempts to sustain rural Newfoundland against the forward march of urbanization, the changes introduced to the provincial education system, and the path to modernization described by Chris Dunn in chapter 2. Careful thought must be given to what institutional reforms are necessary, what the practical implications would be, and whether there is a political will to champion them. In a small polity like Newfoundland, the available evidence suggests that only a premier willing to call a judicial inquiry and act on its recommendations is likely to effect significant institutional change. The alternative is, at best, the incrementalism of ad hoc reforms implemented over an extended period spanning many premierships.

AREAS FOR FURTHER STUDY

There is no academic consensus on the methodology for assessing the legacy of a political leader (Lewis 2012), and the goal of this book was not to render such a judgment. Rather, it was to offer a case study of whether a premier has as much influence over government policy as is popularly perceived, and it has added to the conclusions of other scholars that the answer is no. The case under study was a strong choice for analysis because the dominant critical frame of Premier Williams was that he was a "one man show" running "Dannystan" (e.g., Canadian Press 2009b; Newfoundland and Labrador 2004c) and, importantly, most Newfoundlanders seemed to accept and even welcome this. It is therefore noteworthy that in 2012 a sample of Canadian scholars rated Premier Williams' accomplishments ahead of those of many Canadian premiers who had served in the previous forty years, including Peckford's (Leonard 2012). They awarded high marks for Williams' "winnability," his communications, and his fiscal frameworks. Overall, however, they placed his legacy well behind the accomplishments of Alberta Premier Peter Lougheed (1971–85), Ontario's Bill Davis (1971–85), Saskatch-ewan's Allan Blakeney (1971–82), New Brunswick's Frank McKenna (1987–97), and Quebec's Robert Bourassa (1970–76 and 1985–94), all of whom had left office before Williams assumed it. Within Newfound-land, many citizens felt, and still feel, that Williams was the best premier that their province had ever had (e.g., Roberts 2007). Time will tell how his political leadership and his government's policies will be judged.

While this book represents the first significant analysis of executive authority and public policy in Newfoundland & Labrador, no edited collection can address all worthwhile subject matter. Deeper empirical research about political leadership and public policy is warranted. The production of this volume was limited by the pool of available auth-ors. Consequently, some topics have not been explicitly discussed, such as aboriginal-state relations, Labrador, the oil industry, tourism, the environment, taxation, patronage positions, party financing, and polit-ical journalism.[3] As well, Simon's (2007) observation that much of pub-lic policy decision making is invisible identifies a limitation. None of the authors have reflected perspectives that could have been gathered by interviewing Danny Williams or members of his government or staff, had this been possible. The tiny body of scholarly literature about New-foundland politics means that authors have often had to rely on news sources and government documents to profile their case studies, which is a limitation. The publication of this volume is thus intended to facili-tate deeper research.

This raises some specific issues for consideration by provincial polit-ical actors and scholars concerning strengthening democracy in New-foundland & Labrador. As in chapter 1, we can organize these issues into the areas of economic conditions, executive authority, and political communication.

- Economic conditions: What have been the effects of oil revenues on public policy? What are the implications for government policy when finite oil revenues are exhausted? What conditions must exist for political actors to prioritize long-term policy over short-term benefits?
- Executive authority: What conditions must exist for Newfoundland & Labrador to explore and implement democratic reforms? How can a small province feel valued in the federal system of government? What are the implications of "cabinet government" and/or "premier's government" for public policy design, implementation, and evaluation?
- Political communication: How can government encourage broader pluralism and political efficacy? How can local media organizations be persuaded to support investigative journalism? What can be done to limit perceptions of a premier's superiority over Newfoundlanders and their tacit acceptance of an imperfect democratic system?

In seeking answers to these and other questions, we must be mindful of the classroom tendency for policy idealism to overlook the reality of politics (Stone 1997). Even if research and advocacy leads to public debate about proposals for change, and even if reforms are implemented, it is unclear to what extent the reforms would lead to better public policy. No matter who Newfoundlanders choose to be governed by, we would urge them to be mindful that while the premier's power is more limited than many people think, and is related to his/her public persona, the use of that power must be actively scrutinized in an informed manner.

NOTES

1   In January 2014, PC MHA Paul Lane also joined the Liberals. Soon afterwards, Premier Dunderdale announced her resignation and designated Finance Minister Tom Marshall as interim premier until the selection of a new premier in a PC Party leadership contest. The power of an outgoing premier to choose the next head of government contravenes the basic tenet of democracy that such decisions must be made by the people who are governed (Cheibub, Gandhi, and Vreeland 2010).

2   In June 2012 the Dunderdale government's Bill 29 placed further limits on access to information despite the voices of disapproval conveyed through the news media.

3   The editors commissioned chapters on some of these topics, including two on the oil economy, but were unable to locate substitute authors when that work could not be produced.

Bibliography

Adams, Brian E. 2007. *Citizen Lobbyists: Local Efforts to Influence Public Policy*. Philadelphia: Temple University Press.

Adams, Christopher. 2010. "Realigning Elections in Manitoba." In *Manitoba Politics and Government: Issues, Institutions, Traditions*, edited by Paul G. Thomas and Curtis Brown. Winnipeg: University of Manitoba Press.

Affaires municipales et Régions. 2007. *Politique Nationale de la Ruralité: Une force pour tout le Québec*. Quebec: Gouvernment du Québec.

Agrawal, Arun. 2002. "Common Resources and Institutional Sustainability." In *The Drama of the Commons*, edited by Elinor Ostrom, Thomas Dietz, Nives Dolšak, Paul C. Stern, Susan Stonich, and Elke U. Weber. Washington, DC: National Academy Press.

Alberta. 2008. *Public Agencies Governance Framework*. Edmonton: Government of Alberta. http://www.finance.alberta.ca/business/agency-governance/reports/2008-02-Public-Agencies-Governance-Framework.pdf.

Albo, Gregory. 2005. "A.G. Frank, Dependency Theory and Canadian Capitalism." *Canadian Dimension* 39, no. 6: 20–1.

Alderman, R.K. 1995. "A Defence of Frequent Ministerial Turnover." *Public Administration* 73, no. 4: 497–512.

Alderman, R.K., and J.A. Cross. 1987. "The Timing of Cabinet Reshuffles." *Parliamentary Affairs* 40, no. 1: 1–19.

Almond, Gabriel A., and Sidney Verba. 1963. *The Civic Culture: Political Attitudes and Democracy in Five Nations*. Princeton, NJ: Princeton University Press.

Amable, Bruno. 2003. *The Diversity of Modern Capitalism*. New York: Oxford University Press.

– 2009. "Structural Reforms in Europe and the (In)coherence of Institutions." *Oxford Review of Economic Policy* 25, no. 1: 17–39.

Ambrosio-Albaná, Mateo, and Johan Bastiaensen. 2010. *The New Territorial Paradigm for Rural Development: Theoretical Foundations from Systems and Institutional Theories*. Antwerp, Belgium: Institute of Development Policy and Management, University of Antwerp.

Anderson, Benedict R. 1983. *Imagined Communities: Reflections on the Origin and Spread of Nationalism*. London: Verso.

– 1991. *Imagined Communities: Reflections on the Origin and Spread of Nationalism*. Rev. and extended ed. New York: Verso.

Anderson, Stephen E., and Sophia Ben Jaafar. 2003. "Policy Trends in Ontario Education 1990–2003." ICEC Working Paper no. 1, Ontario Institute for Studies in Education, University of Toronto, Toronto.

Andrews, Ralph L. 1985. *Post-Confederation Developments in Newfoundland Education, 1949–1975*. St John's: Harry Cuff Publications.

Angus Reid. 2007. "Most Popular Canadian Premier Polls." http://www.angus-reid.com/.

– 2010. "Williams and Wall Are Most Popular Premiers in Canada; Charest Lowest." News release, 2 December. http://www.angus-reid.com/wp-content/uploads/2010/12/2010.12.02_Premiers_CAN.pdf.

– 2013. "Wall Maintains Top Spot among Premiers with Highest Job Approval Ratings." 30 September. http://www.angusreidglobal.com/polls/48828/wall-maintains-top-spot-among-premiers-with-highest-job-approval-ratings/ (accessed 10 October 2013).

Antle, Rob. 2004. "Premier Banishes Maple Leaf." *Telegram*, 24 December.

– 2005. "Government Will Overrule Some Boards' Decisions, Says Premier." *Telegram*, 18 June, 4.

– 2008. "Opposition Shocked at Wiseman Testimony." *Telegram*, 11 April, A1.

Association of Seafood Producers. 2004. "Association of Seafood Producers States Processing Capacity Must Be Reduced." News release, 14 December. Accessed 22 August 2011. http://www.seafoodproducers.org/files/ASP-Over-capacity-Dec%2014.pdf.

Association of Universities and Colleges of Canada. 1988. *Statement on Academic Freedom and Institutional Autonomy*.

Atlantic Provinces Economic Council. 2011. "How Atlantic Canada's Economy is Adapting to New Global Realities." Halifax, NS: Atlantic Provinces Economic Council. http://www.apec-econ.ca/files/pubs/%7B2E288FBF-ED85-4847-82EF-11CEEF8E310C%7D.pdf?title=How%20Atlantic%20Canada's%20Economy%20is%20Adapting%20to%20New%2Global%20Realities&publicationtype=Research%20Reports.

Aucoin, Peter. 1995. *The New Public Management: Canada in Comparative Perspective*. Montreal: Institute for Research on Public Policy.

Austin, Roger, and William Hunter. 2012. "Stirring Political Pots: Information and Communications Technology, Denominational Reform, Northern Ireland, Newfoundland and Labrador." In *Education Reform: From Rhetoric to Reality*, edited by Gerald Galway and David Dibbon. London, ON: The Althouse Press.

Baccaro, Lucio, and Chris Howell. 2011. "A Common Neoliberal Trajectory: The Transformation of Industrial Relations in Advanced Capitalism." *Politics and Society* 39, no. 4: 521–63.

Bachrach, Peter, and Morton S. Baratz. 1962. "Two Faces of Power." *American Political Science Review* 56, no. 4: 947–52.

Bailey, Sue. 2010a. "Newfoundland's Danny Williams Quits Politics." *Canadian Press*, 25 November. http://www.thestar.com/news/canada/article/896577--newfoundland-s-danny-williams-quits-politics.

– 2010b. "Williams' Immense Popularity Has Dark Side, Critics Say." *Canadian Press*, 21 March.

– 2011. "Feds Will Support Muskrat Falls: Dunderdale." *Telegram,* 4 June. http://www.thetelegram.com/Business/2011-06-04/article-2558989/Feds-will-support-Muskrat-Falls-Dunderdale/1.

Baines, Paul R., and John Egan. 2001. "Marketing and Political Campaigning: Mutually Exclusive or Exclusively Mutual?" *Qualitative Market Research* 4, no. 1: 25–33.

Baker, Jamie. 2008. "'We Need to Get On with It': Marketing Council, Industry Renewal among Priorities for New Fisheries Minister." *Union Forum* 4, no. 4(November/December): 33–4. http://www.ffaw.nf.ca/userfiles/files/PDF/Forum%20-%20Nov-Dec%202008.pdf.

– 2012. "As Loved Our Fathers: The Strength of Patriotism among Young Newfoundlanders." *National Identities* 14, no. 4: 367–86.

Baker, Melvin. 2003. "History of Newfoundland and Labrador: Chronology of Events." In *Collected Research Papers of the Royal Commission on Renewing and Strengthening Our Place in Canada*. St John's: Government of Newfoundland and Labrador. http://www.exec.gov.nl.ca/royalcomm/research/pdf/bakerchronology.pdf.

Bakvis, Herman. 1989. "Regional Politics and Policy in the Mulroney Cabinet, 1984–88: Towards a Theory of the Regional Minister System in Canada." *Canadian Public Policy* 15, no. 2: 121–34.

– 2001. "Prime Minister and Cabinet in Canada: An Autocracy in Need of Reform?" *Journal of Canadian Studies* 35, no. 4: 60–79.

Bakvis, Herman, and Steven B. Wolinetz. 2005. "Canada: Executive Dominance and Presidentialization." In *The Presidentialization of Politics: A Comparative Study of Modern Democracies*, edited by Thomas Poguntke and Paul Webb. Oxford: Oxford University Press.

Baldacchino, Godfrey. 2010. *Island Enclaves: Offshoring Strategies, Creative Governance, and Subnational Island Jurisdictions*. Montreal and Kingston: McGill-Queen's University Press.

Bannister, Jerry. 2003. "The Politics of Cultural Memory: Themes in the History of Newfoundland and Labrador in Canada, 1972–2003." In *Collected Research Papers of the Royal Commission on Renewing and Strengthening Our Place in Canada*. St John's: Government of Newfoundland and Labrador.

Barnes, Trevor J. 2009. "Focus: A Geographical Appreciation of Harold A. Innis." *The Canadian Geographer* 37, no. 4: 352–64.

Barnes, Trevor, Roger Hayter, and Elizabeth Hay. 2001. "Stormy Weather: Cyclones, Harold Innis, and Port Alberni, BC." *Environment and Planning A* 33 (12): 2127–47.

Barrie, Doreen. 2006. *The Other Alberta: Decoding a Political Enigma*. Regina, SK: Canadian Plains Research Center, University of Regina.

Barro, Robert J. 1999. "Determinants of Democracy." *Journal of Political Economy* 107, no. S6: S158–S183.

Barron, Tracy. 2001. "No Contest: Williams Acclaimed PC Leader." *Telegram*, 1 February.

Battle, Ken, Sherry Torjman, and Micheal Mendelson. 2006. *Towards a New Architecture for Canada's Adult Benefits*. Ottawa: Caledon Institute for Social Policy. http://www.caledoninst.org/Publications/PDF/594ENG.pdf.

Bavington, Dean. 2010. *Managed Annihilation: An Unnatural History of the Newfoundland Cod Collapse*. Vancouver: UBC Press.

Beck, J. Murray. 1985. *Politics of Nova Scotia*. Vol. 1, *1710–1896*. Tantallon, NS: Four East Publications.

Beck, Ulrich. 1994. "The Reinvention of Politics: Towards a Theory of Reflexive Modernization." In *Reflexive Modernization: Politics, Tradition, Aesthetics in the Modern Social Order*, edited by Ulrich Beck, Anthony Giddens, and Scott Lash. Stanford, CA: Stanford University Press.

– 1997. *The Reinvention of Politics: Rethinking Modernity in the Global Social Order*. Cambridge: Blackwell Publishers.

Béland, Daniel, and André Lecours. 2005. "Nationalism, Public Policy and Institutional Development: Social Security in Belgium." *Journal of Public Policy* 25, no. 2: 265–85.

– 2006. "Décentralisation, mouvements nationalistes et politiques sociales: Les cas du Québec et de l'Écosse." *Lien social et politique* 56:135–46.

– 2008. *Nationalism and Social Policy: The Politics of Territorial Solidarity*. New York: Oxford University Press.

Bélanger, Éric. 2009. "The 2008 Provincial Election in Quebec." *Canadian Political Science Review* 3, no. 1: 93–9.

Bélanger, Gérard, and Jean-Thomas Bernard. 1991. "Aluminium ou exportation: De l'usage de l'électricité québécoise." *Canadian Public Policy* 17, no. 2: 197–204.

Bell, David V.J. 1992. *The Roots of Disunity: A Study of Canadian Political Culture.* Oxford University Press.

Beramendi, Pablo, and Christopher J. Anderson, eds. 2008. *Democracy, Inequality, and Representation. A Comparative Perspective.* New York: Russell Sage Foundation.

Berlinski, Samuel, Torun Dewan, and Keith Dowding. 2007. "The Length of Ministerial Tenure in the UK, 1945–1997." *British Journal of Political Science* 37, no. 2: 245–62.

Bernard, Jean-Thomas, and Josee Chatel. 1985. "The Application of Marginal Cost Pricing Principles to a Hydro-Electric System: The Case of Hydro-Quebec." *Resources and Energy* 7, no. 4: 353–75.

Bernard, Jean-Thomas, and Jean-Yves Duclos. 2009. "Quebec's Green Future: The Lowest-Cost Route to Greenhouse Gas Reductions." *C.D. Howe Institute Backgrounder*, no. 118 (October). www.cdhowe.org/pdf/backgrounder_118_English.pdf.

Bernier, Luc. 2005. "Who Governs in Quebec? Revolving Premiers and Reforms." In *Executive Styles in Canada: Cabinet Structures and Leadership Practices in Canadian Government*, edited by Luc Bernier, Keith Brownsey, and Michael Hollett. Toronto: University of Toronto Press.

Bernier, Luc, Keith Brownsey, and Michael Hollett, eds. 2005. *Executive Styles in Canada: Cabinet Structures and Leadership Practices in Canadian Government.* Toronto: University of Toronto Press.

Best, Heinrich, and Maurizio Cotta, eds. 2000. *Parliamentary Representatives in Europe, 1848–2000: Legislative Recruitment and Careers in Eleven European Countries.* Oxford: Oxford University Press.

Beswick, Aaron. 2010. "Custodial Management Dead: Byrne." *Northern Pen*, 4 January. Accessed 12 March 2012. http://www.northernpen.ca/News/2010-01-04/article-1524894/Custodial-management-dead%3A-Byrne/1.

Bickerton, James. 2001. "Nova Scotia: The Political Economy of Regime Change." In *The Provincial State in Canada: Politics in the Provinces and Territories,* edited by Keith Brownsey and Michael Howlett. Peterborough, ON: Broadview Press.

Bienen, Henry, and Nicolas van de Walle. 1989. "Time and Power in Africa." *American Political Science Review* 83, no. 1: 20–34.

Billig, Michael. 1995. *Banal Nationalism*. London: Sage.

Bittner, Amanda. 2011. *Platform or Personality? The Role of Party Leaders in Elections*. Oxford: Oxford University Press.

Black, Edwin R., and Alan C. Cairns. 1966. "A Different Perspective on Canadian Federalism." *Canadian Public Administration* 9, no. 1: 27–44.

Black, Nick. 2001. "Evidence Based Policy: Proceed with Care." *BMJ* 323, no. 7307: 275–9.

Blake, Raymond. 2012. "Canada, Newfoundland, and Term 29: The Failure of Intergovernmentalism." *Acadiensis* 41, no. 1: 49–74.

Blaug, Mark. 1976. "The Empirical Status of Human Capital Theory: A Slightly Jaundiced Survey." *Journal of Economic Literature* 14, no. 3: 827–55.

Bobbit, Philip. 2002. *The Shield of Achilles: War, Peace and the Course of History*. New York: Alfred A. Knopf.

Boeri, Tito, Agar Brugiavini, and Lars Calmfors, eds. 2001. *The Role of Unions in the Twenty-First Century*. New York: Oxford University Press.

Bollman, Ray D., and Heather A. Clemenson. 2008. "Structure and Change in Canada's Rural Demography: An Update to 2006." *Rural and Small Town Canada Analysis Bulletin* 7, no. 7: 1–27. November. Statistics Canada Catalogue no. 21-006-XIE. Ottawa. Accessed 6 November 2012. http://www.statcan.gc.ca/pub/21-006-x/21-006-x2007007-eng.htm.

Bone, Robert M. 2000. *The Regional Geography of Canada*. New York: Oxford University Press.

Bonoli, Giuliano, and David Natali. 2011. *The Politics of the New Welfare State*. New York: Oxford University Press.

Bosch, Gerhard, Steffen Lehndorff, and Jill Rubery. 2009. "European Employment Models in Flux: Pressures for Change and Prospects for Survival and Revitalization." In *European Employment Models in Flux: A Comparison of Institutional Change in Nine European Countries*, edited by Gerhard Bosch, Steffen Lehndorff, and Jill Rubery. New York: Palgrave Macmillan.

Boswell, Peter. 2002. "The Vanishing Report: A Political Analysis of the Newfoundland and Labrador Royal Commission on Renewing and Strengthening Our Place in Canada." *Newfoundland Studies* 18, no. 2: 279–89.

Boswell, Peter, Freida Faour, and Sam Synard. 1997. *Task Force on Municipal Regionalization: Final Report*. St John's: Newfoundland and Labrador Department of Municipal and Provincial Affairs.

Box-Steffensmeier, Janet M., and Bradford S. Jones. 1997. "Time Is of the Essence: Event History Models in Political Science." *American Journal of Political Science* 41, no. 4: 1414–61.

Boyer, Marcel. 2005. "Raise Electricity Prices in Quebec – and Benefit Everyone." C.D. Howe Institute e-brief, 16 March. www.cdhowe.org/pdf/ebrief_13_english.pdf.

Brandolini, Andrea, and Timothy M. Smeeding. 2008. "Inequality Patterns in Western Democracies: Cross-Country Differences and Changes over Time." In *Democracy, Inequality, and Representation: A Comparative Perspective*, edited by Pablo Beramendi and Christopher J. Anderson. New York: Russell Sage Foundation.

Brautigam, Tara. 2009. "Williams Rejects Calls for Health Minister to Quit in Wake of Testing Scandal." *Canadian Press*, 4 March.

Braye, Crystal. 2011. "Is Ye a Schreecher? The Negotiation of Symbolic Identity in a Newfoundland Tradition." Paper presented at the North Atlantic Forum 2011 – Culture, Place, and Identity at the Heart of Regional Development, St John's, NL, 14 October.

Brett, Craig. 2003. "Demographic Trends and Implications for Public Policy." In *Collected Research Papers of the Royal Commission on Renewing and Strengthening Our Place in Canada*. St John's: Government of Newfoundland and Labrador.

Brock, Kathy L. 2008. "The Politics of Asymmetrical Federalism: Reconsidering the Role and Responsibilities of Ottawa." *Canadian Public Policy* 34, no. 2: 143–61.

Brodie, Janine. 1990. *The Political Economy of Canadian Regionalism*. Toronto: Harcourt Brace Jovanovitch.

Brownsey, Keith, and Michael Howlett, eds. 2001. *The Provincial State in Canada*. Peterborough, ON: Broadview Press.

Brubaker, Rogers. 2004. *Ethnicity without Groups*. Cambridge: Harvard University Press.

Budesheim, Thomas Lee, and Stephen J. DePaola. 1994. "Beauty or the Beast? The Effects of Appearance, Personality, and Issue." *Personality and Social Psychology Bulletin* 20, no. 4: 339–48.

Byron, Reginald, ed. 2003. *Retrenchment and Regeneration in Rural Newfoundland*. Toronto: University of Toronto Press.

Cadigan, Sean T. 1992. "The Staple Model Reconsidered: The Case of Agricultural Policy in Northeast Newfoundland, 1785–1855." *Acadiensis* 21, no. 2: 48–71.

– 2006. "Regional Politics Are Class Politics: A Newfoundland and Labrador Perspective on Regions." *Acadiensis* 35, no. 2: 163–8.

– 2009. *Newfoundland and Labrador: A History*. Toronto: University of Toronto Press.

– 2010. "Organizing Offshore: Labour Relations, Industrial Pluralism, and Order in the Newfoundland and Labrador Oil Industry, 1997–2006." In *Work on Trial: Cases in Context*, edited by Judy Fudge and Eric Tucker. Toronto: Osgoode Society for Canadian Legal History and Irwin.

– 2012. "Boom, Bust and Bluster: Newfoundland and Labrador's 'Oil Boom.'" In *Boom, Bust, and Crisis: Canadian Labour in Twenty-First Century Canada*, edited by John Peters. Halifax, NS: Fernwood Publishing.

– Forthcoming. "Newfoundland and Labrador, 1979–2010: Contradiction and Continuity in a Neoliberal Era." In *The End of Expansion: The Political Economy of Canada's Provinces and Territories in a Neoliberal Era*, edited by Bryan Evans and Charles W. Smith. Toronto: University of Toronto Press.

Cairns, Alan C. 1977. "The Governments and Societies of Canadian Federalism." *Canadian Journal of Political Science* 10, no. 2: 695–725.

Cairns, Robert D., and Anthony G. Heyes. 1993. "Why Do We Price Electricity the Way We Do? Canadian Policy in Light of Political-Economic Theories of Governmental Behaviour." *Canadian Public Administration* 36, no. 2: 153–74.

Cameron, David, and Richard Simeon. 2002. "Intergovernmental Relations in Canada: The Emergence of Collaborative Federalism." *Publius: The Journal of Federalism* 32, no. 2: 49–71.

Cameron, Margaret A. 2009. *Commission of Inquiry on Hormone Receptor Testing*. Vol. 1, *Investigation and Findings*. St John's: Government of Newfoundland and Labrador.

Canada. 1993. Task Force on Incomes and Adjustments in the Atlantic Fishery. *Charting a New Course: Towards a Fishery of the Future*. Ottawa: Communications Directorate, Department of Fisheries and Oceans.

– 2001. "Canada Year Book, 2001." Statistics Canada Catalogue no. 11-402-XPE. Ottawa: Statistics Canada.

– 2002. Commission on the Future of Health Care in Canada. *Building on Values: The Future of Health Care in Canada – Final Report*. http://publications.gc.ca/collections/Collection/CP32-85-2002E.pdf.

– 2005. "Minister's Response to the Final Report of the Advisory Panel on Straddling Fish Stocks." News release, 1 September. Accessed 15 May 2011. http://www.marketwire.com/press-release/dfo-ministers-response-final-report-advisory-panel-on-straddling-fish-stocks-553827.htm.

– 2011. Public Health Agency of Canada. "Frequently Asked Questions." Accessed 16 February 2012. http://www.phac-aspc.gc.ca/about_apropos/faq-eng.php.

– 2012a. Department of Finance. *Budget 2012: Budget Plan*. Ottawa: Public Works and Government Services Canada.

– 2012b. Treasury Board of Canada Secretariat. "Federal Identity Program."
   Accessed 9 June 2012. http://www.tbs-sct.gc.ca/fip-pcim/index-eng.asp.
Canadian Association of Petroleum Producers. 2010. "Newfoundland and
   Labrador's Oil and Natural Gas Exploration and Production Industry:
   Contributing to a Strong Provincial Economy." http://www.capp.ca/getdoc.
   aspx?DocId=176807&DT=NTV.
Canadian Health Services Research Foundation. 2000. *Health Services
   Research and Evidence-Based Decision-Making*. Ottawa: CHSRF. http://
   www.cfhi-fcass.ca/migrated/pdf/mythbusters/EBDM_e.pdf.
Canadian Institute for Health Information. 2005. *Exploring the 70/30 Split:
   How Canada's Health Care System is Financed*. Ottawa: Canadian Institute
   for Health Information.
Canadian Judicial Council. 2006. *Alternative Models of Court Administration*.
   Ottawa: Canadian Judicial Council.
Canadian Labour Congress. Social and Economic Policy Department. 2011.
   "Recession Watch Bulletin – Issue 5." Ottawa: Canadian Labour Congress.
   http://www.canadianlabour.ca/sites/default/files/pdfs/recession-watch-
   05-spring-2011-en.pdf.
Canadian Opinion Research Archive. 2010. "Portraits of Canada 1997–2000
   Series, 2003, 2005." In *Canadians' Attitudes toward the Federation*. Kingston, ON: Queen's University. http://www.queensu.ca/cora/.
Canadian Press. 2008. "N.L. Justice Minister Accuses Prime Minister of Trying
   to 'Subdue' Province." 8 September.
– 2009a. "Canada Ratifies NAFO Fishing Changes, Despite Sovereignty
   Concerns from N.L." 12 December. http://www.ngnews.ca/Natural-resour-
   ces/2009-12-12/article-800289/Canada-ratifies-NAFO-fishing-changes-
   despite-sovereignty-concerns-from-NL/1.
– 2009b. "Trouble Brewing in Dannystan?" *Chronicle-Herald*, 26 October, B7.
– 2009c. "Williams Blasts NL Health Board in Its Handling of Missed Cancer
   Tests." 6 April.
– 2010a. "N.L. Doctors Reject Province's Latest Contract Offer." 15 December. http://www.globaltoronto.com/nl+doctors+reject+provinces+latest+
   contract+offer/90959/story.html.
– 2010b. "Williams's Hair Casualty of Operation." 23 February. http://
   www.thetelegram.com/Arts---Life/Well-being/2010-02-23/article-1442066/
   Williamss-hair-casualty-of-operation,-premier-sports-new-post-surgery-hair-
   style/1.
Canadian School Boards Association. 1995. *Who's Running Our Schools?
   Education Governance in the 90s*. Toronto: Canadian School Boards Association.

Canovan, Margaret. 1982. "Two Strategies for the Study of Populism." *Political Studies* 30, no. 4: 544–52.

– 1999. "Trust the People! Populism and the Two Faces of Democracy." *Political Studies* 47, no. 1: 2–16.

Caprara, Gian Vittorio, Michele Vecchione, Claudio Barbaranelli, and R. Chris Fraley. 2007. "When Likeness Goes with Liking: The Case of Political Preference." *Political Psychology* 28, no. 5: 609–32.

Carr, Jan. 2010. "Power Sharing: Developing Inter-Provincial Electricity Trade." C.D. Howe Institute Commentary no. 306. http://www.cdhowe.org/pdf/commentary_306.pdf.

Carter, Angela. 2011. "Environmental Policy in a Petro-State: The Resource Curse and Political Ecology in Canada's Oil Frontier." PHD diss., Government Department, Cornell University, Ithaca, NY.

Carty, R. Kenneth. 1992. "On the Road Again: The Stalled Omnibus Revisited." In *Canadian Political Party Systems: A Reader*, edited by R. Kenneth Carty. Toronto: Broadview Press.

– 2010. "Has Brokerage Politics Ended? Canadian Parties in the New Century." Paper presented at the Canadian Parties and Elections: A New Era? workshop, Memorial University of Newfoundland, St John's, NL, 20–21 August.

Case, Barb. 2009. "Rural Secretariat." 27 October. http://www.vplabrador.ca/home/files/ppoint/panel-_rural_secretariat-_barb_case.ppt.

Cashin, Richard. 2005. Raw Material Sharing (RMS) Review Committee. *Report of the Chairman RMS Review Committee*. St John's: Government of Newfoundland and Labrador. http://www.fishaq.gov.nl.ca/publications/archives/fullreport.pdf.

CBC News. 2003. "Nfld. Premier May Sell Controversial Business Shares." 12 November. http://www.cbc.ca/news/canada/story/2003/11/12/williams_investment031112.html.

– 2004. "Marshall Resigns over Williams' Management." 27 September. http://www.cbc.ca/news/canada/newfoundland-labrador/story/2004/09/27/nf_marshall_20040927.html.

– 2005. "Manning Ejected from Tory Caucus." 5 May. http://www.cbc.ca/news/canada/newfoundland-labrador/story/2005/05/05/nf-manning-caucus-050505.html.

– 2006a. "Byrne Resignation Rocks Political Circles." 22 June. http://www.cbc.ca/news/canada/newfoundland-labrador/story/2006/06/22/nf-williams-byrne-20060622.html.

– 2006b. "Quebecers Form a Nation within Canada: PM." 22 November. Accessed 15 September 2011. http://www.cbc.ca/news/canada/story/2006/11/22/harper-quebec.html.

- 2007a. "One University Enough, Memorial Tells Province." 25 July. http://www.cbc.ca/news/canada/newfoundland-labrador/story/2007/07/25/memorial-grenfell.html.
- 2007b. "Premier's Staff 'Worth Weight in Gold,' MHAs Told." 2 May. http://www.cbc.ca/news/canada/newfoundland-labrador/story/2007/05/02/premier-office.html.
- 2007c. "Tories Offer Baby Bonus to Turn Around N.L. Population." 18 September. http://www.cbc.ca/news/canada/newfoundland-labrador/story/2007/09/18/baby-bonus.html.
- 2008a. "3 Cancer Doctors in St John's Submit Resignations." 29 July. http://www.cbc.ca/news/canada/newfoundland-labrador/story/2008/07/29/cancer-resignations.html.
- 2008b. "Can Cope with Resigning Cancer Docs: N.L. Health Minister." 31 July. http://www.cbc.ca/news/canada/newfoundland-labrador/story/2008/07/31/wiseman-cancer-resign.html.
- 2008c. "Cash Found to Keep Cancer Doctors: Williams." 22 September. http://www.cbc.ca/news/health/story/2008/09/22/williams-doctors.html.
- 2008d. "Deputy N.L. Premier Rideout Quits Cabinet in Spat with Williams." 21 May. http://www.cbc.ca/news/canada/newfoundland-labrador/story/2008/05/21/rideout-future.html.
- 2008e. "MDs Blast 'Divisive' Pathologists Pay Hike." 12 June. http://www.cbc.ca/news/canada/newfoundland-labrador/story/2008/06/12/doctor-divisive.html.
- 2008f. "Misdiagnosed: Anatomy of Newfoundland's Cancer-Testing Scandal." CBC News: In Depth. Last modified 28 April 2008. http://www.cbc.ca/news/background/cancer/misdiagnosed.html.
- 2008g. "Pathologists Offer Moves NL to Top Pay Rates: Williams." 23 May. http://www.cbc.ca/news/canada/newfoundland-labrador/story/2008/05/23/pathologists-offer.html.
- 2008h. "The ABCs of ABC." Features. http://www.cbc.ca/nl/features/abc/.
- 2008i. "Williams Announces Pay Raise for Pathologists, Oncologists." 22 May. http://www.cbc.ca/news/canada/newfoundland-labrador/story/2008/05/22/doctors-raise.html.
- 2008j. "Williams Lashes Cancer Inquiry for 'Inquisitorial Methods.'" 9 May. http://www.cbc.ca/news/canada/newfoundland-labrador/story/2008/05/09/williams-inquiry.html.
- 2008k. "Williams Rejects Bullying Accusations over Cancer Inquiry." 13 May. http://www.cbc.ca/news/canada/newfoundland-labrador/story/2008/05/13/williams-inquiry.html.

– 2009a. "HINI Vaccine Priority Groups Released." 16 September. http://www.cbc.ca/news/health/story/2009/09/16/h1n1-vaccine.html.

– 2009b. "Health-Cuts Reversal Isn't Political: Minister." 2 October. http://www.cbc.ca/news/canada/newfoundland-labrador/story/2009/10/02/health-cuts.html.

– 2009c. "Lewisporte Mayor Vows to Fight Health Cuts." 1 September. http://www.cbc.ca/news/canada/newfoundland-labrador/story/2009/09/01/mayor-health-901.html.

– 2009d. "Lewisporte, Flower's Cove Protest Health Cuts." 3 September. http://www.cbc.ca/news/canada/newfoundland-labrador/story/2009/09/03/protest-cuts-903.html.

– 3009e. "N.L. Marks 60th Confederation Anniversary with Whispers." March 31. http://www.cbc.ca/news/canada/newfoundland-labrador/story/2009/03/31/confederation-anniversary.html.

– 2009f. "N.L. May Ignore Medical Advice on HINI Vaccine." 18 November. http://www.cbc.ca/news/canada/newfoundland-labrador/story/2009/11/18/nl-kennedy-swine-181109.html.

– 2009g. "N.L. Minister May Halt Health Services Review." 15 October. http://www.cbc.ca/news/health/story/2009/10/15/nl-lab-xray-review-1015.html.

– 2009h. "N.L. to Expand H1N1 Shot Eligibility." 10 November. http://www.cbc.ca/news/canada/newfoundland-labrador/story/2009/11/10/nl-vaccine-101109.html.

– 2009i. "Williams Accuses Hydro-Quebec of Protectionism." 3 September. http://www.cbc.ca/news/canada/newfoundland-labrador/story/2009/09/03/williams-quebec-903.html.

– 2009j. "Williams Has 'No Regrets' about On-Air Blow Up." 17 June. http://www.cbc.ca/news/canada/newfoundland-labrador/story/2009/06/17/williams-host-fight-617.html.

– 2009k. "Williams Lashes Out at Quebec-N.B. Power Deal." 30 October. http://www.cbc.ca/news/canada/newfoundland-labrador/story/2009/10/29/nl-newfoundland-nbpower-2910.html.

– 2010a. "Budget Surplus Won't Sweeten MD Offer: N.L." 30 November. http://www.cbc.ca/news/canada/newfoundland-labrador/story/2010/11/30/nlarbitration-rejected-1130.html.

– 2010b. "Doctors Reach Tentative N.L. Contract Deal." 16 December. http://www.cbc.ca/news/canada/newfoundland-labrador/story/2010/12/16/nl-doctors-deal-1216.html.

– 2010c. "Kennedy Softens Tones over MDs." 8 December. http://www.cbc.ca/news/canada/newfoundland-labrador/story/2010/12/08/kennedy-doctors-house-128.html.

– 2010d. "N.L. Children's Care Being Hurt: MD." 29 November. http://www.cbc.ca/news/canada/newfoundland-labrador/story/2010/11/29/nl-pediatric-care-1129.html.

– 2010e. "N.L. Pitting MDs against Each Other: Doctors." 15 November. http://www.cbc.ca/news/canada/newfoundland-labrador/story/2010/11/15/nl-offer-divisive-1115.html.

– 2010f. "Parent Fears MD Dispute May Harm Child." 2 December. http://www.cbc.ca/news/canada/newfoundland-labrador/story/2010/12/02/nl-parent-doctors-1202.html.

– 2010g. "Pay Demands Not Absurd, MDs Tell Williams." 23 March. http://www.cbc.ca/news/canada/newfoundland-labrador/story/2010/03/23/medical-association-contract-323.html.

– 2010h. "Quebec Balked at NB Power Sale Costs." 24 March. www.cbc.ca/news/canada/new-brunswick/story/2010/03/24/nb-nbpower-graham-1027.html.

– 2010i. "Resigning Doctors Vow to Leave." 5 November. http://www.cbc.ca/news/health/story/2010/11/05/nl-thirteen-doctors-1105.html.

– 2010j. "Talks with Docs Back On: N.L." 1 December. http://www.cbc.ca/news/health/story/2010/12/01/kennedy-doctors-talks-121.html.

– 2010k. "Volunteer Sacked over Williams Penis Joke." 1 November. http://www.cbc.ca/news/canada/newfoundland-labrador/story/2010/11/01/pardy-ghent-williams-111.html.

– 2010l. "Williams Should Look at Retirement: Editorial." 23 April. http://www.cbc.ca/news/canada/newfoundland-labrador/story/2010/04/23/williams-editorial-423.html.

– 2011a. "Danny Williams Backs $5B Land Plan in St John's." 13 December. http://www.cbc.ca/news/canada/newfoundland-labrador/story/2011/12/13/nl-danny-williams-land.html.

– 2011b. "Danny Williams Defends Criticized Job Offer." 12 September. http://www.cbc.ca/news/canada/newfoundland-labrador/story/2011/09/12/nl-williams-letter-912.html.

– 2011c. "Dunderdale Takes Risk with Harper Pledge." 4 April. Accessed 9 January 2012. http://www.cbc.ca/news/canada/newfoundland-labrador/story/2011/04/04/dunderdale-harper-risk-404.html.

– 2011d. "Fisheries Workers Confront Dunderdale." 3 October. Accessed 5 October 2011. http://www.cbc.ca/news/canada/newfoundland-labrador/story/2011/10/03/nl-dunderdale-marystown-oci-protest-103.html.

– 2011e. "Fish Cuts on Menu for Ottawa Meeting." 8 June. Accessed 6 October 2011. http://www.cbc.ca/news/canada/newfoundland-labrador/story/2011/06/08/nl-fisheries-meeting-608.html.

– 2011f. "House Debate Not Healthy, Says Dunderdale." 13 October. http://
  www.cbc.ca/news/canada/newfoundland-labrador/story/2011/10/13/nl-
  dunderdale-house-113.html.
– 2011g. "Liberals Call for Judicial Inquiry on Fishery." 16 September.
  Accessed 5 October 2011. http://www.cbc.ca/news/canada/nlvotes2011/
  story/2011/09/16/nl-liberals-fishery-policy-916.html.
– 2011h. "Muskrat Project to Be Exempt from PUB." 17 May. Accessed
  20 May 2012. http://www.cbc.ca/news/canada/newfoundland-labrador/
  story/2011/05/17/nl-muskrat-falls-pub-exemption-517.html.
– 2011i. "N.L. Premier and Opposition Debate on Twitter." 7 November.
  http://www.cbc.ca/news/canada/newfoundland-labrador/story/2011/11/07/
  nl-twitter-debate-1107.html.
– 2011j. "Tuition Freeze Will Stick: Tories." 20 September. http://www.cbc.ca/
  news/canada/newfoundland-labrador/story/2011/09/20/nl-pcs-tuition-fee-
  freeze-920.html.
– 2012a. "Dunderdale Targets Quebec in Defence of Muskrat Falls."
  3 October. http://www.cbc.ca/news/canada/newfoundland-labrador/
  story/2012/10/03/nl-dunderdale-muskrat-falls-quebec-1003.html.
– 2012b. "Get a Thicker Skin, McCurdy Tells King." 29 February. Accessed
  2 April 2012. http://www.cbc.ca/news/canada/newfoundland-labrador/
  story/2012/02/29/nl-earle-mccurdy-darin-king-229.html.
– 2012c. "N.L. Legislature Votes to Approve Muskrat Falls." 5 December.
  http://www.cbc.ca/news/canada/newfoundland-labrador/story/2012/12/05/
  nl-muskrat-falls-debate-assembly-1205.html.
CBC Ombudsman. 2010. "Review: Complaint from The Hon. Danny Williams,
  Premier of Newfoundland and Labrador." 10 March. http://www.cbc.ca/
  ombudsman/pdf/2010-03-10-Williams.pdf.
Centre for Addiction and Mental Health. 2004. "Retail Alcohol Monopolies
  and Regulation: Preserving the Public Interest." Position Paper. http://www.
  camh.ca/en/hospital/about_camh/influencing_public_policy/public_policy_
  submissions/Pages/retail_alcohol_monopolies.aspx.
Chafe, Paul. 2007. "Rockin' the Rock: The Newfoundland Folk/Pop 'Revolution.'" *Newfoundland and Labrador Studies* 22, no. 1: 345–60.
– 2008. "Living the Authentic Life at 'The Far East of the Western World':
  Edward Riche's *Rare Birds*." *Studies in Canadian Literature* 33, no. 2.
  Published electronically. http://journals.hil.unb.ca/index.php/SCL/article/
  view/11235/11996.
Chandler, Marsha A., and William M. Chandler. 1979. *Public Policy and Provincial Politics*. Toronto: McGraw-Hill Ryerson.

Channing, J.G. 1982. *The Effects of Transition to Confederation on Public Administration in Newfoundland*. Toronto: The Institute of Public Administration of Newfoundland.

Cheadle, Bruce. 2011a. "'Harperization' a Classic Branding Exercise." *Telegram*, 1 December, A13.

– 2011b. "Harper's Economic Action Plan Website Got Approval despite Violating Rules." *Whitehorse Star*, 6 January, 8.

2011c. "Government's New 'Economic Action Plan' Ads Dovetail with Tory Campaign." *Canadian Press*, 2 February. http://www.ipolitics.ca/2011/02/02/governments-new-economic-action-plan-ads-dovetail-with-partisan-tory-campaign/.

Cheibub, José Antonio, Jennifer Gandhi, and James Raymond Vreeland. 2010. "Democracy and Dictatorship Revisited." *Public Choice* 143 (April 2010): 67–101.

Chen, Peter John, and Peter Jay Smith. 2010. "Campaigning and Digital Media in Alberta: Emerging Practices and Democratic Outcomes." *Canadian Political Science Review* 2, no. 3: 36–55.

Chiu, Belinda H.Y. 2007. "Brand USA: Democratic Propaganda in the Third Social Space." *Whitehead Journal of Diplomacy and International Relations* (summer/fall): 131–43.

Chronicle Herald. 2001. "Nfld. Grits Lose Two By-Elections." 31 January.

Clapp, R.A. 1998. "The Resource Cycle in Forestry and Fishing." *Canadian Geographer* 42, no. 2: 129–44.

Cleary, Ryan. 2006. "We Are Dead to the Premier." *Independent* (St John's). 13 August.

Clift, Tom. 2011. *Report of the Independent Chair: MOU Steering Committee: Newfoundland and Labrador Fishing Industry Rationalization and Restructuring*. St John's: Newfoundland and Labrador Department of Fisheries and Aquaculture. Accessed 3 November 2011. http://www.fishaq.gov.nl.ca/publications/mou.pdf.

Close, David. 2007. "The Newfoundland and Labrador Strategic Social Plan: Governance Misconceived and Ill-Applied." Paper presented at the annual meeting of the Midwest Political Science Association, Chicago, 12–15 April.

Close, David, Penelope Rowe, and Carla Wheaton. 2007. *Planning the Future of Rural Newfoundland and Labrador by Engaging the Public: From the Strategic Social Plan to the Rural Secretariat*. St John's: Community Services Council. Accessed 14 November 2010. http://envision.ca/pdf/cura/Planning_Future_Rural_NL_Jan08_07.pdf.

Coffen-Smout, Scott. 1998. "Analysis of Public Perceptions of Canadian Coastal and Ocean Management Policy and Practice." http://www.chebucto.ns.ca/~ar120/coa.html.

Colton, Glenn. 2007. "Imagining Nation: Music and Identity in Pre-Confederation Newfoundland." *Newfoundland and Labrador Studies* 22, no. 1: 9–49.

Community Accounts. 2006a. *Census 2006: Labour Market Profile. Employment and Working Conditions by Local Areas.*

– 2006b. "Newfoundland and Labrador Community Accounts." http://nl.communityaccounts.ca/.

Conn, Paul H. 1973. "Social Pluralism and Democracy." *American Journal of Political Science* 17, no. 2: 237–54.

Connections Research and Central Consulting Services. 2003. *Out of Sight, Out of Mind – Community Does Matter! A Study of the Mandate and Roles of the Rural Development Associations and the Newfoundland and Labrador Rural Development Council.* Prepared for Newfoundland and Labrador Rural Development Council.

Conrad, Margaret. 2003. "Mistaken Identities? Newfoundland and Labrador in the Atlantic Region." *Newfoundland and Labrador Studies* 18, no. 2: 159–74.

Conservative Party of Canada. 2006. *Stand Up for Canada.* Federal Election Platform. Accessed 5 January 2012. http://www.cbc.ca/canadavotes2006/leadersparties/pdf/conservative_platform20060113.pdf.

Cooper, Morgan C. 2001. *Labour Relations Processes on Offshore Oil and Gas Fabrication and Construction Projects.* St John's: Newfoundland and Labrador Department of Environment and Labour.

Corbeil, Michel. 2006. "Si Près, Si Loin." *Le Soleil*, 28 August, 3.

Corporate Research Associates. 2012. "Special tabulation, based on opinion surveys administered from 2003 to 2012 as part of the CRA *Atlantic Quarterly*."

Council of Ministers of Education. 2005. *Education at a Glance 2005: Country Profile for Canada.* Accessed 11 June 2013. http://www.cmec.ca/9/Publications/index.html?searchCat=17&searchYr=2005.

Courtney, John C. 1969. "In Defence of Royal Commissions." *Canadian Public Administration* 12, no. 2: 198–212.

Crevier, Raphaël. 2005. "Théorie sur la transformation événementielle des espaces nationaux: du Canada français au Québec contemporain." Master's thesis, Université du Québec à Montréal.

Crocker, Robert K., and Frank T. Riggs. 1979. *Improving the Quality of Education: Challenge and Opportunity. Final Report of the Task Force on Education.* St John's: Queen's Printer.

Crompton, Rosemary. 2006. *Employment and the Family*. New York: Cambridge University Press.

Crosbie, John C. 1997. *No Holds Barred: My Life in Politics*. Toronto: McClelland and Stewart.

– 2009. "Speech from the Throne 2009." Speech. General Assembly, Confederation Building, St John's, 25 March. http://www.exec.gov.nl.ca/throne-speech/2009/speech2009.htm.

– 2011. "Speech from the Throne 2011." Speech. General Assembly, Confederation Building, St John's, 21 March. http://www.releases.gov.nl.ca/releases/2011/exec/0321n06.htm.

Crouch, Colin. 2011. *The Strange Non-Death of Neoliberalism*. Malden, MA: Polity Press.

CTV News. 2002. "Two on Nfld Hydro Board Resign over Power Plan." 21 February.

– 2008. "Danny Williams Apologizes at Breast Cancer Inquiry." 28 October. http://www.ctv.ca/CTVNews/Canada/20081028/williams_inquiry_081028/.

Curran, David, and Associates, Graham Letto, and Ryan Lane. 2009. *Economic Development: Small Towns & Big Industries*. St John's: Municipalities Newfoundland and Labrador.

Dacks, Gurston. 1986. "From Consensus to Competition: Social Democracy and Political Culture in Alberta." In *Socialism and Democracy in Alberta*, edited by Larry Pratt. Edmonton: NeWest.

Dahl, Robert A. 1961. *Who Governs? Power and Democracy in an American City*. New Haven, CT: Yale University Press.

Dahlström, Carl, B. Guy Peters, and Jon Pierre. 2011. *Steering from the Centre: Strengthening Political Control in Western Democracies*. Toronto: University of Toronto Press.

Davies, Gary, and Takir Mian. 2010. "The Reputation of the Party Leader and of the Party Being Led." *European Journal of Marketing* 44, no. 3/4: 331–50.

Davis, Reade, and Kurt Korneski. 2012. "In a Pinch: Snow Crab and the Politics of Crisis in Newfoundland." *Labour/Le Travail*, 69 (spring): 119–45.

Dawson, Robert MacGregor. 1948. *The Government of Canada*. Toronto: University of Toronto Press.

de Peuter, Jennifer, and Marianne Sorensen. 2005. *Rural Newfoundland and Labrador Profile: A Ten-Year Census Analysis (1991–2001)*. Ottawa: Rural Secretariat, Government of Canada.

Delli, Carpini, Michael X., and Bruce A. Williams. 2001. "Let Us Infotain You: Politics in the New Media Environment." In *Mediated Politics:*

Communication in the Future of Democracy, edited by W. Lance Bennett and Robert M. Entman. New York: Cambridge University Press.

Dewan, Torun, and Keith Dowding. 2005. "The Corrective Effect of Ministerial Resignations on Government Popularity." *American Journal of Political Science* 49, no. 1: 46–56.

Dibbon, David, and Gerald Galway. 2012. "Lessons for the Policy Community." In *Education Reform: From Rhetoric to Reality*, edited by Gerald Galway and David Dibbon. London, ON: The Althouse Press.

Dibbon, David, Bruce Sheppard, and Jean Brown. 2012. "The Impact of Education Reform on School Board Governance." In *Education Reform: From Rhetoric to Reality*, edited by Gerald Galway and David Dibbon. London, ON: The Althouse Press.

Diermeier, Daniel, and Randy T. Stevenson. 1999. "Cabinet Survival and Competing Risks." *American Journal of Political Science* 43, no. 4: 1051–68.

Dobbin, Lucy C. 1993. *Report on the Reduction of Hospital Boards*. St John's: Department of Health, Government of Newfoundland and Labrador.

Docherty, David. 2011. "The Canadian Political Career Structure: From Stability to Free Agency." *Regional and Federal Studies* 21, no. 2: 185–203.

Doern, Bruce G., and Peter Aucoin, eds. 1979. *Public Policy in Canada: Organization, Process, and Management*. Toronto: Macmillan.

Dowding, Keith, and Patrick Dumont, eds. 2009. *The Selection of Ministers in Europe: Hiring and Firing*. Abingdon, UK: Routledge.

Dowding, Keith, and Won-Taek Kang. 1998. "Ministerial Resignations 1945–97." *Public Administration* 76, no. 3: 411–29.

Doyle, Arthur T. 1983. *The Premiers of New Brunswick*. Fredericton, NB: Brunswick Press.

du Plessis, Valerie, Roland Beshiri, and Ray D. Bollman. 2001. "Definitions of Rural." *Rural and Small Town Canada Analysis Bulletin* 3, no. 3: 1–17.

Dunderdale, Kathy. 2011. "@KathyDunderdale." 10 August. Deleted 17 April 2013.

Dunn, Christopher. 1996. "Premiers and Cabinets." In *Provinces: Canadian Provincial Politics*, edited by Christopher Dunn. Peterborough, ON: Broadview Press.

– 2001. "Comparative Provincial Politics: A Review." In *The Provincial State in Canada: Politics in the Provinces and Territories*, edited by Keith Brownsey and Michael Howlett. Peterborough, ON: Broadview Press.

– ed. 2002. *The Handbook of Canadian Public Administration*. Don Mills, ON: Oxford University Press.

– 2004. "The Quest for Accountability in Newfoundland and Labrador." *Canadian Public Administration* 47, no. 2: 184–206.

- 2005a. "The Persistence of the Institutionalized Cabinet: The Central Executive in Newfoundland and Labrador." In *Executive Styles in Canada*, edited by Luc Bernier, Keith Brownsey, and Michael Howlett. Toronto: University of Toronto Press.
- 2005b. "Why Williams Walked, Why Martin Balked: The Atlantic Accord Dispute in Perspective." *Policy Options* 26, no. 2: 9–14.
- ed. 2006a. *Provincial Politics*. Toronto: University of Toronto Press.
- 2006b. "Urban Asymmetry and Provincial Mediation of Federal-Municipal Relations in Newfoundland and Labrador." In *Municipal-Federal-Provincial Relations in Canada*, edited by Robert Young and Christian Leuprecht. Montreal and Kingston: McGill-Queen's University Press.
- 2007. "The Williams Effect: Election 2007 in Newfoundland and Labrador." *Policy Options* (November): 35–41.
- Forthcoming. "Deputy Ministers in Newfoundland and Labrador." In *Deputy Ministers in Canada: Comparative and Jurisdictional Perspectives*, edited by Jacques Bourgault and Christopher Dunn. Toronto: University of Toronto Press.
Dunne, Eric. 2003. *Fish Processing Policy Review Final Report*. St John's: Newfoundland and Labrador Fish Processing Policy Review Commission.
Eagles, Munroe. 2002. "Political Geography and the Study of Regionalism." In *Regionalism and Party Politics in Canada*, eds. Keith Archer and Lisa Young, 9–23. Don Mills, ON: Oxford University Press.
Egan, Louise, and Randall Palmer. 2011. "The Lesson from Canada on Cutting Deficits." *Globe and Mail*, 21 November. Accessed 4 February 2011. http://www.theglobeandmail.com/report-on-business/economy/the-lesson-from-canada-on-cutting-deficits/article2243702/page4/.
Elkins, David J. 1980. "The Sense of Place." In *Small Worlds: Provinces and Parties in Canadian Political Life*, eds. David J. Elkins and Richard Simeon, 1–32. Toronto: Methuen Publications.
Elkins, David J., and Richard Simeon. 1980. *Small Worlds: Provinces and Parties in Canadian Political Life*. Toronto: Methuen Publications.
Emmenger, Patrick, Silja Hausermann, Bruno Palier, and Martin Seeleib-Kaiser. 2012a. "Why We Grow More Unequal." In *The Age of Dualization: The Changing Face of Inequality in De-industrializing Societes*, edited by Patrick Emmenger, Silja Hausermann, Bruno Palier, and Martin Seeleib-Kaiser. New York: Oxford University Press.
- eds. 2012b. *The Age of Dualization: The Changing Face of Inequality in De-industrializing Societies*. New York: Oxford University Press.
Entman, Robert. 2007. "Framing Bias: Media in the Distribution of Power." *Journal of Communication* 57: 163–73.

Environics Research Group Limited. 2007. *Overfishing and International Fisheries and Oceans Governance.* Toronto: Environics Research Group Limited. Report prepared for Department of Fisheries and Oceans Canada. http://www.dfo-mpo.gc.ca/por-rop/por-rop068-07-eng.html.

Esselment, Anna. 2010. "Fighting Elections: Cross-Level Political Party Integration in Ontario." *Canadian Journal of Political Science* 43, no. 4: 871–92.

Fagan, Bonaventure. 2012. "The Abolition of Denominational Governance in Newfoundland: Unnecessary, Unwarranted." In *Education Reform: From Rhetoric to Reality,* edited by Gerald Galway and David Dibbon. London, ON: The Althouse Press.

Feehan, James P. 2006. "Federal Government Presence in Newfoundland and Labrador." St John's: Leslie Harris Centre, Memorial University of Newfoundland. Accessed 14 November 2010. http://www.mun.ca/harriscentre/reports/research/2006/federalpresence/HC_FP_FINAL.pdf.

– 2011. "Danny Williams Goes Out On Top." *Policy Options* 32, no. 2: 50–5.

– 2012. "Newfoundland's Electricity Dilemma." C.D. Howe Institute e-brief, 8 January. http://www.cdhowe.org/pdf/ebrief_129.pdf.

Feehan, James P., and Melvin Baker. 2007. "The Origins of a Coming Crisis: Renewal of the Churchill Falls Contract." *Dalhousie Law Journal* 30, no. 1: 207–57.

– 2010. "The Churchill Falls Contract and Why Newfoundlanders Can't Get over It." *Policy Options* (September): 65–70.

Feehan, James P., Jeffrey Braun-Jackson, Ronald Penney, and Stephen G. Tomblin. 2009. "Newfoundland and Labrador." In *Foundations of Governance: Municipal Government in Canada's Provinces,* edited by Andrew Sancton and Robert Young. Toronto: University of Toronto Press.

Ferris, J. Stephen, and Marcel-Cristian Voia. 2009. "What Determines the Length of a Typical Canadian Parliamentary Government?" *Canadian Journal of Political Science* 42, no. 4: 881–910.

Fierlbeck, Katherine. 2011. *Health Care in Canada: A Citizen's Guide to Policy and Politics.* Toronto: University of Toronto Press.

Finlayson, A.C. 1994. *Fishing for Truth: A Sociological Analysis of Northern Cod Stock Assessments from 1977 to 1990.* St John's: Institute of Social and Economic Research.

Fischer, Jörn, and Klaus Stolz. 2010. "Patterns of Ministerial Careers across Territorial Levels in Germany." Paper presented to the Eighty-Second Annual Conference of the Canadian Political Science Association, 1–3 June, Concordia University, Montreal.

Fish, Food and Allied Workers Union (FFAW). 2004. "FFAW/CAW Responds to Dunne Report." News release, 6 February. http://www.ffaw.nf.ca/old/NewsDetails.asp?id=61.

– 2005. "Thousands Protest Williams Government's Crab Plan." News release, 3 May. Accessed 12 July 2011. http://www.ffaw.nf.ca/old/NewsDetails. asp?id=120.

– 2006. "Union Denounces Cuts to DFO Spending." News release, 27 September. http://www.ffaw.nf.ca/default.aspx?Content=News_and_Events/Current_News/General_News/Union_Denounces_Cuts_to_DFO_Spending.

– 2009. "Meet the New Boss ... Jackman Calls for Collective Approach; Says Government Money Not 'Only Solution.'" Convention 2009. *Union Forum* 5, no. 4 (winter): 15–16. http://www.ffaw.nf.ca/userfiles/files/PDF/Union%20Forum%20-%20Winter%202009.pdf.

Flecker, Jörg, Christoph Hermann, Torsten Brandt, Nils Böhlke, and Christer Thörnqvist. 2009. "Privatisation of Public Services and the Impact on Quality, Employment, and Productivity (PIQUE)." *European Commission's 6th Framework Programme*. Vienna. http://pique.at/reports/reports.html.

Fleming, Thomas. 1997. "Provincial Initiatives to Restructure Canadian School Governance in the 1990s." *Canadian Journal of Educational Administration and Policy*, no. 11. Published electronically. Accessed 25 May 2012. http://umanitoba.ca/publications/cjeap/articles/fleming.html.

Fleming, Thomas, and B. Hutton. 1997. "School Boards, District Consolidation, and Educational Governance in British Columbia, 1872–1995." *Canadian Journal of Educational Administration and Policy*, no. 10. Published electronically. http://www.umanitoba.ca/publications/cjeap/articles/fleming10.htm.

Foot, Richard. 2009. "Danny Williams, Rock Star; The Premier of Newfoundland and Labrador, One of Canada's Smallest Provinces, Holds an Outsized National Political Influence." *Ottawa Citizen*, 5 February.

Franks, C.E.S. 2007. "Members and Constituency Roles in the Canadian Federal System." *Regional & Federal Studies* 17, no. 1: 23–45.

– 2008. "*Quis custodiet ipsos Custodes?* The Contribution of Newfoundland and Labrador to the Reform of Management of Canadian Legislatures." *Canadian Public Administration* 51, no. 1: 155–69.

Freeman, Richard. 2008. "Labor Market Institutions around the World." NBER Working Paper No. 13242, Centre for Economic Performance, London School of Economics and Political Science, London.

Frege, Carola M., and John Kelly, eds. 2004. *Varieties of Unionism: Strategies for Union Revitalization in a Globalizing Economy*. New York: Oxford University Press.

Freshwater, David, Alvin Simms, and Kelly Vodden. 2011. *Defining Regions for Building Economic Development Capacity in Newfoundland and Labrador*. St John's: Leslie Harris Centre, Memorial University of Newfoundland.

Furedi, Frank. 2005. *Politics of Fear: Beyond Left and Right*. London: Continuum International Publishing Group Ltd.

Fürst, Bojan, and Kelly Vodden, with A. Khan, D. Smith and M. Woodrow. 2011. *Viability of Newfoundland and Labrador Coastal and Small Island Communities: The Case of Change Islands, NL, the Viability of Coastal and Small Island Communities*. Policy Brief. http://gracilis.carleton.ca/tgeog/downloads/Using%20Local%20Knowledge,%20PB%204%20(February%202012).pdf.

Gagnon, Alain-G. 2010. *The Case for Multinational Federalism: Beyond the All-Encompassing Nation*. London: Routledge.

Gagnon, Alain-G., Montserrat Guibernau, and François Rocher, eds. 2003. *The Conditions of Diversity in Multinational Democracies*. Montreal and Kingston: IRPP/McGill-Queen's University Press.

Gagnon, Alain–G., and Raffael Iacovino. 2007. *De La Nation à La Multination: Les Rapports Québec-Canada*. Montreal: Boréal.

Gagnon, Alain-G., and James Tully, eds. 2001. *Multinational Democracies*. Cambridge: Cambridge University Press.

Gainer, Karen, Mamoru Watanabe, Robert G. Evans, Margaret McDonald, Eric M. Maldoff, Tom W. Noseworthy, Noralou P. Roos, Lynn Smith, Krista Estrin, and Krista Locke. 1997. "Creating a Culture of Evidence-Based Decision Making in Health." In *National Forum on Health Canada. Health Action – Building on the Legacy*. Vol. 2, *Synthesis Reports and Issues Papers*. Ottawa: National Forum on Health Canada.

Galbraith, John Kenneth. 1993. *Capitalism: The Concept of Countervailing Power*. New Brunswick, NJ: Transaction Publishers.

Galway, Gerald. 2006. "An Investigation of the Uses of Evidence and Research in the Education Decision Making of Policy Elites." PHD diss., University of South Australia, Adelaide.

– 2011. "One Heart among Us: Holy Heart of Mary High School, Then and Now." *Aspects (Newfoundland Quarterly)* 46, no. 3: 48–54.

– 2012. "Lessons in Leadership: Insider Perspectives on Corporate Managerialism and Educational Reform." *Canadian Journal of Educational Administration and Leadership*, no. 130. Published electronically. http://www.umanitoba.ca/publications/cjeap/pdf_files/galway.pdf.

Galway, Gerald, and David Dibbon. 2012. "A Perfect Storm: Conceptualizing Educational (Denominational) Reform in Newfoundland and Labrador." In

Educational Reform: From Rhetoric to Reality, edited by Gerald Galway and David Dibbon. London, ON: The Althouse Press.

Galway, Gerald, Bruce Sheppard, John Wiens, and Jean Brown. 2012. "School District Governance, Autonomy and Decision Making in the Canadian Context: Preliminary Findings from a Canada-Wide Study." Paper presented at the American Educational Research Association Conference, Vancouver, 13–17 April.

Garcia, Claude. 2009. "How Would the Privatization of Hydro-Québec Make Quebecers Richer?" Montreal Economic Institute Research Paper. www.iedm.org/files/cahier0209_en.pdf.

Gaudreau, Karine. 2010. "Danny Williams Insulte Les Québécois en Français." *Le Gaboteur*. 14 October. http://www.gaboteur.ca/journal-francophone/politique/toutes-les-nouvelles/danny-williams-insulte-les-quebecois-en-francais.aspx.

Gautie, Jerome, and John Schmitt, eds. 2010. *Low-Wage Work in the Wealthy World*. New York: Russel Sage Foundation.

Gavin, Neil T., and David Sanders. 1997. "The Economy and Voting." *Parliamentary Affairs* 50, no. 4: 631–40.

Gebel, Olivier. 2005. *Separatism in Canada: A Nation at Stake? The Example of Québec and Newfoundland and Labrador*. Seminar Paper. Germany: GRIN Verlag.

Geertz, Clifford. 1973. *The Interpretation of Cultures*. New York: Basic Books.

Gellner, Ernest. 1983. *Nations and Nationalism*. Ithaca, NY: Cornell University Press.

Gibbins, Roger. 1982. *Regionalism: Territorial Politics in Canada and the United States*. Toronto: Butterworths.

Gibbins, Roger, and Loleen Berdahl. 2003. *Western Visions, Western Futures: Perspectives on the West in Canada*. 2d ed. Peterborough, ON: Broadview Press.

Gibson, Ryan, and Greg Dominaux. 2010. *Exploring Regionalism in Rural Newfoundland: The Case of the Burin Peninsula*. St John's: Memorial University of Newfoundland. http://regionalismburinpen.files.wordpress.com/2010/07/ttns-regionalism-in-the-burin-23-oct-20101.pdf.

Gillingham, Rosie. 2006. "Provincial Pride: Reaction to Williams' Performance on Larry King Live 'Overwhelming.'" *Telegram*, 6 March.

Glass, Gene V., and A.G. Rud. 2012. "The Struggle between Individualism and Communitarianism: The Pressure of Population, Prejudice, and the Purse." *Review of Research in Education* 36, no. 1: 95–112.

Glenn, Ted. 2005. "Politics, Personality and History in Ontario's Administrative Style." In *Executive Styles in Canada: Cabinet Structures and*

Leadership Practices in Canadian Government, edited by Luc Bernier, Keith Brownsey, and Michael Howlett. Toronto: University of Toronto Press.

Glyn, Andrew. 2006. *Capitalism Unleashed: Finance Globalization and Welfare*. New York: Oxford University Press.

Gomery, John. 2006. "The Pros and Cons of Commissions of Inquiry." *McGill Law Journal* 51, no. 4: 783–98.

Grabe, Maria Elizabeth, and Erik Page Bucy. 2009. *Image Bite Politics: News and the Visual Framing of Elections*. New York: Oxford University Press.

Graesser, Mark. 1992. "Leadership Crises in an Opposition Party: The Liberal Party of Newfoundland." In *Leaders and Parties in Canadian Politics: Experiences of the Provinces*, edited by R. Kenneth Carty, Lynda Erickson, and Donald E. Blake. Toronto: Harcourt Brace Janovich Canada.

Green, J. Derek. 2004. "Judicial Notice and Financial Support for the Courts." Presentation to the Newfoundland Branch of the Canadian Bar Association, 29 January, Fairmont Newfoundland Hotel, St John's.

– 2007. *Rebuilding Confidence: Report of the Review Commission on Constituency Allowances and Related Matters*. St John's: Government of Newfoundland and Labrador.

Green, M. 2012. "Discourses of Care in Educational Reform." In *Education Reform: From Rhetoric to Reality*, edited by Gerald Galway and David Dibbon. London, ON: The Althouse Press.

Greenwood, Robert. 1991. "The Local State and Economic Development in Peripheral Regions: A Comparative Study of Newfoundland and Northern Norway." PHD diss., University of Warwick, Coventry, UK.

Grimes, Roger. 2012. "Quebec Putting Up Roadblocks? A Political Fiction." *Telegram*. 23 August, A6.

Gunton, Thomas. 2003. "Natural Resources and Regional Development: An Assessment of Dependency and Comparative Advantage Paradigms." *Economic Geography* 79, no. 1: 67–94.

Gwyn, Richard. 1972. *Smallwood: The Unlikely Revolutionary*. Rev. ed. Toronto: McClelland and Stewart.

– 1999. *Smallwood: The Unlikely Revolutionary*. 2nd. rev. ed. Toronto: McClelland and Stewart.

Hacker, Jacob, and Paul Pierson. 2010. *Winner-Take-All Politics: How Washington Made the Rich Richer – and Turned Its Back on the Middle Class*. New York: Simon & Schuster.

Hamman, Kerstin, and John Kelly. 2011. *Parties, Elections, and Policy Reforms in Western Europe. Voting for Social Pacts*. New York: Routledge.

Hancock, Edward. 2012. "A Call for Reform: Teachers and Denominational Schools." In *Education Reform: From Rhetoric to Reality*, edited by Gerald Galway and David Dibbon. London, ON: The Althouse Press.

Hardin, Garrett. 1968. "The Tragedy of the Commons." *Science* 162, no. 3859: 1243–8.

Harris, Leslie. 1989. Independent Review of the State of the Northern Cod Stock. *Final Report*. Department of Fisheries and Oceans. Ottawa: Minister of Supply and Services, Government of Canada.

HayGroup. 2002. *Operational Review of the Health Care Corporation of St John's*. Department of Health and Community Services, Government of Newfoundland and Labrador.

Hayter, R., and T. Barnes. 1990. "'Innis' Staple Theory, Exports, and Recession: British Columbia, 1981–1986." *Economic Geography* 66:156–73.

Health Canada. 2003. "First Ministers Health Accord." Accessed 30 September 2013. http://www.hc-sc.gc.ca/hcs-sss/delivery-prestation/fptcollab/2003accord/fs-if_1-eng.php

– 2004. "Severe Acute Respiratory Syndrome (SARS)." Accessed 12 February 2012. http://www.hc-sc.gc.ca/hl-vs/iyh-vsv/diseases-maladies/sars-sras-eng.php#ba.

Hechter, Michael. 2000. *Containing Nationalism*. Oxford: Oxford University Press.

Hede, Karyn. 2008. "Breast Cancer Testing Scandal Shines Spotlight on Black Box of Clinical Laboratory Testing." *Journal of the National Cancer Institute* 100, no. 12: 836–8.

Hiesz, Andrew, and Sébastien LaRochelle-Côté. 2006. "Work Hours Instability in Canada." Ottawa: Statistics Canada.

Higgins, Jenny. 2008. "Economic Impacts of the Cod Moratorium." St John's: Newfoundland and Labrador Heritage, Memorial University of Newfoundland. http://www.heritage.nf.ca/society/moratorium_impacts.htm

Hiller, Harry H. 1987. "Dependence and Independence: Emergent Nationalism in Newfoundland." *Ethnic and Racial Studies* 10, no. 3: 257–75.

Hobsbawm, Eric. 1983. "Introduction: Inventing Traditions." In *The Invention of Tradition*, edited by Eric Hobsbawm and Terence Ranger. London: Cambridge University Press.

– 1990. *Nations and Nationalism since 1780: Programme, Myth, Reality*. Cambridge: Cambridge University Press.

Hodder, Bryce. 2012. "The Impact of Educational Reform on Religious Education and Religious Observances." In *Education Reform: From Rhetoric to Reality*, edited by Gerald Galway and David Dibbon. London, ON: The Althouse Press.

House, Douglas. 2006. "Oil, Fish and Social Change in Newfoundland and Labrador: Lessons for British Columbia." Presentation sponsored by Simon Fraser University's Centre for Coastal Studies, Burnaby, BC, 11 January.

House, J.D. 1982. "Premier Peckford, Petroleum Policy, and Popular Politics in Newfoundland and Labrador." *Journal of Canadian Studies* 17, no. 2: 12–31.

– 1985. "The Don Quixote of Canadian Politics? Power in and Power over Newfoundland Society." *Canadian Journal of Sociology* 10, no. 2: 171–88.

– 1992. *Against the Tide: Battling for Economic Renewal in Newfoundland and Labrador.* Toronto: University of Toronto Press.

– 1999. *Against the Tide: Battling for Economic Renewal in Newfoundland and Labrador.* Reprint. Toronto: University of Toronto Press.

– 2005. "Change from Within the Corridors of Power: A Reflective Essay of a Sociologist in Government." *Canadian Journal of Sociology* 30, no. 4: 471–90.

House, Douglas, and Alison Earle. 2004. "Understanding the Strategic Social Plan in the Framework of the New Rural Secretariat." 3 June. http://www.envision.ca/pdf/cura/RuralSecretariatSeminarReport.pdf.

Howlett, Michael, M. Ramesh, and Anthony Perl. 2009. *Studying Public Policy: Policy Cycles & Policy Subsystems.* 3rd ed. Don Mills, ON: Oxford University Press.

Hoy, Claire. 1992. *Clyde Wells: A Political Biography.* Toronto: Stoddart.

Huber, Evelyne, and John D. Stephens. 2001. *Development and Crisis of the Welfare State: Parties and Policies in Global Markets.* Chicago: University of Chicago Press.

Huber, John D., and Arthur Lupia. 2001. "Cabinet Instability and Delegation in Parliamentary Democracies." *American Journal of Political Science* 45, no. 1: 18–33.

Huber, John D., and Cecilia Martinez-Gallardo. 2008. "Replacing Cabinet Ministers: Patterns of Ministerial Stability in Parliamentary Democracy." *American Political Science Review* 102, no. 2: 169–80.

Hueglin, Thomas O. 1986. "Regionalism in Western Europe: Conceptual Problems of a New Political Perspective." *Comparative Politics* 18, no. 4: 439–58.

Hunt, Clayton. 2011. "Jackman Rejects MOU Report." *Coaster*, 8 March. Accessed 12 December 2011. http://www.thecoaster.ca/News/2011-03-08/article-2311621/Jackman-rejects-MOU-Report/1.

Huo, Jingjing. 2009. *Third Way Reforms: Social Democracy after the Golden Age.* New York: Cambridge University Press.

Indridason, Indridi H., and Christopher Kam. 2008. "Cabinet Reshuffles and Ministerial Drift." *British Journal of Political Science* 38, no. 4: 621–56.

Innis, Harold. 1930. *The Fur Trade in Canada: An Introduction to Canadian Economic History.* New Haven, CT: Yale University Press.

– 1954. *The Cod Fisheries: The History of an International Economy.* Toronto: University of Toronto Press.

Iversen, Torben, and David Soskice. 2008. "Electoral Institutions, Parties, and the Politics of Class: Explaining the Formation of Redistributive Coalitions." In *Democracy, Inequality, and Representation*, edited by Pablo Beramendi and Christopher J. Anderson. New York: Russell Sage Foundation.

Jaccard, Mark. 1995. "Oscillating Currents: The Changing Rationale for Government Intervention in the Electricity Industry." *Energy Policy* 23, no. 7: 579–92.

Jackson, Craig. 2005. "Tories Scrap Planned School Closure in Contested Exploits District." *Western Star,* 18 June.

Jackson, F.L. 1984. *Newfoundland in Canada: A People in Search of a Polity.* St John's: Harry Cuff Publications.

– 1986. *Surviving Confederation: A Revised and Extended Version of "Newfoundland in Canada."* St John's: Harry Cuff Publications.

Jacobs, Alan M., and J. Scott Matthews. 2012. "Why Do Citizens Discount the Future? Public Opinion and the Timing of Policy Consequences." *British Journal of Political Science* 42, no. 4: 903–35.

Jenkins, Glenn P. 1985. "Public Utility Finance and Economic Waste." *Canadian Journal of Economics* 18, no. 3: 484–98.

Jentoft, Svein. 1993. *Dangling Line: The Fisheries Crisis and the Future of the Coastal Communities: The Norwegian Experience.* St John's: Institute of Social and Economic Research.

Johnson, Ross A. 1976. "Cabinet Decision-Making Structures: Taking Issues out of Politics?: The Newfoundland Case." Paper presented at the annual meeting of the Canadian Political Science Association, Quebec, 30 May–2 June.

Joint Review Panel. 2011. *Lower Churchill Hydroelectric Generation Project: Report of the Joint Review Panel.* Ottawa: Minister of Environment and Conservation, Government of Canada. http://www.ceaa.gc.ca/050/ documents/53120/53120E.pdf.

Kaid, Lynda Lee, and Monica Postelnicu. 2005. "Political Advertising in the 2004 Election: Comparison of Traditional Television and Internet Messages." *American Behavioral Scientist* 49, no. 2: 265–78.

Kam, Christopher, and Indridi H. Indridason. 2005. "The Timing of Cabinet Reshuffles in Five Westminster Parliamentary Systems." *Legislative Studies Quarterly* 30, no. 3: 327–63.

Kassam, Karim-Aly. 2001. "North of 60 Degrees: Homeland or Frontier?" In *Passion for Identity: Canadian Studies for the Twenty-first Century*, edited by David Taras and Beverly Rasporich. Scarborough, ON: Nelson Thompson.

Kearley, Wade. 2008. *"Where Do You Draw the Line? Regionalization in Newfoundland and Labrador: A Comparative Synopsis of Selected*

Stakeholders' Input." St John's: Leslie Harris Centre, Memorial University of Newfoundland.

Keating, Michael. 1988. *State and Regional Nationalism: Territorial Politics and the European State.* New York: Harvester Wheatsheaf.

– 1996. *Nations against the State: The New Politics of Nationalism in Quebec, Catalonia and Scotland.* New York: St Martin's Press.

– 2008. "Thirty Years of Territorial Politics." *West European Politics* 31, 1/2: 60–81.

Keenan, Robert. 2011. *Census of Municipalities in Newfoundland and Labrador.* St John's: Municipalities Newfoundland and Labrador.

Kellert, Stephen R., James P. Gibbs, and Timothy J. Wohlgenant. 1995. "Canadian Perceptions of Commercial Fisheries Management and Marine Mammal Conservation in the Northwest Atlantic Ocean." *Anthrozoos: A Multidisciplinary Journal of The Interactions of People & Animals,* 8, no. 1: 20–30.

Kelly, James B., and Christopher P. Manfredi. 2009. "Should We Cheer? Contested Constitutionalism and the Canadian Charter of Rights and Freedoms." In *Contested Constitutionalism: Reflections on the Canadian Charter of Rights and Freedoms,* edited by James B. Kelly and Christopher P. Manfredi. Vancouver: UBC Press.

Kelly, Nathan. 2009. *The Politics of Income Inequality in the United States.* New York: Cambridge University Press.

Kelso, William. 1978. *American Democratic Theory: Pluralism and Its Critics.* Westport, CT: Greenwood Press.

Kerby, Matthew. 2009a. "Calls of the Wild: Resignation Requests in the Canadian House of Commons: 1957–2008." Paper presented to the Annual Conference of the Canadian Political Science Association, Ottawa, 27 May.

– 2009b. "Worth the Wait: The Determinants of Ministerial Appointment in Canada, 1935–2008." *Canadian Journal of Political Science* 42, no. 3: 593–611.

– 2011. "Combining the Hazards of Ministerial Appointment and Ministerial Exit in the Canadian Federal Cabinet." *Canadian Journal of Political Science* 44, no. 3: 595–612.

– Forthcoming. "Les Carrière provinciale et la durée des ministres." *Revue Internationale de Politique Comparée.*

Kerby, Matthew, and Kelly Blidook. 2011. "It's Not You, It's Me: Determinants of Voluntary Legislative Turnover in Canada." *Legislative Studies Quarterly* 36, no. 4: 621–43.

King, Desmond, and David Rueda. 2008. "Cheap Labor: The New Politics of 'Bread and Roses' in Industrial Democracies." *Perspectives on Politics* 6, no. 2: 279–97.

King, Gary, James E. Alt, Nancy E. Burns, and Michael Laver. 1990. "A Unified Model of Cabinet Dissolution in Parliamentary Democracies." *American Journal of Political Science* 34, no. 3: 846–71.

King, Ruth, and Sandra Clarke. 2002. "Contesting Meaning: Newfie and the Politics of Ethnic Labelling." *Journal of Sociolinguistics* 6, no. 4: 537–58.

Kingdon, John W. 1995. *Agendas, Alternatives and Public Policy*. 2d ed. Boston: Little, Brown & Co.

Kiousis, Spiro, Michael Mitrook, and Xu Wu. 2006. "First- and Second-Level Agenda-Building and Agenda-Setting Effects: Exploring the Linkages among Candidate News Releases, Media Coverage, and Public Opinion during the 2002 Florida Gubernatorial Election." *Journal of Public Relations Research* 18, no. 3: 265–85.

Kirby, Michael. 1982. *Navigating Troubled Waters: A New Policy for the Atlantic Fisheries*. Task Force on Atlantic Fisheries. Ottawa: Minister of Supply and Services, Government of Canada.

Kitchen, Harry. 2002. "Canadian Municipalities: Fiscal Trends and Sustainability." *Canadian Tax Journal* 50, no. 1: 156–80.

Köhler, Nicholas. 2006. "Go Ahead, Take Your Best Shot." *Maclean's*, 31 July, 17.

Koop, Royce. 2011. *Grassroots Liberals: Organizing for Local and National Politics*. Vancouver: UBC Press.

Kornberg, Allan, William Mishler, and Harold D. Clarke. 1982. *Representative Democracy in the Canadian Provinces*. Scarborough, ON: Prentice-Hall Canada.

Korpi, Walter. 1983. *The Democratic Class Struggle. Swedish Politics in a Comparative Perspective*. London: Routledge and Kegan Paul.

Krashinsky, Michael, and William J. Milne. 1986. "The Effect of Incumbency in the 1984 Federal and 1985 Ontario Elections." *Canadian Journal of Political Science* 19, no. 2: 337–43.

Lambert, Carolyn. 2008. "Emblem of Our Country: The Red, White and Green Tricolour." *Newfoundland and Labrador Studies* 23, no. 1: 21–43.

LaRochelle-Côté, Sébastien, and Claude Dionne. 2009. "International Differences in Low-Paid Work." *Perspectives on Labour and Income* 10, no. 6: 5–13. Ottawa: Statistics Canada. http://www.statcan.gc.ca/pub/75-001-x/2009106/pdf/10894-eng.pdf.

Laver, Michael. 2003. "Government Termination." *Annual Review of Political Science* 6 (June): 23–40.

Lawson, James. 2005. "Power, Political Economy, and Supply Chains: Staples as Media of Power." Paper presented at the Annual Meeting of the Canadian Political Science Association, University of Western Ontario, London, ON, 2–5 June. Accessed 14 August 2006. http://www.cpsa-acsp.ca/papers-2005/Lawson.pdf.

Lecours, André, and Daniel Béland. 2009. "Federalism and Fiscal Policy: The Politics of Equalization in Canada." *Publius: The Journal of Federalism* 40, no. 4: 569–96.

Lee, Philip. 2001. *Frank: The Life and Politics of Frank McKenna*. Fredericton, NB: Goose Lane.

Léger Marketing. 2007. "Nearly All Canadians Concerned about State of Fisheries in Canada." *Canada News Wire*. 21 November. http://www.newswire.ca/en/story/42429/nearly-all-canadians-concerned-about-state-of-fisheries-in-canada-union-of-environment-workers-calls-on-federal-government-to-put-more-money-into-fish.

Léger, Pierre Thomas. 2011. *Physician Payment Mechanisms: An Overview of Policy Options for Canada*. Ottawa: Canadian Health Services Research Foundation.

Leonard, Jeremy. 2012. "Ranking Provincial Premiers of the Last 40 Years: The Numbers Speak." *Policy Options* (June/July): 21–3.

Lessard, Claude, and André Brassard. 2005. "Education Governance in Canada: Trends and Significance." Accessed 28 November 2011. http://www2.crifpe.ca/html/chaires/lessard/pdf/AERAgouvernanceang3.pdf.

Levin, Benjamin. 2001. *Reforming Education: From Origins to Outcomes*. London: Routledge-Falmer.

– 2003. "Knowledge and Action in Educational Policy and Politics." In *Towards Evidence-Based Policy for Canadian Education*, edited by Patrice de Broucker and Arthur Sweetman. Montreal and Kingston: McGill-Queen's University Press.

– 2004. "Making Research Matter More." *Education Policy Analysis Archives* 12, no. 6: 1–21.

Levin, Benjamin, and J.A. Riffel. 1997. *Schools and the Changing World: Struggling towards the Future*. London: Falmer.

Lewis, J.P. 2012. "If We Could All Be Peter Lougheed: Provincial Premiers and Their Legacies, 1967–2007." *British Journal of Canadian Studies* 25, no. 1: 77–114.

Liberal Party of Newfoundland and Labrador (Liberal Party). 2011. *People's Platform*. St John's: Liberal Party. http://nlliberals.ca/wp-content/uploads/2011/08/peoples_platform_download.pdf.

Lijphart, Arend. 2012. *Patterns of Democracy: Government Forms and Performance in Thirty-Six Countries*. Grand Rapids, MI: Yale University Press.

Lindblom, Charles E. 1980. *The Policy-Making Process*. New York: Prentice Hall.

Lindblom, Charles E., and Edward J. Woodhouse. 1993. *The Policy-Making Process*. 3rd ed. Englewood Cliffs, NJ: Prentice Hall.

Lindvall, Johannes. 2010. *Mass Unemployment and the State*. New York: Oxford University Press.

Lingard, Bob, and Shaun Rawolle. 2004. "Mediatizing Educational Policy: The Journalistic Field, Science Policy and Cross-Field Effects." *Journal of Education Policy* 19, no. 3: 361–80.

Linz, Juan J. 2000. *Totalitarian and Authoritarian Regimes*. Boulder, CO: Lynne Rienner Publishers.

Lipset, Seymour Martin. 1959. "Democracy and Working-Class Authoritarianism." *American Sociological Review* 24, no. 4: 482–501.

Lisac, Mark. 2004. "Don Getty, 1985–1992." In *Alberta Premiers of the Twentieth Century*, edited by Bradford J. Rennie. Regina, SK: Canadian Plains Research Center, University of Regina.

Lock, Andrew, and Phil Harris. 1996. "Political Marketing – Vive la Différence!" *European Journal of Marketing* 30, no. 10/11: 14–24.

Locke, Wade. 2011. *Municipal Fiscal Sustainability: Alternative Funding Arrangements to Promote Fiscal Sustainability of Newfoundland and Labrador Municipalities: The Role of Income and Sales Taxes*. St John's: Municipalities Newfoundland and Labrador.

Lomas, Jonathan. 1990. "Finding Audiences, Changing Beliefs: The Structure of Research Use in Canadian Health Policy." *Journal of Health, Politics, Policy and Law* 15, no. 3: 525–42.

– 2000. "Connecting Research and Policy." *ISUMA* 1, no. 1: 140–4.

Lomas, Jonathan, Tony Culyer, Chris McCutcheon, Laura McAuley, and Susan Law. 2005. *Conceptualizing and Combining Evidence for Health System Guidance*. Ottawa: Canadian Health Services Research Foundation.

Luchak, Andrew A. 2003. "Newfoundland and Labrador: Shifting Tides." In *Beyond the National Divide: Regional Dimensions of Industrial Relations*, edited by Mark Thompson, Joseph B. Rose, and Anthony E. Smith. Montreal and Kingston: McGill-Queen's University Press.

Lucifora, Claudio, and Wiemar Salverda. 2009. "Low-Pay." In *The Oxford Handbook of Economic Inequality*, edited by Wiemer Salverda, Brian Nolan, and Timothy M. Smeeding. New York: Oxford University Press.

Lukacs, John. 2005. *Democracy and Populism: Fear and Hatred*. New Haven, CT: Yale University Press.

Lusztig, Michael, Patrick James, and Jeremy Moon. 1997. "Falling from Grace: Nonestablished Brokerage Parties and the Weight of Predominance in Canadian Provinces and Australian States." *Publius: The Journal of Federalism* -27, no. 1: 59–81.

MacDermid, Robert. 1997. "TV Advertising Campaigns in the 1995 Ontario Election." In *Revolution at Queen's Park*, edited by Sid Noel. Toronto: James Lorimer & Company.

MacEachern, Daniel. 2010. "Dunderdale to Seek Top Job." *Telegram*, 31 December, A1.

Mackenzie, Hugh. 2004. *Newfoundland and Labrador Fiscal Review.* Ottawa: Canadian Centre for Policy Alternatives. Accessed 14 November 2010. https://www.policyalternatives.ca/sites/default/files/uploads/publications/National_Office_Pubs/nl_fiscal_review.pdf.

MacKinnon, Wayne. 2005. *Between Two Cultures: The Alex Campbell Years.* Stratford, PE: Tea Hill Press.

Mackintosh, W.A. 1923. "Economic Factors in Canadian History." *Canadian Historical Review* 4, no. 1: 12–25.

– 1953. "Innis on Canadian Economic Development." *Journal of Political Economy* 61, no. 3: 185–94.

Macpherson, C.B. 1953. *Democracy in Alberta: The Theory and Practice of a Quasi-Party System.* Toronto: University of Toronto Press.

Majone, Giandomenico. 1989. *Evidence, Argument, and Persuasion in the Policy Process.* New Haven, CT: Yale University Press.

Makin, Kirk. 2008. "Harper Blasted over Hasty Top-Court Nomination." *Globe and Mail,* 6 September, 4.

Malloy, Jonathan. 2003. "High Discipline, Low Cohesion? The Uncertain Patterns of Canadian Parliamentary Party Groups." *Journal of Legislative Studies* 9, no. 4: 116–29.

– 2004. "The Executive and Parliament in Canada." *Journal of Legislative Studies* 10, no. 2: 206–17.

Malone, Greg. 2012. *Don't Tell the Newfoundlanders: The True Story of Newfoundland's Confederation with Canada.* Toronto: Alfred A. Knopf Canada.

Manin, Bernard. 1996. *Principes du gouvernement représentatif.* Paris: Flammarion.

Manitoba. 2003. Intergovernmental Affairs. *Building Strong Communities: A Vision for Rural Manitoba.* Winnipeg: Government of Manitoba. http://www.gov.mb.ca/agriculture/ri/pdf/rurstrat.pdf.

Mares, Isabela. 2003. *The Politics of Social Risk: Business and Welfare State Development.* New York: Cambridge University Press.

Marier, Patrik. 2009. "The Power of Institutionalized Learning: The Uses and Practices of Commissions to Generate Policy Change." *Journal of European Public Policy* 16, no. 8: 1204–23.

Marissal, Vincent. 2010. "Le Québec perd son meilleur ennemi." *La Presse*, 26 November, A12.

Markey, Sean, John Pierce, and Kelly Vodden. 2000. "Resources, People and the Environment: A Regional Analysis of the Evolution of Resource Policy in Canada." *Journal of Regional Science* 23, no. 3: 427–54.

Markey, Sean, John Pierce, Kelly Vodden, and Mark Roseland. 2005. *Second Growth: Community Economic Development in Rural British Columbia.* Vancouver: UBC Press.

Marland, Alex. 2007a. "Scandal and Reform in the Newfoundland and Labrador House of Assembly." *Canadian Parliamentary Review* 30, no. 4: 37–41.

– 2007b. "The 2007 Provincial Election in Newfoundland and Labrador." *Canadian Political Science Review* 1, no. 2: 75–85.

– 2009. "Voting in Newfoundland and Labrador: Turned Off by Canadian Elections? Tune In to Canadian Idol!" *Newfoundland and Labrador Studies* 24, no. 2: 219–37.

– 2010. "Masters of Our Own Destiny: The Nationalist Evolution of Newfoundland Premier Danny Williams." *International Journal of Canadian Studies* 42: 155–81.

– 2011. "Order, Please! The Newfoundland and Labrador House of Assembly." *Studies of Provincial and Territorial Legislatures.* Canadian Study of Parliament Group. Accessed 22 November 2010. http://www.studyparliament.ca/English/pdf/Newfoundland_Marland-e.pdf.

– 2012a. "Political Photography, Journalism and Framing in the Digital Age: The Management of Visual Media by the Prime Minister of Canada." *The International Journal of Press/Politics* 17, no. 2: 214–33.

– 2012b. "A Race for Second place: The 2011 Provincial Election in Newfoundland and Labrador." *Canadian Political Science Review* 6, nos. 2–3: 117–30.

– Forthcoming. "If Seals Were Ugly, Nobody Would Give a Damn: Propaganda, Nationalism and Political Marketing in the Canadian Seal Hunt." *Journal of Political Marketing.*

Marland, Alex, and Matthew Kerby. 2010. "The Audience is Listening: Talk Radio and Public Policy in Newfoundland and Labrador." *Media, Culture & Society* 32, no. 6: 997–1016.

Marsh, David, Paul 't Hart, and Karen Tindall. 2010. "Celebrity Politics: The Politics of Late Modernity?" *Political Studies Review* 8, no. 3: 322–40.

Martin, Don. 2002. *King Ralph: The Political Life and Success of Ralph Klein.* Key Porter Books.

Martin, Lawrence. 2010. *Harperland: The Politics of Control.* Toronto: Viking Canada.

Maxwell, Judith, and Carole Pestieau. 1980. *Economic Realities of Contemporary Confederation.* Montreal: C.D. Howe Research Institute.

May, A.W., Dawn A. Russell, and Derrick H. Rowe. 2005. *Breaking New Ground: An Action Plan for Rebuilding the Grand Banks Fisheries.* Report of the Advisory Panel on the Sustainable Management of Straddling Fish Stocks in the Northwest Atlantic. Ottawa: Department of Fisheries and Oceans, Government of Canada.

Mayo, H.B. 1949. "Newfoundland's Entry into the Dominion." *Canadian Journal of Economics and Political Science* 15, no. 4: 505–22.

McBride, Stephen. 2005. *Paradigm Shift: Globalization and the Canadian State.* Halifax, NS: Fernwood Publishing.

McCann, Phillip. 1988. "The Politics of Denominational Education in the Nineteenth Century in Newfoundland." In *The Vexed Question: Denominational Education in a Secular Age,* edited by William McKim. St John's: Breakwater.

– 1998. "Education." Newfoundland and Labrador Heritage. http://www.heritage.nf.ca/society/education.html.

– 2002. "The Background to the Royal Commission on Education." *Morning Watch* 29, no. 3/4. Faculty of Education, Memorial University of Newfoundland. http://www.mun.ca/educ/faculty/mwatch/win22/mccann.htm.

McCormick, Peter. 2004. *Judicial Independence and Judicial Governance in the Provincial Courts.* Lethbridge, AB: Canadian Association of Provincial Court Judges.

McCorquodale, Susan. 1972. "Newfoundland: The Only Living Father's Realm." In *Canadian Provincial Politics: The Party Systems of the Ten Provinces,* edited by Martin Robin. Scarborough, ON: Prentice-Hall Canada.

– 1989. "Newfoundland: Personality, Party, and Politics." In *Provincial and Territorial Legislatures in Canada,* edited by Gary Levy and Graham White. Toronto: University of Toronto Press.

McCrank, Neil, Linda Hohol, and Allan Tupper. 2007. *At a Crossroads: The Report of the Board Governance Review Task Force.* Edmonton: Board Governance Task Force, Government of Alberta. http://www.assembly.ab.ca/lao/library/egovdocs/2007/alz/162424.pdf.

McCrorie, James. 1969. *An Experiment in Development Planning.* Ottawa: Canadian Council on Rural Development, Government of Canada.

McLeod, James. 2010. "Kennedy Asks Doctors Back to Table." *Telegram*, 2 December. http://www.thetelegram.com/News/Local/2010-12-02/article-2011047/Births-1847.

– 2011a. "Grimes Gets Serious on Muskrat Falls." *Telegram*, 2 March, A3.

– 2011b. "Two in Tory Race?" *Telegram*, 11 January, A1.

Meisel, John. 1963. "The Stalled Omnibus: Canadian Parties in the 1960s." *Social Research* 30, no. 3: 367–90.

Memorial University of Newfoundland. 2008. *Balancing Autonomy and Accountability: Report of the Ad Hoc Committee of the Board of Regents at Memorial University of Newfoundland*. St John's: Memorial University of Newfoundland.

Mendelson, Michael, Ken Battle, and Sherri Torjman. 2009. "Canada's Shrunken Safety Net: Employment Insurance in the Great Recession." Ottawa: Caledon Institute of Social Policy. http://www.caledoninst.org/Publications/PDF/773ENG%2Epdf.

Michels, Robert. 1915. *Political Parties*. English ed. London: Collier-Macmillan 1962.

Miljan, Lydia. 2008. *Public Policy in Canada: An Introduction*. Toronto: Oxford University Press.

Milne, David A. 2001. "Prince Edward Island: Politics in a Beleaguered Garden." In *The Provincial State in Canada: Politics in the Provinces and Territories*, edited by Keith Brownsey and Michael Howlett. Peterborough, ON: Broadview Press.

Mitchell, David J. 1987. *Succession: The Political Reshaping of British Columbia*. Vancouver: Douglas & McIntyre.

Molot, Henry. 2010. "The Public Service of Canada." In *The Handbook of Canadian Public Administration*, edited by Christopher Dunn. Don Mills, ON: Oxford University Press.

Moncrief, Gary F. 1994. "Professionalization and Careerism in Canadian Provincial Assemblies: Comparison to US State Legislatures." *Legislative Studies Quarterly* 19, no. 1: 33–48.

– 1998. "Terminating the Provincial Career: Retirement and Electoral Defeat in Canadian Provincial Legislatures, 1960–1997." *Canadian Journal of Political Science* 31, no. 2: 359–72.

Monitoring and Evaluation Subcommittee. 1997. *Monitoring and Evaluation Framework for the Strategic Regional Diversification Agreement and Regional Economic Development Board Performance Contracts*. Draft in preparation for the Management Committee of the Strategic Regional Diversification Agreement. Unpublished. Government of Newfoundland and Labrador.

Moody, Kim. 2007. *US Labor in Trouble and Transition: The Failure of Reform from Above, the Promise of Revival from Below*. New York: Verso.

Moore, Dene. 2005. "Nfld. Tory Kicked out of Government Caucus for Breaking Ranks on Crab." *Canadian Press*, 5 May.

Morley, J. Terence, and Walter D. Young. 1983. "The Premier and the Cabinet." In *The Reins of Power: Governing British Columbia*, edited by J. Terence Morley, Norman J. Ruff, Neil A. Swainson, R. Jeremy Wilson, and Walter D. Young. Vancouver: Douglas and McIntyre.

Moss, B. 2009. "Expedition Sailors: The Ombudsman in Newfoundland and Labrador." In *Provincial and Territorial Ombudsman Offices in Canada*, edited by Stewart Hyson. Toronto: University of Toronto Press.

Mothers against Drunk Driving (MADD). 2012. "Provincial Liquor Boards: Meeting the Bests Interests of Canadians." MADD Canada Policy Backgrounder. http://www.madd.ca/media/docs/MADD-Canada_Provincial-Liquor-Boards-Paper_August-2012.pdf.

Müller, Wolfgang. 2000. "Political Parties in Parliamentary Democracies: Making Delegation and Accountability Work." *European Journal of Political Research* 37, no.3: 309–33.

Mullins, Kimberley. 2008. "The Voting Audience." *Media/Culture Journal* 11, no. 1. Published electronically. http://journal.media-culture.org.au/index.php/mcjournal/article/view/23.

Municipalities of Newfoundland and Labrador (MNL). 2005. *Strengthening Our Communities: President's Task Force on Municipal Sustainability*. St John's: MNL.

– 2011b. "Municipal Fiscal Framework Review – Dr Wade Locke's Recommendations for Reforming Municipal Fiscal Framework." News release, 4 October.

– 2011a. *What's the Plan?* St John's: MNL.

– 2012. "MNL Calls for a Real Plan for Municipalities." News release, 26 January.

Nalcor Energy. 2010. *2010 Business and Financial Report: The Energy behind Our Year*. St John's: Nalcor.

Nanos, Nik. 2009. "Canadians Overwhelmingly Choose Water as Our Most Important Natural Resource." *Policy Options* 6 (July/August): 12–15.

Nanos Research. 2011. "McGuinty, Hudak Close as Best Premier." 4 October. http://www.nanosresearch.com/library/polls/POLONT-F11-T516.pdf.

Naváez, Peter. 1986. "Joseph R. Smallwood, The Barrelman: The Broadcaster as Folklorist." In *Media Sense: The Folklore-Popular Culture Continuum*, edited by Peter Naváez and Martin Laba. Bowling Green State University: Popular Press.

Needham, Catherine. 2005. "Brand Leaders: Clinton, Blair and the Limitations of the Permanent Campaign." *Political Studies* 53, no. 2: 343–61.

Netherton, Alexander. 2007. "The Political Economy of Canadian Hydro-Electricity: Between Old 'Provincial Hydros' and Neoliberal Regional Energy Regimes." *Canadian Political Science Review* 1, no. 1: 107–24.

Neville, Doreen, Gwynedd Barrowman, Brenda Fitzgerald, and Stephen Tomblin. 2005. "Regionalization of Health Services in Newfoundland and Labrador: Perceptions of the Planning, Implementation and Consequences of Regional Governance." *Journal of Health Services Research and Policy* 10, supplement no. 2: 12–21.

New Democratic Party of Newfoundland and Labrador (NDP). 2011. *It's Time: The NDP Plan for Newfoundland and Labrador*. St John's: NDP. http://nl.ndp.ca/sites/default/files/NDP_Plan_2011.pdf.

Newfoundland and Labrador. 1967. *Report of the Royal Commission on Education and Youth*. St John's: Government of Newfoundland and Labrador.

– 1972. *White Paper on the Organization of the Public Service of Newfoundland and Labrador*. St John's: Government of Newfoundland and Labrador.

– 1986. Royal Commission on Employment and Unemployment (RCEU). *Building on Our Strengths: The Report of the Royal Commission on Employment and Unemployment*. St John's: Government of Newfoundland and Labrador.

– 1989. *Towards an Achieving Society: Report of the Task Force on Mathematics and Science Education*. St John's: Government of Newfoundland and Labrador.

– 1991. *House of Assembly Proceedings (Hansard)*. 41st General Assembly, 3rd Session. Vol. 41, no. 2. 4 March. (Lynn Verge). http://www.assembly.nl.ca/business/hansard/ga41session3/91-03-04.htm.

– 1992a. *Challenge and Change: A Strategic Economic Plan for Newfoundland and Labrador*. St Johns: Government of Newfoundland and Labrador.

– 1992b. *House of Assembly Proceedings (Hansard)*. 41st General Assembly, 4th Session. Vol. 41, no. 53. June 9. (Lynn Verge). http://www.assembly.nl.ca/business/hansard/ga41session4/92-06-09.htm.

– 1992c. *Our Children, Our Future: Report of the Royal Commission of Inquiry into the Delivery of Programs and Services in Primary, Elementary, Secondary Education*. St John's: Government of Newfoundland and Labrador.

– 1995. Task Force on Community Economic Development (CED) in Newfoundland and Labrador. *Community Matters: The New Regional Economic Development*. St John's: Atlantic Canada Opportunities Agency.

– 1999. Department of Education. *Postsecondary Indicators '98: University, Public Colleges, Private Colleges.* St John's: Government of Newfoundland and Labrador.

– 2000. Department of Education. *Supporting Learning: Report of the Ministerial Panel on Educational Delivery in the Classroom.* St John's: Government of Newfoundland and Labrador.

– 2002. Department of Mines and Energy. "Minister Questions the Merits of Opposition Leader's Public Protest." News release, 29 November. http://www.releases.gov.nl.ca/releases/2002/mines&en/1129no5.htm.

– 2003. Treasury Board. Budgeting Division. *Estimates 2003–04.* St John's: Government of Newfoundland and Labrador. http://www.budget.gov.nl.ca/budget2003/download/Estimates2003.pdf.

– 2003–04 to 2008–09. Department of Fisheries and Aquaculture. *Annual Reports.* Government of Newfoundland and Labrador. St John's: Government of Newfoundland and Labrador.

– 2004a. Treasury Board. Budgeting Division. *Estimates 2004–05.* St John's: Government of Newfoundland and Labrador. Accessed 11 May 2012. http://www.budget.gov.nl.ca/Budget2004/estimates2004.pdf.

– 2004b. Department of Health and Community Services. "Government Transforms Health Boards' Administrative Structure." News release, 10 September.

– 2004c. *House of Assembly Proceedings (Hansard).* 45th General Assembly, 1st Session. Vol. 45, no. 33. 19 May. http://www.assembly.nl.ca/business/hansard/ga45session1/04-05-19.htm.

– 2004d. Office of the Auditor General. "Reports for 2004." St John's: Government of Newfoundland and Labrador. http://www.ag.gov.nl.ca/ag/2004.htm.

– 2004e. "Premier Danny Williams State of the Province Address." 5 January. http://www.gov.nl.ca/financialsituation/premieraddress.html.

– 2004f. Department of Education. "School Board Consolidation." News release, 30 March. Accessed 12 May 2012. http://www.releases.gov.nl.ca/releases/2004/edu/0330n20.htm.

– 2004g. *School Board Consolidation: Orientation Information for Transitional Committees.* St John's: Government of Newfoundland and Labrador.

– 2004h. Executive Council. "Williams Brings Openness, Accountability to Premier's Office." News release, 30 March. http://www.releases.gov.nl.ca/releases/2004/exec/0330n28.htm

– 2005a. *Foundation for Success: White Paper on Public Post-Secondary Education.* St John's: Government of Newfoundland and Labrador.

– 2005b. *House of Assembly Proceedings (Hansard)*. 45th General Assembly, 2nd Session. Vol. 45, no. 12. 18 April. http://www.assembly.nl.ca/business/hansard/ga45session2/05-04-18.htm.

– 2005c. "Minister Taylor Updates Federal Minister about Fisheries and Aquaculture Issues." News release, 5 April. http://www.releases.gov.nl.ca/releases/2005/fishaq/0405n03.htm.

– 2005d. "Overview of Renewed Fish Processing Policy Framework." News release backgrounder, 3 February. http://www.releases.gov.nl.ca/releases/2005/fishaq/0222n03back1.htm.

– 2005e. *Reducing Poverty in Newfoundland and Labrador: Working towards a Solution.* St John's: Government of Newfoundland and Labrador.

– 2005f. Treasury Board. Budgeting Divison. *Budget Estimates 2005–06.* St John's: Government of Newfoundland and Labrador. Accessed 11 May 2012. http://www.budget.gov.nl.ca/budget2005/pdf/estimates2005.pdf.

– 2005g. *Working Together for Mental Health: A Policy Framework for Mental Health and Addiction Services in Newfoundland and Labrador.* http://www.health.gov.nl.ca/health/publications/working_together_for_mental_health.pdf.

– 2006a. Department of Health and Community Services. *Achieving Health and Wellness: Provincial Wellness Plan for Newfoundland and Labrador.* http://www.health.gov.nl.ca/health/publications/nlprovincialwellnessplan.pdf.

– 2006b. Executive Council and Department of Business. "Creative, Resilient and Inventive: New Brand Embodies Essence of Newfoundland and Labrador." News release, 3 October. Accessed 9 June 2012. http://www.releases.gov.nl.ca/releases/2006/exec/1003n01.htm.

– 2006c. Department of Finance. Economics and Statistics Branch. *Demographic Change – Issues and Implications.* St John's: Government of Newfoundland and Labrador.

– 2006d. Department of Environment and Conservation. "Environmental Assessment Bulletin." News release, 1 December. http://www.releases.gov.nl.ca/releases/2006/env/1201n08.htm.

– 2006e. Executive Council and Department of Natural Resources. "Newfoundland and Labrador Will Lead Lower Churchill Development." News release, 8 May. http://www.releases.gov.nl.ca/releases/2006/exec/0508n03.htm.

– 2006f. Executive Council and Department of Fisheries and Aquaculture. "Premier's Meeting with Fishery Stakeholders Explores New Direction for Future." News release, 24 May. Accessed 11 May 2012. http://www.releases.gov.nl.ca/releases/2006/exec/0524n08.htm.

– 2006g. Department of Fisheries and Aquaculture. "Province Can Learn
    Many Lessons from Icelandic Fishery." News release, 6 September. http://
    www.releases.gov.nl.ca/releases/2006/fishaq/0906n07.htm.
– 2006h. Department of Health and Community Services. *2006–2008 Stra-
    tegic Plan.* St John's: Government of Newfoundland and Labrador.
– 2006i. Department of Innovation, Trade, and Rural Development, Depart-
    ment of Fisheries and Aquaculture, and Department of Natural Resources.
    "The Right Choices: Building Rural Regions." News release, 30 March.
    http://www.releases.gov.nl.ca/releases/2006/intrd/0330no11.htm.
– 2007a. Department of Natural Resources. *Focusing Our Energy: Energy
    Plan.* http://www.nr.gov.nl.ca/nr/energy/plan/pdf/energy_report.pdf.
– 2007b. Department of Health and Community Services. 2007. "Government
    to Undertake Judicial Commission of Inquiry on Estrogen and Progesterone
    Receptor Testing for Breast Cancer Patients." News release, 22 May.
– 2007c. *House of Assembly Proceedings (Hansard).* 45th General Assembly,
    4th Session. Vol. 45, no. 14. 16 May. St John's: Government of Newfound-
    land and Labrador.
– 2007d. Executive Council. "Provincial Government Prepares for Commission
    of Inquiry and Announces New Task Force on Health System." News release,
    30 May. http://www.releases.gov.nl.ca/releases/2007/exec/0530n04.htm.
– 2007e. Department of Health and Community Services. Aging and Seniors
    Division. *Provincial Healthy Aging Policy Framework.* St John's: Govern-
    ment of Newfoundland and Labrador. http://www.health.gov.nl.ca/health/
    publications/ha_policy_framework.pdf.
– 2007f. Department of Fisheries and Aquaculture. "Renewing the Newfound-
    land and Labrador Fishing Industry." News release, 12 April. http://www.
    releases.gov.nl.ca/releases/2007/fishaq/0412n03.htm.
– 2008a. *House of Assembly Proceedings (Hansard).* 46th General Assembly,
    1st Session. Vol. 46, no. 25. 12 May. St John's: Government of Newfound-
    land and Labrador.
– 2008b. Executive Council and Department of Natural Resources. "Nal-
    cor Energy – The Future of Energy Development in Newfoundland and
    Labrador." News release, 11 December. http://www.releases.gov.nl.ca/
    releases/2008/exec/1211n11.htm.
– 2008c. Executive Council and Department of Health and Community Servi-
    ces. "Province's Package for Pathologists to Rival Any in the Country." News
    release, 22 May. http://www.releases.gov.nl.ca/releases/2008/exec/0522n11.
    htm.
– 2008d. Executive Council and Department of Health and Community
    Services. "Provincial Government Reaches Compensation Agreement with

Gynecological Oncologists." News release, 22 September. http://www.
releases.gov.nl.ca/releases/2008/exec/0922n05.htm.

– 2008e. Department of Fisheries and Aquaculture. "Significant Trade Offs
for Modest Gains Once Again Compromise Provincial Objectives at NAFO."
News release, 6 October. http://www.releases.gov.nl.ca/releases/2008/
fishaq/1006n07.htm.

– 2008f. "Submission of Her Majesty in Right of Newfoundland and Labrador." 1 December. Office of the Secretary to Cabinet for the Management
of Health Issues. http://www.cihrt.nl.ca/Submissions%20for%20Website/1_
Her%20Majesty_The%20Province.pdf.

– 2009a. Department of Human Resources, Labour and Employment.
Empowering People, Engaging Community, Enabling Success. St John's:
Government of Newfoundland and Labrador.

– 2009b. Department of Fisheries and Aquaculture. "Government of Canada
and Province of Newfoundland and Labrador Join with Cooke Aquaculture to Invest in a Cod Demonstration Farm on Newfoundland's South
Coast." News release, 2 March. http://www.releases.gov.nl.ca/releases/2009/
fishaq/0227n17.htm.

– 2010a. *Canada – Newfoundland and Labrador Labour Market Agreement 2010–2011 Annual Plan*. St John's: Government of Newfoundland
and Labrador. Accessed 3 December 2011. http://www.hrle.gov.nl.ca/hrle/
publications/lmd/LMA_Annual_Plan_2010_2011.pdf.

– 2010b. Department of Natural Resources. "Electricity." Government of
Newfoundland and Labrador. http://www.nr.gov.nl.ca/nr/energy/electricity/.

– 2010c. Department of Finance. Budgeting Division. *Estimates of the
Program Expenditure and Revenue of the Consolidated Revenue Fund
2010–11*. St John's: Government of Newfoundland and Labrador. Accessed
11 May 2012. http://www.budget.gov.nl.ca/budget2010/estimates/estimates
2010.pdf.

– 2010d. Department of Health and Community Services. *Gaining Ground: A
Provincial Cancer Control Policy Framework for Newfoundland and Labrador*. St John's: Government of Newfoundland and Labrador. http://www.
health.gov.nl.ca/health/publications/gaining_ground_provincial_cancer_
control_policy.pdf.

– 2010e. Department of Natural Resources, Department of Fisheries and
Aquaculture, and Department of Business. "Managing Our Natural Resources – For Our Children and Our Future." News release, 29 March. http://
www.releases.gov.nl.ca/releases/2010/nr/0329n12.htm.

– 2010f. *Rural Secretariat, Executive Council Activity Report 2009–10*. St
John's: Government of Newfoundland and Labrador.

- 2010g. Department of Health and Community Services. "Significant Progress Made on Cameron Report Recommendations." News release, 24 March.
- 2010h. Department of Works, Services, and Transportation. "Telephone Directory." Accessed 15 November 2010. http://telephonedirectory.gov.nl.ca/.
- 2010i. Department of Finance. Economic Research and Analysis Division. *Economic Review 2010*. St John's: Government of Newfoundland and Labrador.
- 2010j. Department of Human Resources, Labour and Employment and Department of Education. "Williams Government Makes Further Investments in Youth." News release, 8 July. http://www.releases.gov.nl.ca/releases/2010/hrle/0708n06.htm.
- 2011a. Department of Advanced Education and Skills. "Advance Studies – Fast Facts." Accessed 11 July 2013. http://www.aes.gov.nl.ca/postsecondary/fastfacts.html#enrolment.
- 2011b. Department of Finance. Budgeting Division. *Estimates of the Program Expenditure and Revenue of the Consolidated Revenue Fund 2011–12*. http://www.budget.gov.nl.ca/budget2011/estimates/estimates2011.pdf.
- 2012a. Department of Education. "Education Statistics: Elementary-Secondary 2011–2012." St John's: Government of Newfoundland and Labrador. http://www.ed.gov.nl.ca/edu/publications/k12/stats/1112/stat_1112_full.pdf.
- 2012b. "Government of Newfoundland and Labrador." Accessed 9 June 2012. http://www.gov.nl.ca/.
- 2013a. "Brand Signature." Accessed 11 June 2013. http://www.gov.nl.ca/brand/.
- 2013b. "Land Area." http://www.gov.nl.ca/aboutnl/area.html.
- 2013c. Rural Secretariat. "Rural Lens." Last updated 13 May 2013. http://www.exec.gov.nl.ca/rural/publications/rurallens.html.
Newfoundland and Labrador Board of Commissioners of Public Utilities. 2011. "Muskrat Falls Review Underway." News release, 26 July. http://www.pub.nf.ca/press/PUB-Press-MFR-July26-11.pdf.
Newfoundland and Labrador Housing Corporation. 2011. *Strategic Plan 2011–2014*. St John's: Newfoundland and Labrador Housing Corporation.
Newfoundland and Labrador Statistics Agency. 2012. "Annual Average Unemployment Rate Canada and Provinces 1976–2011." St John's: Economics and Statistics Branch. http://www.stats.gov.nl.ca/statistics/Labour/PDF/UnempRate.pdf.
Newfoundland and Labrador Teachers' Association (NLTA). 1986. *Exploring New Pathways: A Brief Presented to the Government of Newfoundland and Labrador by the Newfoundland Teachers' Association*. St John's: NLTA.

– 2003. *Putting the Teacher Back in Teaching*. Accessed 16 March 2009. St John's: NLTA. https://www.nlta.nl.ca/files/documents/reports/brief_tchr_bk_tching_feb03.pdf.

Newfoundland Labrador Liquor Corporation. 2012. "Responsibility." http://www.nlliquor.com/corporate/responsibility.

Newfoundland and Labrador Medical Association. 2010. "Book of Reports for the Annual General Meeting." 12 June 2010. Accessed 30 September 2013. http://www.nlma.nl.ca/documents/annual_reports/annual_report_12.pdf.

Noel, S.J.R. 1971. *Politics in Newfoundland*. Toronto: University of Toronto Press.

Norris, Pippa. 1997. *Passages to Power: Legislative Recruitment in Advanced Democracies*. Cambridge: Cambridge University Press.

Noseworthy, John. 2007. Office of the Auditor General. *Report of the Auditor General to the House of Assembly on a Review of Constituency Allowance Claims, 1989–90 Through to 2005–06*. St John's: Government of Newfoundland and Labrador.

– 2009. Office of the Auditor General. *Report of the Auditor General to the House of Assembly: Reviews of Departments and Crown Agencies for the Year Ended 31 March 2009*. St John's: Government of Newfoundland and Labrador.

Nova Central School District. 2005. *Minutes of Special School Board Meeting*. 11 April 2006. Proposed Year 2 Changes – 5 Year Plan. http://www.ncsd.ca/docs/minutes/2006/SpecialBoardMeetingMinutes_04-11-2006.pdf.

O'Connor, Dennis R. 2007. "Some Observations on Public Inquiries." Presentation to the Annual Conference of the Canadian Institute for the Administration of Justice, Halifax, NS, 10 October.

O'Dea, Shane. 1994. "Newfoundland: The Development of Culture on the Margin." *Newfoundland Studies* 10, no. 1: 73–81.

O'Neill, Paul. 2005. "Flying the Pink, White and Green." *Evening Telegram*, 9 January.

Oesch, Daniel. 2006. *Redrawing the Class Map: Stratification and Institutions in Germany, Britain, Sweden, and Switzerland*. London: Palgrave Macmillan.

Ommer, Rosemany E., and the Coasts under Stress Research Project Team. 2007. *Coasts under Stress: Understanding Restructuring and the Social-Ecological Health of Coastal Communities*. Montreal and Kingston: McGill-Queen's University Press.

Ontario. 2011. Ministry of Finance. "Ontario Economy is Turning Corner, Creating Jobs." News release, 29 March. http://www.fin.gov.on.ca/en/budget/ontariobudgets/2011/nr1.html.

Organization for Economic Cooperation and Development (OECD). 2006. *Supporting the Contribution of Higher Education Institutions to Regional Development: Peer Review Report – Atlantic Canada*. Paris: OECD.

– 2008. *Growing Unequal: Income Distribution and Poverty in OECD Countries*. Paris: OECD.

– 2010. OECD *Rural Policy Review: Québec, Canada*. Paris: OECD.

Ormrod, Robert P., and Stephan C.M. Henneberg. 2006. "'Are You Thinking What We're Thinking?' or 'Are We Thinking What You're Thinking?' An Explanatory Analysis of the Market Orientation of the UK Parties." In *The Marketing of Political Parties: Political Marketing at the 2005 British General Election*, edited by Darren G. Lilleker, Nigel A. Jackson, and Richard Scullion. Manchester: Manchester University Press.

Osberg, Lars, and Andrew Sharpe. 2011. *Beyond GDP: Measuring Economic Well-Being in Canada and the Provinces, 1981–2010*. CSLS Research Report 2011. Ottawa: Centre for the Study of Living Standards. Accessed 22 October 2011. http://www.csls.ca/reports/csls2011-11.pdf.

Ostrom, Elinor. 1990. *Governing the Commons: The Evolution of Institutions for Collective Action*. Cambridge: Cambridge University Press.

– 2000. "The Danger of Self-Evident Truths." *Political Science and Politics* 33, no. 1: 33–44.

Overton, James. 1979. "Towards a Critical Analysis of Neo-Nationalism in Newfoundland." In *Underdevelopment and Social Movements in Atlantic Canada*, edited by Robert J. Brym and R. James Sacouman. Toronto: New Hogtown Press.

– 1980. "Promoting 'The Real Newfoundland.' Culture as Tourist Commodity." *Studies in Political Economy*, 4 (autumn 1980): 115–37.

– 1985. "Progressive Conservatism? A Critical Look at Politics, Culture, and Development in Newfoundland." In *Ethnicity in Atlantic Canada*, 84–102. Social Science Monograph Series V. Fredericton: University of New Brunswick.

– 1988. "A Newfoundland Culture?" *Journal of Canadian Studies* 23 (spring/summer): 5–22.

– 2000. "Sparking a Cultural Revolution: Joey Smallwood, Farley Mowat, Harold Horwood and Newfoundland's Cultural Renaissance." *Newfoundland Studies* 16, no. 2: 166–204.

Ozga, Jennifer. 2000. *Policy Research in Educational Settings: Contested Terrain*. Buckingham, UK: Open University Press.

Paine, Robert. 1981. *Ayatollahs and Turkey Trots: Political Rhetoric in the New Newfoundland*. St John's: Breakwater Books.

Pal, Leslie A. 2006. *Beyond Policy Analysis: Public Issue Management in Turbulent Times*. 3rd ed. Toronto: Nelson.

Palda, Kristian S. 1973. "Does Advertising Influence Votes? An Analysis of the 1966 and 1970 Quebec Elections." *Canadian Journal of Political Science* 6, no. 4: 638–55.

Pammett, Jon H., and Christopher Dornan, eds. *The Canadian Federal Election of 2011*. Toronto: Dundurn Press.

Panitch, Leo, and Donald Swartz. 2003. *From Consent to Coercion: The Assault on Trade Union Freedoms*. 3rd ed. Aurora, ON: Garamond Press.

Parent, Christophe. 2011. *Le Concept d'État Fédéral Multinational: Essai Sur L'union des Peuples*. Bruxelles: P.I.E. Peter Lang.

Parfrey, Patrick, Brendan Barrett, and Deborah Gregory. 2005. "Restructuring Acute Care Hospitals in Newfoundland and Labrador." *Journal of Health Services Research and Policy* 10, supplement 2: 1–3.

Peckford, Brian. 2012. *Some Day the Sun Will Shine and Have Not Will Be No More*. St John's: Flanker Press.

Penney, Neil. 1981. "The Parliamentary Tradition in Newfoundland." *Canadian Parliamentary Review* 4, no. 2: 11–16.

Perlin, A.B. 1958. *The Story of Newfoundland*. St John's: A.B. Perlin.

Perlin, George. 1974. "Patronage and Paternalism: Politics in Newfoundland." In *Perspectives on Newfoundland Society and Culture*, edited by Maurice A. Sterns. St John's: Memorial University of Newfoundland.

Peters, B. Guy. 2005. *Institutional Theory in Political Science: The "New Institutionalism."* London: Continuum.

Peters, John. 2010. "Down in the Vale: Corporate Globalization, Unions on the Defensive, and the USW Local 6500 Strike in Sudbury, 2009–2010." *Labour/Le Travail* 66 (fall): 73–106.

– 2012. "Neoliberal Convergence in North America and Western Europe: Fiscal Austerity, Privatization, and Public Sector Reform." *Review of International Political Economy* 19, no. 2: 208–35.

Pinkerton, Evelyn, and Danielle N. Edwards. 2009. "The Elephant in the Room: The Hidden Costs of Leasing Individual Transferable Fishing Quotas." *Marine Policy* 33, no. 4: 707–13.

Poguntke, Thomas, and Paul D. Webb, eds. 2005. *The Presidentialization of Politics: A Comparative Study of Modern Democracies*. Oxford: Oxford University Press.

Ponting, Rick J. 2006. *The Nisga'a Treaty: Polling Dynamics and Political Communication in Comparative Context*. Peterborough, ON: Broadview Press.

Pontusson, Jonas. 2005. *Inequality and Prosperity: Social Europe vs Liberal America*. Ithaca, NY: Cornell University Press.

Porter, Michelle, and Kelly Vodden. 2012. *The Analysis of Municipal Readiness for Development Opportunities in the Communities Located in the Isthmus of Avalon Region*. St John's: Rural Secretariat, Memorial University of Newfoundland.

Powell Jr, G. Bingham, and Guy D. Whitten. 1993. "A Cross-National Analysis of Economic Voting: Taking Account of the Political Context." *American Journal of Political Science* 37, no. 2: 391–414.

Pratte, André. 2010. "Le Lévesque de Terre-Neuve." *La Presse*, 27 November: PLUS6.

Progressive Conservative Party of Newfoundland and Labrador (PC Party). 2003. *Real Leadership: A New Approach. Our Blueprint for the Future*. St John's: PC Party.

– 2007. *Proud, Strong, Determined: The Future is Ours*. St John's: PC Party.

– 2011. *New Energy: 2011 Policy Blue Book*. St John's: PC Party. http://www.newenergynl.ca.

Putnam, Robert. 1977. *The Comparative Study of Political Elites*. Englewood Cliffs, NJ: Prentice Hall.

Quinn, Mark. 2011. "Health System a 'Mess,' Michaels Tells Forum." CBC News, 27 September. http://www.cbc.ca/news/canada/newfoundland-labrador/story/2011/09/27/nl-health-platforms-927.html.

Quinton, Stephen, and Ryan Lane. 2009. *Municipal Sustainability Self-Assessment Project – Final Report*. St John's: Municipalities Newfoundland and Labrador and the Federal-Provincial Gas Tax Secretariat.

Radio-Canada. 2012. "Ottawa: Un Drapeau Associé à L'indépendance de Terre-Neuve Soulève la Controverse." Accessed 22 February 2013. http://www.radio-canada.ca/nouvelles/Politique/2012/05/26/002-drapeau-terre-neuve-ottawa.shtml.

Rasmussen, Ken, and Gregory P. Marchildon. 2005. "Saskatchewan's Executive Decision-Making Style: The Centrality of Planning." In *Executive Styles in Canada: Cabinet Structures and Leadership Practices in Canadian Government*, edited by Luc Bernier, Keith Brownsey, and Michael Howlett. Toronto: University of Toronto Press.

Reid, Ross. 2011. "Response to MNL's What's the Plan." Letter from Progressive Conservative Party of Newfoundland and Labrador to MNL. Accessed 6 November 2012. http://www.municipalitiesnl.com/userfiles/files/PC%20response%20to%20MNL.pdf.

Research & Development Corporation of Newfoundland and Labrador (RDC). 2012. "R&D Project Funding." Accessed 6 November 2012. http://www.rdc.org/funding/index.htm.

Resnick, Philip. 2000. *The Politics of Resentment: British Columbia Regionalism and Canadian Unity*. Vancouver: UBC Press.

Richards, John. 1985. "The Staple Debates." In *Explorations in Canadian Economic History: Essays in Honour of Irene M. Spry*, edited by Duncan Cameron. Ottawa: University of Ottawa Press.

– 2008. "Cracks in the Country's Foundation: The Importance of Repairing Equalization." *Canadian Political Science Review* 2, no. 3: 68–83.

Ritcey, Joan. 2002. "Recent Publications and Works Relating to Newfoundland and Labrador." *Newfoundland and Labrador Studies* 18, no. 1: 108–29.

Roberts, Terry. 2005. "Packed House for Manning." *Telegram*, 11 May.

– 2007. "Williams Hints at Third Term." *Telegram*, 23 September, A1.

– 2010. "Mayor Describes Decision as Callous." *Telegram*, 16 April, A1.

Robin, Martin, ed. 1978. *Canadian Provincial Politics: The Party Systems of the Ten Provinces*. 2nd ed. Scarborough, ON: Prentice-Hall Canada.

Robinson, Claire. 2010. "Political Advertising and the Demonstration of Market Orientation." *European Journal of Marketing* 44, no. 3/4: 451–9.

Rochon, Joel, and Sakie Tambakos. 2004. "Give Newfoundland a Supreme Court Voice." *Globe and Mail*, 10 August, 13.

Rose, G.A. 2003. *Fisheries Resources and Science in Newfoundland and Labrador: An Independent Assessment*. In *Collected Research Papers of the Royal Commission on Renewing and Strengthening Our Place in Canada*. St John's: Government of Newfoundland and Labrador.

Ross, Marc Howard. 2009. "Culture in Comparative Political Analysis." In *Comparative Politics: Rationality, Culture, and Structure*, Cambridge Studies in Comparative Politics, edited by Mark Irving Lichbach and Alan S. Zuckerman. Cambridge : Cambridge University Press.

Rothney, Gordon O. 1962. "The Denominational Basis of Representation in the Newfoundland Assembly, 1919–1962." *Canadian Journal of Economics and Political Science* 28, no. 4: 557–70.

Rowat, Bill, Scott Parson, Bob Applebaum, and Earl Wiseman. 2007. "Running Out of Fish." *Ottawa Citizen*, 20 September. Accessed 19 November 2011. http://www.nafo.int/about/media/oth-news/2007/overfishing.html.

Rowe, Bill. 2010. *Danny Williams, The War with Ottawa: The Inside Story by a Hired Gun*. St John's: Flanker Press.

Rowe, Frederick W. 1964. *The Development of Education in Newfoundland*. Toronto: Ryerson Press.

– 1980. *A History of Newfoundland and Labrador*. Toronto: McGraw-Hill Ryerson.

Ruddle, Kenneth. 1989. "Solving the Common-Property Dilemma: Village Fisheries Rights in Japanese Coastal Waters." In *Common Property*

Resources: Ecology and Community-Based Sustainable Development, edited by Fikret Berkes. London: Belhaven Press.

Ruggie, John Gerard. 1993. "Territoriality and Beyond: Problematizing Modernity in International Relations." *International Organization* 47, no. 1: 139–74.

Ryan Research and Communications. 2003. "Provincial Opinion Study." In *Royal Commission on Renewing and Strengthening our Place in Canada*. St John's: Government of Newfoundland and Labrador. http://www.exec.gov.nl.ca/royalcomm/research/pdf/ryan.pd

Sabatier, Paul A. 2007. "The Need for Better Theories." In *Theories of the Policy Process*, 2nd ed., edited by Paul A. Sabatier. Boulder: Westview Press.

Sampert, Shannon. 2005. "King Ralph, the Ministry of Truth, and the Media in Alberta." In *The Return of the Trojan Horse: Alberta and the New World (Dis)Order*, edited by Trevor W. Harrison. Montreal: Black Rose Books.

Saunders, Phillip M. 2003. "Policy Options for the Management and Conservation of Straddling Fisheries Resources." In *Collected Research Papers of the Royal Commission on Renewing and Strengthening Our Place in Canada*. St John's: Government of Newfoundland and Labrador. Accessed 16 May 2012. http://www.gov.nl.ca/publicat/royalcomm/research/Saunders.pdf.

Savage-Hughes, Denise, and David Taras. 1992. "The Mass Media and Modern Alberta Politics." In *Government and Politics in Alberta*, edited by Allan Tupper and Roger Gibbons. Edmonton: University of Alberta Press.

Savoie, Donald J. 1999. *Governing from the Centre: The Concentration of Power in Canadian Politics*. Toronto: University of Toronto Press.

– 2005. "The Federal Government: Revisiting Court Government in Canada." In *Executive Styles in Canada: Cabinet Structures and Leadership Practices in Canadian Government*, edited by Luc Bernier, Keith Brownsey, and Michael Howlett. Toronto: University of Toronto Press.

– 2008. *Court Government and the Collapse of Accountability in Canada and the United Kingdom*. Toronto: University of Toronto Press.

– 2010. *Power: Where is It?* Montreal and Kingston: McGill-Queen's University Press.

– 2011. "Steering from the Centre: The Canadian Way." In *Steering from the Centre: Strengthening Political Control in Western Democracies*, edited by Carl Dahlström, B. Guy Peters and Jon Pierre. Toronto: University of Toronto Press.

Scammell, Margaret. 2007. "Political Brands and Consumer Citizens: The Rebranding of Tony Blair." *The Annals of the American Academy of Political and Social Science* 611, no. 1: 176–92.

Scheufele, Dietram A., and David Tewksbury. 2007. "Framing, Agenda Setting, and Priming: The Evolution of Three Media Effects Models." *Journal of Communication* 57, no. 1: 9–20.

Schwartz, Mildred A. 1974. *Politics and Territory: The Sociology of Regional Persistence in Canada.* Montreal and Kingston: McGill-Queen's University Press.

Sheppard, Bruce. 2012. "Systems Challenges to the Sustainability of Meaningful School Reform." In *Educational Reform: From Rhetoric to Reality*, edited by Gerald Galway and David Dibbon. London, ON: The Althouse Press.

Siaroff, Alan. 2009. "Seat Imbalance in Provincial Elections since 1900: A Quantitative Explanation." *Canadian Political Science Review* 3, no. 1: 77–92.

Simms, David. 1986. *Rural Development in Newfoundland: "A Legitimation Crisis."* St John's: Royal Commission on Employment and Unemployment, Government of Newfoundland.

Simon, Christopher A. 2007. *Public Policy: Preferences and Outcomes.* New York: Pearson Education.

Simpson, Jeffrey. 2001. *The Friendly Dictatorship.* Toronto: McClelland and Stewart.

– 2008. "Will a Newfoundlander Receive the Prized Appointment?" *Globe and Mail,* 30 April, 19.

Skogstad, Grace. 2000. "Canada: Dual and Executive Federalism, Ineffective Problem-Solving." In *Public Policy and Federalism*, edited by Dietmar Braun. Aldershot, UK: Ashgate Publishing.

Smith, Anthony D. 1987. *The Ethnic Origins of Nations.* Oxford: Blackwell.

Smith, Gareth. 2001. "The 2001 General Election: Factors Influencing the Brand Image of Political Parties and Their Leaders." *Journal of Marketing Management* 17, nos. 9–10: 989–1006.

Smith, Gareth, and Alan French. 2009. "The Political Brand: A Consumer Perspective." *Marketing Theory* 9, no. 2: 209–26.

Soroka, Stuart N. 2002. *Agenda-Setting Dynamics in Canada.* Vancouver: UBC Press.

Sproule-Jones, Mark. 2008. "Property Rights for Water Resources Management." In *Canadian Water Politics*, edited by Mark Sproule-Jones, Carolyn Johns, and B. Timothy Heinmiller. Montreal and Kingston: McGill-Queen's University Press.

Stanford, Jim. 2008a. "Picking Winners? The Distorting Effects of Federal Corporate Tax Cuts." *Behind the Numbers* 9, no. 1. Ottawa: Canadian Centre for Policy Alternatives.

– 2008b. "Staples, Deindustrialization, and Foreign Investment: Canada's Economic Journey Back to the Future." *Studies in Political Economy* 82 (fall): 7–34.

Statistics Canada. 2006a. *Census of Population*. Ottawa: Statistics Canada.

– 2006b. "Population, Urban and Rural, by Province and Territory." http://www.statcan.gc.ca/tables-tableaux/sum-som/l01/cst01/demo62b-eng.htm.

– 2007. *2006 Census: Portrait of the Canadian Population in 2006*. Ottawa: Statistics Canada.

– 2009. "Federal, Provincial and Territorial General Government Revenue and Expenditures, for Fiscal Year Ending March 31." CANSIM, table 385-0002.

– 2011a. *Summary Public School Indicators for the Provinces and Territories, 2002/2003 to 2008/2009*. Elementary-Secondary Education Survey (ESES), Statistics Canada catalogue no. 81-595-MWE2010083, table A.2. Published 20 December 2010, updated 29 April 2011. http://www.statcan.gc.ca/pub/81-582-x/2011001/tbl/tblc2.1-eng.htm.

– 2011b. "Table 1: Gross Domestic Product, Income-based, Newfoundland and Labrador." *Provincial and Territorial Economic Accounts: Data tables*. Statistics Canada Catalogue no. 13-018-x.

– 2012a. "Census Profile. 2011 Census." Statistics Canada Catalogue no. 98-316-XWE. 8 February. Ottawa: Statistics Canada.

– 2012b. "Employment Insurance Beneficiaries Receiving Regular Benefits by Age, Sex and Province and Territory (Monthly)." CANSIM, table 276-0001. Accessed 29 June 2012. http://www.statcan.gc.ca/tables-tableaux/sum-som/l01/cst01/labor02a-eng.htm.

– 2012c. "Persons in Low Income Families." CANSIM, table 282-0802.

– 2012d. "Public Sector Employment, Wages and Salaries, Seasonally Unadjusted and Adjusted." CANSIM, table 183-0002.

– 2013a. "Employment (SEPH), Unadjusted for Seasonal Variation, by Type of Employee for Selected Industries Classified Using the North American Industry Classification System (NAICS)." CANSIM, table 281-0024.

– 2013b. "Labour Force Survey Estimates (LFS), by North American Industry Classification System (NAICS), Sex and Age Group." CANSIM, table 282-0008.

– 2013c. "Labour Force Survey Estimates (LFS), Employees by Union Coverage, North American Industry Classification System (NAICS), Sex and Age Group." CANSIM, table 282-0078.

Stewart Jr, Joseph, David M. Hedge, and James P. Lester. 2008. *Public Policy: An Evolutionary Approach*. 3rd ed. Boston: Thomson Wadsworth.

Stokes Sullivan, Deanna. 2010a. "Minister Rejects Binding Arbitration." *Telegram,* 16 November. http://www.thetelegram.com/News/Local/2010-11-16/article-1967545/Minister-rejects-binding-arbitration/1.

– 2010b. "Doctors Worried about Loss of ICU Specialist." *Telegram,* 30 November. http://www.thetelegram.com/News/Local/2010-11-30/article-2004078/Doctors-worried-about-loss-of-ICU-specialist/1.
– 2010c. "Departing Geneticist Praised." *Telegram,* 2 December. http://www.thetelegram.com/News/Local/2010-12-02/article-2011048/Departing-geneticist-praised/1.
– 2010d. "Patient Calls for Better Treatment of Doctors." *Telegram,* 7 December. http://www.thetelegram.com/News/Local/2010-12-07/article-2022999/Patient-calls-for-better-treatment-of-doctors/1.
Stoltz, Klaus. 2001. "The Political Class and Regional Institution-Building: A Conceptual Framework." *Regional and Federal Studies* 11, no. 1: 80–100.
Stone, Deborah. 1988. *Policy Paradox and Political Reason.* Boston: Scott Foresman.
– 1997. *Policy Paradox: The Art of Political Decision Making.* New York: W.W. Norton.
– 2002. *Policy Paradox: The Art of Political Decision Making.* Rev. ed. New York: W.W. Norton.
Storey, Keith. 2008. "Managing Growth and Promoting Development: Avoiding Boom and Bust." Presentation at the Canadian Rural Revitalization Foundation Conference, Inuvik, Northwest Territories.
Storey, Keith, and Mark Shrimpton. 2008. "Industrial Benefits Planning in North America: Current Practice and Case Studies." Presentation to the seminar Regional Planning in Greenland, Nuuk, Greenland, 23–24 January.
Strøm, Kaare. 2000. "Delegation and Accountability in Parliamentary Democracies." *European Journal of Political Research* 37: 261–89.
Studlar, Donley T. 2001. "Canadian Exceptionalism: Explaining Differences over Time in Provincial and Federal Voter Turnout." *Canadian Journal of Political Science* 34, no. 2: 299–319.
Studlar, Donley T., and Gary F. Moncrief. 1996. "Women Cabinet Ministers in Canadian Provinces 1976–1994." *Canadian Parliamentary Review* 19, no. 3: 10–13.
– 1997. "The Recruitment of Women Cabinet Ministers in the Canadian Provinces." *Governance: An International Journal of Policy and Administration* 10, no. 1: 67–81.
– 1999. "Women's Work? The Distribution and Prestige of Portfolios in the Canadian Provinces." *Governance: An International Journal of Policy and Administration* 12, no. 4: 379–95.
Summers, Valerie A. 2001. "Between a Rock and a Hard Place: Regime Change in Newfoundland." In *The Provincial State in Canada: Politics in the*

Provinces and Territories, edited by Keith Brownsey and Michael Howlett. Peterborough, ON: Broadview Press.

Sutherland, S.L. 1991. "Responsible Government and Ministerial Responsibility: Every Reform Is Its Own Problem." *Canadian Journal of Political Science* 24, no. 1: 91–120.

Sweet, Barb. 2004. "Cabinet Shuffle." *Telegram,* 2 October, A1.

– 2008a. "More Briefing Note Problems Come to Light." *Telegram,* 28 May, A1.

– 2008b. "ADM Knew Numbers Were Wrong." *Telegram,* 29 May, A1.

– 2008c. "Witness Didn't Agree with Deletion of Information." *Telegram,* 21 June, A3.

– 2008d. "No Extraordinary Interference from Premier: Witness." *Telegram,* 26 September, A3.

– 2010. "The Alarm Should Come On." *Telegram,* 2 December. http://www.thetelegram.com/News/Local/2010-12-02/article-2011051/%26lsquo%3BThe-alarm-should-come-on%26rsquo%3B/1.

– 2012. "Province Loses Bid to Force Abitibi to Clean Up Contamination." *Telegram,* 8 December, C1.

Taft, Kevin. 1997. *Shredding the Public Interest: Ralph Klein and Twenty-five Years of One-Party Government.* Edmonton: The University of Alberta Press and Parkland Institute.

Taggart, Paul. 2000. *Populism.* Philadelphia: Open University Press.

Taylor, Sanda, Fazal Rizvi, Bob Lingard, and Miriam Henry. 1997. *Educational Policy and the Politics of Change.* London: Routledge.

Tayner, Jeremy, and Tina L. Beaudry-Mellor. 2009. "Hope and Fear Revisited: Did the Provincial Election of 2007 Mark the Transition to a Stable Two-Party System in Saskatchewan?" *Canadian Political Science Review* 3, no. 1: 17–33.

Telegram. 2008. "Cheers Jeers." Editorial, 20 May, A6.

– 2010. "And Now It Begins." 3 December. http://www.thetelegram.com/Opinion/Editorial/2010-12-03/article-2014432/Births-1847.

Thomas, Paul G. 2003. "Governing from the Centre." *Policy Options* (December): 79–85.

Thomsen, Robert. 2001. "Cultural and Political Nationalism in Stateless Nations: Nationalism in Newfoundland and Scotland." *Canadian Review of Studies in Nationalism* 28, nos. 1/2: 57–75.

– 2010. *Nationalism in Stateless Nations: Images of Self and Other in Scotland and Newfoundland.* Edinburgh: West Newington House.

Thomson, Pat. 2004. "Introduction." *Journal of Education Policy* 19, no. 3: 251–2.

Tibbets, Janice. 2008. "The Rock Lobbies for Top Court Vacancy; 'Harper Would Be Silly Not to Appoint' a Newfoundlander." *Ottawa Citizen*, 5 May, 3.

"Time to Flip: The Voters May Be Tiring of the Prime Minister's Bullying." 2012. *Economist*, 7 July.

Tobin, Brian, with John Lawrence Reynolds. 2002. *All In Good Time*. Toronto: Penguin Canada.

Tomblin, Stephen G. 1990. "W.A.C. Bennett and Province-Building in British Columbia." BC *Studies* 85 (Spring): 45–61.

Tomblin, Stephen G., and Jeffrey Braun-Jackson. 2006. *Managing Change through Regionalization: Lessons from Newfoundland and Labrador*. St John's: Leslie Harris Centre, Memorial University of Newfoundland. Accessed 14 November 2010. http://www.mun.ca/harriscentre/reports/arf/2005/FinalReportTomblinRegionalization.pdf.

– 2009. "Renewing Health Governance: A Case-Study of Newfoundland and Labrador." *Canadian Political Science Review* 3, no. 4: 15–30.

Trapasso, Raffaele. 2010. "OECD Rural Reviews: Lessons from the Past Decade." Presented at the Dynamics of Rural Transformation in Emerging Economies International Conference, New Delhi, India, 14–16 April.

Tremblay, Jacinthe. 2008. "Totalement, fièrement et délicieusement Newfie. Aux armes, musiciens et conteurs!" *Le Devoir*, 15 August, A-1 and A-10.

Tucker, Amy, Ryan Gibson, Kelly Vodden, and June Holley. 2011. *Network Weaving for Regional Development on the Tip of the Northern Peninsula*. St John's: Department of Geography, Memorial University of Newfoundland.

Tumilty, Joseph. 2008. *President's Letter – Detailed Report on Government Decision to Increase Salaries for Pathologists, Medial and Radiation Oncologists*. St John's: Newfoundland and Labrador Medical Association.

Tupper, Allan. 2004. "Peter Lougheed, 1971–1985." In *Alberta Premiers of the Twentieth Century*, edited by Bradford J. Rennie. Regina, SK: Canadian Plains Research Center, University of Regina.

Ungerleider, Charles. 2003a. *Failing Our Kids: How We Are Ruining Our Public Schools*. Ottawa: McClelland and Stuart.

– 2003b. "Large-Scale Student Assessment: Guidelines for Policymakers." *International Journal of Testing* 3, no. 2: 119–28.

Vallinder, Torbjorn. 1994. "The Judicialization of Politics – A World-Wide Phenomenon: Introduction." *International Political Science Review* 15, no. 2: 91–9.

Vardy, David A. 2011. "Making Best Use of the Lower Churchill: The Muskrat Falls Development." Prepared for Action Canada as part of the *Action Canada Papers*. St John's: Leslie Harris Centre, Memorial University of

Newfoundland. www.mun.ca/harriscentre/reports/research/2011/Action-CanadaReportOct2011Web.pdf.

Verser, Rebecca, and Robert H. Wicks 2006. "Managing Voter Impressions: The Use of Images on Presidential Candidate Web Sites during the 2000 Campaign." *Journal of Communication* 56, no. 1: 178–97.

Vining, Aidan R. 1981. "Provincial Hydro Utilities." In *Public Corporations and Public Policy in Canada,* edited by Allan Tupper and G. Bruce Doern. Montreal: Institute for Research on Public Policy.

Vodden, Kelly. 2009. "New Spaces, Ancient Places: Collaborative Governance and Sustainable Development in Canada's Coastal Regions." PHD diss., Simon Fraser University, Burnaby, BC.

– 2010. "Heroes, Hope and Resource Development in Canada's Periphery." In *The Next Rural Economies: Constructing Rural Place in Global Economies,* edited by Greg Halseth, Sean Markey, and David Bruce. Oxfordshire, UK: CABI International.

Vodden, Kelly, and John C. Kennedy. 2006. "From Resignation to Renewal: First Nations Strategies for Resilience." In *Power, Agency and Environment: Restructuring Canada's East and West Coasts,* edited by Peter R. Sinclair and Rosemary E. Ommer. St John's: ISER Books.

Vodden, Kelly, Ryan Lane, and Matthew Beck. 2008. "The 2007 Municipal Census of Newfoundland and Labrador." St John's: Community Cooperation Resource Centre, MNL.

Vosko, Leah F., ed. 2006. *Precarious Employment: Understanding Labour Market Insecurity in Canada.* Montreal and Kingston: McGill-Queen's University Press.

Walsh, Deata. 2011. "What Restructuring? Whose Rationalization? Newfoundland and Labrador's Memorandum of Understanding on Its Fishing Industry." In *World Small-Scale Fisheries: Contemporary Visions,* edited by Ratana Chuenpagdee. CW Delft, The Netherlands: Eburon.

Wangersky, Russell. 2009. "The Moral of the Story? Don't Provoke the Premier." *Telegram,* 7 March, A20.

– 2011. *Danny Williams: A Profile.* St John's: Breakwater Books.

Wanna, John. 2006. "Insisting on Traditional Ministerial Responsibility and the Constitutional Independence of the Public Service: The Gomery Inquiry and the Canadian Sponsorship Scandal." *Australian Journal of Public Administration* 65, no. 3: 15–21.

Ward, Neil, and David L. Brown. 2009. "Placing the Rural in Regional Development." *Regional Studies* 43, no. 10: 1237–44.

Warren, Philip. 2012. "The Politics of Educational Change: Reforming Denominational Education." In *Education Reform: From Rhetoric to*

Reality, edited by Gerald Galway and David Dibbon. London, ON: The Althouse Press.

Warwick, Paul. 1994. "Government Survival in Parliamentary Democracies." Cambridge: Cambridge University Press.

Watkins, Melville H. 1963. "A Staple Theory of Economic Growth." *Canadian Journal of Economic and Political Science* 29, no. 2: 141–58.

– 1982. "The Innis Tradition in Canadian Political Economy." *Canadian Journal of Political and Social Theory* 6, no. 1/2: 12–34.

Watts, Ronald L. 1999. *Comparing Federal Systems*. Kingston: Institute of Intergovernmental Relations.

Webb, Jeff. 1997. "Constructing Community and Consumers: Joseph R. Smallwood's Barrelman Radio Programme." *Journal of the Canadian Historical Association* 8, no. 1: 165–86.

– 2001. "Provincial Government: The Smallwood Years, 1949–1972." Accessed 4 October 2008. http://www.heritage.nf.ca/law/prov_gov.html.

– 2008. *The Voice of Newfoundland: A Social History of the Broadcasting Corporation of Newfoundland, 1939–1949*. Toronto: University of Toronto Press.

Weir, Erin. 2008. "Profits vs. Wages in Saskatchewan and Newfoundland." Progressive Economics Forum. 8 May. http://www.progressive-economics. ca/2008/05/18/profits-wages-saskatchewan-newfoundland/.

Weller, Patrick. 2003. "Cabinet Government: An Elusive Ideal?" Public Administration 81(4): 701–22.

Wells, Janice. 2008. *Frank Moores: The Time of His Life*. Toronto: Key Porter.

Wesley, Jared J. 2009. "In Search of Brokerage and Responsibility: Party Politics in Manitoba." *Canadian Journal of Political Science* 42, no. 1: 211–36.

– 2010. "Political Culture in Manitoba." In *Manitoba Politics and Government: Issues, Institutions, Traditions,* edited by Paul G. Thomas and Curtis Brown. Winnipeg: University of Manitoba Press.

– 2011. *Code Politics: Campaigns and Cultures on the Canadian Prairies*. Vancouver: UBC Press.

Western, Bruce. 1997. *Between Class and Market: Postwar Unionization in the Capitalist Democracies*. Princeton, NJ: Princeton University Press.

White, Graham. 1994. "The Interpersonal Dynamics of Decision Making in Canadian Provincial Cabinets." In *Cabinet Ministers and Parliamentary Government*, edited by Michael Laver and Kenneth Shepsle. New York: Cambridge University Press.

– 2005. *Cabinets and First Ministers*. Vancouver: UBC Press.

Williams, Danny. 2009. "Premier Danny Williams – St John's Board of Trade."
    Speech. 9 September. www.releases.gov.nl.ca/releases/speeches/2009/
    premiersept10.htm.
– 2010a. "Premier Danny Williams – Canadian Club of Ottawa." Speech. 9
    June. www.releases.gov.nl.ca/releases/speeches/2010/canadianclub_speech.
    htm.
– 2010b. "The Honourable Danny Williams." Speech. 25 November. http://
    www.releases.gov.nl.ca/releases/speeches/2010/1125s01.htm.
Williams, T.R. 2003. "Educational Governance." Paper prepared for the Panel
    on the Role of Government. October. Accessed 6 December 2011. http://
    www.law-lib.utoronto.ca/investing/reports/rp46.pdf.
Wisenthal, M. 2008. *Historical Compendium of Education Statistics*. Ottawa:
    Statistics Canada.
Woodrow, Maureen, Kelly Vodden, Derek Smith, and Ahmed Khan. 2011.
    "Rationalization of the Fishing Industry: The Case of Change Islands."
    Policy Brief. http://gracilis.carleton.ca/tgeog/downloads/Using%20Local%20
    Knowledge,%20PB%201%20(February%202012).pdf.
World Bank. 2012. "World Bank Commodity Price Data (Pink Sheet)." http://
    econ.worldbank.org/.
World Health Organization. n.d. "Summary of Probable SARS Cases with
    Onset of Illness from 1 November 2002 to 31 July 2003." Accessed 16 Feb-
    ruary 2012. http://www.who.int/csr/sars/country/table2004_04_21/en/index.
    html.
Young, Victor. 2003a. *Collected Research Papers of the Royal Commission on
    Renewing and Strengthening Our Place in Canada*. St John's: Government
    of Newfoundland and Labrador.
– 2003b. "What We Heard." St John's: Royal Commission on Renewing and
    Strengthening Our Place in Canada, Government of Newfoundland and
    Labrador. Accessed 12 November 2011. http://www.gov.nl.ca/publicat/royal-
    comm/WhatWeHeard.pdf.
Zavattaro, Staci M. 2010. "The Implications of a Branded President." *Admin-
    istrative Theory & Praxis* 32, no. 1: 123–8.
Zuker, R.C., and M.H. Pastor. 1985. "Financial Policies in the Canadian
    Electric Utility Sector: Origins, Practices, and Questions." *Canadian Public
    Policy* 11, supplement: 427–37.

Contributors

KARLO BASTA is assistant professor in the Department of Political Science at Memorial University of Newfoundland. His research investigates the institutional management of difference in multinational states, with an emphasis on federal institutions in ethnically complex societies.

SEAN CADIGAN is professor in the Department of History at Memorial University of Newfoundland. His research interests include the social and ecological history of fishers and fishing communities and the development of fisheries science.

ANGELA CARTER is assistant professor in the Department of Political Science at the University of Waterloo. She researches comparative environmental policy regimes surrounding oil developments in key oil-dependent cases.

CHRISTOPHER DUNN is professor in the Department of Political Science at Memorial University of Newfoundland. He is a leading academic in Canadian public administration and the politics of Newfoundland and Labrador.

JIM FEEHAN is professor in the Department of Economics at Memorial University of Newfoundland. His expertise is in public finance with emphasis on benefit taxation, fiscal federalism, and the economics of public investment.

GERALD GALWAY is associate professor and associate dean in the Faculty of Education at Memorial University of Newfoundland. His interests include educational policy and governance, educational change, public sector accountability, and educational reform.

RYAN GIBSON is completing doctoral studies in the Department of Geography at Memorial University of Newfoundland and beginning as a postdoctoral fellow with the International Centre for Northern Governance and Development, University of Saskatchewan. He is interested in regional development, collaboration, governance, cooperatives, and rural philanthropy.

JAMES KELLY is professor in the Department of Political Science at Concordia University. His research focuses on the judicialization of politics associated with the introduction of the Charter of Rights and Freedoms in 1982.

MATTHEW KERBY is associate professor in the School of Political Studies at the University of Ottawa. He teaches and researches on the subjects of research methods and political elites.

ROYCE KOOP is assistant professor in the Department of Political Studies at the University of Manitoba. He researches representation and political parties, municipal politics, and government communication online.

MARIO LEVESQUE is assistant professor in the Department of Politics and International Relations at Mount Allison University. He is interested in environmental policy change and implementation processes focusing on common pool resources (fisheries, water) and intergovernmental relations surrounding social policy changes.

ALEX MARLAND is associate professor in the Department of Political Science and associate dean of arts at Memorial University of Newfoundland. His research interests concern the use of communication, marketing, and electioneering in Canadian politics and government.

MARIA MATHEWS is professor of health policy/health care delivery in the Division of Community Health & Humanities, Faculty of Medicine, Memorial University of Newfoundland. Her research interests include physician supply and access to care.

JOHN PETERS is assistant professor in the Department of Political Science at Laurentian University. He researches political economy, labour movements, and public policy in North America and Western Europe.

MICHELLE PORTER is a PHD student in the Department of Geography at Memorial University of Newfoundland. Her research interests include community development and resilience.

KATE PUDDISTER is a PHD student in the Department of Political Science at McGill University. Her research focuses on judicial politics and the litigation strategies of political actors.

VALÉRIE VÉZINA is a PHD student in the Department of Political Science at the Université du Québec à Montréal. She is interested in island nationalism and has researched the development of nationalist movements in Newfoundland and Puerto Rico.

KELLY VODDEN is associate professor in environmental studies at Memorial University of Newfoundland, Grenfell Campus, and in the Department of Geography at Memorial University of Newfoundland. Her research focuses on collaborative governance and sustainable community and regional development, particularly in Canadian rural and small-town communities and coastal regions.

Index